An Ac

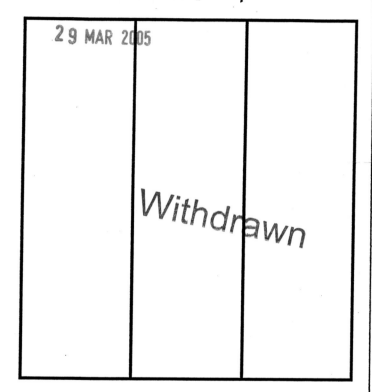
Man

THE
OPEN
LEARNING
FOUNDATION

An Active Learning Approach

MANAGEMENT ACCOUNTING

Peter Atrill and Eddie McLaney

Copyright © Open Learning Foundation Enterprises Ltd 1994

First published 1994

Blackwell Publishers, the publishing imprint of
Basil Blackwell Ltd
108 Cowley Road
Oxford OX4 1JF
UK

Basil Blackwell Inc.
238 Main Street
Cambridge, Massachusetts 02142
USA

British Library Cataloguing in Publication Data

A CIP catalogue record for this book is available from
the British Library.

Library of Congress Cataloging-in-Publication Data

A catalog record for this book is available from the
Library of Congress

ISBN 0-631-19538-6

Typeset in 10 on 12 pt Times New Roman

Printed in Great Britain by T.J. Press, Cornwall

This book is printed on acid-free paper

CONTENTS

Unit 3   Investment Decisions   55

Unit 4   Further Aspects of Investment Decision Making   101

Unit 5   Cost–Volume–Profit Analysis   **143**

Unit 6   Full (Total) Costing   **189**

Unit 7   Budgets and Budgetary Control   231

Unit 8   Control Through Variances   271

Unit 9 Divisional Performance Measurement and Control 315

Reader 359

GUIDE FOR STUDENTS

Course Introduction

Welcome to *Management Accounting*. The objectives of this guide are:

- to give you an outline of the subject of management accounting;

- to explain why it is necessary for you to study management accounting as part of your degree;

- to describe the nature of the material on which this workbook is based;

- to outline the programme which you will be following;

- to offer some practical hints and advice on how to study management accounting using the open learning approach; and

- to point out some of the advantages to you of studying management accounting by the method used in this book.

What is management accounting?

MANAGEMENT ACCOUNTING IS CONCERNED with providing financial information about a particular organisation to managers to help them to manage. Management can be seen as a series of activities which involve:

- Decision making

- Planning

- Control

Thus management accounting is the collection, analysis, dissemination and interpretation of information for managers of an organisation which will help them to make decisions, to make plans based on those decisions and to control their part of the organisation so as to try to ensure that the plans come to fruition.

The precise area in which a particular manager will make decisions, plan and control will depend on whether that manager is a sales manager, a production manager, a personnel manager etc. All of these managers should find that they are much more effective as managers if they are provided with accurate, relevant and timely information to help them.

Thus accounting plays a useful, if not vital, role in enabling managers to make sensible decisions in their crucially important choices as to how to allocate the scarce resources which are under their control.

The distinction between management accounting and financial accounting is that the former is specifically related to the informational needs of managers within the organisation, whereas financial accounting is more concerned with needs of outsiders, eg shareholders, creditors, the Inland Revenue etc.

In this workbook you will be dealing with the following aspects of management accounting:

- The nature and role of management accounting.

- Financial decision making in general.

- Making long-term, strategic decisions.

- Making short-term, tactical decisions.

- Planning and budgeting.

- Using accounting information to help managers to exercise control.

Why do I need to know anything about accounting?

FROM THE BRIEF STATEMENT of what accounting is (given above) it should be clear that the accounting function of the organisation is a central part of its management information system. It is important, therefore, that all business students should have a fairly clear idea of various aspects of accounting. These aspects include:

- where accounting data comes from;

- the way in which the data is processed to generate accounting reports which are used by decision makers;

- how accounting reports should be read and interpreted;

- the reliability of accounting statements as a basis for decision making, planning and control.

Many, perhaps most, business students have a career goal of being a manager within some organisation, perhaps a personnel manager or a marketing manager. If you are one of these students, an understanding of management accounting is very important. When you become a manager, even a junior one, it is almost certain that you will need to use accounting reports to help you to carry out your management tasks. It is equally sure, that it is substantially on the basis of accounting information and reports that your performance as a manager will be judged.

If you do not understand what the statements really mean and to what extent the accounting information is reliable, you will find yourself at a distinct disadvantage to others who know their way round the system. This is not to say that you cannot be an effective and successful personnel or marketing manager unless you are a qualified accountant as well. But it does mean that you need to acquire a bit of 'street wisdom' in management accounting in order to succeed.

Private sector/public sector manufacturing industry/service industry

ACCOUNTING, INCLUDING MANAGEMENT ACCOUNTING, seeks to achieve the same objectives irrespective of whether the organisation is privately or publicly owned, is involved in manufacturing (including mineral extraction and farming) or it offers a service. The need to make decisions and plans and to exercise control is critically important irrespective of whether the organisation is:

- a private sector company which manufactures hi-fi equipment;

- a publicly owned hospital offering health care;

- a private sector company which produces television advertisements for its clients;

- a publicly owned coal mine; or

- any other type of organisation.

In the units that follow, examples are given relating to all types of organisation. Private sector manufacturing organisations are well represented. This is because private sector organisations tend to have more focussed financial objectives than their public sector counterparts, thus decisions are often more clear cut. The other reason is that a manufacturing environment often provides more graphic examples than service industry environments.   However, you should not see the preponderance of examples involving private sector manufacturers to imply either that this is the most important sector of the economy or that the principles of management accounting only apply to that sector.

What is in this workbook?

The core of the workbook are nine study units. These were written specifically for undergraduate business students and have been tried and tested over a couple of years on BA (Hons) courses. The content has been revised to accommodate students' comments on it and to keep it up to date, and the material has been very well received by nearly all students.

The units are particularly useful to students, like you, who may be following a course where an 'open learning' approach is being adopted. The features which make it particularly suitable for open learning include:

- Very careful sequencing of the material so that there is a clear and logical progression.

- A step by step approach so that you will be able to understand each new point thoroughly before proceeding to the next one.

- A very clear layout with relatively short headed sections and paragraphs.

- Many worked examples, particularly in the computational areas, with an emphasis on understanding rather than on computation.

- Lots of opportunities for you to check that you understand what you have just read using the large number of 'activities' and 'self-assessment questions' which are interspersed through the units, to which solutions are provided at the back of the relevant unit.

- Plenty of opportunities for you to test your progress through end-of-unit exercises to which solutions are provided.

READER

At the back of the book there is a Reader, which is a collection of journal articles and extracts from texts. This allows you the opportunity of wider reading without having to fight your way past a large number of your course colleagues in the library to find the one copy of the journal which contains the article which you have been asked to read! Particular features of the Reader are:

- A significant number of journal articles and extracts from texts, each dealing with a significant issue in management accounting.

- Up-to-date material, some of which will deal with topical issues.

- Fairly short articles and extracts.

- Articles and extracts written in clear, non-technical language.

- Material particularly relevant to users of management accounting information (ie to managers) rather than to accountants.

Using the workbook

You should work through the units in the order which best fits in with your course. You should begin by noting the points which the unit outlines identify as the crucial aspects of the material. This will put the contents of the units into context and guide you through them.

Each unit is interspersed with a number of 'activities' and 'self-assessment questions'. There are 'additional exercises' at the end of each unit. All of these are intended to be attempted by you as they arise and completed before you move on. The suggested solutions to each activity are given immediately following the relevant activity. The solutions to the self-assessment questions and additional exercises are given at the end of the relevant unit.

The activities are intended to be a combination of a check that you are following the unit and understanding it, on the one hand, and a way of making your learning a more active experience for you, on the other. By working through the activities you can effectively divide your study time between that necessary to taking on new ideas and that which is necessary to reinforce those ideas.

The self-assessment questions are intended to give you the opportunity to see whether you have really grasped the content of the unit. The additional exercises are intended to give you further practice and the opportunity to reinforce your knowledge and understanding.

Typically, the activities will only take you a few minutes to deal with. By contrast, the self-assessment questions and additional exercises may quite easily take 20 minutes or more to complete. It is important that you discipline yourself to complete each activity, self-assessment question or exercise before you refer to the solution provided. If you get stuck part way through a question you should try to get help from the solution only on the point causing you difficulty and then continue to complete the question before referring to the solution again.

You should read the items in the Reader when recommended.

AVOID ROTE LEARNING

In respect of each topic in the workbook, it is important that you thoroughly understand what you are doing and why you are doing it. If you are clear on the underlying logic you will find it unnecessary to learn up a list of rules to be followed. This will mean that preparation for tests and for final examinations will be easier for you. It will also mean that you will be fairly comfortable in dealing with unfamiliar problems. This is an important point since dealing with problems which require the application of principles and techniques which you have learned, but which are of a type which you have not specifically encountered before, will certainly be a feature of your assessment.

SET ASIDE TIME FOR YOUR ACCOUNTING STUDIES

It is necessary for you to spend an amount of time during each study period in mastering the material concerned. The flexibility which the open learning system of study allows should not lead you to overlook this fact. Clearly at the start of the study period you will not know how long it will take to do the necessary work. It is sensible therefore, to make a start on the work at an early stage in the study period. Try to discipline yourself to set aside particular times in the week to study accounting, though not necessarily the same times each week.

UNIT 1

AN INTRODUCTION TO MANAGEMENT ACCOUNTING

THIS UNIT IS CONCERNED with the role and nature of management accounting.

On completion of this unit you should be able to:

- define and explain the role and nature of management accounting

- explain how to assess whether a particular accounting report represents value for money

- show the importance of information technology in management accounting

- explain the role of the management accountant in relation to the individual managers of the organisation

- describe and explain the decision making and control process

Outline of the unit

THIS UNIT IS CONCERNED WITH the role and nature of management accounting. As such it attempts to 'set the scene' for Management Accounting. It deals with a number of broad issues which need to be addressed before we consider the concepts and techniques of management accounting in detail.

The unit attempts to explain what management accounting really tries to do. This is important, since it should help you gain a perspective on management accounting. When studying this subject, it is easy to become too concerned with detailed technical aspects and to lose sight of the really important question of the purpose of management accounting.

The unit begins by describing the major purpose of management accounting. In essence, management accounting is concerned with providing economic information to managers to help them manage the organisation in an effective and an efficient manner.

Management accounting information should, therefore, be of value to managers in carrying out two primary tasks. These are:

- Decision making and planning; and

- Control.

DECISION MAKING AND PLANNING
Decision making and planning involves the consideration of the options available and then deciding which of the options available should be pursued. It should be seen as a prelude to action. Planning often involves assessing the costs and benefits of each course of action available. The accountant should have an important

contribution to make in this process. Indeed, as mentioned later in the unit, the evaluation of costs and benefits lies at the heart of management accounting.

Although the accountant may not be the sole provider of information for planning and decision making purposes, accounting information will usually be an important element of the total information available for these purposes.

Control

Control is closely linked to the planning process. It is concerned with attempts to ensure that actual outcomes correspond to earlier plans. This involves the comparison of planned performance and actual performance and the taking of corrective action where necessary. The role of the accountant in the control process involves providing 'feedback' information to managers concerning actual results.

Although the accountant is mainly concerned with providing managers with financial data, other information which is relevant to an economic decision may also be produced. Examples include details of physical resources held, details of market share and qualitative data such as morale of workforce etc.

The distinction between financial and management accounting is also considered. It is important to recognise that both forms of accounting have common features. Financial and management accounting are both concerned with providing users with economic information which can be used:

- to help predict future outcomes, and

- to compare earlier predictions with actual outcomes.

The basic objective of both forms of accounting is really to help improve the quality of economic decisions.

However, there are important differences between financial and management accounting in the form and nature of the information supplied and the people who use the information. These differences are considered in some depth in this unit. You may have already dealt with this issue in your earlier studies of accounting. Even if you have met financial accounting already, it is probably worthwhile to remind yourself of the main differences between financial and management accounting.

We shall also consider the fact that accounting information is often an expensive commodity and that this expense must be justified in some way. To be of value, the accounting information supplied must be capable of influencing management decisions in such a way that it is beneficial to the organisation. Unless this is the case, management accounting becomes a pointless exercise. However, benefit to the organisation is not a *sufficient* justification for providing accounting information. The benefits must be weighed against the costs. Unless the benefits of supplying the information outweigh the costs involved the accounting information should not be supplied. Although these criteria may seem quite straightforward they are difficult to apply for reasons which we shall consider in the unit.

We shall also look at the main elements of a management accounting information system. We shall see that, despite differences in the size and nature of organisations and the type of information technology employed, there are particular elements which are common to all management accounting systems. These main elements are:

- Information collection

- Information recording

- Information evaluation

- Information reporting.

Each of these elements is discussed.

The unit also discusses the tremendous impact of information technology on the development of management accounting. It is important to appreciate that it is not simply the more mechanical aspects of management accounting which have been affected by IT (ie information collection and information recording). The reporting and evaluation of management accounting information is also improved as a result of advances in information technology.

Accounting can be seen as a service function. By this we mean that it must seek to meet the needs of its users. In the case of management accounting, the users are the managers within the organisation. The management accountant must therefore attempt to establish what the needs of the managers are and to provide information which meets those needs.

Although the particular needs of managers will vary there are certain qualitative characteristics of accounting information which are generally applicable. These characteristics are important to ensure useful information is provided. Thus, management accounting information should be:

- Relevant,

- Reliable,

- Timely and,

- Understandable.

We shall consider the relationship between decision making, planning and control in some detail. Briefly the decision making, planning and control process can be viewed as a series of interrelated activities which involve the following:

● Defining the objective(s)

● Identifying the options

● Selecting the relevant data

● Assessing the relevant data (*At this point, a decision will be made concerning the particular option(s) to be pursued.*)

● Monitoring the outcome of the decision .

The unit discusses each of these steps in some detail.

This section considers the possible objectives which organisations may wish to pursue. The objectives of profit-seeking organisations, ie businesses are discussed in some detail. Although various possible objectives for businesses have been put forward in the literature, maximisation of the value of the business is assumed to be the key financial objective of a business in this module. Note that this module focuses on profit-seeking businesses. Non-profit seeking organisations, both in the private and public sectors, are likely to have other financial objectives.

Control may be defined as 'compelling events to conform to a plan'. The control process involves a series of steps. These are:

● Make plans

● Perform in pursuit of those plans

● Provide feedback on actual performance

● Compare actual performance with planned performance and identify any areas which are 'out of control'

● Take steps to establish control.

In order for the control process to be effective, good quality accounting information must be available in the form of 'feedback' so as to identify problem areas. Effective control, however, requires more than just good quality information. It requires good management and effective processes.

Now that you have a broad idea of what this unit is about, you can make start on the detail.

Management accounting

MANAGEMENT ACCOUNTING IS CONCERNED with the collection, analysis and reporting of economic (financial) information for managers of an organisation.

Managers require economic information because they are responsible for achieving the objectives which have been set for the organisation. This involves planning and controlling the activities of the organisation and its resources. In order to ensure the activities of the organisation are effective in fulfilling the objectives of the organisation and the resources are used as efficiently as possible, managers need information on such matters as the costs and benefits of particular products, investments, policies, etc. The management accounting system should provide managers with this economic information to help guide their decisions.

Thus, management accounting information should help managers in carrying out two primary tasks. These are:

- *Planning and decision making* This involves making plans about such matters as which investments to make, which products to make, which services to provide and in what quantities, what prices to charge for the output of the organisation, etc. Planning obviously involves decision making, ie selecting between possible courses of action.

- *Control* This involves ensuring the actual outcomes correspond to earlier planned outcomes.

Now try this 'activity'. Activities are intended to be short questions or tasks for you to do. Some of the activities are intended to give you the opportunity to test how well you have understood the contents of the unit so far. Other activities try to get you to think a bit more widely and relate your own experience and background knowledge to the material of the unit.

Activity 1

Just to satisfy yourself that you are fairly clear on the role of management accounting, see if you can remember the main points.

Jot down on a piece of paper the main points on the role of management accounting.

Your points should include:

Management accounting is concerned with

- the collection of economic information

- the analysis of economic information

- the reporting of economic information

With the purpose of helping managers to

- make decisions and plans

- exercise control.

The overall aim being to help managers to achieve the objectives of the organisation for which they work.

The role of the management accountant is, therefore, to provide managers with information which will help them to manage.

Most of the information supplied by the management accountant of an organisation will be expressed in monetary terms, probably derived from the accounting system of the business. However, this need not always be the case. For some decisions, information relating to physical units of resources may be useful. Similarly, qualitative information relating to such factors as customer goodwill, workforce morale, etc, may be useful for certain decisions. The management accountant should try to ensure that *all* information which is relevant to an economic decision is made available to managers. The information provided should not be constrained by the output of the accounting system.

Activity 2

From what you have learned so far in this unit, do you think that management accounting is likely only to be used in private sector businesses, or do you think that public sector organisations may also use it?

Try to justify your answer.

Your answer should have been along these lines:

- Public sector organisations have objectives which they are trying to meet, despite suffering from a limitation of economic resources (basically money). Thus public sector organisations face similar management problems as do managers of private sector businesses.

● Hospitals, universities and local government, are concerned with planning and controlling activities and have economic resources which must be used in as an efficient way as possible. This means that the managers of these organisations will require economic information to guide their decisions in much the same way as managers in a private sector business. Thus, management accounting has a crucial role to play in public sector organisations.

The same points are true in respect of not-for-profit organisations in the private sector, such as churches, charities and trade unions.

Financial accounting and management accounting

ACCOUNTING MAY BE DEFINED AS *'the process of identifying, measuring and communicating economic information to permit informed judgements and decisions by the users of the information'* (The American Accounting Association). This definition emphasises the decision making role of accounting and applies both to financial and management accounting. This definition also contains the important implication that accounting information has no place unless it helps managers to make better decisions.

Accounting is usually subdivided into two areas:

● Financial accounting

● Management accounting.

Activity 3

If you have studied financial accounting already, from your recollection of your accounting studies and that which you have read so far in this unit, what do you think is the essential difference between financial accounting and management accounting?

If you have not met financial accounting before, try an intelligent guess at this question.

(Hint: there is a good clue in the word 'management', as in management accounting.)

The essential difference is as follows:

● Management accounting seeks to provide information to those in positions of authority within the organisation, ie managers.

● Financial accounting, on the other hand, seeks to provide information to other interested groups, including shareholders, government, customers, suppliers of goods and services, lenders of finance and employees.

FINANCIAL ACCOUNTING

Financial accounting provides a broad overview of the performance and position of the organisation. The financial statements provided tend to be published relatively infrequently (annually, semi-annually or, occasionally, quarterly) and are, in essence a financial history of the organisation.

Limited companies provide a very good example, though by no means the only one, of organisations which have a need to account externally for their actions. Since financial accounting statements of limited companies are for the use of 'outsiders' such as shareholders and creditors, the law and certain regulatory bodies such as the Accounting Standards Board and the Stock Exchange provide some protection by prescribing such matters as frequency of financial statement reporting, the format and nature of the statements, details of what information must be included in the statements and how that information is to be derived. This prescription is intended to make companies disclose at least a minimum amount of information and to provide it in a standard format, thus promoting comparability between one company and another.

The objective of financial accounting is, broadly speaking, to enable 'outsiders' who are interested in an organisation to make judgements concerning its general position and performance on the basis of its recent past history. Financial accounting rarely contains forecast information or information concerning the future plans of the organisation. Such information is normally regarded as too sensitive to divulge as it may adversely affect the competitive advantage of the organisation, a point particularly relevant for private sector organisations. There may also be the fear that users of the information would misunderstand the nature of forecast information.

MANAGEMENT ACCOUNTING

Management accounting differs from financial accounting in an important number of respects. Accounting information can be provided to managers as frequently as they want it. In order for managers to make timely decisions, the reporting cycle for management accounting is usually much shorter than for financial accounting. Thus, in organisations of any size, it is common for certain management accounting reports to be produced on a monthly basis. The accounting reports produced are usually provided in the form in which managers require and with the information which they believe they will find useful to help them to make decisions and plans, and to control the progress of the organisation towards the achievement of those plans.

Managers normally expect to set financial targets for the future and to assess forecast outcomes of decisions made. The accounting system will provide forecast information for managers in addition to information concerning past events. Thus management accounting information is much more future oriented than financial accounting information. The information provided for managers would often be of benefit to other users. However, for reasons mentioned earlier, the information is rarely disclosed to outsiders. Occasionally, managers will be prepared to reveal to others information produced for internal purposes if they feel it is appropriate to do so. For example, managers may reveal cash flow forecasts to prospective lenders in negotiations concerning a future loan.

Financial accounting statements tend to be *general purpose* in nature, ie they are aimed at providing information which can be used for a variety of different decisions. Management accounting information, on the other hand tends to be *specific purpose* in nature. The reports produced often address specific matters. For example, reports may be provided on the results of just one small department or an assessment of the likely viability of making an investment in a new computer. Typically, the reports are aimed at particular managers and are not intended to be used at all by other managers, for whom they would have no interest or benefit. Thus a junior manager will normally receive reports about his or her relatively small area of responsibility. The junior manager's manager will receive a report which will include this middle manager's sphere of responsibility. This will include the areas of responsibility of all of the junior managers who report to this particular middle manager. This approach continues up the organisation's hierarchy, so that the chief executive/managing director will receive a report which covers the whole of the organisation.

The value of accounting information

ACCOUNTING INFORMATION IS AN expensive commodity. There are many reasons for this. Accountants command fairly large salaries. Computers, used to collect, process and disseminate information can be costly to buy and maintain. Systems designed specifically for the organisation are often expensive. In addition to these costs directly attributable to providing accounting information, it is also common for non-accounting staff to be involved in the preparation of accounting reports, if only to the extent of providing raw data, such as the number of hours worked by hourly paid staff. Finally, if accounting information is being produced, managers are likely to spend some time considering it. In view of the costs involved, it is important for managers to be convinced of the benefits they receive from the accounting system.

For accounting information to be of value, it should be capable of causing users to alter their behaviour as a result of considering the information provided. Thus, management accounting information should be capable of affecting the behaviour of managers. Sometimes the word *data* is used for the system output, where that output is not capable of affecting behaviour.

To have a positive value, accounting information should be capable of causing managers to alter their behaviour in a way which is favourable to the organisation, ie it is *functional*. Sometimes management accounting can have a *dysfunctional* effect on managers, ie it can lead them to alter their behaviour in a way which is detrimental to the organisation. Here it would have a negative value and, logically, the organisation should be prepared to pay money to avoid having the information. We shall look at some examples of dysfunctional information in later units of this module.

Clearly, management accounting reports which produce data, as opposed to information, have no value and are a waste of money to produce. Dysfunctional reports have a negative value and are an even more significant waste of money. Functional reports, on the other hand, do have a positive value, ie they are beneficial to the organisation.

Activity 4

Should all management accounting reports which are believed to be 'functional' be produced by an organisation? How should this decision be made?

● You should have concluded that the answer to this question is no. If the reports are functional, they have a value to the organisation. The organisation's managers must, however, assess whether or not the benefit to be derived outweighs the cost.

The idea that the additional (incremental) benefits of an activity or investment should exceed the additional (incremental) costs lies at the heart of management accounting and we shall return to this issue in later units. This cost/benefit criterion can equally be applied to the accounting system as to any other activity.

In practice, however, there are problems to be faced in applying the cost/benefit criterion. It is not always obvious whether accounting reports provide genuine information or just data. Whether information is functional or dysfunctional is frequently difficult to judge. The psychological and behavioural effects of accounting information must be considered. The way in which humans process the information provided and the impact of accounting information on attitudes, motivation and actions are important factors which will determine whether the information is functional or dysfunctional. We shall consider some of these issues in later units.

Even, what would appear to be a very straightforward matter, the question of the costs and benefits of functional information is highly problematical. Assessing the value of a particular piece of information can be very difficult and imprecise. Sometimes it is virtually impossible to know what action would have been taken without a particular piece of information. Even if this can be assessed, the economic effect of making a better decision can be hard to measure. The cost of providing accounting information is likely to be no easier to assess. Many of the costs of operating an accounting system are set-up costs or costs which will be incurred whether or not the particular report in question is produced. On the other hand, if a decision were made to abandon the production of a whole series of reports there might be sufficient savings to enable a less sophisticated system to be used, leading to cost savings.

At this stage, perhaps all that we can do is to recognise that accounting reports are expensive to produce and that they do not automatically represent value for money.

The management accounting information system

THE MANAGEMENT ACCOUNTING INFORMATION system can be viewed as an information gathering and communication system. It is a means by which economic information is collected and then communicated to managers for decision making purposes. Each organisation will develop a system according to what is perceived as meeting the requirements of its particular managers. These requirements can vary considerably and will be influenced by such factors as the nature and size of the organisation, the economic environment in which the organisation operates and the degree of financial sophistication of its managers. The technology employed to operate the management accounting system can also vary significantly between organisations.

Differences in managers' needs and in the technology employed will mean that management accounting systems can differ widely between organisations. However, management accounting systems of all types have certain functions which are common to all information systems. These common functions are as follows:

> ● *Information collection* This function is concerned with ensuring that the economic information which is relevant to managers, decisions, is correctly identified and captured by the system.

> ● *Information recording* This function involves recording the information which has been captured in a systematic and logical manner. It is important to be able to gain access to information acquired without undue difficulty when necessary. Unless the accounting system allows easy access to relevant information, the information captured by the system may not ultimately be used when making decisions.

> ● *Information evaluation* This function involves analysing and interpreting the information recorded, in the context of the decisions which have to be made. This can involve the assessment of the costs and benefits associated with different options. It may also

involve an assessment of the effects of the information on the decisions and behaviour of particular managers.

● *Information reporting*   This function involves preparing financial reports which can be used by managers as a basis for decision making. The information collected and evaluated must be relevant to the particular decision and should be put in a form which is comprehensible to managers.

In this module we are primarily concerned with the last two functions mentioned above – information evaluation and information reporting. The perspective adopted in the module is that, as a potential *user* of management accounting information, you will be required to understand the way in which information is evaluated and reported for decision making purposes. The way in which information is collected and recorded is important but is of more concern to a *preparer* of such information. The collection and recording of management accounting information will be mentioned at certain points in the module but are not considered in detail.

Management accounting and information technology (IT)

THERE CAN BE FEW areas of business where the introduction of IT has had such profound effects as it has in the area of management accounting. Management accounting systems based on IT have undoubtedly revolutionised the way in which information is collected and recorded. However, the impact of IT is not confined simply to these areas. IT can also be of use in evaluating the information captured. It has enabled managers to alter particular variables in plans (eg price, quantity, levels of inflation, etc) to see the likely outcome of different possible scenarios ('what-if? analysis'). These benefits have been achieved by a combination of standard 'off-the-shelf' packages, bespoke systems and of the extensive use of spreadsheets.

IT has enabled the more traditional management accounting reports to be produced more promptly and more efficiently. It has also enabled reporting at a level of specificity and detail which would not even have been attempted with a manual system. Under a manual system, managers would often have to make what use they could of generalised reports.

In the future, it is likely that IT will play an even larger role in management accounting. Computer hardware and software are becoming cheaper so the benefits of computerised accounting systems are now reaching a wider market. In addition, the increasing sophistication of IT has meant an increase in the potential applications available. In the area of decision making, for example, IT has developed to a point where it can now be used to make judgements which, hitherto, were considered to be the exclusive domain of humans.

Management accounting as a service function

WE HAVE SEEN THAT management accounting exists to serve managers, helping them in their work as decision makers, planners and controllers of their respective departments or areas of responsibility. Management accountants, to be effective, must clearly recognise that this is their role. This means that management accountants must become familiar with the problems and needs of their 'clients' – the line managers. The management accountants must discover, and then try to meet, the needs of the managers to whom they supply information.

Activity 5

Commercial Services plc supplies various goods and services to its business clients. Responsibility for meeting the clients and negotiating sales with them lies with a number of sales staff, each of whom is responsible to the relevant regional sales manager. There is one sales manager for each geographical area. The company's management accountant provides the regional managers with information to help them with their work.

What sort of information will each of the regional sales managers want from the management accountant? Make a list of the points that you think of.

Your list might include such matters as:

● The amount of stock/service that is available for sale.

● Possible delivery times.

● Manufacturing/service provision cost, possibly giving a 'floor' for price negotiations.

● Sales and profit achieved in the region last month and how this compared with the target.

● Sales and profit achieved by each of the regional manager's subordinates last month and how this compared with the target

● Sales and profit achieved by other regions.

Management accountants should be particularly aware of the fact that they are specialists providing an information service for managers, who are laymen as far as accounting is concerned. They must therefore provide the information in the form required by managers for the purpose in hand, in a clear, logical manner. Unless management accounting information is comprehensible it will not have a positive value to the organisation. For some managers, the portrayal of information in the form of charts, graphs, etc, may help in developing a better understanding of the issues.

Decision making and planning

We have seen above that management accounting is concerned with the provision of information which will help managers in decision making, planning and control. In this section we shall consider these processes in outline.

Making decisions involves selecting the option which will best fulfil whatever it is that the decision maker sees as the goal or objective. If there is not a choice of options because only one possible course of action can be identified, no decision needs to be made. Thus decision making always involves choices between two or more courses of action.

The steps in the decision making process are as follows:

DEFINE THE OBJECTIVES
Organisations, like individuals, have goals or objectives. All decisions should seek to work towards the fulfilment of those objectives. It is impossible to make rational decisions unless the goal or goals of the organisation are clear in the decision maker's mind. Take, for example, a decision for a local government authority to buy a labour saving machine. Analysis of the costs of buying and operating the machine suggests that acquiring it will lead to significant financial savings as compared with using labour to perform the same task. Should the machine be bought or not? In order to make this decision we need to know the objective of that local authority. If the objective is to meet its obligations at the minimum possible cost without any other considerations, then the decision will logically be to buy the machine, presumably leading to some staff redundancies. If, on the other hand, the local authority has as a primary objective, perhaps because it operates in an area of high unemployment, of employing as many people as possible the decision would be the opposite.

This is not to raise the question as to what objectives a local authority *should* have. Rather it is intended to illustrate that unless the decision maker is clear as to what the objectives are, decisions which will fulfil those objectives will only be made by chance. In practice, it is often the case that the final decision is likely to represent a compromise between two or more objectives, some of which may be in conflict with one another, as in our labour saving machine example.

Later in this unit we shall consider likely objectives for private sector organisations and possibly for many public sector organisations as well.

IDENTIFY THE OPTIONS

Organisations must constantly be looking for new opportunities to fulfil their objectives. These opportunities may involve the development of new products or new markets. However, the opportunities may be technological (eg new manufacturing processes) or financial (eg different means of financing the organisation) or in other facets of the organisation. Successful organisations do not stand still; those organisations which do not innovate tend to fall into decline.

The identification of viable options will take account of the strengths and weaknesses of the organisation and the capabilities of its competitors. Ideally, new opportunities should match the particular capabilities of the organisation.

SELECT THE RELEVANT DATA

Having identified a point where a decision needs to be made it is necessary to collect the relevant data. To be relevant the data must:

- relate to the objectives of the organisation

- relate to the future; and

- be different between the options under consideration.

Going back to the local authority example, and assuming that cost effectiveness is the only objective being pursued, the decision makers should only be interested in cost effectiveness. Matters not relevant to the authority's objective are irrelevant to the decision. For example whether the machine under consideration is made in the UK or not is irrelevant because 'buying British' is not the authority's objective. This is not to say that a local authority should not have an objective of favouring UK manufacturers, simply that *if* this is not an objective, the origin of the machine is irrelevant.

Only the future financial ramifications of the decision are relevant. Thus, for example, what the staff in question have been paid in the past is irrelevant to the decision, only what they will be paid in the future if they are to be kept on and any future redundancy costs, if they are to be laid off, are relevant. This is by no means the same thing as saying that the present and future effects of past events are irrelevant. The fact that, as a result of past actions, the local authority employs staff to do the work which could be carried out by the machine is highly relevant. It is relevant because it has potential effects on the future. What is irrelevant is how much it costs to recruit those staff, because this will be the same irrespective of whatever course of action is now taken.

As we have just seen, some information about the options, even though it may relate both to the objectives being pursued and to the future, is nevertheless irrelevant. This is information which is common to all of the options. It is only possible to select between options on the basis of differences between them. For example the future cost (salary etc) of employing the member of staff who presently supervises the labour which might be replaced by the machine seems relevant in that it relates to the local authority's presumed objective (cost effectiveness) and it relates to the future. If, however, the individual concerned would be retained, at the same salary, to supervise the machine, this salary would be irrelevant.

In fact the reason why past data is always irrelevant is that it must be common between the possible courses of action. That which has already occurred must be the same, irrespective of what the future may hold.

Activity 6

Can you think of any reasons why it is important to restrict the data to that which is strictly relevant? Write down such reasons you can think of; we think that there are two main reasons.

The two reasons why it is important to restrict the data to the strictly relevant are:

● Data can be expensive to gather, in staff time if nothing else. If irrelevant information is being gathered this is unnecessarily increasing the cost of making the decision.

● Irrelevant information can 'muddy the water' and make it more difficult for the decision maker to reach the right conclusion.

In Unit 2 of this module we shall give some detailed consideration to relevance in financial decision making.

ASSESS THE RELEVANT DATA AND MAKE THE DECISION
How this is done in detail depends on exactly the type of decision being taken and much of the remainder of this module will be concerned with looking at how the data is assessed in a range of financial decision making areas. Broadly, it is a matter of comparing the anticipated outcomes of the options identified to see which will best achieve the objective or objectives of the organisation. An option (or options) will then be selected according to this criterion.

MONITOR THE OUTCOME OF THE DECISION
Most decision makers would feel that the task is not completed merely by the taking of the decision.

Activity 7

Can you think of reasons why most decision makers would not feel the task to be complete? We think that there are three basic reasons why decision makers will need to, or want to, go further than just making the decision.

The three reasons are:

- to get things underway

- to take 'damage limitation' actions if things go wrong

- to see how well the decision making process has worked.

In more detail the reasons are:

TO IMPLEMENT THE DECISION PROPERLY

If the labour-saving machine is to be bought, steps must be taken to try to ensure that the machine is bought and properly operated to do the required task. This reason for monitoring the outcome of the decision really falls into the area of control.

TO LIMIT THE DAMAGE OF BAD DECISIONS

If a particular decision is not having the desired effect of working towards the organisation's objectives, it may be possible to take steps to amend the plans to improve matters. If our local authority were to decide in favour of the labour saving machine, this decision may prove to be a disaster if, say, the machine proved to be unreliable. A year after taking and implementing the original decision it will not be possible to decide not to buy the machine and make the employees redundant – these things will have already happened. It may be possible, however, to make a decision to abandon the machine and re-employ the labour. This will not stop the original decision from having been a bad one, but it may well be able to avoid good money being thrown after bad.

TO ASSESS THE EFFECTIVENESS OF THE DECISION MAKING PROCESS

Though the decision already made and implemented cannot be unmade, it is still very valuable to try to see whether future decision making could be improved. Decision making is such a crucial aspect of any organisation that it is vital that, if possible, a critical assessment of each significant past decision is undertaken and that the conclusions are taken seriously. The assessment might include such questions as:

- Were forecasts made at the time of the decision reliable? Could some other forecasting techniques or approaches have been more reliable?

- Was the assessment of the data carried out appropriately? Could some other method of assessment have led to a decision which would have better achieved the organisation's objectives?

This first reason (taking steps to implement the decision) really comes under the heading of 'control'. We shall return to the subject of control after we have considered what organisations seek to achieve through their decisions.

Organisational objectives

OBVIOUSLY, THE PARTICULAR OBJECTIVE or objectives which an organisation will pursue will vary from one organisation to the next. The type of organisation will greatly influence the objectives which will be pursued. Firstly, we shall concentrate on private sector businesses.

What businesses seek to achieve, and therefore what decisions will help achieve them has been a matter of considerable debate over recent years. The following objectives have been suggested:

PROFIT MAXIMISATION

The **profit maximisation** suggestion is based on the fact that the business is owned and controlled by the owners (shareholders, in the case of a company). They appoint the senior level of management of the business (the board of directors in the case of a company). The managers will, therefore, do what is in the best interests of the shareholders. Since the owners are the beneficiaries of the profits, maximising profit is seen as the most logical objective for the business to pursue.

This idea is reasonable up to a point. It assumes that profit maximisation is necessarily in the best interests of the owners. This may not, however, be true in all cases. Some strategies may increase profits in the short-term but in the longer term the opposite effect may be achieved. For example, a business which has been reliant on internally developed product innovation (eg, a pharmaceutical manufacturing business) may decide to cut back significantly on its expenditure on research. This would undoubtedly improve current profits because it takes so long for new drugs to be developed and then to obtain clearance from government agencies, that current research will not normally manifest itself in profitable sales for the business in much less than 10 years. However the increased short-term profitability is likely to be at the expense of longer term benefits.

Profit maximisation also fails to take account of the problem of risk. Strategies which increase profits in the short term may be very risky and may lead to a decline in profits over the long-term. For example, a business may borrow heavily during a period of economic boom and make additional short-term profits as a result of the additional funds available. However, during a period of economic recession the additional borrowing may prove a burden and lead to the demise of the business.

It may be possible to increase the net profit figure, merely as a result of expanding the size of the business, by raising additional long-term finance. Such expansion would not necessarily increase the profit attributable to each of the original owners.

MAXIMISE RETURN ON CAPITAL EMPLOYED

The **maximisation of return on capital employed** may be a more realistic owner-related objective because it relates profit to size of investment. Like profit maximisation, however, it completely ignores questions of risk and longer term prosperity.

SURVIVAL

All businesses, in normal circumstances, would seek to **survive**. However this is more likely to be a minimum objective. In periods of economic/trade recession some businesses may be forced to see survival as all that they can hope to achieve in the short-term. It seems unlikely that any private sector business would see mere survival as its goal in the longer term, however.

LONG-TERM STABILITY

Most businesses would see **long-term stability** as a highly desirable part of its future. However, like *survival*, few businesses would see stability in the long-term as all that are striving to achieve. A business may be stable in terms of economic achievement, but that level of achievement could be unacceptably low.

GROWTH

Organic growth, both of assets and of earnings, is likely to figure in the objectives of most businesses. Research evidence shows that business managers in practice seem to be concerned with growth. However growth suffers from some of the defects of *profit maximisation* in that short-term growth may be at the expense of longer term benefits, particularly if risks are taken in order to grow.

'SATISFICING'

The objectives which we have so far considered put owners as the key participants in the business. There are many people, or groups of people who have some interest in a particular business and in its future. Thus a modern business can be viewed as an alliance of a number of interested parties who have a 'stake' in the business.

Activity 8

Can you identify who these 'stakeholders' are?

In answering this activity you may have identified the following:

- Owners

- Labour

- Suppliers of goods and services

- Suppliers of loan finance

- Customers

- Other members of the public.

Some people would argue that the owners are not necessarily more important than any of the other interested parties. For this reason, it has been suggested that managers of businesses need to seek to satisfy all of the participants rather than seeking to maximise the returns to any one of them, possibly at the expense of others. This is known as **satisficing**.

MAXIMISATION OF THE VALUE OF THE BUSINESS

If managers are going to concentrate on the welfare of the owners, probably the best approach is to seek to **maximise the value of the business to its owners**, either in terms of the market value of the business (value of the shares in the case of a company) or in drawings made by the owners (dividends paid to the shareholders in the case of a company). This objective combines notions of maximisation of long-term profitability with those of growth and stability. A business with strong, stable growth would be highly valued in the stock market.

Though from an owner's perspective, maximisation of the value of the business may be a highly acceptable goal, it does seem inconsistent with the notion of *satisficing*. This is because value maximisation appears to benefit owners at the expense of the other participants. On reflection, however, this may not be true. Consider, for example a supplier of a raw material or service to the business. At first sight it seems likely that a management following a value maximising goal would ruthlessly seek to exploit all opportunities to obtain its supplies at the cheapest possible price with total disregard for the welfare of the suppliers. Though this might make the business more profitable in the short term it seems unlikely that in the longer term this will be the case. Suppliers would seek to retaliate whenever the opportunity were to arise, restricting supplies to the business when demand was high, seeking to charge the highest possible price on all occasions. Other participants in the business would have similar relations with it. Such hostile, resentful relationships would be likely, in the medium-term, to be damaging to the business. This would have an adverse effect on the value of the business.

Thus it seems likely that *value maximising* and *satisficing* are not necessarily in conflict; in fact they can reasonably be seen as complementary to one another. It is not being suggested here that there are no businesses which ruthlessly seek to exploit other participants in favour of the owners. These are not, however, businesses which can be observed to be successful in the long-term.

Activity 9

Consider a successful business with which you are familiar. By 'successful' is meant a business which is profitable, has been around for some time and seems likely to continue to do so. (You might think of certain of the high street chains.)

How does this business treat its customers, employees, suppliers and other stakeholders, as far as you know?

● We should be surprised if you answer, that the business treats
them badly, in respect of any of the stakeholders. The stable,
successful businesses seem to build their stability and success on
good treatment of those on whom they depend.

For the remainder of this module we shall assume that maximisation of the value of
the business is the key financial objective which is being pursued by private sector
organisations. It seems likely that businesses may well have other objectives which
their managements will need to balance against the financial one when making a
decision. Even if it could be argued that value maximisation is not the crucial
business objective, perhaps not even the key financial one, what is without doubt is
that if businesses consistently make decisions which have the effect of reducing
their value, eventually all value will be lost from the business and it will collapse.

Even where the organisation concerned is not in the private sector or is not pursuing
profit, most of its decisions will need to take account of the organisation's wealth.
As with private sector organisations, even where it is clear that wealth maximisation
is not a primary objective, wealth is a limited, finite resource and most, if not all,
decisions should take account of the effect of possible courses of action on the
organisation's wealth.

Activity 10

Why is maximisation of the value of the business accepted as the primary
financial objective in the private sector ?

● It strikes a balance between short and long term profitability. It
also strikes a balance between returns and risk.

Control

EARLIER IN THE UNIT we saw that management accounting has an important role to
play in helping managers to control the organisation. Control may be defined as
'compelling events to conform to a plan', ie making things happen as was intended.
Thus, an activity is out of control if things are not going according to plan. We shall
consider in detail the whole question of control and how management accounting
can help managers in the exercise of control in Unit 8. For the time being, however,
it may be useful to take an overview of control.

The control process involves the following steps:

● *Make plans* This involves pursuit of the organisation's
objectives. These plans will usually be quantified in monetary
terms.

● *Perform in pursuit of those plans.*

● *Provide feedback on actual performance.* Usually this is in the form of a management accounting report.

● *Compare actual performance with the planned performance and identify any areas which are 'out of control'.* The management accounting system should be capable of helping to identify the possible problem areas.

● *Take steps to establish control where it has been lost* (ie take management action to put things back on course).

We can see from the above that the role of management accounting in providing 'feedback' on actual performance and in helping to identify problem areas is an important element in the control process. Managers may be physically removed from the activities over which they have responsibility. Even where they are not physically removed, managers may find it impossible to assess what is going on by physical observation. Thus many, probably most, managers rely heavily on management accounting information. In effect, management accounting becomes the 'eyes and ears' of managers by informing them about what is happening.

The quality of the information provided by the management accounting system is important for managers wishing to use it as a basis for planning and control. The information provided to managers must be reliable, timely and relevant to the decisions being made. In the US, there is a saying 'garbage in, garbage out'. When applied in the context of management accounting, this means that the decisions made by managers will only be as good as the information on which it is based. Where quality standards are poor, managers will lose confidence in the accounting system.

Reading

You should now read Reader Article 1.1 'The link between management and management accounting' by Mark Lee Inman.

This article was published in the Students' Newsletter of the Chartered Association of Certified Accountants. This explains the references to specific examination. Despite this, the article has general relevance, particularly to you.

The article will provide you with a useful overview of management accounting and, to some extent, its historical development. This should help you to put the subject of this module into context.

You may come across a few technical words or expressions which are new to you. Do not be concerned about this; you can understand the main thrust of the article even if the odd word or two escapes you.

Points to consider:

● How does the author (an accounting academic) see the relationship between the accountant and managers?

● What view does the author take of communication of accounting information?

● Does the nature of the organisation in which the managers work affect their management accounting needs?

Management accounting in practice

IN MOST OF THE units of this module, after having reviewed the theory of each topic, we shall conclude with a brief outline of what happens in practice in the UK. Our main source for this is the report of a major research project which was funded by the Chartered Association of Certified Accountants, one of the leading UK professional accountancy bodies. The report is called 'A survey of management accounting practices in UK manufacturing companies' and it was researched and written by Colin Drury, Steve Braund, Paul Osborne and Mike Tayles. It was published in 1993.

The research was conducted by postal questionnaire. There were responses from accountants at 260 different UK manufacturing companies. These companies, between them, represented all major areas of manufacturing. In size they ranged from quite small companies (sales turnover between £10 million and £15 million) to very large ones (sales turnover in excess of £1,000 million).

The survey is particularly useful to us because it is up-to-date, which in a rapidly changing world is very helpful. The survey does have the disadvantage of involving only UK private sector manufacturing companies, when the private sector service and the public sector represent such large components of the economies of most countries. Despite this disadvantage we feel that the survey provides us with some extremely valuable insights to what happens in practice.

In subsequent units we shall refer to this survey as 'the ACCA survey'.

It is well worth mentioning that the survey report is extremely readable, partly because it is pretty free of technical jargon. We very much recommend that you read the report. You should find a copy in the library of your institution.

Summary of the unit

IN THIS UNIT WE have seen that management accounting is concerned with the provision of information to help managers to manage. Not all reports produced by management accountants represent value for money, some reports do not provide anything useful and some even provide misleading signals. Accounting information is expensive and even where it is useful its expense may not be justified by the benefit provided.

Management accountants should not lose sight of the fact that they are rendering a service to other managers in the organisation whom the accountants should see as 'clients'. Management accountants should avoid the use of unnecessary specialist terminology and reporting styles. It is very important for the management accountants to ensure that the information is communicated in a way which is comprehensible to their clients, the other managers.

We have seen that planning and decision making are important functions of management. Planning involves a series of steps, including the identification of the organisation's objectives. Whatever the nature of the organisation, an objective which is concerned with optimising the use of the organisations wealth is very likely to be an important one to be taken account of when making decisions. The other important area of management is that of control, ie ensuring that events conform to earlier plans. Managers rely on good quality accounting information for planning, decision making and control purposes.

UNIT 2

RELEVANT COSTS FOR DECISION MAKING

THIS UNIT IS CONCERNED with identifying the relevant costs of particular courses of action. We will see how those costs can be used to assess different courses of action for decision making purposes. On completion of this unit you should be able to:

- define and provide examples of outlay costs, sunk costs, committed costs and opportunity costs

- identify and to measure the costs and benefits which are relevant to a particular decision under consideration

- explain and justify the costs identified

- prepare a cost statement in a logical form, for management

- discuss the importance of qualitative factors in decision making.

Outline of the unit

THE UNIT BEGINS BY reviewing the steps in the decision making process that were dealt with in Unit 1. The point is made that the accountant has an important role to play in the selection of relevant data for decision making purposes. Deciding what data are relevant and what data are irrelevant for decision making purposes is the essence of this unit.

Next we shall develop a concept which was mentioned in Unit 1. You may remember that, whether a cost or benefit is relevant or irrelevant to a particular decision depends on three factors. These factors are:

- does it relate to the objectives of the organisation?

- does it relate to the future?

- is it different between the options under consideration?

A great deal of information may be available concerning a particular project, product or service which is to be the subject of a decision. The role of the accountant is often to sift through this information and to identify what is relevant. The three factors above provide the necessary guidance in identifying relevant costs and benefits.

SUNK COSTS

Sunk costs are costs which have been incurred in the past. Sunk (past) costs are irrelevant as they cannot be affected by any future decision. Sometimes students have difficulty with this idea. They see it as being necessary for an organisation to recoup all costs when setting prices for contracts, products, services, etc. Whilst it would be *desirable* to ensure that all costs incurred are fully recouped this is not always possible.

Let us say, for example, that you purchased a new car for £10,000 and, after a few miles of driving, managed to write it off by hitting a tree. Assuming you were not insured against this type of accident, your only course of action may be to sell the car to a scrap dealer. If you were offered £50 by the scrap dealer for the vehicle it would be pointless rejecting this offer on the grounds that the vehicle cost you £10,000 a few hours earlier. Failure to accept £50 from the scrap dealer may mean receiving nothing at all! Thus, when making a decision about whether or not to sell to the scrap dealer only *future* costs and benefits must be considered.

COMMITTED COSTS

Committed costs are costs arising from some earlier decision. For example, the decision to lease a shop for four years will result in committed costs in the form of lease payments in each of the four years. The amount of the committed costs are predetermined and cannot usually be avoided. As a result they are normally irrelevant to decisions being made. Committed costs can only usually be altered by some major change of policy.

OPPORTUNITY COST

An *opportunity cost* is the amount lost or sacrificed as a result of undertaking one course of action rather than an alternative course of action. Where a number of options could be pursued the opportunity cost is the loss or sacrifice associated with the best of the options foregone. This type of cost is not captured by the accounting system as no transaction takes place, nevertheless, it is a 'real' cost and must be separately identified. Opportunity costs are relevant costs for decision making purposes.

OUTLAY COSTS

Outlay costs, unlike opportunity costs, involve out-of-pocket expenditure. As we shall see, such costs will be relevant if they relate to the future and vary with the options under review.

The identification of relevant costs and benefits is based on the view that it is only differential (incremental) costs and benefits which should be taken into account. The decision rule is that where the differential benefits exceed the differential costs, a particular course of action should be pursued because the owners will be better off as a result. However, application of this rule will not automatically ensure long-term survival for the organisation.

Consider a situation where a business has leased premises for £10,000 per annum and wishes to sublet these premises as they are surplus to requirements. If the business receives only one offer to sublease for an annual income of £4,000 what should it do? Applying the relevant cost ideas in this unit, the answer will be to accept the sublease offer. However, it is important to recognise that this decision will only minimise the loss of the business in leasing the premises. In other words, it will be making the best of a bad job. Whilst this is the most appropriate course of action at this stage, the business will not be able to afford to continue to make commitments which cannot be covered by future revenues.

We must keep in mind the fact that, over the longer term, the survival of a business will depend on its ability to ensure that total revenues exceed total costs. Unless a business is profitable, the owners will not support its continued operation.

There is a saying that, when making management decisions, 'the things that count are the things that get counted'. In other words, it is quantitative data rather than qualitative data which dominates the minds of managers. This may be because managers can usually see the impact of quantitative data on the 'bottom line', ie the net profit of the organisation.

However, qualitative factors can be extremely important in shaping the profitability and viability of an organisation. Indeed, qualitative factors are often the main determinants of profitability and viability. Thus, it is important to identify these factors and to evaluate them when making decisions.

Qualitative factors can cover a very wide range. Examples of such factors include:

- the reputation of the business in its dealings with customers, employees and suppliers

- the attitude and morale of the workforce

- the quality of the workforce

- the quality of the product or services being offered

- the degree of competition etc.

By giving these factors explicit consideration the quality of management decisions will be enhanced.

Although this unit is fairly short you may well find that it is quite tough! As was mentioned earlier, the application of the relevant cost concept is not always easy. When dealing with problems you must always keep in mind the three factors which distinguish relevant costs and apply them rigorously to each item presented to you. Although the factors provide clear rules to apply, students do not usually find the application of these rules to particular situations a simple task. It is easy to become confused by the volume of data or the 'red herrings' contained in an exercise. Practice is very important in helping you to get to grips with this area. You really must work through the activities and exercises contained in the unit and check your answers carefully against the solutions provided.

The relevant cost concept will emerge at various points in future units and so it is important that you get to grips with it.

Now that you have a broad idea of what this unit is about, you can make start on the detail.

Decision making

IN UNIT 1 WE SAW that making decisions involves a series of logical steps.

Activity 1

See if you can remember what making a decision involves.

Jot down a list of the steps

Your list should include the following:

- Define the organisation's objective

- Identify the options

- Select the relevant data

- Assess the relevant data and make the decision

- Monitor the outcome of the decision.

We can see from this that the selection and assessment of relevant data is a crucial part of the decision making process. The accountant has an important role to play in both the selection of relevant data and the preparation of reports which assess the effect of possible courses of action. The accountant must ensure that only relevant data is employed to guide management decisions. It is the managers, however, who must decide which course of action should be followed.

The selection and assessment of relevant data is the main subject of this unit.

Relevant and irrelevant costs

WE SAW IN UNIT 1 that, in the context of a particular decision, whether a financial cost or benefit is relevant or irrelevant depends on three factors.

Activity 2

Can you identify what these three factors are?

Jot them down.

The three factors are as follows:

- does it relate to the objectives of the organisation?

- does it relate to the future?

- is it different between the options under consideration?

The third factor requires some elaboration. It is only *differential* (or *incremental*) costs and benefits which must be taken into account. Differential (incremental) costs are the additional costs arising from a particular course of action being taken. Differential (incremental) benefits are the additional revenues or cost savings arising from a particular course of action being taken. Costs and benefits which are not different between the options can be ignored.

Life would be easier if it were possible to identify certain types of costs (eg materials, labour, overheads) which could be classed as being relevant or irrelevant for decision making purposes. However, this is not really possible. As we shall see, costs such as materials etc may be regarded as relevant costs in one set of circumstances, but may be regarded as irrelevant costs in another set of circumstances. For each problem, therefore, we must try to identify the *future*, *differential* costs from the information provided.

Let us consider the following example.

Example 1

A business owns a machine which cost £6,000 two years ago. There is no further use for the machine as it stands and it could either be sold for £3,000 or converted at a cost of £1,500 so that it could be used as a perfect substitute for a machine which the management has definitely decided it needs. The new machine will cost £5,000 if bought. What should the management do?

Probably the best approach to dealing with this problem is to compare the benefits and costs which would occur with each course of action.

	Sell machine £	Convert machine £
Sales proceeds	3,000	-
Cost of new machine	(5,000)	-
Conversion cost	-	(1,500)
	(2,000)	(1,500)

NB Brackets round figures implies that they are negative. This convention will be used throughout this module.

Thus the lower cost lies with converting the machine. Given the business is seeking a wealth maximising objective, the business will convert the machine since this will have a beneficial effect on the value of the business (ie costs will be minimised).

Note that we are not making the decision on whether it is desirable to have the 'new' machine or not, merely how it is best to get it, by converting an existing machine or by buying a brand new one.

You should note that the above solution ignores the original cost of £6,000. This is because it is a *past* cost and like all past costs it must be the same irrespective of the course of action taken, ie it does not vary with the present decision. Decisions made at the present time cannot influence costs incurred at some earlier date. Whichever course of action is chosen, and it is presumably conversion which would be chosen, the £6,000 cost will be the same. It would be possible to take account of the £6,000 in the above solution but this would be pointless since it would need to appear in both columns so the difference will be identical (£500 in favour of conversion).

What is true of past costs is also true of future costs where they will be the same irrespective of the decision. Thus in the above example, if it will cost £100 to disconnect and remove the existing machine, an action which will need to be taken irrespective of what is done with it, the £100 is irrelevant to the decision and should be ignored.

Sunk costs

A SUNK COST IS A past cost, which, therefore, cannot be recovered. A sunk cost cannot be affected by any future decision and, therefore, should not be taken into account when making such decisions. An example of a sunk cost was the original cost of the machine in the activity above. Sunk costs may also be referred to as *historical costs* or *past costs*.

Activity 3

Can you think of any circumstances in which past costs may be useful when making decisions concerning the future?

Past costs, of themselves, are irrelevant to future decisions for the reasons mentioned above. However, they may be useful to managers when formulating predictions about future costs. These predictions may then be relevant in making decisions concerning the future. Thus, past costs may have an indirect influence on future decisions.

Reading

You should now read Reader Article 2.1 'Fixed costs and sunk costs in decision making' by Robert Luther.

When Luther mentions fixed costs he is referring to those costs which are not affected by the level of output. Similarly variable costs are those which vary as output rises or falls. We shall be dealing with this distinction in some detail in Unit 5, but these definitions will enable you to appreciate the points which the article makes.

Concorde, which is referred to in the article is a supersonic civil aircraft, which has now been in operation for some years. It was developed as an Anglo-French joint venture. The costs of the development of this aircraft continually overran the budget and called the plane's commercial viability into question. The two governments were, however, unwilling to 'waste' the money already spent by abandoning the project. Although the plane was finally developed and became successful in operational terms, it was and remains a financial disaster.

Points to consider:

Can knowledge of sunk costs ever be useful? What is the danger of knowing the size of sunk costs?

Committed costs

COMMITTED COSTS ARE COSTS to which the organisation is committed as a result of some past action. An example of a committed cost would be the amounts payable under a lease or rental contract. Depreciation of fixed assets already owned by an organisation is another example of a committed cost.

Committed costs are irrelevant to the decision because they will not vary according to which decision is made.

Activity 4

Johnson Ltd rents a building on a lease which still has ten years to run at a rent of £5,000 pa. The company has no use for the building during the next year but will continue to use it as a store thereafter. The only use to which it can be put during the next year is to sublet it to another business which is only prepared to pay £2,000 for the year's rental.

Should Johnson Ltd sublet the building?

The rent which Johnson Ltd is contracted to pay to the owner of the building is an example of a committed cost. It is, therefore, irrelevant to the decision.

On the basis of the information provided, and presuming that the company is seeking to maximise the wealth of its shareholders, it should sublet the premises. Doing this will make the company £2,000 more wealthy than not doing so.

Opportunity costs

SOMETIMES A COST OF pursuing a particular course of action is the failure to benefit from pursuing the alternative. In Example 1 (above), an effective cost of converting the machine is the sales proceeds (£3,000) foregone. This is as much a cost of the converted machine as is the £1,500 cost of the conversion work. Costs such as the £3000 are usually referred to as 'opportunity' costs because they represent the effective cost of foregoing an opportunity to pursue an alternative course of action.

Opportunity costs may take the form of either revenue foregone or cost savings foregone as a result of pursuing a particular course of action. Although opportunity costs do not involve out-of-pocket expenditure, they, nevertheless, represent real costs to the business and must be taken into account. Opportunity costs are not captured by the conventional accounting system. This is because accounting is transactions based. This means that there has to be a financial transaction with an external entity before an item is recorded by the accounting system (eg the purchase of an asset the sale of goods, the receipt of a loan, etc). Opportunity costs do not involve a transaction with another entity and, therefore, must be separately identified.

One of the difficulties with identifying opportunity costs is that they may not always be very obvious. If a business is assessing the commercial viability of launching a new product to extend an existing range of products, it is likely that sales of the new products could have an adverse effect on sales of existing products. Think, for example of a business which produces a range of models and types of household electrical appliances. If this business introduced a brand new model it is quite likely that it would compete for market with some of its own existing range of products. The cost of the profit lost from any lost sales of appliances in the existing range is an opportunity cost of a project to make and market the new model. The extent of this opportunity cost may be very difficult to assess. Furthermore such opportunity costs can be overlooked, which could lead to wrong decisions being taken. Probably all that can be said about identifying opportunity costs is that the task should be formally approached, not left to chance. This should be done by people who have sufficient knowledge of the circumstances to be able to recognise where a possible opportunity cost might exist, and of the financial values involved.

Activity 5

What would be the appropriate opportunity cost of conversion in Example 1, had there been an alternative buyer for the machine who was prepared to pay £3,200 ?

To answer this we simply need to ask ourselves which of the two options would be chosen if the conversion were not to go ahead. Clearly, all other things being equal, the old machine would be sold for the higher price of £3,200. Thus £3,200 is the opportunity cost of conversion, not £3,000.

It should now be clear that the effective opportunity cost is the value of the benefit foregone as a result of failing to pursue the next best option to the one which is under consideration.

Outlay costs

OUTLAY COSTS, UNLIKE OPPORTUNITY costs, involve out-of-pocket expenditure. Costs such as the £1,500 for conversion in the activity above are usually referred to as 'outlay' costs. Outlay costs will be relevant to a decision if they relate to the future and if they vary with the options under consideration. Thus the opportunity cost is that which is foregone by failing to pursue the best alternative.

Activity 6

Adams Ltd holds a stock of 200 kg of material Gamma. This cost £2/kg to buy two months ago. It is proposed to use all 200 kg in project X. The scrap value of Gamma is £1.80/kg but it will cost £2.20/kg to replace it. Gamma is a material which is used regularly by the company in its normal production.

What is the cost of using material Gamma in project X ?

If the material were not to be used in Project X it could either be scrapped or used in normal production. In fact it is the latter which would occur. Using the 200 kg in Project X engenders replacing it at a cost of £2.20/kg and this must, therefore, be the cost of using it in Project X. The figure of £1.80/kg is not relevant as scrapping the Gamma is not the alternative which would be pursued if the Gamma were not used in Project X, since to sell it at £1.80/kg to replace it at £2.20/kg would be illogical and would not occur. The original purchase price (outlay cost) of £2.00/kg is irrelevant since it is a past cost.

Activity 7

Job 106 requires the use of the following materials

Material		
	X	10 tonnes
	Y	2 tonnes
	Z	5 tonnes

There is no material X in stock; it will need to be purchased for the job at a cost of £2.10/tonne.

Material Y is in stock. It cost £5.50 a tonne to buy. It is in general use and could be used for other jobs immediately. It could be sold for £6/tonne less selling costs of £0.20/tonne. It would cost £6/tonne to replace.

Material Z is in stock. It cost £4.50 a tonne to buy. If not used on Job 106 it could not be used by the company. It could be sold for £1.50/tonne (net). Current replacement cost is £4/tonne.

What is the relevant material cost of Job 106 ?

Your answer should look something like this:

Material
X	10 tonnes @ £2.10/tonne	£21.00
Y	2 tonnes @ £6.00/tonne	12.00
Z	5 tonnes @ £1.50/tonne	7.50
		£40.50

Material X would need to be purchased so there is a clear outlay cost of £2.10/tonne.

Material Y would be used from stock, but would need to be replaced more or less immediately for the other purposes at £6.00/tonne.

Material Z would be scrapped if this job does not go ahead thus there is an opportunity cost of £1.50/tonne of using it in Job 106.

Cost information

A MANAGER MAY BE provided with a considerable amount of cost information concerning a particular project or product. In the context of a particular decision, however, the information provided may contain both relevant and irrelevant information. This can often be misleading for managers and there is a risk that incorrect decisions will be made. In Activity 7 above, for example, some of the information relating to the material required for Job 106 was irrelevant when attempting to determine the material cost of this job. (Even though it may have been useful for other reasons eg stock valuation.) It is important, therefore, to be able to examine cost information and be able to distinguish between the relevant and irrelevant costs for a particular decision. The self-assessment question below deals with this issue.

Now try this self-assessment question. This is intended to give you the opportunity to see whether you have grasped the material so far. You should probably be able to complete this in a half to three-quarters of an hour. Don't worry if it takes you longer. The main point is that, once you have completed it, you are clear on all of the points which it involves. It is not really helpful to look at the answer to this until you have completed your answer.

Self-assessment question 1

Dynamic Ltd is a manufacturer of specialist equipment for use in making plastic window frames. The company had just completed an order for Clearview Windows Ltd when the order was cancelled. The equipment concerned is so specialised that there is no ready market for it. The only potential buyer is a German company which said that it might be prepared to buy the equipment if certain conversion work were to be carried out first.

The following information has been prepared to help management decide on the minimum price that could be charged to the German company

Cost of manufacturing the equipment (see note (a) below)	£32,000
Deposit retained when order cancelled	£5,000

Conversion costs:
Materials	(see note b)
Labour	(see note c)
Fixed overheads	(see note e)

Normal mark up for profit	15%

Notes

(a) The material used in the equipment was of two types:
    (i) Alpha type, which could now be sold to a scrap merchant for £2,000, but would take 60 hours of labour to put the material into a suitable form for sale. The work could be undertaken by the company's maintenance department, which is very slack at this time. Maintenance staff are paid £6.00 per hour.

Continued over . . .

(ii) Beta type, which could be sold to the scrap merchant for £1,500 again after 60 hours of labour had been spent on it by the maintenance department. Alternatively it could be kept for use next year as a substitute for a material which is expected to cost £2,000; an additional 50 hours of highly skilled labour which would have to be specifically hired for the work over and above that spent rendering the material suitable for resale would have to be hired at £7.00 an hour.

(b) The material that would be used for the conversion was ordered a year ago at a price of £4,200. Delivery was delayed and its realisable value has fallen to £1,000. In recognition of this the supplier has given the company a discount of £1,600. The material could be used only for this one job. It is not possible to avoid the contract with the supplier.

(c) Labour for the conversion will be temporarily transferred from another department for one month. This labour is paid £1,000 per month. The other department makes a product, sales of 40 units of which will be lost if the labour is transferred. Each unit would sell for £100 and would use materials which would be bought in for £40 per unit. Only 25 units of the output will be lost if the company were to hire a special machine at a cost of £600 for the month partially to make up for the smaller labour force.

(d) The plans, patents and specifications of the equipment could be sold for £1,750 if the vehicles were scrapped, but passed to the German company if the machines are converted and sold.

(e) Overheads:
   (i) Additional supervisors would have to be hired for £900 for the conversion. It is the company's practice to charge such costs to fixed overheads.
   (ii) No other overheads would be affected by the conversion.

You are required to prepare an assessment of the absolute minimum price which the company should charge for the converted equipment, bearing in mind that the German company is the only possible customer.

Your assessment should be in the form of a list of all of the relevant costs of conversion, which add up to a total which will be the minimum price.

(The answers to self-assessment questions are provided at the end of the unit.)

Relevant costs and long-term profitability

WHAT WE HAVE SEEN so far, including the suggested solution to Self-assessment question 1, might be taken to mean that provided an organisation can cover the relevant future costs, in any particular situation, it will be successful in the long run. This is not necessarily the case. To be successful in the long run, the cash coming into the organisation will need to exceed the cash going out. Thus in Self-assessment question 1, if Dynamic Ltd continues to make equipment which it cannot sell at a price which enables it to recover all of its costs, it will go bankrupt. This means that when organisations are committing costs to particular activities management must make judgements about the likelihood of recouping those costs from customers. A company like Dynamic cannot spend £32,000 making equipment which it cannot sell, or at least it cannot do this too often before disaster will ensue.

When Dynamic found itself in the position outlined in the question, the £32,000 had already been spent (was a sunk cost). Now it might be a matter of making the best of a bad job. You should be clear that the suggested solution to this question is not suggesting that Dynamic should seek only to sell the converted equipment for £9,400. Since the company is presumably seeking to maximise its wealth, it will sell the converted equipment for as much as it possibly can. However, it remains the case, given the circumstances, that the company will be better off by selling the converted equipment at any price over £9,400 than it will be by pursuing the only alternative, which is scrapping it.

You might think that Dynamic's situation in this question is untypical of that in which organisations normally find themselves. Perhaps to some extent this is true. However, unless we are considering a brand new organisation, we never start with a 'blank sheet of paper'. An existing organisation will almost always be committed to something and/or be in a particular position as a result of some past decision. Ford has a number of vehicle factories around the world as a result of past decisions. When that company is considering the introduction of a new model, it should not ignore the existence of these factories and assess the viability of the new model as if they did not exist.

Now try this self-assessment question. You should probably be able to do it in half an hour or so. Don't look at the answer until you have completed the question.

Self-assessment question 2

James plc is engaged in a research project which so far has cost £180,000 but is currently under review. It is estimated that if the project is to be completed, which will take a further year, the findings will be sold to the European Commission for £200,000.

The research director of the company estimates that the following will be necessary during the forthcoming year to complete the project:

Materials – original cost £55,000. This material, which is currently in stock, is highly unstable, if it is not used in the project it will have to be rendered stable by a special process, costing £10,000 to undertake, before it can be disposed of. The stabilised material can be disposed of at no cost to the company. There is no market for the material, in either its unstable or stable state.

Labour – wage cost £40,000. This labour is highly skilled and is in great demand within the company. The production director has stated that were the project to be abandoned the labour could be used in making a product which would sell for £20 each and have a material cost of £10 each. It is estimated that the released labour could produce 10,000 units of the product during the year, all of which could be sold.

Research staff – salaries £65,000. A decision has been taken that, whenever the current research project ceases, the research staff will be declared redundant. Redundancy pay has been estimated at £50,000.

Share of rent – £40,000. This represents the appropriate proportion of the rent of the entire premises occupied by James plc.

Assuming that the estimates are correct and that the research done so far cannot be sold, advise the company on whether it should complete the project or not.

Clearly explain your reason for the treatment of each item of cost.

Your assessment should be in the form of a list of all of the relevant items, treating benefits of completing the project as positive and costs as negative. These should add up, taking account of pluses and minuses, to a figure which will lead you to a decision.

Each figure which you use in your analysis should have a few words of explanation as to why it is relevant.

(The answers to self assessment questions are provided at the end of the unit.)

Qualitative factors in decision making

SO FAR, WE HAVE seen how cost and benefits which can be quantified can be used to evaluate a particular course of action. However, we must recognise that there may be certain factors which cannot be easily expressed in financial terms but may, nevertheless, be important for a particular decision. These factors must not be excluded from the decision making process simply because they cannot be quantified. It is quite possible for certain qualitative factors to assume greater importance, when evaluating possible courses of action, than the quantitative factors.

Qualitative factors can have a significant effect on the profitability of the business in the longer term. For example, a business may make a decision to close down its transport division and use outside haulage companies to transport goods to customers. However, this decision may result in redundancies and conflict with the workforce. It may also make the business heavily dependent on outside companies for ensuring a prompt and reliable delivery service to customers. If the service proves unreliable, customer goodwill and future sales may be lost. The risks of such a policy must, therefore, be weighed against any quantifiable cost savings which may be achieved.

Activity 8

A business has a maintenance contract for certain specialised equipment with X Ltd. However, another company, Y Ltd, has recently approached the business and has offered to undertake the maintenance of the equipment at a price which is 20% lower than is currently being charged by X Ltd.

What are the qualitative factors which the business should take into account when assessing this offer?

Write down the points which occur to you.

There are numerous factors which you may have considered in answering this activity. Possible qualitative factors include:

● the reputation of Y Ltd concerning the quality of workmanship, reliability of maintenance work undertaken and response times in dealing with equipment breakdowns

● the nature of the maintenance work offered by Y Ltd. Will they offer an identical service to that of X Ltd?

● the experience of Y Ltd in dealing with the type of equipment used by the business

● the level of satisfaction with the existing maintenance contractors and the prospects of finding other maintenance contractors in the future if the business is dissatisfied with Y Ltd

● the reputation of the business for its loyalty to suppliers of goods and services.

This is not an exhaustive list. You may have thought of other factors which are not mentioned above

---

Activity 9

A company installs security systems for factories and other commercial premises. The basic security system for a shop is £800. The company is currently operating below capacity and has been approached by the owner of a small chain of newsagents to provide security systems for each of her shops at a price of £650 per shop. The relevant cost of installing the security system for each shop has been established as being £500.

What qualitative factors should be taken into account before a final decision is made concerning acceptance/rejection of the proposal?

The suggested price is greater than the relevant cost of producing the security systems and so acceptance of the contract will increase the wealth of the owners (at least in the short-term). However, when considering this proposal a number of qualitative factors should be considered.

These include:

● the reaction of other potential customers who may demand a similar price

● the reaction of rival businesses to the company's decision to cut prices

● the possibility of the excess capacity being taken up in the near future

● the timing of the contract. Will it coincide with the period of excess capacity?

● the possibility of making employees redundant if the contract is not accepted.

Once again, this list is not meant to be exhaustive and you may well have thought of other factors which are relevant to the final decision.

Wherever possible it is useful to try to quantify the impact of different factors on the business. By so doing we reduce the number of factors where judgement must be applied.

Summary of the unit

THIS UNIT HAS BEEN concerned with identifying relevant costs (and benefits) for decision making purposes. We have seen that, in order to be relevant to a particular decision, costs (and benefits) must:

- relate to the objective(s) being pursued

- relate to the future

- vary according to which decision is made.

In making financial decisions, it is necessary not only to consider the explicit, outlay costs and benefits, it is also necessary to take account of opportunity costs and benefits. These are items which **will not** arise if a particular decision is taken, but **will** arise if it is not. Sunk and committed costs should be ignored when making decisions.

The concept of relevant costs is important when we are making decisions. Thus, where the differential benefits exceed the differential costs of a particular course of action, we should make a decision to proceed as the total profits of the business will be increased (or total losses decreased). However, over the longer term, managers must seek to ensure that total revenues exceed total costs. Failure to do so will result in the failure of the business.

In making financial decisions, it is also necessary be aware that there may be factors which cannot be quantified in monetary terms but which may, nevertheless, be relevant to the final decision. These factors must be identified and evaluated as part of the decision making process.

The concept of relevant costs is important and it will re-appear in subsequent units when we concern other decision making problems. In particular, we will be concerned with the identification of relevant costs when we consider investment appraisal (Units 3 and 4) and cost–volume–profit analysis (Unit 5).

Suggested solutions to self-assessment questions

Self-assessment question 1

Dynamic Ltd

The absolute minimum price which should be charged to the German company should reflect only the future costs of conversion including opportunity costs, but ignoring costs which will be (or have been) incurred irrespective of conversion. This price, calculated below, is not the price which Dynamic might see as a very desirable one, nor the price which it would seek to charge. It is the price however which will make the company as well off by doing the conversion as pursuing the alternative. Anything above this price, logically should be accepted since there is no other customer.

Minimum price for converted equipment.

	£	Note to solution
Opportunity cost of scrapped material:		
Type Alpha material	2,000	(a)
Type Beta material	1,650	(b)
Conversion material	1,000	(c)
Labour	2,100	(d)
Opportunity cost of plans ètc	1,750	
Overheads	900	(e)
	£9,400	

Notes to the solution

(a) Since the labour to put type Alpha material in a suitable form is employed and paid by the company whether it does the work or not, the labour cost is irrelevant.

(b) There are two possibilities here:
(i) sell the type Beta material for £1,500 again with no relevant labour cost, ie a net benefit of £1,500.
(ii) use the material to save £2,000 at the relevant labour cost of £350, ie a net benefit of £1,650 (note that saving £2,000 is equivalent to receiving £2,000.)

Clearly possibility (ii) is the opportunity which would be pursued if the vehicles are not converted and £1,650 is the relevant opportunity cost.

(c) Since this material will have to be bought in any case the relevant cost is £1,000 ie how much it could be sold for if not used in the conversion. This is because selling the material for scrap is the only logical alternative to using it for the conversion.

(d) If the labour is transferred and the machine hired, sales of 25 units will be lost, a net financial loss of £1,500 (ie 25 × (£100 - 40)) after material cost savings have been taken into account. Hiring the machine will increase this by £600 to £2,100. This is less costly than losing 40 sales.

The labour cost of £1,000 is irrelevant since this amount will be paid irrespective of what the labour does during the month.

(e) Only overhead costs which alter with the decision to convert should be taken into account ie £900. Other overheads such as rent, heating, managerial salaries etc. will not apparently be altered by the decision to convert.

Self-assessment question 2

James plc

Net financial benefit (detriment) of continuing the project

Revenue	200,000
Material disposal cost saving	10,000
Labour opportunity cost	(100,000)
Research staff salaries	(65,000)
Net benefit of continuing	£45,000

Since there is a net financial benefit of continuing with the project, all other things being equal, it should continue.

Notes

1. The £180,000 already spent is irrelevant since it has been spent irrespective of whether the project is completed or not.

2. The £55,000 cost of materials is irrelevant since it has been spent irrespective of whether it is used or not. The cost of stabilising is relevant since, if the project continues, there will be no cost, but there will if the project is abandoned.

3. The £40,000 labour cost is irrelevant since it will be spent in either case. If the project does not continue the labour can produce net benefits of £100,000 (ie (£20 - 10) × 10,000), not possible if the project is completed.

4. Research staff redundancy cost is irrelevant since they will be made redundant in either case. The salary bill, for the forthcoming year, is relevant since it will only be incurred if the project continues.

5. The rent is irrelevant unless (very unlikely) the rent is reduced as a result of abandoning the project.

Additional exercises

THESE ARE QUESTIONS FOR you to do after you have completed your work on the main body of the section. By that time you should broadly have mastered the material but you will, almost certainly, find a bit more practice to be useful.

Exercise 1

Rhodes Ltd, which normally produces fibreglass sailing dinghies, is considering a special order from Crete Ltd for cabin cruiser hulls which has been offered to the firm. The hulls are to be built and delivered during the forthcoming year.

Following investigation, the management accountant of Rhodes Ltd has established the following information relating to the special order:

(1) **Materials:** Only two basic materials are necessary for the Crete contract, 20 tonnes of Alpha and 30 tonnes of Beta. Alpha is in constant use by Rhodes which is already under a binding contract for the purchase of 50 tonnes at £850 per tonne, but since the contract was placed the price has dropped to £800 per tonne.

Rhodes already has 30 tonnes of Beta in stock, but will only need to use 15 tonnes on dinghies over the next year; thereafter there would be no other use for the material apart from the Crete contract. The material originally cost £750 a tonne a year ago, since when the purchase price has risen to £1,000 a tonne.

The company could sell its stock of Beta for £800 a tonne.

(2) **Labour:** Skilled and unskilled labour and one supervisor will be required for the contract. Skilled workers (four of them), will be employed on special contracts which will terminate when the Crete contact is complete. Each skilled worker will be paid £8,900 for the contract.

The unskilled labour is already employed by Rhodes but would need to be moved from routine dinghy work to work on the Crete contract. These will be replaced on the dinghy work by paying overtime to the remaining dinghy workers. The overtime payments will amount to £19,200 during the Crete contract. The supervisor is due to retire at an annual pension of £4,800 but has agreed to stay on an extra year (forfeiting the year's pension) for a salary of £10,400.

(3)   **Overheads:** Rhodes has a policy of adding 50% of material and labour cost to cover overheads on all contracts. Management believe that the Crete contract will not give rise to additional overheads.

(4)   **Machinery:** A special machine will need to be hired for the duration of the Crete contract at a rental cost of £14,000. This machine will not be used full-time on the Crete contract and can be used on dinghy work. This will give rise to labour cost savings of £4,800 on dinghies.

Prepare a schedule to show whether the Crete contract would be acceptable to Rhodes if the maximum that Crete would pay for the contract is £125,000.

(Ignore the time value of money.)

Exercise 2

Cooper Ltd makes wooden barrels. The company has been approached by a customer who wants 100 barrels made to a particular specification, with a one week delivery deadline. The company, like its competitors, is short of work at the moment and is keen to get the contract.

Cooper's accountant has produced the following information:

Materials

The barrels will require the use of a special type of oak wood, which is no longer used on any of the company's other work.

Amount needed for the contract   500 square metres
Amount held in stock   300 square metres

The stock held originally cost £2.00 per square metre when it was bought for an order which did not materialise three years ago. It now costs £4.00 per square metre, but the company could only get £3.00 per square metre if it wanted to sell any.

Labour

The contract would require 100 hours of skilled labour. Skilled staff work a guaranteed 40 hour week. Since work is slack at present, there is 50 hours available among staff who would otherwise be unoccupied. The other 50 hours could come from overtime. The staff concerned are paid £5 an hour, with a 50% premium for overtime working. The company knows of a suitably qualified freelance worker who would do the work, in time to meet the customer's deadline for a total of £500. This person is not interested in the job unless all of it is available.

Other costs

	£
Steel strip	500
Design costs (already incurred, but not yet paid)	150
Overheads which vary with the level of production	360

Cooper normally adds 50% of the material and labour cost to cover things like rent, rates, insurance, etc.

You are required to deduce the minimum price which Cooper Ltd could quote for the barrels in order not to be economically worse off by getting the contract.

Exercise 3

Cherry Ltd, an engineering company, wishes to tender for an order with a French company. Before meeting to negotiate the price, the sales negotiator wishes to know the price at which the company would be neither better nor worse off as a result of taking the order.

One of the company's engineering estimators has already worked 50 hours in connection with the quotation and it has incurred travelling expenses of £630 on a visit to the customer's premises in France.

The estimator has produced the following statement relating to the contract:

French company estimate

	£	£
Materials and components		
7,500 kg of Gamma at £10 per kg	75,000	
1,000 kg of Delta at £3 per kg	3,000	
Components which will need to be to be bought-in	10,000	
		88,000
Labour		
Skilled labour: 500 hours at £6.00 per hour	3,000	
Unskilled labour: 700 hours at £4.00 per hour	2,800	
		5,800
Overheads		
Variable with the level of output	5,000	
Fixed irrespective of the level of output	40,000	
		45,000
Estimating costs		
50 hours at £20 per hour	1,000	
Travelling expenses	630	
		1,630
Total		£140,430

The following information has also been identified:

Material Gamma: This is used regularly by the company. There is currently 9,000 kg in stock which cost £10 per kg. The buying price has recently increased by 20%. If the company wanted to scrap any of this material it would expect to get £8 per kg for it.

Material Delta: A stock of 400 kg is in stock at present, though the material is never used by the company in its normal work. It was bought several years ago for £2 per kg, but its current buying price is £4 per kg. Its scrap value is only £3.50 per kg. It had been suggested that this material could be used as a perfect substitute for material Beta, which is in constant use on one of the company's normal products. Beta costs £3 per kg.

Labour: Labour is paid by the hour. Even though work is slack at present the company tends to keep on its skilled staff in order to maintain its pool of skilled labour. Even though the estimate identifies a particular mix of labour, it is likely that the contract, if it is to be undertaken, will be staffed only by skilled staff who would otherwise have nothing to do.

Variable overheads: These are items which vary with the level of output. If the job is not obtained, the overheads will not be incurred on it. If the job is not obtained, however, the facilities of the company will be sublet to another business which will pay £7 00 for their use. This would cause the variable overheads to be incurred at exactly the same level as if the job had been obtained.

Fixed overheads: This figure represents a share of rent, rates and general administrative costs.

Estimating costs: The estimators are charged to contracts at £20 per hour, even though they are paid, on average, £8 per hour. The difference is to cover the overheads associated with having a team of estimators.

Prepare a schedule showing the minimum price which could charge for the job such that it would not be economically worse off as a result of getting the job.

Solutions to additional exercises

Exercise 1

Assessment of the Crete contract

		£	£	Notes
Labour				
	Skilled 4 × £8,900		35,600	
	Unskilled		19,200	
	Supervisors	10,400		
	Less: pension saving	4,800	5,600	(a)
			60,400	
Materials				
	A 20 tonnes @ £800 per tonne	16,000		(b)
	B 15 tonnes @ £1,000 per tonne	15,000		(c)
	15 tonnes @ £800 per tonne	12,000		(d)
			43,000	
Overheads				
				(e)
Machinery				
	Rentals	14,000		
	Less: Labour cost savings	4,800		
			9,200	
Total			112,600	

Since the contract price offered is £125,000, the contract would be beneficial to Rhodes.

Notes

(a) The relevant cost of the contract is the **additional amount** which keeping the supervisor for the next year will give rise. Since if the supervisor would receive a pension if not kept on the relevant cost is the salary less the savings from the non-payment of the pension.

(b) Any material Alpha used on the Crete contract will need to be replaced, presumably at a price of £800 per tonne. The binding contract price of £850 is irrelevant since irrespective of the Crete contract this purchase will have to be made.

(c) If the Crete contract were not undertaken 15 tonnes of the stock of Beta will be sold at £800 per tonne. This represents the relevant cost of using it in the Crete contract.

(d) There will be a requirement to buy an additional 15 tonnes of Beta in order to fulfil the Crete contract. This will have to be bought at the current price of £1,000 per tonne.

(e) The manner in which Rhodes normally allows for overheads in pricing is irrelevant to the minimum price for the contract. The point is the additional cost of overheads for the contract. This appears to be nothing.

Exercise 2

Total differential cost of undertaking the order

		£
Oak:	300 @ £3.00 (opportunity cost)	900
	200 @ £4.00 (outlay cost)	800
Labour:	50 hours @ £7.50 (this is less costly than paying £500 to a subcontractor)	375
Steel strip		500
Variable overheads		360
Total differential cost of undertaking the order		**£2,935**

(absolute minimum price)

Note

The above items are only those which will differ according to whether the order is undertaken. Thus, for example, the non-overtime labour is ignored because the cost will be the same irrespective of the order.

Exercise 3

Revised French company estimate

		£	Notes
Materials			
Gamma	7,500 kg at £12 per kg	90,000	(1)
Delta	400 kg at £3.50 per kg	1,400	(2)
	600 kg at £4.00 per kg	2,400	
Components		10,000	
Sublet facilities		700	(3)
Minimum tender price		**104,500**	

Notes

1. This material is in general use and will need to be replaced at £20 per unit.

2. For the 400 kg which is in stock and is not much used the relevant cost is the scrap value since scrapping is the better option than using it as a substitute for the material costing £3 per kg. The relevant cost for the other 600 kg is its buying-in cost.

3. If the tender is successful the company will lose the opportunity to sublet the facilities for £700. The overheads will be the same in either case.

4. The company has surplus capacity and has a 'no redundancy' policy for its skilled employees. It seems that if the tender is successful the work will be done by skilled labour who would otherwise be idle. Thus there is no relevant labour cost.

5. The fixed overheads clearly will not vary with the success of the tender and are, therefore, irrelevant.

6. The estimating department costs are past and, therefore, irrelevant.

UNIT 3

INVESTMENT DECISIONS

THIS UNIT IS CONCERNED with investment decision making, both the theoretical and practical aspects.

On completion of this unit you should be able to:

- explain the concept of the time value of money

- deduce the present value of any future cash flow from first principles and explain the meaning of the net present value (NPV) of a project

- deduce the internal rate of return (IRR) of a project.and.explain the theoretical strengths and weaknesses of IRR relative to those of NPV

- define and to calculate the payback period and the accounting rate of return of a project and to discuss their usefulness relative to that of NPV

- discuss and to apply the practical aspects of using the NPV approach to investment decision making.

Outline of the unit

THE UNIT BEGINS BY pointing out that a business can be viewed as an investment agency in so far that it obtains funds from shareholders and lenders and then invests these amounts in a portfolio of projects. Deciding which projects to invest in is vitally important to a business. The size of the projects undertaken are often substantial and the time scale over which they are undertaken will often be long. It is, therefore, vitally important for the future profitability and survival of the business that investment decisions are made in a logical systematic way.

Businesses are concerned with generating wealth. This means that, when considering an investment project, the financial benefits must exceed the costs involved, if it is to be worthwhile. Only if there is a net benefit arising from an investment will the value of the business be enhanced and wealth generated. Thus investment decisions are, in essence, concerned with an evaluation of benefits and associated costs. We shall see later in this unit that the main techniques of investment appraisal are really only applying this cost/benefit principle.

Where all benefits and costs arise at the same point in time the evaluation process is quite straightforward. However, this rarely occurs in practice. It is often the case that the costs are incurred first and the benefits will begin to flow at some later point in time. This timing difference is important because £1 today is not the same as £1 at some future date. Most people would prefer to have £1 now rather than in the future. One reason for this is simply that £1 received today can grow into a larger amount at some future date. Other reasons for preferring £1 today are also discussed.

Given that £1 today is not the same as £1 in (say) one years time we might ask: 'What is the maximum worth of £1 receivable in one years time to an individual?' This question can be answered by using a simple and logical approach which deduces the *present value* of a sum of money receivable at some, specific, date. When evaluating an investment project, it is necessary to establish the present value of all future sums. It is only by establishing the present value of these future sums that we can compare like with like. Where, for example, an investment involves an immediate outlay followed by future benefits, the present value of the future benefits will be established and then netted off against the outlay cost. (Where the outlay is immediate it will already be expressed in present terms.)

NET PRESENT VALUE

The resultant figure is known as the *net present value* (NPV) of the project. The NPV can be related to the primary objective of a business. If the NPV is positive the value of the business will be increased and, therefore, on the basis of the quantitative information available, the project should be accepted. Where there are two mutually exclusive projects being considered, the project with the higher NPV should be chosen. If the NPV of a project is negative the value of the business will be decreased if the project is undertaken. The project should therefore be rejected, unless there are other, compelling, reasons for undertaking it. The figures never tell the whole story and other, qualitative factors must also be taken into account. The final decision is usually the result of some balancing of figures and other factors.

As we shall see later in the unit, it is theoretically superior to any other approach available.

INTERNAL RATE OF RETURN

Another approach to investment appraisal is through the *internal rate of return* (IRR). This method also involves discounting future cash flows, however, it views the investments proposal from a slightly different perspective than the NPV method. The IRR method adopts the view that, for a project to be worthwhile, the rate of return on cash invested must be higher than the interest foregone.

The internal rate of return is that rate of return which, when used to discount future cash flows, will give the project a zero NPV. This rate can then be compared with the interest rate foregone (hurdle rate) to see which is higher. The decision rule is that only those projects which provide a higher IRR than the 'hurdle rate' should be accepted as only these will lead to an increase in the value of the business.

We shall discuss the fact that, in most cases, the NPV and IRR methods both promote the maximisation of value objective. However, there are certain situations where IRR will not do this, ie NPV and IRR methods will give conflicting answers. As the NPV method will always promote the maximisation of value objective it can be regarded as theoretically superior and should be the preferred method.

PAYBACK

A third method of assessing investment opportunities is the *payback* method. This method calculates the time it takes for the net cash inflows from a project to repay the initial outlay. The shorter the payback period the more attractive the project. A business may set a particular payback period which projects are expected to achieve in order to be acceptable.

The payback period for a particular opportunity is difficult to interpret. This is because the method is not directly related to the primary objective of businesses. Payback period's weaknesses, as a method, are discussed.

ACCOUNTING RATE OF RETURN

The fourth method of investment appraisal is the *accounting rate of return*. This method takes the expected average accounting profit from the proposed investment and expresses it as a percentage of the initial investment. To be acceptable, a project would be expected to achieve a minimum rate of return. Once again, the calculations are fairly straightforward, but they are difficult to interpret as the method does not directly relate to the primary objective of a business. The problems of this method are discussed in the unit.

The unit ends with consideration, in more detail, of how the discounting methods are applied to practical problems. This is important as it will help you in getting to grips with computational problems in this area.

The importance of investment decision making to a business cannot be overstated. This unit is, therefore, a very important part of Management Accounting. The unit is quite long compared to the previous two units. You will need to devote a fair amount of time to it.

Now that you have a broad idea of what this unit is about, you can make start on the detail.

The nature and importance of investment decision making

IN A VERY IMPORTANT respect, businesses can be viewed as investment agencies. They obtain funds from various sources, most significantly from the shareholders and from long-term lenders. Businesses then use those funds to make investments. Sometimes a business will make investments of the type which individuals associate with the word investment; buying shares in other businesses or putting money on deposit in a bank. More typically however, businesses use the funds to make investments in, so-called, 'real' investments, eg factories, machinery, shops, offices, theatres, films. The role of the business is to manage those investments so as best to achieve its objectives. Decisions affecting the choice of investments which businesses make is of vital importance to the ability of those businesses to achieve their objectives and to prosper.

Investment decisions are vitally important to a business for several reasons:

● They tend to involve very large amounts of finance, given the size of the particular business concerned

● They tend to be financially costly to abandon once funds have been committed to them. For example, a business which buys and equips a new factory will normally find that, if a decision is made to reverse the original decision, it will not get all of its money back. Typically, there would be a significant financial loss in reversing the decision. This is likely to be the case even where the reversing decision is taken very shortly after the factory has been established and equipped

● Investment decisions tend to have fairly long time scales. Businesses establish and equip new offices, shops, factories etc, in the expectation of profitable use of their investment for perhaps 20 years.

These points emphasise that many of the investment decisions of a business are likely to go to the very essence of its ability to survive and to prosper.

Business objectives and the nature of investment decisions

WE HAVE ALREADY SEEN (Unit 2) that most businesses seem to follow an objective of seeking to maximise the value of the business. They may do this in conjunction with other objectives, but they will need to ensure that the value of the business is maintained, if only to survive.

In order for a particular investment to be beneficial to the business (in the sense of enhancing its value) the financial benefits coming from the investment must be greater than the cost of making the investment. In the very simplest case, where the cost and the benefit are made at the same time, assessment of a project is easy.

Example 1

A business can buy an item of stock-in-trade for £1,000 which it can sell (with immediate cash settlement) for £1,500. Should it make the investment ?

The answer is that the business should make the investment since this will have the effect of increasing its value by an immediate £500. Only if there are special reasons would it be logical for the business not to enter into this investment because the value of the financial benefit exceeds the value of the financial detriment.

Suppose now that exactly the same opportunity exists *except* that now the £1,500 is not due for payment until one year after making the investment. Is the straightforward comparison of the two amounts still valid ?

Is £1,500 to be received in a year's time as valuable as the same amount receivable immediately? In practice most people would not regard these two as equivalently acceptable or attractive.

Activity 1

Most people would prefer to receive £1,500 immediately than to wait a year for it?

Can you think of three reasons for this? Jot down your reasons.

The three reasons for this are

● **Interest foregone.** If the business had the money immediately it could put it on deposit and earn a year's interest on it. This could not be done if it were not to be received until next year.

● **Inflation.** The goods and services which the business could buy with £1,500 in a year's time would generally be less than could be bought now. This makes the amount effectively less valuable if it is not available for a year, even though it is nominally the same number of pounds.

● **Risk.** An amount of money, either in the hands of the business, or due to be received immediately, is generally much more certain, and logically much more valuable, than the same amount due in one year's time. Obviously this point does not always apply, or at least is not always significant. For example an amount to be received from a very secure source like the UK government is not very risky. In most commercial contexts however, risk is a very important consideration.

We shall come back to the topics of inflation and risk later. For the time being we shall concentrate on just the first of these three, ie the opportunity cost of the interest foregone. We shall see later that how we deal with this factor is also the logical way of coping with the presence of the other two.

The time value of money

We have seen that most rational people (including business managers) do not regard £1,500 to be received in a year's time as being equivalent to the same amount now. Put another way, most people would not be prepared to pay £1,500 now to buy the right to receive £1,500 in a year's time. So that we can proceed towards some logical basis for dealing with such decisions, we need to answer the question as to how much people would be prepared to pay to buy this right.

Activity 2

If there were a prevailing interest rate of 10% per annum (ie you could put money on deposit which would earn 10% per annum), ignoring inflation, risk and taxation, how much do you think would be the logical maximum amount to spend on buying the right to receive £1,500 in a year's time?

The logical value of next years receipt is the amount which would grow with interest to become £1,500 after one year.

If we call this amount X, then:

$$X + (10\% \times X) = £1,500.$$

so,

$$X + 0.1X = £1,500$$

If we rearrange this slightly, by taking X outside of a bracket on the left-hand-side, then:

$$X(1 + 0.10) = £1,500$$
$$X = £1,500/(1 + 0.10)$$
$$X = £1,363.6$$

Thus a logical person would be as happy to have £1,363.6 now as to have £1,500 in one year's time. In this sense £1,363.6 is the **present value** of £1,500 in a year's time.

Net present value

If £1,500 receivable in one year's time is worth £1,363.6 to us now, we should presumably be pleased to buy the stock-in-trade (in Example 1, above) because we are being offered something worth this amount for just £1,000. Taking on this deal will make the business richer by £363.6 (in today's terms). All things being equal, the business will be eager to take on this investment.

The £363.6 is known as the *net present value* (NPV) of the investment because it is the present value of the investment after netting the present value of the future benefits with the present value of the cost of making the investment. It is the standard convention to treat costs as negative and benefits as positive. Thus, the investment we are considering has a positive net present value.

Obviously investment opportunities with a positive NPV are beneficial, in the sense of increasing the value of the business, and should, in principle, be undertaken. By the same token investment projects with a negative NPV should be rejected. A project with a zero NPV should leave the business indifferent as to whether the project is undertaken or not. Thus a business should seek to undertake all available projects which have positive NPVs. By doing this the value of the business will be maximised.

Where a business has two competing investment opportunities the one with the higher NPV should be selected.

Logically the value of a business should be the sum of all of the projects which it has in operation at the particular time.

Activity 3

What is the NPV of an investment opportunity which involves an immediate outflow of £260,000, which will give rise to an inflow of £300,000 after one year, assuming an interest rate of 8%?

$$\text{NPV} = -260,000 + \frac{300,000}{1 + \frac{8}{100}}$$

$$= -260,000 + 277,778$$

$$= £17,778$$

All other things being equal, the investment should be undertaken.

Activity 4

What is the NPV of an opportunity which involves *receiving* £10m immediately and *paying* £12m after one year assuming a 12% pa interest rate?

$$NPV = £10m + \frac{£12m}{1 + \frac{12}{100}}$$

$$= £10m - £10.7$$

$$= -£0.7m$$

The 'investment' should not be undertaken. Note that this 'discounting' approach is just as valid irrespective of whether the future cash flow is a positive or a negative one.

Investment opportunities lasting more than one year

In reality, few investment opportunities last for only one year. Suppose that an investment opportunity involves an immediate cash outflow C_o which will give rise to inflows C_1 and C_2 after one and two years respectively. We already know that the present value of C_1 (effect on the value of the business), is $C_1/(1 + i)$. By the same logic as we derived this, an amount, say Y, which would grow with interest compounded annually to C_2.

Y invested now will grow to $Y + Yi$ or $Y(1 + i)$ after one year. During the second year this amount will be reinvested and it will then grow to $Y(1 + i) + (Y(1 + i) \times i)$. This equals

$$C_2 = Y + Yi + (Y + Yi)i$$

(i.e. the original borrowing plus interest on that amount for the first year plus interest on these two during the second year).

This expression expands to:

$$C_2 = Y + Yi + Yi + Yi^2$$

taking Y outside brackets:

$$C_2 = Y(1 + 2i + i^2)$$
$$C_2 = Y(1 + i)^2$$
and $$Y = C_2/(1 + i)^2$$

Following this logic, it can be shown that the present value of any amount of cash receivable after n years (C_n) would be $C_n/(1 + i)^n$.

If we wish to define NPV in a formal, mathematical way, we can say that the NPV of any investment opportunity is given by:

$$\text{NPV} = \sum_{n=0}^{n=t} \frac{C_n}{(1+i)^n}$$

(where t is the life of the opportunity in years)

If we wish to put it in plain English, we can say that the NPV of an opportunity is the sum of all of the cash flows associated with it, each one discounted according to how far into the future it one will occur.

Example 2

Antonio plc has estimated that it could achieve cost savings by investing in either of two automatic machines. The accountant's estimate of the actual savings and of the cost of the machines is as follows:

	Type Alpha £	Type Beta £
Cost of the machine (payable now)	50,000	60,000
Estimated annual savings:		
Year 1	14545 16,000	16,000
2	9917 12,000	16,000
3	9016 12,000	16,000
4	6833 10,000	14,000
5	6209 10,000	10,000

1 3483

Which, if either, of these two machines should be bought if the relevant interest rate is 10% per annum throughout?

Note that the savings listed above are not actual inflows (receipts) of cash. They are however 'opportunity' cash inflows. As such, we should recall from Unit 2, they are highly relevant to the present decision.

The NPV of each machine is as follows:

	Type Alpha £	Type Beta £

Present value
of cash flows:

		Type Alpha		Type Beta	
Now (Year 0)		(50,000)		(60,000)	

1	$\dfrac{16{,}000}{(1 + 0.10)} = 14{,}545$	$\dfrac{16{,}000}{(1+ 0.10)} = 14{,}545$
2	$\dfrac{12{,}000}{(1 + 0.10)^2} = 9{,}917$	$\dfrac{16{,}000}{(1 + 0.10)^2} = 13{,}223$
3	$\dfrac{12{,}000}{(1 + 0.10)^3} = 9{,}016$	$\dfrac{16{,}000}{(1 + 0.10)^3} = 12{,}021$
4	$\dfrac{10{,}000}{(1 + 0.10)^4} = 6{,}830$	$\dfrac{14{,}000}{(1 + 0.10)^4} = 9{,}562$
5	$\dfrac{10{,}000}{(1 + 0.10)^5} = 6{,}209$	$\dfrac{10{,}000}{(1 + 0.10)^5} = 6{,}209$
	£(3,483)	£(4,440)

This process of converting future cash flows to their present value is known as *discounting*. Tables are readily available which give the factor $1/(1 + i)^n$ for a range of values of i and n. Such a table appears on the very last page of this unit. However, it is not really worth bothering to use a table when it is just as easy to use a calculator to discount from first principles.

It can be seen that both machines have a negative NPV. To purchase either machine would reduce the value of the business. Neither of these two machines should, therefore, be bought on the basis of these estimates of costs (including the relevant interest rate) and of the benefits.

Activity 5

The supplier of the Alpha type machine has told Antonio plc that it might be prepared to reduce the price of the machine. On the basis of the above calculations, what is the maximum price that Antonio plc should logically be prepared to pay for a machine?

The maximum price which the business should be prepared to pay is the value of the savings which would be expected to result from buying the machine; it would be illogical to pay more for an economic asset than it is worth. To do so would reduce the value of the business, which is precisely the opposite of what businesses seek to do. On the basis of the above calculations, an Alpha type machine is worth £46,517 (ie the sum of the present values of the savings). It may be to another business, or even to Antonio plc under other circumstances, the machine may be worth more or less than this. You should note that the value of any economic asset should logically be deduced in this way.

Advantages of using the NPV approach

WE CAN CONCLUDE THAT NPV is a valuable means of assessing investment opportunities because:

● It is directly derived from, what appears to be the main financial objective of private sector organisations

● It seems to take account of all the relevant, measurable information about an investment opportunity. This includes the timing of the estimated cash flows and the cost of financing the investment

● It gives clear unambiguous results, which are simple and logical to interpret.

Discounting and compounding

WE HAVE SEEN THAT the major objective of discounting future cash flows is to express all cash flows, irrespective of when in the future they are estimated to occur, in the same terms so that a comparison can be made. (Remember our original problem in Example 1 was trying to compare £1,000 to be spent immediately with £1,500 to be received a year later).

An alternative to discounting, ie expressing all cash flows in present value terms, is to *compound*, ie to express all cash flows in terms of their value at some specific date in the future. If, as we previously did in respect of Example 1, we assume an interest rate of 10%, we should compound the present cash flow by adding 10% interest to it and then compare it with the unadjusted future cash flow.

Future value (after one year) of £1,000 (assuming a 10% per annum interest rate) = £1,000 + (£1,000 × 10%) = £1,100. This can now be compared with the £1,500 cash flow, after one year, to show that as the future value of the receipt (£1,500) is greater than the future value of the payment (£1,100), it would be worth buying the stock-in-trade. This is, of course, the same conclusion as we came to when we discounted to enable us to make the comparison. The actual difference between the figures is not the same as it was when we discounted because now the difference is expressed in future values, as compared with present values, but this does not affect the decision, and it never will in any example.

The following diagrams illustrate the relationship between discounting and compounding:

Figure 1

Discounting, expressing all cash flows in present value terms

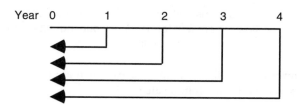

Figure 2
Compounding, expressing all cash flows in future value terms.

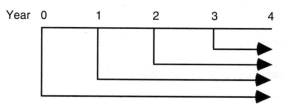

You will probably agree that compounding cash flows is as logical a method of expressing cash flows in the same terms, in order that valid comparisons to be made, as is discounting. Thus it can, in principle, be used equally as effectively as discounting. For example, if you were to rework Example 2 (above) compounding all cash flows to year 5, you would find that the sum of the compounded annual savings would be less than the compounded value of the machine. This is to say that both machines have a negative *net future value*, as well as a negative *net present value*. Thus you would reach exactly the same conclusion for very much the same reason.

All this, of course, raises the question, why discount instead of compounding? If they both tell you the same thing, does it matter which one you use?

There are probably two reasons for discounting being favoured over compounding. These are:

● Since we are making the decision now, it seems logical to express everything about the decision in terms of now, ie in present value terms. If you are trying to compare the price of a particular product in Germany, with its price in the UK, you have the choice of converting the UK price into DMarks or of converting the German price into sterling. It really does not matter which you do, the cheaper price will still be cheaper irrespective of the currency in which it is expressed. However, if you are living in the UK and are used to thinking in sterling terms you may feel that sterling is the more relevant. Similarly if you are at the 'present' point in time, you may feel it more logical to express things in present value terms.

● If we are going to compound we must decide to which point in the future we are going to compound. Logically this would be to the end of a particular project eg five years in the case of Example 2. Projects which are being compared are not necessarily of the same length, however. In these circumstances the future date to be selected becomes more arbitrary. In principle this is not a problem, but to assess all projects by expressing their cash flows in the same terms does make for more consistency. Expressing cash flows in present terms (ie discounting) has tended to be the most popular basis in practice.

Nevertheless, all of the advantages which are claimed for NPV could equally well be claimed for net future value.

We shall go on to consider three other approaches to assessing investment opportunities which are widely used in the UK. We shall seek to assess how valid each one is by the attributes of NPV listed above.

Now try this self-assessment question. You can probably do it in about 20 minutes.

Complete it before you check with our solution.

Self-assessment question 1

Patterson Ltd has the opportunity to make an investment, the anticipated cash flows relating to which are as follows:

	£
Year 0	-70,000 (ie an outflow)
1	+20,000
2	+30,000
3	+20,000
4	+10,000
5	+10,000

Calculate the NPV assuming:

(a)   an interest rate of 10%
(b)   an interest rate of 15%

Comment on the difference between the two NPVs.

(The answers to self assessment questions are provided at the end of the unit.)

Internal rate of return

This approach seeks to identify the effective rate of return on the cash invested in a project, taking account of the precise length of time for which it is committed to the project. Those who use internal rate of return (IRR) as the criterion for making their investment decisions would require that for any project to be worth undertaking, it must have an IRR of at least the interest rate which would be available to the business if it were to put the cash on deposit in a bank. If two or more projects are competing for consideration, as for example in the case of the Alpha and Beta type machines in Example 2 (above), the one with the higher IRR should be selected.

To understand IRR, it may be useful to think of a particular investment opportunity in terms of depositing and withdrawing funds from an interest bearing bank deposit account. The implied interest rate from those cash flows is the IRR of the investment.

Example 3

An investment project requires an initial investment of £1,000. The only expected inflow from the project is £1,200 after one year. What is the IRR of this project?

If we were to place £1,000 on bank deposit which grew to £1,200 after one year we should deduce that the interest rate which the original investment was earning must be:

$$\frac{(£1,200 - 1,000)}{1,000} (\times 100) = 20\% \text{ per annum}$$

Thus the IRR of the investment opportunity is 20% per annum.

Now consider a slightly more complicated but more realistic example.

Example 4

An investment project requires an initial investment of £2,000. The expected inflows from the project are £1,200 after one year and a further £1,100 after a further year. What is the IRR of this project ?

Perhaps our first instinct is to believe that the IRR is as follows:

$$\frac{(£1,200 + 1,100 - £2,000)/2}{2,000} (\times 100) = 7.5\% \text{ per annum}$$

ie the net benefit from the project divided by 2 (because there are two years), expressed as a percentage of the investment.

This would be wrong however. If we think in terms of the bank deposit account we realise that the £1,200 withdrawn from the account at the end of the first year is not just interest. A part of it is a withdrawal of some of the original deposit of £2,000. As a result the amount still left on deposit during the second year is less than £2,000. This means that the calculation carried out above is wrong to the extent that it is based on the assumption that the whole £2,000 on deposit for the whole of the two years, whereas in fact much of it has been withdrawn at the end of the first year.

Deducing the IRR for this example is not very straightforward. In fact IRR is the discount rate which gives the investment a zero NPV.

The investment which we are considering here can be expressed as:

$$-2,000 + \frac{1,200}{(1 + i)} + \frac{1,100}{(1 + i)^2} = 0$$

Where i is the IRR of the investment (or the implied rate of interest paid by the bank (to continue the analogy)).

It is possible to calculate i directly in this case. In fact the correct result is 10% per annum.

Thus the IRR is 10% per annum. Just to demonstrate the similarity of IRR to the interest rate on a deposit account, let us see what happens if we take the cash flows from the example and assume that they are in fact a deposit and two withdrawals from a bank deposit account yielding an interest rate of, what we now know to be, 10% per annum.

	£
Amount deposited in the bank	2,000
Interest earned during the first year (2,000 × 10%)	200
	2,200
Amount withdrawn at the end of the first year	1,200
Amount left on deposit during the second year	1,000
Interest earned during the second year (1,000 × 10%)	100
	1,100
Amount withdrawn at the end of the second year	1,100
Amount left in the bank at the end of the second year	ZERO

This shows that the investment project yields a return of 10% on the cash committed to the project, but only for as long as it is committed.

It was relatively easy to deduce the IRR for the two projects outlined in these two examples because they lasted only for one or two years. Where a project last for longer, the IRR can only be found by trial and error. This can be done manually, as we shall shortly see. In practice it is usually done on a computer. Many of the modern 'spreadsheet' packages incorporate a facility for deducing IRRs, if the cash flows and their timing are entered.

If we return to the Alpha type machine in Example 2 (above), here the IRR is the solution (for i) of the statement:

$$-50{,}000 + \frac{16{,}000}{(1+i)} + \frac{12{,}000}{(1+i)^2} + \frac{12{,}000}{(1+i)^3} + \frac{10{,}000}{(1+i)^4} + \frac{10{,}000}{(1+i)^5} = 0$$

The only way that we can deduce the value of i (the IRR) is by trial and error.

We know from Example 2 that if we use a value for i of 10% we obtain a value of £3,483 (negative) for the left hand side of this statement This means that the project does not have an IRR as high as 10%.

Let us try 5%

ie
$$-50{,}000 + \frac{16{,}000}{(1+0.05)} + \frac{12{,}000}{(1+0.05)^2} + \frac{12{,}000}{(1+0.05)^3} + \frac{10{,}000}{(1+0.05)^4} + \frac{10{,}000}{(1+0.05)^5}$$

$$= \quad -50{,}000 + 15{,}238 + 10{,}884 + 10{,}366 + 8{,}227 + 7{,}835$$

$$= \quad +2{,}550.$$

Thus the IRR for the Alpha type machine lies somewhere between 5% and 10%. It is obviously a bit closer to 5% since +2,550 is rather closer to zero than is -£3,483. We can see by looking at these figures that the IRR lies quite close to 7%, an assertion which could be checked by doing the calculations again using 7%.

From what we have just seen, it is fairly obvious that IRR is quite closely linked to NPV. In fact the IRR of a particular project is the discount percentage which gives the project a zero NPV.

Activity 6

Have a go at deducing the IRR of the Beta type machine project, the cash flows for which were given in Example 2 (earlier in this unit)?

Use the same approach as we just did for the Alpha type machine.

The IRR for the Beta is the solution for i in the following statement:

$$-60{,}000 + \frac{16{,}000}{(1+i)} + \frac{16{,}000}{(1+i)^2} + \frac{16{,}000}{(1+i)^3} + \frac{14{,}000}{(1+i)^4} + \frac{10{,}000}{(1+i)^5} = 0$$

We know from Example 2 that if we use a value for i of 10% we obtain a value of £4,440 (negative) for the left hand side of this statement. This means that like the Alpha, the Beta project does not have an IRR as high as 10%.

Let us try 5%

ie -60,000 + $\dfrac{16,000}{(1+0.05)}$ + $\dfrac{16,000}{(1+0.05)^2}$ + $\dfrac{16,000}{(1+0.05)^3}$ + $\dfrac{14,000}{(1+0.05)^4}$ + $\dfrac{10,000}{(1+0.05)^5}$

=   -60,000 + 15,238 + 14,512 + 13,821 + 11,518 + 7,835

=   +2,924.

As with the Alpha, since the NPV at 10% was negative, but at 5% it was positive, the IRR must lie between these two percentages. It is obviously closer to 5%, perhaps about 7%.

We can easily prove this point by trying 7%.

ie -60,000 + $\dfrac{16,000}{(1+0.07)}$ + $\dfrac{16,000}{(1+0.07)^2}$ + $\dfrac{16,000}{(1+0.07)^3}$ + $\dfrac{14,000}{(1+0.07)^4}$ + $\dfrac{10,000}{(1+0.07)^5}$

=   -60,000 + 14,953 + 13,975 + 13,061 + 10,681 + 7,130

=   -200

We can say that the IRR for this project is about 7%.

Where IRR is used to assess projects, the decision rule is that only those with an IRR above a predetermined 'hurdle rate' would be accepted. Where projects are competing, the project with the higher IRR is selected, provided the higher IRR exceeds the hurdle rate.

Since both of these machines have an IRR of about 7%. IRR cannot select between them. It does tell us, however, that neither of them is acceptable if the business has to pay more than 7% for its finance.

Activity 7

Why is it acceptable to say that 'about 7%' (answer to Activity 6), when we know that, strictly, the IRR is below 7%, because the NPV at 7% is less than zero (-£200)?

It is true that IRR is strictly below 7%. However you should bear in mind the fact that the data which was used to deduce the IRR is all forecast and, therefore, unlikely to be totally reliable. In fact it may prove to be rather unreliable. It is based on estimates of cost savings stretching five years into the future. In these circumstances it is pointless concerning ourselves about precise accuracy in the IRR, when it is based on such unreliable information.

The unreliability of input data is a problem, but it is a constant problem of all decision making. There are ways of dealing with this problem, and we shall consider some of these in Unit 4. Meanwhile it is worth mentioning that to imply a high degree of reliability by deducing an IRR to several decimal places could mislead people into believing that the figure is highly precise and reliable.

An example of such spurious accuracy is provided when a accountant visited his hill-farmer client to help with the annual stock taking. The farmer and the accountant went into a large field in which there was a large number of sheep. The accountant asked the farmer how many he thought were in the field, to which the farmer replied '1,005'. When the accountant asked how the farmer knew this, the farmer replied 'well, there's 5 down here by the river and there's about 1,000 over there on the hill-side'.

The point about spurious accuracy is equally valid in all situations where statements are being made, which are based on forecast data.

Now try this self-assessment question. It might take you about 20 minutes. Make sure that you complete it before you look at the answer.

Self-assessment question 2

A project has the following anticipated cash flows:

Year	£000
0	(12)
1	5
2	6
3	4
4	2

(a) What is the project's IRR?

(b) If the business has to pay 15% per annum to finance its activities and it uses IRR, would it find this project acceptable?

(The answers to self assessment questions are provided at the end of the unit.)

Attributes of the IRR approach

WE CONCLUDED EARLIER THAT NPV is a valuable means of assessing investment opportunities because:

● It is directly derived from, what appears to be the main financial objective of private sector organisations

● It seems to take account of all the relevant, measurable information about an investment opportunity. This includes the timing of the estimated cash flows and the cost of financing the investment

● It gives clear unambiguous results, which are simple and logical to interpret.

Having outlined the IRR method it might now be useful to compare it to NPV in respect of these attributes.

● IRR does not directly relate to the value maximisation criterion. Since IRR resembles NPV it will in most cases promote value maximisation. Consider, however, the following two competing projects:

	Project A	Project B
Investment required (now)	£10.0m	£15.0m
Cash inflow (next year)	£12.0m	£17.8m
The prevailing rate of interest is 10% per annum		
The NPVs (at a 10% discount rate) are	£0.91m	£1.18m
The IRRs are	20.0%	18.7%

There is conflict here between the two methods. IRR favours Project A, but Project B would be selected under the NPV criterion. In essence the conflict lies in the fact that IRR favours high yielding projects, without reference to their size. However, given an objective of seeking to maximise value, this can lead to wrong decisions where decision makers are selecting between competing projects.

A useful analogy might be a self-employed person. On a particular day there are two possibilities: work 8 hours for £5 an hour **or** work for the morning only (4 hours) for a rate of £7 an hour. These two are mutually exclusive possibilities. If we assume that the person wants to earn (increase wealth) by as much as possible clearly, the 8 hours earning £40 would be preferred to 4 hours earning £28, even though the latter is at a higher hourly rate.

● IRR does take all relevant information into account, including the timing of the cash flows.

● IRR generally gives clear results which are easy to interpret. As we have already seen, in the context of a value maximisation criterion, the results could be misleading.

● IRR can have other interpretation problems. Projects with particular (and unusual) patterns of cash flows can lead to problems with IRR. There are cases where a project has more than one IRR. There are other cash flow patterns which can lead to particular projects not having an IRR at all, or, at least, not one which has any economic meaning.

In general we may reasonably conclude that IRR will tend to promote the value maximisation objective. However, it only does so by coincidence and on occasions may not promote it at all. In other circumstances IRR may give ambiguous signals. For these reasons, NPV is a more logical approach for the value maximising business to adopt.

Research evidence shows IRR to be quite a popular method in practice; rather more popular than is NPV. It is not obvious why this should be the case. It may be that managers feel more comfortable with measures which are expressed in percentage terms, even though percentages can mislead.

Now try the following self-assessment question. You can probably do it in about half an hour or so. Do not look at the answer until you have completed it.

Self-assessment question 3

Turners Ltd is considering the purchase of a new machine which is expected to save labour on an existing project. The estimated data for the two machines available on the market are as follows:

	Machine A	Machine B
	£000	£000
Initial cost (year 0)	120	120
Residual value of machines (year 5)	20	30

Continued over . . .

	Machine A	Machine B
	£000	£000
Annual labour cost savings:		
Year 1	40	20
2	40	30
3	40	50
4	20	70
5	20	30

Which machine will be selected under the following criteria:

(a) NPV, assuming a cost of finance of 10% pa
(b) IRR

(The answers to self assessment questions are provided at the end of the unit.)

Payback period

THE PAYBACK PERIOD (PBP) is concerned with how long it takes for a particular investment opportunity's net cash inflows to repay the initial investment (cash outflow). A business using PBP to help to make its investment decisions would favour a project with a short recovery period over a longer one. It may also require that to be acceptable any project must have a PBP not exceeding a predetermined time.

Consider the two projects which were set out in Example 2. The details of these are set out again as Example 5:

Example 5

Antonio plc has estimated that it could achieve cost savings by investing in either of two automatic machines. The accountant's estimate of the actual savings and of the cost of the machines is as follows:

	Type Alpha £	Type Beta £
Cost of the machine(payable now)	50,000	60,000

Estimated annual savings:

	Type Alpha	Type Beta
Year 1	16,000	16,000
2	12,000	16,000
3	12,000	16,000
4	10,000	14,000
5	10,000	10,000

What is the PBP for each of these machines?

The cumulative net cash flows for these projects are as follows:

Year	Type Alpha	£	Type Beta	£
0		(50,000)		(60,000)
1	(50,000 - 16,000)	(34,000)	(60,000 - 16,000)	(44,000)
2	(34,000 - 12,000)	(22,000)	(44,000 - 16,000)	(28,000)
3	(22,000 - 12,000)	(10,000)	(28,000 - 16,000)	(12,000)
4	(10,000 - 10,000)	ZERO	(12,000 - 14,000)	2,000
5	(ZERO + 10,000)	10,000	(2,000 +10,000)	12,000

Thus the payback period for the Alpha type machine is exactly 4 years.

For the Beta type machine it is also exactly 4 years if we assume that the annual savings from using the machine manifest themselves at exactly the end of the years. If, in fact, they accrue fairly evenly over the year, the £12,000 outstanding at the end of year 3 will be cleared 12/14 of the way through year 4, ie the PBP will be about 3 years 10 months.

Earlier in this unit, we identified factors relating to NPV which commended it as a useful and a logical approach to investment decision making. These factors are:

● It is directly derived from, what appears to be the main financial objective of private sector organisations

● It seems to take account of all the relevant, measurable information about an investment opportunity. This includes the timing of the estimated cash flows and the cost of financing the investment

● It gives clear, unambiguous results, which are simple and logical to interpret.

If we try to assess PBP by reference to these same factors we find that:

● PBP has the weakness of not relating in any way to the main objective of most private sector organisations, value maximisation. PBP will promote projects which are short-term and will tend to lead to a maximisation of liquidity rather than of value.

● Much relevant information is ignored. For example, with the Alpha type machine (above), the PBP would remain at 4 years even if the machine were capable of continuing to achieve significant savings for very many years into the future. Similarly, if the machine were capable of achieving no savings in years 1 to 3, but achieved savings of £50,000 in year 5, it would still have a 4 year PBP, but most people would see it as a very different project to the actual one. It is possible to deduce a discounted payback period, but this only partially overcomes the very limited way in which PBP deals with the timing of cash flows.

● Though the result of a PBP analysis is fairly clear in that the output is a straightforward figure (the PBP, normally in years), it is not easy to interpret this outcome. This is mainly because the PBP method relates so little to what most businesses are seeking to achieve.

In general we can conclude that the PBP method is badly flawed. However, it is very widely used in practice, a fact which has confused writers on the subject of investment appraisal. Several possible explanations for this paradox have been suggested including the following:

● Possibly it is only used in conjunction with a discounting method (NPV or IRR) and as such gives a different and additional perspective on an investment project

● It is used as a 'screening' device. Only projects which have a PBP below some agreed maximum are actually assessed in detail. This seems not a particular likelihood, since in order to carry out a PBP analysis nearly all of the information required to carry out a discounted cash flow analysis would need to be to hand. The additional step of calculating the NPV or IRR once the information is available does not involve much effort

● Some decision makers are so unsophisticated that they fail to recognise the weaknesses of the method

● It may be seen by some decision makers as identifying less risky projects. This may be a reason for the popularity of PBP, but it is not particularly logical for decision makers to take this view. PBP only deals with the risk that the project may end prematurely. This is only one of an enormous number of things which could go wrong with a project.

Activity 8

Ludwig Ltd is trying to assess an investment opportunity which involves buying a new machine to replace some labour. The machine will cost £80,000 and the labour savings are expected to amount to the following:

Year	£
1	10,000
2	20,000
3	20,000
4	30,000
5	40,000
6	20,000

(a) What is the payback period of the machine?

(b) What is the discounted payback period of the machine, assuming a discount rate of 10%?

Treat the annual savings as if they will occur at the end of the relevant year.

The payback period is 4 years (ie £10,000 + 20,000 + 20,000 + 30,000 = £80,000).

Discounted payback period

Year	Saving	Discount factor	Discounted saving	Cumulative discounted saving
1	10,000	0.909	9,090	9,090
2	20,000	0.826	16,520	25,610
3	20,000	0.751	15,020	40,630
4	30,000	0.683	20,490	61,120
5	40,000	0.621	24,840	85,960
6	20,000	0.564	11,280	97,240

The discounted payback period is 5 years. This is because it takes 5 years before the discounted cash flows add up cumulatively to the £80,000 initial outlay.

Note that this solution uses the discount factors from the table. It would have been just as easy to work it out without the table.

Accounting (unadjusted) rate of return

THIS APPROACH TAKES THE average accounting profit anticipated from the investment and expresses it as a percentage of the initial investment. Some users of ARR use the average investment as the denominator of the fraction on the basis that not all of the investment is outstanding for all of the time.

Users of ARR would require that a project, to be acceptable, must have a minimum ARR. When selecting between competing projects the one with the higher or highest ARR would be selected.

Example 6

A business is assessing an investment of £5m in some plant to manufacture Product X. The project is expected to last for 7 years during which profits from the manufacture of Product X are expected to be:

	£m
Year 1	0.7
2	0.8
3	0.9
4	0.7
5	0.6
6	0.3
7	0.2

What is the ARR of manufacturing product X?

Solution 6

$$ARR = \frac{(0.7 + 0.8 + 0.9 + 0.7 + 0.6 + 0.3 + 0.2)/7}{5.0} \times 100 = 12\%$$

Alternatively, the average investment (£2.5m, assuming that the plant has no residual value at the end of the project) could be used instead of the initial investment (£5.0) which would result in an ARR of 24%. It would be up to any particular business, which used ARR, to decide which approach to use and to use it consistently.

If we compare ARR to NPV using the same three criteria (relationship with value maximisation, extent of using all relevant information and ease of interpretation) we can say that:

● ARR does not relate directly to value maximisation but pursues maximisation of a rate of return, measured by accounting profits. This may appear to be more or less the same thing. However because accounting's objective is to measure increases in value over a short period it can be very misleading when applied to the relatively long-term future, perhaps mainly because it takes little account of timing.

● ARR fails to take timing into account properly and, therefore, fails to take proper account of the cost of financing the investment.

In the above example, the same ARR would have been calculated with both the original and the alternative profit figures set out below, because they have the same total.

	Original profits	Alternative profits
	£m	£m
Year 1	0.7	0.1
2	0.8	0.1
3	0.9	0.1
4	0.7	0.1
5	0.6	0.1
6	0.3	0.1
7	0.2	3.6

Any rational investor would greatly prefer the original to the alternative profit profile, yet ARR cannot distinguish between them.

● As with PBP, ARR gives a clear figure as a result of the analysis yet interpreting it is very difficult. This is particularly so when we consider the fact that the original and alternative profit profiles given above yield the same ARR result. The 12% (or 24%) may be acceptable if the profits fall as in the original profile, but it may not be if the profits are like the alternative profile. A very confusing situation!

Activity 9

Ajax plc is assessing an investment of £12m in some plant to render a new service to its customers. The project is expected to last for 6 years, during which profits from the provision of the service are estimated to be:

	£m
Year 1	0.9
2	1.2
3	1.5
4	1.7
5	1.1
6	0.8

What is the ARR of manufacturing product X?

ARR = (0.9 + 1.2 + 1.5 + 1.7 + 1.1 + 0.8) = 1.2
                          6

million £s

divided by 12 = 0.1 (ie 10%)

Relative merits of the four appraisal methods

IT MIGHT BE HELPFUL to set out the relative merits, from a theoretical point of view of the four appraisal methods.

NPV is clearly the most valid of the four. As we have already seen, it relates directly to wealth enhancement, it takes account of all relevant information and it gives clear results.

IRR probably ranks second, because it will usually give the same results as NPV. On occasions it gives misleading results, however. Its flaw lies in the fact that, unlike NPV, it does not directly pursue wealth enhancement.

Payback probably ranks third. It is seriously flawed as an appraisal method. It does not relate to wealth, it ignores a lot of information and it is difficult to interpret. On the other hand it has the merit of highlighting liquidity, which many managers are very concerned about.

ARR probably ranks last. It has little going for it. This is because it takes a measure, accounting profit, which is deduced for one purpose and attempts to use it for an entirely different purpose. It is rather like trying to play cricket with a football. There is nothing wrong with the football; if you wish to play football it is perfect. It simply was not designed with cricket in mind.

Reading

You should now read Reader Article 3.1 'Is there a 'correct' method of investment appraisal?' by David Dugdale.

The article starts with a brief outline of the four methods which we have already discussed. This should be useful to you because it gives you a slightly different perspective on the methods. Note how inflation is dealt with in the assessment of a project in a period of inflation. We shall look at this topic in a little more detail in Unit 4.

Points to consider:

How does the author view IRR relative to NPV?
What case is there for the use of ARR?

Some practical aspects of appraising investment opportunities using the discounted cash flow techniques

HAVING REVIEWED THE FOUR methods of investment appraisal which are found in practice, we shall now go on to see how these methods are applied to practical problems.

Since we have concluded that NPV is the most sound of the four methods, we shall approach this on the assumption that NPV is the method to be used. In fact, virtually all of the points which we shall consider in the remainder of this unit, and in Unit 4, are equally valid whether we are using NPV, IRR or PBP. Many of them are also appropriate if we are using ARR . This distinction between NPV, IRR and PBP on the one hand, and ARR on the other, is that ARR is the only one which is based on accounting flows, rather than on cash flows.

CONSIDER CASH FLOWS, NOT ACCOUNTING FLOWS

The logic of using both NPV and IRR demands that we should consider relevant cash outflows and inflows and their timing in the analysis. This is because it is not until cash actually flows into a particular investment project that the business has to borrow it or is deprived of the opportunity to use it elsewhere. Similarly it is not until cash actually flows from the project that it can be used in some way to generate benefits elsewhere.

As you may have seen before, cash flows are not the same as accounting flows.

Activity 10

See if you can identify the type of things which mean that accounting flows are different to cash flows.

Jot down a list of the things that you can think of.

The factors which cause the most important differences are:

- Sales being made on credit

- Purchases of stock and expenses being incurred on credit

- Holding stock of various types

- Accounting for fixed assets by depreciating them over a number of accounting periods.

These factors are explained more fully in the next couple of paragraphs.

Financial accounting flows take account of accruals and prepayments, sales are usually deemed to have occurred when the goods or service passes to the customer, not when the cash is received. Accounting flows include depreciation of wasting fixed assets even though the cash expended on them may have occurred years earlier. Emphasising the difference between accounting flows and cash flows is by no means a criticism of financial accounting. Financial accounting has as its objective giving interested readers an assessment of the economic effectiveness of the operations of the business over a relatively short period, eg one year. Capital investment appraisal has an entirely different objective, however. Here the objective is to assess one particular self contained investment project over its entire life, possibly of many years.

In practice, it is particularly important to appreciate the distinction between accounting flows and cash flows. This is because it seems that many investment plans are set out in accounting terms rather than in cash flow terms. Where this is the case, it is necessary to adjust accounting flows to deduce the equivalent cash flows.

Broadly, the difference between accounting flows and cash flows is concerned with timing. In the final analysis, the net cash flows over the entire life of a project will equal the total net profit deriving from the project. To consider the timing differences it is probably useful to look at the issues in two stages, capital costs and operating revenues and expenses.

CAPITAL COSTS

When a depreciating fixed asset is used by a business (which owns the asset) it is standard accounting practice to depreciate the asset in some logical way over its useful life in that business. This is usually done by taking the actual cost, less any anticipated disposal proceeds and spreading this 'capital loss' over the useful life of the asset in the business. The spreading is most usually done in the UK by charging each year with an equal portion (ie straight line depreciation).

In cash flow terms, which are the relevant terms for NPV and IRR, we are only interested in when and how much cash is paid out to acquire the asset and the amount and timing of any cash receipt from disposal of the asset.

OPERATING REVENUES AND EXPENSES

Most sales of goods and services by businesses are made on credit with the goods or service passing to the customer at one point in time, but the cash being received at a later time, typically a couple of months later. In financial accounting we tend to take account of any particular sale, and of the profit or loss on it, when the goods or service passes to the customer. When we are interested in the success of the business over a month or a year, this is a perfectly reasonable view to take. Since NPV and IRR need to take account of cash flows and their timing, using accounting flows instead of cash flows will be distorting where the accounting recognition of a sale and the resultant cash are out of step, as they frequently will be in practice.

It is necessary, therefore, if the data on which the decision is to be made is expressed in accounting terms, to convert it to cash flow terms by adjusting for the amount of the trade debtors figure associated with the project. This is because the trade debtors figure associated with sales from the project will, at any particular time, represent the value of the timing difference.

For example, the plans for a particular project include selling 100 units of a product each month at a price of £10 each, giving customers two months' credit. Thus at any point in the life of the project the extent to which the 'accounting' sales figure will be ahead of the 'cash flow' sales figure will be £2,000 (ie 100 × £10 × 2 months). Thus in the first year of the project the accounting sales figure will be £12,000, whereas the cash flows from sales will only be £10,000, because no cash will be received in the first two months. By contrast in the final year of the project, the accounting sales figure will be £12,000, but the cash coming from sales will be £14,000. This is because sales cash from sales made in the last two months of the penultimate year will actually manifest itself in cash in the final year.

A similar phenomenon will also occur in respect of other working capital items, namely stock and creditors. The fact that purchases of goods and services will be made on credit means that cash flows will lag behind accounting flows to an extent equal to the value of the trade creditors. This itself will however, be offset to some extent by the fact that most organisations which manufacture and/or sell goods hold a stock-in-trade in some form or another.

Converting accounting flows into cash flows

FROM WHAT WE HAVE just seen, it is obvious that if we are confronted with accounting information, we must carry out a conversion process to turn it into cash flow information, in order that we can use it to assess an investment opportunity.

To correct for the depreciation charge against profit, we must calculate what the profit would have been had depreciation not been charged. We can do this simply by adding the amount of the depreciation, charged in the profit and loss account, to the net profit figure.

To correct for the timing discrepancy relating to operating revenues and expenses we need to make an adjustment for the investment which the business will need to make in working capital to support the project. Remember that working capital is basically stock plus debtors minus creditors. Taking on most real investment opportunities will mean that the business will be obliged to carry larger stocks and debtors, which will be partially offset by the fact that the business will probably also increase its trade creditors. Once the investment project has ended, the working capital requirement of that particular project will disappear and the working capital will flow back into the business.

Example 7

Johnson plc is contemplating an investment project. The net profit from the project is expected to be £1.2m for each of the six years' life of the project. The project will involve the immediate purchase of, and payment for, depreciating capital equipment at a cost of £5.0m. This equipment is expected to be sold for £2.0m at the end of the six years. The company uses a straight-line (equal yearly amounts) basis of depreciation. It is estimated that the average investment in working capital will be £0.3m.

The annual cash flows will be as follows:

Year	£m	comment
0 (ie now)	(5.3)	ie capital cost [£5.0m] + working capital [£0.3m]
1	1.7	ie annual net profit [£1.2m] + annual depreciation [[£5.0m - 2.0m]/6 = £0.5m]
2	1.7	ditto
3	1.7	ditto
4	1.7	ditto
5	1.7	ditto
6	4.0	ie £1.7 + working capital [£0.3] + disposal proceeds [£2.0]

It could be argued that the working capital 'outflow' should be included as a Year 1 cash flow rather than one for Year 0. The need to adjust for working capital at all stems from the fact that during the first couple of months cash outflows tend to be greater than accounting outflows justifies treating it as a Year 0 cash flow.

The year-end assumption

IN ALL OF THE examples of investment opportunities which we have so far considered and in most of those which we shall go on to look at, cash flows have occurred at the ends of years. This is not very realistic. Most of the types of investment project with which we are dealing include in their cash flows cash receipts from sales and payments to suppliers of a whole range of goods and services, including labour. These sort of cash flows do not occur in large amounts at annual intervals, but fairly steadily as the project progresses.

Strictly following the logic of NPV and IRR we should discount cash flows according to their precise timings. Though this tends to be impractical and not particularly valuable, to relate cash flows to the month of inflow or outflow is more practical and will probably give a significantly more reliable result. Despite this, we shall continue generally to treat cash flows occurring within a year as occurring at the year end. Where there are significant cash flows occurring close to the start of a year, eg the initial capital outlay or the initial adjustment for working capital these should be taken to the previous year end.

In practice, it may well be worth carrying out the analysis by identifying and discounting cash flows month-by-month. In this case the discount factor will still be $1/(1 + i)^n$, however, the value for n would include numbers other than whole numbers.

Relevant cash flows

AS WE SAW IN Unit 2, the cash flows which we must take into account are the relevant ones, basically those which relate to the objectives of the business concerned and vary according to the decision under review. This may well include various opportunity costs and benefits.

Taxation

IN THE CONTEXT OF capital investment decisions, the effects of taxation, to the extent that they vary with the decision must be taken into account. This is very important since tax is levied on corporate profits at relatively high rates. Since a study of the tax system is beyond the scope of this module, we shall pursue this point no further. You should be clear, however, that in practice tax must be taken account of in all decisions which have a finance perspective.

Financing costs

WHEN DISCOUNTING, USING EITHER NPV or IRR, we are making an allowance for the financing cost. We are in fact making allowance for it in a most logical and complete way. Therefore it is wrong to take interest cash flows into account in deducing the projects estimated cash flows; to do so will be double counting of, what is likely to be, a significant item of cost. We shall take a look at how the discount rate is deduced, so that it does logically and completely allow for all aspects of the financing cost of the investment, in Unit 5.

Now have a try at the last self-assessment question of this unit. It will probably take you around 45 minutes to complete.

Self-assessment question 4

Angelo Ltd recently commissioned a market survey into a new product the 'gadget'. The survey, costing £15,000 which Angelo has yet to pay, revealed that at the proposed selling price of £3 each it could expect sales of 50,000 gadgets in each of the next two years, 40,000 in the third year and 30,000 in each of the following two years, after which demand would fall away completely. On the basis of the market survey and its own estimates Angelo's management accounting department has produced the following budgeted income statements for gadget sales:

Year	1	2	3	4	5
	£000	£000	£000	£000	£000
Sales	150	150	120	90	90
Cost of Sales	100	100	80	60	60
Gross Profit	50	50	40	30	30
Variable overheads	10	10	8	6	6
Fixed overheads	20	20	20	20	20
Depreciation	16	16	16	16	16
	46	46	44	42	42
Net profit/loss	4	4	(4)	(12)	(12)

Production will require the purchase of a new machine costing £80,000 (payable immediately) which is not expected to have any scrap value at the end of five years.

Production will give rise to an additional working capital requirement of £20,000 which will cease with the end of production in Year 5.

The fixed overheads are mainly a reallocation of the existing overheads of the business. Production of gadgets is expected to give rise to additional fixed overheads of £5,000 in each year of production. (Note that variable overheads vary directly with the level of output of gadgets; fixed overheads remain the same irrespective of the level of output of gadgets.)

Assume that all operating cash flows will occur at the end of the year to which they relate.

Ignore taxation.

Angelo's management estimates that the cost of finance for this project is 12% per annum.

Continued over . . .

You are required:

(a) to calculate the net present value of the project to manufacture gadgets and to comment on the implications of this value

(b) to estimate the internal rate of return of the project.

You will probably find it most practical to set out the cash flows in columns, one for each year, including Year 0 (now), in the same way as the question is set out.

(The answers to self assessment questions are provided at the end of the unit.)

Reading

You should now read Reader Article 3.2 'Discordant voices: accountants' views of investment appraisal' by David Dugdale and Colwyn Jones.

This article outlines the results of some research carried out by the article's authors in which they interviewed a number of accountants who are involved, in some way or another, in investment decision making.

Points to consider:

Do all of the accountants seem fully to understand NPV?
What arguments do some of the accountants give for the use of payback?

Investment decision making in practice

THE ACCA SURVEY (SEE UNIT 1) showed that companies typically use more than one of the appraisal methods (NPV etc). The average is 2.46 methods per company, with larger companies above this and smaller companies below this, on average. Whether this means that there is a tendency to use more than one method in each decision or whether a different method is used for different decisions is not clear. Of course the input data for the different methods is similar, ie the same forecast information. Once this information has emerged, it is little extra effort in applying several appraisal techniques to it. Possibly some companies use payback as well as using a discounting method (NPV or IRR).

The survey also shows that when asked to rank the methods from the most important to the least important, the average ranking was:

1 Payback
2 IRR
3 NPV
4 'Intuitive managerial judgement'
5 ARR

For the larger companies, the ranking was:

1 IRR
2 Payback
3 NPV
4 ARR
5 'Intuitive managerial judgement'

The attraction of payback is surprising, given its obvious theoretical weaknesses, but it is interesting to note that among the larger, and presumably more sophisticated, companies it is rather less important. Reader article 3.2 might provide the reason for this phenomenon, namely that many managers, including some accountants, do not really understand NPV.

The relative popularity of IRR over NPV is not too surprising. In most real-life cases they will give similar signals. It has been argued that people prefer to express investment returns in percentage terms than in terms of amounts of money.

You should note that the survey results are consistent with a fairly large number of similar studies of investment appraisal in practice.

Summary of the unit

WE STARTED BY CONSIDERING the importance of investment decisions and saw that businesses actually use four main methods of assessing investment opportunities. These are NPV, IRR, PBP and ARR. We explored the time value of money and the importance of this concept in the assessment of investment opportunities. We then saw that, given the principal financial objective of most private sector organisations of increasing their value, NPV is by far the most logical of the methods to use. The NPV of a project is deduced by relating the present value (ie what we logically would be prepared to pay for them) to the cost of obtaining the opportunity to have them. Having established that NPV is the best method of assessing investments, in theory at least, we then compared the other methods with NPV. We concluded the unit by considering some practical aspects of using NPV to make decisions, particularly the need to identify the prospective cash flows rather than the accounting flows.

Suggested solutions to self-assessment questions

Self-assessment question 1

Patterson Ltd

(This solution uses the discount factors derived from the present value table given at the end of this Unit. Discounting the cash flows from first principles would have been just as straightforward, but may result in slightly different solutions due to rounding differences.)

Time	Cash flow (£)	10% Dis. Factor	PV (£)	15% Dis. Factor	PV (£)
0	(70,000)	1.000	(70,000)	1.000	(70,000)
1	20,000	0.909	18,180	0.870	17,400
2	30,000	0.826	24,780	0.756	22,680
3	20,000	0.751	15,020	0.658	13,160
4	10,000	0.683	6,830	0.572	5,720
5	10,000	0.621	6,210	0.497	4,970
	NPV =		£ 1,020		£(6,070)

Thus, if the interest rate were 10% the investment opportunity should be accepted; if it is 15% it should be rejected.

Note that as the discount rate increases the NPV decreases. This is because a higher interest rate means a higher opportunity cost of making the investment and the less attractive the investment becomes. Thus if there were an opportunity to use the money to make an investment at 15%, Patterson would be better off doing this than investing in the above project.

Self-assessment question 2

(This solution uses the discount factors derived from the present value table given at the end of this Unit. Discounting the cash flows from first principles would have been just as straightforward.)

Try 20%

NPV $= -12{,}000 + (5{,}000 \times 0.833) + (6{,}000 \times 0.694) + (4{,}000 \times 0.579) + (2{,}000 \times 0.482)$

$= 391$ (negative)

Try 18%

NPV =-12,000 + (5,000 × 0.847) + (6,000 × 0.718) + (4,000 × 0.609) + (2,000 × 0.516)

   = 11 (positive)

Thus the IRR is marginally above 18%. It is not important (in theory) which discount rate is used in the first trial. Obviously, it is best to try to make some sensible guess rather than to pick a figure completely at random.

A business which had to pay 15% for its funds would be prepared to undertake this project, if it used IRR as its investment decision criterion.

Self-assessment question 3

Turners Ltd

(This solution uses the discount factors derived from the present value table given at the end of this Unit. Discounting the cash flows from first principles would have been just as straightforward.)

NPV

Year	Discount factor	Machine A Cash flow £000	Machine A PV (£) £000	Machine B Cash flow £000	Machine B PV (£) £000
0	1.000	(120)	(120.00)	(120)	(120.00)
1	0.909	40	36.36	20	18.18
2	0.826	40	33.04	30	24.78
3	0.751	40	30.04	50	37.55
4	0.683	20	13.66	70	47.81
5	0.621	40	24.84	50	31.05
	NPV =		17.94		39.37

Machine B shows itself to be significantly more desirable from an economic viewpoint than does Machine A. Since both machines have a positive NPV either would be worth buying.

IRR

Clearly the IRR of both machines lies well above 10% (the NPV at 10% is fairly large relative to the initial outlay).

For our second trial 10% (above) being the first, let us try 20%.

Year	Discount factor	Machine A		Machine B	
		Cash flow £000	PV (£) £000	Cash flow £000	PV (£) £000
0	1.000	(120)	(120.00)	(120)	(120.00)
1	0.833	40	33.32	20	16.66
2	0.694	40	27.76	30	20.82
3	0.579	40	23.16	50	28.95
4	0.482	20	9.64	70	33.74
5	0.402	40	16.08	50	20.10
	NPV =		(10.04)		0.27

The IRR of Machine A lies below 20%, but above 10%. That of Machine B is just above 20%. Further trials using other discount rates could be undertaken. Alternatively, a short-cut can be made to a reasonable approximation, ie linear interpolation. This assumes that there is a straight line relationship between the discount rate and the NPV. This is not strictly true, though over short ranges it is nearly true. This approach works as follows:

Figure 3

NPV for machine A against discount rate

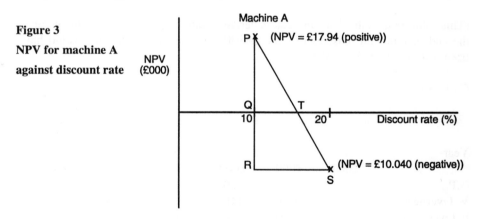

This is a graph of the NPV for machine A plotted against the discount rate. As with most projects, when we increase the discount rate we reduce the NPV.

Points P and S on the graph are the calculated NPVs at 10% and 20%. The IRR for this project at point T, and this is what we want to know. It is clear from the graph that the two triangles PRS and PQT are identical in shape. Thus relationships between the lengths of corresponding sides will be identical. Therefore QT/PQ = RS/PR. We need to know QT and we know all of the other lengths. Therefore:

QT/17,940 = (20 - 10)/(17,940 + 10,040)

QT = 6.4% ie the IRR is 6.4% above 10% or 16.4%.

This approach can be used whenever you are trying to deduce the IRR longhand. It may be helpful to draw a rough sketch of the graph whenever you use this approach. But remember, you can simply keep trying different discount rates until you come to one which gives you a close to zero NPV, thus avoiding the interpolation calculation.

Machine B

$$IRR = 10\% + \{(20\text{-}10).\frac{39.37}{(39.37 - 0.27)}\}\%$$

$$= 10 + 10.1 = 20.1\%$$

On the basis of the IRR criterion machine B would be preferred.

Self-assessment question 4

Angelo Ltd

(This solution uses the discount factors derived from the present value table given at the end of this Unit. Discounting the cash flows from first principles would have been just as straightforward.)

Cash flows

Year	0	1	2	3	4	5
	£000	£000	£000	£000	£000	£000
G.P.		50	50	40	30	30
V. Overheads		(10)	(10)	(8)	(6)	(6)
F. Overheads		(5)	(5)	(5)	(5)	(5)
Initial Investment	(80)					
Working capital	(20)					20
	(100)	35	35	27	19	39

Discount factor						
12%	1.00	0.89	0.79	0.71	0.64	0.57
PV	(100.00)	31.15	27.65	19.17	12.16	22.23
NPV	12.36					

This implies that the project should be undertaken other things being equal.

Clearly the IRR lies above 12%.

Try 15%

Year	Cash flow £000	Discount factor	PV £000
0	(100)	1.00	(100.00)
1	35	0.87	30.45
2	35	0.76	26.60
3	27	0.66	17.82
4	19	0.57	10.83
5	39	0.50	19.50
			5.20

This implies that IRR is above 15%

By extrapolation:

$$\text{IRR} = 15\% + (3\% \times \frac{5.20}{(12.36 - 5.20)}) = 17\%$$

Additional exercises

Exercise 1

Auto Products plc has just developed a new device for facilitating cold starting of motor cars. It is now necessary to make a decision on whether or not to go ahead with commercial production. The following information is available:

(a) The development work cost £8,000 in labour and £5,000 in materials purchased specifically for that purpose.

(b) The selling price will be £75 per device, 5,000 are expected to be sold in each of the next 5 years.

(c) Production of the device will involve two types of material:

(i) Alpha which will need to be bought in specifically. Each device requires 0.5 kg of alpha and the price is £20 per kg.

(ii) Beta, of which the firm holds a stock of 10000 kg which cost £5 per kg. There is no use for this material to the firm other than in production of the device, so if production does not go ahead, it will be sold immediately for £4 per kg. Further supplies are expected to cost £6 per kg. Each device requires 1 kg of beta.

(d) 10 hours of labour are required to make each device at a wage rate of £3 per hour. During the first 2 years, production labour could only be made available by diverting it away from other production which would otherwise yield a contribution of £2 per hour. (Contribution is measured as sales revenue less all costs which vary proportionately with the level of production, including labour.) This labour shortage will disappear from year 3 onwards.

(e) The total fixed costs (ie those which do not vary proportionately with the level of production) would be expected to increase by £50,000 pa if production of the device goes ahead.

(f) Additional working capital of £50,000 will be required immediately if production goes ahead but this will be released at the end of the production period.

(g) Production of the device will require the use of a machine already owned by the firm. This machine cost £800,000 when it was bought 2 years ago. It is being depreciated at the rate of £120,000 pa. Since there is no other use for the machine, if production does not go ahead it will be sold immediately for £200,000. If it is retained, it is expected that it will have a residual sales value of £20,000 when production ceases.

Assume that all operating cash flows occur at the end of the year concerned. Ignore taxation.

Auto Product plc's cost of finance is 10% pa.

You are required:

(a) to assess whether, on the basis of net present value, the production should go ahead.

(b) to estimate the internal rate of return of this investment opportunity.

Exercise 2

The project manager of your company has asked you to take a quick look at some calculations, regarding an investment project, which are to be presented at a board meeting tomorrow. You have been asked to check the arithmetic. This you have done and found it all to be correct. You attention could not help but be drawn, however, to what seem to you to be errors of principle.

The calculations are set out as follows:

Year	0	1	2	3	4
	£000	£000	£000	£000	£000
Sales revenue		450	540	540	360
Less: Material		100	120	120	80
Labour		75	90	90	60
Overheads		75	90	90	60
Depreciation		100	100	100	100
Working capital	200				
Interest		60	60	60	60
Development costs		25	25	25	25
	200	435	485	485	385
Net cash flow	(200)	15	55	55	(25)
Discount factor	1.0	0.8	0.6	0.4	0.2
Discounted	(200.0)	12.0	33.0	22.0	(5.0)
NPV	(138.0)	ie negative			

You decide to make some discreet enquiries into some of the figures and discover the following:

(i) The overheads are apportioned on a labour cost basis. The actual increase in overheads which the project will engender is estimated at £30,000 per annum.

(ii) The project requires the use of a machine already owned by the company which appears in the books of the company at cost, less depreciation, a net figure of £400,000. If the project does not go ahead the machine will not have any other use to the company and will therefore be sold immediately for an estimated £500,000. If it is used in the project it is not expected to be worth anything by year 4. The company uses a straight-line basis of depreciation.

(iii) Development costs associated with this project have cost £100,000 and it is company policy to write off such costs over the life of a viable project.

(iv) The company uses a discount rate of 20% per annum to assess the NPV of its capital projects.

You are required to rework the Project Manager's calculations of the NPV making such alterations as seem necessary. You should make a short note to explain any adjustments which you have made. You should indicate, on the basis of your calculations, whether or not in your opinion, the project should go ahead.

Solutions to additional exercises

Exercise 1

(This solution uses the discount factors derived from the present value table given at the end of this Unit. Discounting the cash flows from first principles would have been just as straightforward.)

Auto Products plc

(a) Differential cash flow arising from the project

Year	0	1	2	3	4	5
	£000	£000	£000	£000	£000	£000
Machine	(200)					20
Working capital	(50)					50
Sales		375	375	375	375	375
Alpha		(50)	(50)	(50)	(50)	(50)
Beta*	(40)			(30)	(30)	(30)
Labour		(250)	(250)	(150)	(150)	(150)
Overheads		(50)	(50)	(50)	(50)	(50)
	(290)	25	25	95	95	165
Discount factor (at 10%)	1.00	0.91	0.83	0.75	0.68	0.62
PV	(290.0)	22.75	20.75	71.25	64.60	102.30
NPV	(8.35)					

On the basis of NPV, production of the device should not go ahead.

* Note that if the material Beta is not used in this project, it will be sold immediately.

(b) Clearly the IRR of this project lies below 10% but not much below it, try 9%:

Discount factor (at 9%)	1.00	0.92	0.84	0.77	0.71	0.65
PV	(290.0)	23.0	21.0	73.2	67.45	107.3
NPV	1.95					

Thus IRR is marginally above 9%.

Exercise 2

Reworked calculation of net present value

(This solution uses the discount factors derived from the present value table given at the end of this Unit. Discounting the cash flows from first principles would have been just as straightforward.)

Year	0	1	2	3	4	Note
	£000	£000	£000	£000	£000	
Sales revenue		450	540	540	360	
Less: Material		100	120	120	80	
Labour		75	90	90	60	
Overheads		30	30	30	30	1
Working capital	200				(200)	2
Machine	500					3
	700	205	240	240	(30)	
Net cash flow	(700)	245	300	300	390	
Discount factor	1.00	0.83	0.69	0.58	0.48	
Discounted	(700.0)	203.35	207.0	174.0	187.2	4
NPV	74.3					

On the basis of the revised calculations the project should be undertaken since it has a significant NPV.

Notes:

1. Only the overheads which will vary with the decision should be included in the analysis. How the company may apportion overheads to various products for costing purposes is not relevant here.

2. Account must be taken of the working capital 'inflow' at the end of the project.

3. The opportunity cost of the machine to be used in the project must be treated as a cash outflow of the project.

4. A 20% discount rate does not imply a rate which reduces by 20% for each year into the future. The discount factor to be applied is $1/(1 + i)^n$, where i is the per annum interest rate and n the number of years into the future that the particular cash flow will occur.

5. Depreciation is not a cash flow and should be ignored. It is, in effect, taken into account by including the opportunity cost of the asset as an outflow and the disposal proceeds (none in this case) as an inflow.

6. The development cost should be ignored because it is not relevant to the present decision. Irrespective of whether or not the project is undertaken the development expenditure has already been incurred. Past costs can never be relevant.

Present value table

Present value of £1 receivable (payable) after t years at i% per annum discount rate.

Time years	Discount rate (%)									
	1	2	3	4	5	6	7	8	9	10
1	0.990	0.980	0.971	0.962	0.952	0.943	0.935	0.926	0.917	0.909
2	0.980	0.961	0.943	0.925	0.907	0.890	0.873	0.857	0.842	0.826
3	0.971	0.942	0.915	0.889	0.864	0.840	0.816	0.794	0.772	0.751
4	0.961	0.924	0.888	0.855	0.823	0.792	0.763	0.735	0.708	0.683
5	0.951	0.906	0.863	0.822	0.784	0.747	0.713	0.681	0.650	0.621
6	0.942	0.888	0.837	0.790	0.746	0.705	0.666	0.630	0.596	0.564

Time years	Discount rate (%)									
	11	12	13	14	15	16	17	18	19	20
1	0.901	0.893	0.885	0.877	0.870	0.862	0.855	0.847	0.840	0.833
2	0.812	0.797	0.783	0.769	0.756	0.743	0.731	0.718	0.706	0.694
3	0.731	0.712	0.693	0.675	0.658	0.641	0.624	0.609	0.593	0.579
4	0.659	0.636	0.613	0.592	0.572	0.552	0.534	0.516	0.499	0.482
5	0.593	0.567	0.543	0.519	0.497	0.476	0.456	0.437	0.419	0.402
6	0.535	0.507	0.480	0.456	0.432	0.410	0.390	0.370	0.352	0.335

UNIT 4

FURTHER ASPECTS OF INVESTMENT DECISION MAKING

THIS UNIT CONTINUES THE consideration of various practical issues relating to businesses making decisions on investment in 'real' assets. Much of the unit is devoted to considerations of risk in investment decision making and how it can be dealt with.

On completion of this unit you should be able to:

- explain the importance of formal assessment of risk in decision making and deal with risk through sensitivity analysis and the use of probabilities and expected values

- describe briefly the relationship between risk and the discount rate

- explain the problem for investment decision makers caused by inflation and the approach which needs to be taken to the selection of the discount rate

- modify the NPV rule when there are shortages of investment finance relative the beneficial projects available

- discuss the nature and purpose of management of the investment process.

Outline of the unit

THE UNIT STARTS BY pointing out that the future is uncertain and so we cannot predict with total accuracy the outcome of an investment project. There is always a risk that, when making decisions concerning the future, things will not turn out as planned. Let us say a business was considering the purchase of a machine to make a particular product. There are numerous factors which the business must attempt to predict when evaluating the purchase. These include:

- the likely sales volume for the product

- the selling price of the product

- the useful life of the machine

- the residual value of the machine at the end of its useful life

- the machine running costs etc.

In some cases the predictions made may be little more than informed guesses. Thus, it is possible that a project which is predicted to increase the value of the business may turn out to reduce it, or vice versa.

We need to take account of risk because the degree of risk will affect the value which is placed on the project. The more risky the project the lower the price decision makers will normally be prepared to pay. Thus, it is important to take account of the level risk when evaluating investment opportunities.

SENSITIVITY ANALYSIS

One method of dealing with risk is *sensitivity analysis*. This looks at the effect of a change in each of the key inputs related to the project (sales volume, sales price, useful life of machine, etc). When using the NPV method, the decision maker may attempt to establish the value of the input which reduces the NPV to zero. Sensitivity analysis gives a measure of the safety margin which exists before the project becomes non-viable. A worked example of this method is provided in the section and should be studied carefully.

The advantage of this method is that it gives the decision maker a 'feel' for the riskiness of the project. However, it does not provide clear decision rules concerning acceptance or rejection of the project. The method considers only one input at a time and all other inputs are held constant. However, in practice, it is likely that more than one input relating to the project will vary from the planned outcome.

STATISTICAL PROBABILITY

Another approach to risk assessment is through the use of statistical probabilities. A level of probability can be ascribed to each of the outcomes which may arise. For example, it may be that a project has a 0.3 probability of yielding an NPV of £2m, a 0.5 probability of yielding a NPV of £5m and a 0.2 probability of yielding a NPV of £6m. The sum of the probabilities will be equal to 1.0 (ie at least one of the outcomes must occur). The way in which probabilities may be determined are discussed in detail. This method can help build up a picture of the possible outcomes and likelihood of occurrence.

Having assigned a level of probability to each possible outcome it is possible to derive an 'expected value'. The calculation of ENPV is quite straightforward, once the probabilities are known. The expected value is simply a weighted average of the possible outcomes where the probabilities are used as weights. In the example used above the ENPV will be $(0.3 \times £2m) + (0.5 \times £5m) + (0.2 \times £6m) = £4.3m$.

Although expected value is a method which provides a clear single figure value for decision making purposes, there are problems associated with the use of expected values. One problem is that the expected value is an average figure which may not actually be capable of occurring. Another problem is that the use of an average figure may obscure the underlying riskiness of the project. It may be, for example that, although the ENPV calculation indicates a profit is expected to arise, there may be a high degree of probability that a loss will arise. This information may be extremely important when deciding whether or not to embark on the project. However, these problems may not be significant where a business has a portfolio of projects. They can be lost in the averaging process.

The unit next goes on to consider the use of an adjusted discount rate to deal with the problem of risk. A 'risk premium' can be added to the discount rate to help assess an investment project. The greater the level of risk the higher the risk premium that should be used.

Problems are posed by inflation when evaluating investment projects. The problems are really of three types:

● Difficulties in forecasting

● Difficulties in predicting demand and other factors affected by the rate of inflation

● Problems in carrying out the analysis; ie to express future cash flows in 'real' terms or money terms.

The first two points make the forecasting problem more difficult. The third point raises an issue of principle. Future cash flows may be expressed in either real terms or money terms. However, the choice of the discount rate must be consistent with the approach used. Where future cash flows are expressed in real terms the discount rate must be a 'real' discount rate. Where future cash flows are expressed in money terms a 'money' discount rate (which includes an allowance for inflation) must be used.

In practice, a business may have only a limited amount of finance to invest in projects for a given period. Thus, it may not be possible to invest in all projects which yield a positive NPV. The decision rule for NPV must, therefore, be modified to take account of shortages of finance. Where there is limited finance in a particular period we must try and get the best use of the finance available. This means we must seek the highest benefit per £ of finance from the investment opportunities.

The relationship between corporate strategy and NPV is also considered in the unit. It is sometimes suggested that NPV is a rather narrow form analysis which is incompatible with a broader strategic approach. However, in so far that the strategy of the business is concerned with enhancing its wealth, the NPV method supports the strategic approach.

Lastly, but not least, the unit considers the practical aspects of investment decision making. In order for a business to fully exploit the opportunities available it must ensure that a systematic approach is taken to the investment process. This means that new investments proposals must be actively encouraged and recognised, the proposals should be formally screened using the techniques of investment appraisal and risk analysis dealt with earlier, responsibility must be assigned for the implementation of the proposal, and the results of the investment must be properly reviewed at each stage of its life and at the end of its life to see whether any lessons can be learned.

The investment techniques dealt with in this unit and the earlier unit must be kept in perspective. They form part of the screening process which is, in turn, part of the overall investment decision making, planning and control process. Proper weight must be given to these other aspects of the investment process.

Risk in decision making

UNTIL NOW WE HAVE ignored risk in our consideration of how decisions should be made. What we mean by risk in this context is the phenomenon which arises from the fact that no matter how good a predictor the decision maker may be, he or she can never be sure of the future so there is the prospect that what is planned to happen may not actually occur. The greater the probability that predicted outcomes will not occur and the larger the difference between the predicted and actual outcomes could be, the larger the risk. Of course decision makers are not concerned that a better-than-predicted outcome might occur. It is the 'downside' risk which they worry about.

For an example of the sort of risks facing the decision maker, say a business is contemplating an investment in a machine which renders some service to customers, an activity so far carried out by people. The data inputs on which the decision will rely include such things as predicted labour cost savings and the predicted ability of the machine to do the work adequately. These predictions must inevitably be guesses, though very possibly informed ones, of what actually will happen. What effect would there be on these predicted savings if:

- the machine does not work as well as expected

- labour costs (and therefore potential savings) are not as predicted

- the market for which the machine is to render the service is not as predicted?

These are just three examples in a very simple case, where the uncertainty of the future makes decision making difficult.

An attractive sounding solution to the problem of uncertain outcomes (ie risk) is to make no decisions but clearly this is not a realistic option.

Why take account of risk?

THE RISKINESS OF A project fundamentally affects people's judgement of it and how much the project is worth. People will pay less for a project whose cash inflows are uncertain than for one whose cash flows are certain. The greater the riskiness which decision makers perceive, the less they are willing to invest. By riskiness here we mean both the extent of the range of possible out comes and the likelihood of each possible outcome actually occurring.

We shall now go on to consider one way in which risk in investment decisions can be dealt with.

Sensitivity analysis

ONE APPROACH TO ASSESSING risk is known as sensitivity analysis. Though this technique seems to be used fairly widely in the context of investment appraisal, it can equally usefully be applied in most decision making contexts.

When using sensitivity analysis to help to deal with risk in a net present value assessment of a project, the following approach is taken:

1) The 'best estimate' for each input (initial investment, volume of output, life of the market for the output, sales value per unit of output, individual operating costs, required amount of working capital, discount rate) is estimated.

2) The NPV for the project is calculated using the best estimates for each of the inputs.

3) If there is a positive NPV when using the best estimates, the question is now asked, by how much can each of the estimates prove in reality to be incorrect before the project starts to become non-viable in the sense of failing to generate an increase in the value of the business (zero NPV)?

In practice, this last step would require that the value is established for each input which will cause the project to have a zero NPV, usually on the assumption that none of the other inputs deviates from the best estimate of its value.

Activity 1

Can you think of anything, which we have looked at so far in the context of investment appraisal, which considers the value of one of the inputs which would give rise to a zero NPV?

Internal rate of return (IRR) can be seen as an example of sensitivity analysis. The IRR of a particular project is, of course, the maximum value that the discount rate (financing cost) can have before the project ceases to be viable.

Let us take a look at an example of sensitivity analysis.

Example 1

NHB Ltd has the opportunity to make an investment in some equipment which will enable the company to market a product on behalf of the manufacturer. The best estimates of the inputs to the NPV calculation are as follows:

capital cost of the equipment is £40,000 payable immediately;

annual sales demand is for 300 units for each of the first and fourth years of the project and 400 units for each of the second and third years;

the sales price of each unit to the customers will be £200;

the rate of commission which NHB will earn on sales will be 30% of the gross sales price – the commission will be paid to NHB at the end of each year based on that year's sales;

fixed costs relevant to the project will be £5,000 each year. These will be payable at the end of each year;

the residual value of the equipment will be £3,000 which will be received at the end of the fourth year of the project;

the financing cost of the project will be 20% per annum.

The NPV calculation based on these best estimates is as follows:

Year	0	1	2	3	4
	£000	£000	£000	£000	£000
Equipment	(40)				3
Commission		18	24	24	18
Fixed costs		(5)	(5)	(5)	(5)
Net cash flows	(40)	13	19	19	16
Discount factor		$(1/1.20)^1$	$(1/1.20)^2$	$(1/1.20)^3$	$(1/1.20)^4$
Present value	(40)	10.8	13.2	11.0	7.7
Net present value	2.7				

Thus, on the basis of the best estimates for the inputs, the project has a positive NPV.

The level of risk can now be examined by taking each of the inputs in turn and assessing how far each one could move in an adverse direction before the project would become non-viable.

Let us start by considering the sales demand in the first year of the project. We need to identify the commission receivable for year 1 which will cause the project to break even (NPV = 0), on the assumption that all other inputs remain at the best estimate.

Since the effect on the NPV of the first year inputs is after they have been discounted, we need to express the NPV of 2.7 (thousand pounds) in terms of its value in year 1.

The minimum value for the year 1 commission which will yield a non-negative NPV is 18 - [2.7 / (1/1.20)^1] (ie the original value for the year 1 commission less the original NPV divided by the discount factor for year 1) = 14.7. In other words the commission for the first year could drop by 3.3 (18% of the best estimate) before the project would become non-viable.

Since the commission is based on three factors (sales volume, sales price and commission rate), the *actual value* of any one of those factors falling 18% below the best estimate for year 1 would result in a non-viable project.

Suppose that we wished to look at the sensitivity of the positive NPV to the sales price over all four years, ie to see how far the price would need to fall below £200 in all four years for the project to become non-viable.

There is only one way to approach this which is by trial and error. Had the annual cash flow been equal throughout the project, the minimum sales price at which the project would remain viable could have been calculated directly. It is rare in practice for cash flows to be constant from year to year so the trial and error approach is the only possibility in most cases where we want to assess the sensitivity to a change effecting all years of the project.

We need to recalculate the NPV for the project assuming another commission receivable level, say 10% below the best estimate.

The revised NPV calculation based on the best estimates for all factors except commission and 10% below best estimate for commission is as follows:

Year	0	1	2	3	4
	£000	£000	£000	£000	£000
Equipment	(40)				3
Commission		16.2	21.6	21.6	16.2
Fixed costs		(5)	(5)	(5)	(5)
Net cash flows	(40)	11.2	16.6	16.6	14.2
Discount factor		(1/1.20)^1	(1/1.20)^2	(1/1.20)^3	(1/1.20)^4
Present value	(40)	9.3	11.5	9.6	6.8
Net present value	(2.8)				

We can get to an acceptable approximation of the percentage fall in commission which will give a zero NPV by linear interpolation.

We have seen that a 10% fall in the commission each year lowers the NPV by 5.5 (ie 2.7 + 2.8). We need to know what percentage fall in commission is consistent with a drop in NPV of 2.7 (ie from 2.7 to zero). This will be 10 × (2.7/5.5) = 4.9%. Thus commission needs to fall by 4.9% to 95.1% of the best estimate before the project starts to become non-viable. Thus, if the sales price over the four years proved in reality to be below £190.20 (ie 95.1% of £200), the project would give a negative NPV.

We could obviously go through each of the inputs, one by one, to discover the sensitivity of the projects NPV, based on the best estimates, to an adverse change in each input.

Having carried out a complete sensitivity analysis of the project we could try to reach some conclusions on its riskiness.

Activity 2

How sensitive is the outcome of NHB Ltd's project to the amount which is received for the equipment at the end of the fourth year?

How would you interpret your findings ?

The minimum value for the year 4 equipment disposal proceeds which will yield a non-negative NPV is $3 - [2.7/ (1/1.20)^4]$ (ie the original value for the equipment proceeds less the original NPV divided by the year 4 discount factor) = -5.6 (£000).

In other words instead of actually receiving something for the old equipment, it would be necessary for the company to have to pay as much as £5,600 to *take the old equipment away before the project would become non-viable. Probably, unlike some of the other inputs, the decision maker would know whether it would be feasible for such an outcome to be capable of causing the project to be disadvantageous to the company.*

The advantages and disadvantages of using sensitivity analysis

THE REAL ADVANTAGE OF using sensitivity analysis is that it enables the decision maker to take the project apart and look at each of the inputs individually. In this way the decision maker can get a 'feel' for the project which may not be obtainable in any other way.

Having done this the decision maker can identify the estimates on which a favourable assessment of the project most crucially depends, ie the sensitive factors. Armed with this information it may be possible to make some judgement about the riskiness of the project. This in turn may cause the decision maker to try to be more confident about particularly sensitive elements. For example, if a particular project depends crucially on the level of sales demand, it may be worth spending money on further market research, in an attempt to gain greater insight to the quality of the original estimates. Perhaps the price of a raw material is a crucial factor. Here it may be possible to place an advance order for the necessary quantities at a fixed contract price, thus guaranteeing that the estimated and actual material price are the same.

The disadvantages of using sensitivity analysis include:

> ● The fact that having calculated the individual sensitivities the decision maker has no rule as to how to interpret them. For example, what is an acceptable sensitivity? Is it 10% different from the best estimate? Is it 20%? Is it 30%?

This point gains greater weight when we consider that different judgements will probably be made from one input to the next. In the example, the fact that the project's outcome is fairly sensitive to changes in the commission **rate** may be unimportant to the decision maker because the manufacturer may be prepared to enter into a binding contract throughout the four years fixing the rate at 30% of sales price. On the other hand, the same level of sensitivity attaches to the sales volume, but it is unlikely that the manufacturer will guarantee under binding contract that the best estimates of the sales volume will actually occur. Thus very different judgements will be made between different inputs, despite the fact that the 'sensitivity factor' is identical from one to the next.

On the other hand, it can be argued that all risk analysis is a subjective activity and that sensitivity analysis merely provides fairly solid information to which decision makers can apply their judgement.

> ● The static nature of sensitivity analysis, as we have considered it here, is unrealistic. We have assumed that only one of the input variables is susceptible to being incorrectly estimated, to the extent that we have held all other variables steady while concentrating on the particular one in question. In most investment appraisal exercises there will be many variables, vastly more than in the example which we considered. It is clearly nonsense to believe that all but one of them will actually have the value predicted for it. It seems likely that all the estimates made before a particular project is undertaken will in the event prove to be wrong, perhaps by a little, perhaps by a lot.

An alternative approach to the one which we took is to look at what would be the outcome for the project if various possible outcomes were to occur in respect of a number of the inputs. This process, known as 'scenario building', can only realistically be done using a computer. However a cheap 'spreadsheet' computer package would be capable of providing a practical and effective way of handling a range of different sets of possible outcomes for each of the inputs, and assessing the overall outcome from each of them.

Use of probabilities

ANOTHER WAY TO ASSESS risk is through statistical probabilities. If each possible outcome from a particular investment project can be identified and have a statistical probability ascribed to it, the whole range of possible results can be seen. Since we should know the likelihood of each one's occurrence we could also work out the 'weighted average' (ie the average, weighted by the probability of occurrence of each possible outcome). This would give a single representative value for the NPV of a project on which a decision could be based.

In relating probabilities to particular outcomes, decision makers might use either objective or subjective probabilities:

OBJECTIVE PROBABILITIES

Objective probabilities are based on actual past experience of the events. If we wanted to know the likely market demand for a particular commodity it might be useful to look at experience of the past. If over recent years demand has been 5 million units of the commodity for 60% of years and 6 million for the other 40%, we might feel it reasonable to assume that for the future the probabilities of the demand are:

5 million units	0.6
6 million units	0.4

It is obviously important when using past data to be fairly confident that the past is a reliable guide to the future.

SUBJECTIVE PROBABILITIES

Subjective probabilities would be based on opinion, preferably expert opinion. Perhaps the sales force would be asked their opinion of the likely range and probabilities for the size of the market.

Irrespective of how the probabilities are deduced, using them to build up a picture of the possible outcomes and likelihoods of occurrence, gives decision makers valuable insights on a project.

Example 2

Project X

Life	2 years (certain)
Initial outlay	£9,500 (certain)
Annual cash flows	£5,000 (p = 0.30) or £6,000 (p = 0.70)
Cost of capital	10% (certain)

This project has four possible outcomes for annual cash flows:

Outcome	Year	Cash Flow	Probability		
I	1	£5,000	0.3×0.3	=	0.09
	2	£5,000			
II	1	£5,000	0.3×0.7	=	0.21
	2	£6,000			
III	1	£6,000	0.7×0.3	=	0.21
	2	£5,000			
IV	1	£6,000	0.7×0.7	=	0.49
	2	£6,000			1.00

Thus even this very simple example has four possible *different* outcomes.

The possible NPVs will be:

I $-9,500 + (5,000 \times (1/1.10)^1) + (5,000 \times (1/1.10)^2) = -£826$ (unacceptable)

II $-9,500 + (5,000 \times (1/1.10)^1) + (6,000 \times (1/1.10)^2) = +£1$ (acceptable)

III $-9,500 + (6,000 \times (1/1.10)^1) + (5,000 \times (1/1.10)^2) = +£86$ (acceptable)

IV $-9,500 + (6,000 \times (1/1.10)^1) + (6,000 \times (1/1.10)^2) = +£910$ (acceptable)

This project is obviously difficult to assess. We know that there are only four possible outcomes, one of which must occur, but we do not know which one it is. All we have is the likelihood of each possible outcome.

There is a fairly high probability (0.91) that the project will turn out to be favourable (positive NPV). There is only a small (0.09) probability of an unfavourable outcome. Though it remains difficult to assess, it is probably more satisfactory to make a judgement on the basis of the possible outcomes and their probabilities than to base the decision, say, on the most likely outcome.

From this very simple example we can see that if there were more uncertainties the range of possible outcomes could become enormous. In real life where everything about the future is more or less uncertain the volume of possible individual outcomes can become so vast as to make identification of each one an impractical proposition.

Expected value

A WAY OF OVERCOMING the problem of the vast range of outcomes is to average the NPVs weighted according to the probability of occurrence. The resultant figure is known as the expected (net present) value (ENPV).

For the Example 2 (above), the ENPV would be:

$$(-826 \times 0.09) + (1 \times 0.21) + (86 \times 0.21) + (910 \times 0.49) = £390$$

A more direct approach, which would not require that the individual NPVs are identified, is to find the expected value of the inputs. In the example the expected value of the annual cash inflows is:

$$(5,000 \times 0.3) + (6,000 \times 0.7) = £5,700$$

So the project becomes:

Year	£
0	-9,500
1	5,700
2	5,700

$$NPV = -9,500 + (5,700 \times 0.909) + (5,700 \times 0.826) = £390$$

From this we can see that the 'direct approach' gives the same expected NPV as does the approach which identifies all of the possible outcomes individually.

Problems with expected value

(a) ENPV may not be capable actually of occurring. In the above example the ENPV is £390. This is not a value which could actually occur. There are four possible outcomes and +£390 is not one of them.

(b) Averaging positive outcomes with negative ones masks the risk. In the above example the fact that the ENPV is +£390 does not tell us that there is a 9% probability of a quite major (-£826) adverse outcome.

The counter argument to these two points is that businesses do not typically just make one investment but have a portfolio of different investments in plant, machinery, land, vehicles, etc. This means that while the ENPV of a particular project may be incapable actually of occurring, the ENPV of the whole portfolio of projects could reasonably occur. For example, there is a 0.5 probability of a fair coin landing heads, thus the wager which pays £1 if the coin lands heads and zero if it lands tails has an expected value of £0.50 even though this is an outcome which could not occur. If this wager were repeated 20 times we should be surprised if the expected value of £10 (implying 10 heads and 10 tails) were very far away from the actual outcome. Thus the fact that ENPV may not be capable of occurring for a particular project and that the individual outcomes get lost in the averaging process may not matter in real situations.

Where a particular project being assessed is large relative to the size of the business concerned, this counter argument does not work. In these circumstances decision makers will want some feel for the range of possible outcomes, particularly how bad the worst possible outcome could be. Decision makers will also want to have some feel for how far away from the predicted outcome the actual outcome is likely to be. Thus a measure of the dispersion of outcomes, like standard deviation, is likely to be very valuable to decision makers.

Activity 3

Cleancar Ltd is to purchase a machine to clean upholstery in saloon cars. There is a choice of two machines, the Super and the De Luxe. Each machine has an estimated life of 3 years with no estimated scrap value.

A Super machine will cost £25,000 and De Luxe machine will cost £32,000 payable immediately in either case. The relevant costs of cleaning one set of car seats is £2 if the Super machine is used, but only £1 if a De Luxe machine is used. This is because the De Luxe works faster and therefore engenders a lower labour cost.

The company plans to charge £5 for cleaning one set of car seats.

The company is uncertain of the likely demand for the service, but estimates have been made as follows:

Annual demand	Probability of occurrence
2,000	0.25
4,000	0.50
6,000	0.25

It is expected that, whichever level of demand applies in the first year will be repeated in each of the subsequent years.

Cleancar's cost of finance is estimated at 10% per annum.

You are required:

(a) to deduce the NPV for each of the three activity levels for each machine and to state a conclusion.

(b) to calculate the 'expected' NPV for each machine and to state your conclusion.

Cleancar

Differential cash flows of the Super machine

Demand (units)		2,000	4,000	6,000
		£000	£000	£000
Year 0		(25,000)	(25,000)	(25,000)
Year 1 (£5 - 2) per unit		6,000	12,000	18,000
Year 2		6,000	12,000	18,000
Year 3		6,000	12,000	18,000
Discounted	Factor			
Year 0	1.000	(25,000)	(25,000)	(25,000)
Year 1	0.909	5,454	10,908	16,362
Year 2	0.826	4,956	9,912	14,868
Year 3	0.751	4,506	9,012	13,518
		£(10,084)	£4,832	£19,748

Expected value   = (0.25 × (10,084)) + (0.50 × 4,832) + (0.25 × 19,748)
                 = £4,832

At the lowest level of demand the project would yield a significant adverse NPV.

Differential cash flows of De Luxe machine

Demand (units)		2,000	4,000	6,000
		£000	£000	£000
Year 0		(32,000)	(32,000)	(32,000)
Year 1 (£5 - 1) per unit		8,000	16,000	24,000
Year 2		8,000	16,000	24,000
Year 3		8,000	16,000	24,000
Discounted	Factor			
Year 0	1.000	(32,000)	(32,000)	(32,000)
Year 1	0.909	7,272	14,544	21,816
Year 2	0.826	6,608	13,216	19,824
Year 3	0.751	6,008	12,016	18,024
		£(12,112)	£7,776	£27,664

Expected value   = (0.25 × (12,112)) + (0.50 × 7,776) + (0.25 × 27,664)
                 = £10,776

If the level of demand were to prove to be 2,000 units per annum, investing in the De Luxe machine would be adverse.

On the other hand at the other possible levels of demand the De Luxe would be preferred to the Super.

Now try this self-assessment question. It might take you about 40 minutes. Do not worry too much if it takes longer. The main point is that you should understand all of the issues involved.

Try to complete the question before looking at our version of the answer.

Self-assessment question 1

Falco plc is considering the introduction of a new product to add to its existing range.

Demand

A market survey, which cost £20,000 but has yet to be paid for, has been undertaken. The survey suggests that the demand will last for the next four years with annual demand as follows:

Quantity (Number of units)	Probability
8,000	0.2
10,000	0.5
12,000	0.3

The market survey report suggests that whichever level of demand actually occurs it will stay at that level throughout the four year market life of the product.

The selling price will be £17 per unit of the product.

Capital equipment

The machinery which could be used in the manufacture of the new product is already owned by the company. If it is not used for the new product the company has no other use for it and it will be sold immediately for £100,000. If it is used for the new product it is expected to have a residual value of £20,000 at the end of the four years. Since the production cycle is very short, both production and sales could start more or less immediately, should the decision be made for production to go ahead.

Continued over . . .

Labour

Each unit of the new product will require 2 hours labour which will need to be taken on specifically for the purpose. Management is of the opinion that there will be adequate genuine vacancies to absorb these workers when the 4 years have elapsed. The grade of labour concerned is paid £2.50 per hour.

Materials

Each unit of the new product will require the use of one component A and 2 metres of material B. The company has a stock of 15,000 components A which were bought for £3 each for another project which was subsequently abandoned. These have no second-hand value because they are very specialised. Any component A which needs to be bought will cost £4 each. The company holds no stock of material B which costs £2 per metre to buy.

Overheads

It is estimated that the company's overheads will increase by a total of £20,000 per annum if the project goes ahead.

The company estimates its cost of finance to be 15% for the project under review.

Assume that all operating cash flows occur on the last day of the year concerned.

Ignore taxation.

You are required to calculate the expected NPV of the project and to comment on it.

(The answers to self-assessment questions are provided at the end of the unit.)

Now try this self-assessment question. Again it will probably take you about 40 minutes, but do not worry if it takes a bit longer.

You should make a real effort to complete the question before looking at our version of the answer.

Self-assessment question 2

Empall plc is a civil engineering business based in the UK. The company has been offered the opportunity to apply for a contract to build a tunnel under the Zimzam river in the Third World country of Zimzamia. The total contract price is £40 million, payable in sterling on completion of the contract. The contract payment would be guaranteed by the UK government. The contract would take three years to complete.

Empall has recently had a survey undertaken to assess the nature of the rock, through which the tunnel will need to pass. It was conducted by the local office of a very reliable rock surveying company. The survey cost £2 million, only half of which has been paid at present. The report of the survey points out that the situation is impossible to assess with absolute reliability. However the survey shows that the tunnel will either have to pass through Alpha type rock or Beta type rock. The survey company's results show that Alpha type rock is 60% likely, whereas Beta type rock is 40% likely to be encountered. Whichever type of rock is actually encountered, it will be consistently encountered throughout the contract.

Labour would be employed locally. It would cost £4 million for each year of the contract if Alpha type rock were encountered. If Beta type rock were encountered tunnelling would be more difficult and labour costing £6 million each year would be required. These labour costs assume normal weather conditions.

Zimzamia sometimes suffers from very severe rainfall in the spring. If it should so suffer during any of the three years of the contract, work would have to stop, though the labour would still need to be employed during the stoppage to satisfy local employment laws.

In order to stay on the necessary time schedule should severe rainfall occur, additional labour and overtime would be required. This would give rise to 25% additional local labour cost for any year in which the problem arose.

United Nations Weather Bureau statistics, based on observations over the past 120 years, indicate that severe rainfall occurred in the springs of 30 different years and that those years fell randomly over the observation period.

The tunnelling would require the use of plant which would need to be bought especially for the contract at a price of £10 million, payable immediately, including shipping costs. The plant would not be expected to have any value at the end of the contract.

Continued over . . .

The management of the contract would be undertaken by staff already employed by Empall. They would be paid their normal salaries totalling £1 million each year. An additional £1 million would be spent on travel to Zimzamia and living expenses paid by the company.

Empall is short of work at the moment to the extent that if the contract were not undertaken the managers would be made redundant immediately at a cost to the company of £1 million in redundancy pay. If the contract were undertaken it is believed that the managerial staff would be made redundant at the end of the contract, at which time the same £1 million redundancy pay would arise.

Any costs not mentioned above, including fuel for the plant, will be met by the Government of Zimzamia.

Empall's financing cost is 15% pa.

You are required:

(a) to deduce the 'expected' net present value of the contract and to comment on it; (hint – it is not necessary to calculate the value of the NPV of each of the possible outcomes in order to be able to deduce the expected NPV)

(b) to deduce the net present value of the contract assuming that the worst possible combination of events were to occur (ie Beta type rock encountered and severe rainfall in all three years), its likelihood of occurrence and comment on them;

(c) to say what further steps could be taken, on the basis of the available data, to put Empall in a better position to make the decision.

(The answers to self-assessment questions are provided at the end of the unit.)

Just before we move away from our brief consideration of some methods of handling risk in the context of investment decisions, it may be helpful to emphasise that the problem of risk is by no means restricted to investments decisions. Risk may be a particular problem with investment decision making, because investment decisions tend to relate to the longer term future. However, all decisions relate to the future and so risk must be considered in all decisions. The particular techniques which we have considered in this unit (basically sensitivity analysis and the use of probabilities) can usefully be brought to the aid of decision makers in most contexts, financial and non-financial decisions. Risk has been formally raised in the context of investment decisions only because this is the first decision making topic which we have considered the more practical aspects.

Risk and the discount rate

THERE ARE STRONG THEORETICAL reasons, which go beyond the scope of this module, for believing it logical to assess projects, whose cash flows are particularly risky, using a discount rate which is weighted to take account of the risk level. Evidence that this theory holds true in practice is not difficult to see. For example, typically banks when giving overdraft facilities to clients set the rate of interest at a level which reflects the amount of risk perceived by the bank.

When assessing an investment opportunity using NPV we should use a discount rate where:

discount rate to be applied to investment i	= risk-free rate	+ a risk premium which takes account of the riskiness of investment i

So a really safe investment (ie where there was little doubt about the outcome) would be assessed using a discount rate not much above the risk-free rate. The risk-free rate is usually seen as being the return on short-term loans to a very stable government, eg that of the UK, France or Germany.

Inflation and investment appraisal

PRICE INFLATION, THE EROSION of the purchasing power of money, can cause problems for the financial decision maker. This is particularly true when assessing investment decisions. This is because investment decisions can easily rely on predicted cash flows over several years into the future. Over just a few years a fairly modest rate of inflation can have pretty profound effects on the purchasing power of money. Specifically the problems which inflation causes the investment decision maker are of three types:

● Difficulty in forecasting the future rates of inflation. As we shall see shortly, this is not a problem which can be avoided.

● Difficulty of predicting demand and other factors when these may be affected by the level of inflation. Inflation seems to help to promote economic uncertainty, which is the reason why governments seem so eager to try to solve the inflation problem. This tends to make forecasts even more difficult to make than they would be otherwise.

● Problems with carrying out the analysis. A decision needs to be made as to whether to express forecast cash flows in 'real' terms, or in 'money' (or 'nominal') terms. Real, in this context, means expressing the cash flow in terms of £s of today's purchasing power. Money or nominal means the number of £s which are forecast to be paid and received at various future times.

Activity 4

A project is expected to generate a cash inflow of £150,000 in one year's time. The inflation rate for the next year is estimated at 5% per annum.

Have a try at expressing this cash inflow, both in real and in money terms.

The £150,000 is already expressed in money terms, since it is the amount of money which is actually expected next year. In real terms this would be £142,857 (ie £150,000/1.05).

Let us return to the three problems which inflation causes the investment decision maker. The first two of these make forecasting more difficult than it otherwise would be, but they do not raise any points of principle. The third one does raise a fundamental point, however.

It is perfectly correct to use either real cash flows or money cash flows in an investment appraisal. Clearly, whether the decision maker expresses the cash flows in real or in money terms, will make a difference to the NPV calculated, unless there is some adjustment made somewhere. In fact the adjustment is made in the choice of discount rate. The costs of finance which we observe in the market place, eg bank and building society lending rates, include an allowance for the rate of inflation which lenders expect. This is because lenders need to be compensated for three factors:

● Delaying consumption, by a pure risk-free rate of interest.

● Bearing the risk that the borrower may not meet all of the obligations under the loan contract, by a risk premium.

● For the fact that the money lent will be worth less in its ability to buy goods and services when it is repaid than when it was borrowed, ie for inflation.

If the investment decision maker is using real cash flows in the analysis, then a discount rate which excludes an allowance for inflation, ie a 'real' discount rate, must be used. On the other hand, if the decision maker prefers to deal in money cash flows, a 'money' discount rate which includes an allowance for inflation must be included.

It should now be clear as to why it is not possible to avoid having to make judgements about likely future inflation rates. If the 'real' route is taken, the decision maker will need to adjust observable market rates of interest by the expected rate of inflation in order to arrive at the real discount rate. If the 'money' route is taken the money cash flows will need to be estimated. This will involve the decision maker in estimating the actual number of £s which will be paid or received at various times, which in turn requires some estimate of the rate of inflation.

The crucial point about investment appraisal in an inflationary environment is that the decision maker must be scrupulously consistent, whichever approach is taken, real or money.

Money cash flows must be discounted using a money discount rate, real cash flows must be discounted using a real discount rate.

Shortages of investment capital

WE SAW IN UNIT 3 that a business which is seeking to increase its wealth should accept all investment opportunities which will yield a positive NPV. This assumes that the business has access to unlimited finance. Where it is not the case that the business can find as much finance as it needs to make all of the favourable investments open to it, the basic NPV rule must be modified.

Example 3

A business has identified three investment opportunities. They are typical of the projects undertaken by the business in that they require injections of cash over the first two years, after which they start to produce positive net cash flows over the subsequent four years. The company uses a discount rate of 10% per annum for investments of the level of risk inherent in these three projects. The estimated cash flows are as follows:

Project		A	B	C
	Year	£m	£m	£m
	0	(6)	(8)	(5)
	1	(2)	(2)	(3)
	2	1	1	2
	3	3	4	5
	4	5	6	3
	5	3	5	2
	NPV	0.54	1.21	0.97

Investment funds are limited to £10m for year 0. Each of the projects could be partially undertaken.

All three projects are beneficial to the business in that they all show positive a NPV. If there were sufficient funds the business would be advised to undertake them all. Clearly this cannot happen if there is only £10m available.

Activity 5

What advice would you give the management of this business if there is no other source of finance?

It is tempting to suggest that project B is undertaken in full, since this project gives the highest NPV. However this would be wrong. Where there is a limited resource (investment finance in this case) the best use of it is to get the highest benefit per unit of the scarce resource. Thus we need to look to see which project gives the highest NPV per £ of year 0 investment (see overleaf).

Project	A £m	B £m	C £m
Year 0 investment	6	8	5
NPV	0.54	1.21	0.97
NPV/year 0 investment	0.54/6 =0.09	1.21/8 =0.15	0.97/5 =0.16

Thus the order of 'merit' is C, then B and A last. This means that the highest possible NPV can be obtained by investing £5m in project C and the remaining £5m in project B.

Suppose now that investment finance in year 1 is expected to be limited to £4m, as well as the £10m limitation in year 0. If we approached the year 1 problem as we just did for the year 0 one we should have the following:

Project	A £m	B £m	C £m
Year 0 investment	2	2	3
NPV	0.54	1.21	0.97
NPV/year 0 investment	0.54/2 =0.27	1.21/2 =0.61	0.97/3 =0.32

This seems to imply that the business should undertake all of investment B and part of investment C. This is, however, in conflict with the conclusion which we reached when we considered the year 0 finance shortage. Bearing in mind that there is a shortage of finance in both years, what should the business do? In the context of the year 0 finance shortage, one course of action is best. In the context of the year 1 problem another, conflicting, course of action is best.

Activity 6

Do you remember coming across a technique for dealing with situations like this one where there are two or more constraints? It is likely that you have met this technique in another module of your course.

The technique is known as linear programming. This is a mathematical technique for solving problems exactly like the present one, supplying the decision maker with the ability to invest in the projects so as to maximise the NPV given the impossibility of making all three investments in full.

Corporate strategy and NPV

Senior management of the organisation, having identified its overall objectives, will seek to set out long/medium term strategic plans for the achievement of those objectives. In doing this management will tend to take account of such factors as the strengths and weaknesses of the organisation and of the opportunities and threats which the environment confronts it with. The strategic plans which result will tend to involve such issues as at which end of its market the organisation will operate, what market share it will seek to have and whether the organisation will produce its product or service 'in house' or whether it will buy it in. It is against this strategic framework that the organisation will make its decisions, including its investment decisions. Since the primary financial objective of the organisation is to enhance wealth, the strategy will be selected on the basis of its ability to achieve wealth enhancement.

Some people seem to suggest that NPV analysis seeks to take each opportunity as an independent venture, unrelated to the organisation's strategy. Thus they see corporate strategy, which takes the broad view, and NPV analysis, which they believe to take the narrow one, as incompatible. Clearly organisations must develop strategic plans, so to those who see corporate strategy and NPV as incompatible, NPV is a seriously flawed approach.

This view is not logical. Corporate strategy is important, because it sets the framework for the organisation's planning and decision making. However, once this framework has been established, the use of NPV to seek to make decisions which enhance the wealth of the organisation and which are consistent with the strategy, is the correct approach. Thus corporate strategy, on the one hand, and the use of NPV, on the other, far from being incompatible in fact support one other.

Reading

You should now read Reader Article 4.1 'Evaluating and controlling investments in advanced manufacturing technology' by Graham Motteram and John Sizer. Note that Graham Motteram is a manager with Rolls-Royce plc.

Advanced manufacturing technology includes such areas as computer controlled production facilities and robotics. The authors have chosen to deal with this area of investment because it is seen by some people as raising issues which do not apply to more traditional assets.

Points to consider:

The authors advocate 'major sequential steps' (Figure 1). Do you think that these are likely to be, more or less, the same steps which all business should take in respect of all types of investment appraisal?

What is the view of the relationship between corporate strategy and the appraisal of the financial aspects (eg by NPV) of a project? Does their view differ from ours (outlined in section 4.14)?

The notion of having a series of steps in the investment process, explained in the article, gives a useful introduction to the next section of this unit.

Management of the process of identifying, assessing, implementing and reviewing investment projects

IT WAS POINTED OUT at the beginning of Unit 3, that businesses are organisations which raise funds from various sources and invest those funds with the intention of increasing their wealth as a result. Thus, the whole process of making suitable investments requires careful management. In principle, a system needs to be set in place where:

- Good investment opportunities can be identified

- Proposed projects can be assessed in a formal, unbiased way to identify beneficial projects

- Beneficial projects can be implemented

- Projects once in operation are reviewed.

It is not appropriate for us to be too dogmatic as to precisely what system any particular business should implement to achieve these goals. We can, however, outline the type of approach which would appear sensible for the typical business.

IDENTIFICATION OF POTENTIAL PROJECTS

Effort should be put into the identification of potential projects. It is crucial for almost all businesses to innovate. This may mean introducing new products and services, serving new markets or using new processes to generate the products and services. In general, business is highly competitive and those businesses which fail to innovate will not survive. This means that steps should actively be taken to identify new projects. This can be done, at least partly, through a department or section of the business being charged with the task of identifying new projects. Alternatively, or in addition, ordinary members of staff can be encouraged to come up with ideas. The ordinary members of staff may well be able to identify new projects because they are actively involved, on a day-to-day basis, with some aspect of the work of the business, eg marketing or production. Technical assistance should be made available to the originator of an idea to help develop it into a serious proposal. It should be possible for all reasonable ideas to have the opportunity to be assessed. People will tend not to come up with a second proposal if their first one was ignored.

Proposals would normally be formalised by requiring the proposer to complete a standard proposal form. This will require various details about the proposal which will help at the assessment stage.

ASSESSING THE PROPOSALS

Serious proposals should be formally screened using NPV analysis. The technical process of estimating cash flows, assessing risk, etc should be carried out by an expert who is independent of the originator of the idea. This person obviously needs technical skills to be able to discover and handle the data. The person also needs to be unbiased. There is the danger that the originator of the idea will be so committed to the proposal that bias could creep into the analysis if he or she were asked to carry out this technical task. Sometimes the politics of the particular business can play a part in the process, with individuals keen to promote their own ideas in order to gain influence and prestige.

Once the technical analysis has been completed a decision must be made. In many cases, the formal proposal will be presented to a committee which has the power to make investment decisions. This might be the board of directors for significantly large or far reaching proposals. The committee should reach a decision and set a timetable for the implementation of successful proposals.

Some projects are difficult to assess because the benefits are hard to identify. Here we are not referring to the general uncertainty, which surrounds virtually all projects, relating to such matters as the level of sales revenue or cost saving to which the project might give rise. This is a problem, but it is one which can be handled through risk analysis. The problem which is now being raised concerns projects where, even after they are fully operating, it remains unclear as to what the benefit is. An example of such a project is an investment in creating a subsidised canteen for staff use. Estimating the costs of creating and operating the canteen pose no more than the usual problems. However what is the value of the benefit, in terms of staff morale, goodwill, etc, which can be compared to the costs in order to make a valid decision?

There is no simple answer to this problem. It may be possible to find some formula through which estimates of benefits may be assessed. Quite likely, in the end, the decision makers will be forced to rely heavily on their judgement in balancing quantitative factors (the costs in this case) against qualitative factors (staff morale etc) to reach a decision.

IMPLEMENTING OF SUCCESSFUL PROPOSALS

It is not enough for the proposed project to be successfully assessed. Once the decision has been made it should become part of a formal capital expenditure schedule. Someone should be required to take responsibility for putting the project in place. This could involve the original proposer. It is important that the expenditure is carefully controlled. The proposed project would have been accepted for implementation because, amongst other things, it had the potential to generate more wealth than it would cost to implement it. Clearly this potential will be lost as the cost of implementation increases. The person responsible for implementation needs to be held accountable for any excess spending.

REVIEWING THE PROJECT IN OPERATION

When we discussed the subject of financial decision making in the first unit, it was suggested that review of the decision, once implemented, is an important part of the decision making process. Three reasons were given for this assertion.

Activity 7

Can you remember what these three reasons were?

Jot down what you think that they were.

The three reasons are:

1) To assess the effectiveness of the decision making process.

2) To limit the damage of bad decisions.

3) To take steps properly to implement the decision.

Here they are repeated in the specific context of investment decisions. They are:

● To review the quality of the decision to try to identify strong and weak features of the decision making process. This is sometimes known as 'post-audit' in the investment context. The post-audit process should seek to compare the actual outcomes of the project with that which was claimed to be the likely outcome. It is far from being the case that a project which has shown itself to be a failure means that the wrong decision was made at the assessment stage. In real life, the future is uncertain. At the time of the decision the circumstances which caused the project to fail may not have been capable of being known. Nevertheless decision makers must ask themselves whether there was any way in which the bad decision could have been avoided. If the decision making process is capable of being improved, and few human endeavours are not, it is likely to be the post-audit which will provide the clues to where the areas of improvement lie.

● If the project is turning out to be less beneficial than was originally planned, review should identify this fact and enable efforts to be made to try to rescue the project. Again the budgetary control routines should highlight failures, which should initiate the search for ways of improving matters.

● To try to ensure that the decision is actually being implemented as planned. To a great extent the operation of the project, once implemented, will become the responsibility of the manager into whose sphere of responsibility the project falls. Review of this aspect would normally be carried out on a continuous and routine basis, as part of the budgetary control system of the business.

Reading

You should now read Reader Article 4.2 'Post-completion auditing: a source of strategic direction' by Alison Kennedy and Roger Mills.

The article reviews some research carried out by its authors, and by others, into the nature and extent of the review of investment projects once they are under way – 'post audits' as they are known.

Points to consider:

Is 'post-auditing' a very widely practised activity in UK companies? Is the practice on the increase? What do people seem to think is the hardest part of the capital budgeting process?

Further aspects of investment decision making in practice

THE ACCA SURVEY (see Unit 1) showed that companies dealt with assessment and/or adjustment for risk as follows:

	Percentage of companies
Sensitivity analysis	51
Adjusting the payback period	37
Conservative estimates of cash flows	32
Adjusting the discount rate	18

The fact that these percentages add up to more than 100 implies that the 'average' company uses more than one of these approaches. The larger companies tend to use a larger number of approaches, on average, than the small companies do. Of course, these approaches are not mutually exclusive. A company might carry out a sensitivity analysis to try to assess the riskiness of a particular project. Having done this, the discount rate can be adjusted to reflect this level of risk.

The survey also addressed itself to the problem of dealing with inflation. The results showed that among all companies, only about 40% dealt with inflation correctly or in a way which probably was not significantly incorrect. For the larger companies in the sample, about 60% were correct or not significantly incorrect in their treatment. Given the rates of inflation which have recently been experienced in the UK, it seems likely that many investment decisions have been made on the basis of potentially misleading analysis.

Summary of the unit

THIS UNIT HAS MAINLY been concerned with some of the more practical aspects of investment decision making. Risk is an important aspect of virtually all real world decisions. One way to try to assess it is through sensitivity analysis, ie trying to see the effects on the predicted outcome of changes in various of the inputs. Another technique is to try to identify each of the possible actual values for each item of input data and to ascribe statistical probabilities to each of these. By doing this it is possible to identify all of the possible outcomes for the particular project under review and to deduce the likelihood of each ones occurrence. (This is not necessarily very practical, due to the vast number of possible outcomes there may be in practice.) Whether or not the individual outcomes are all identified, it is possible to calculate an 'expected value' for the project, ie a weighted average of all of the possible outcomes. We then went on to consider how the discount rate is affected by the riskiness of a project. Following this we considered how decision makers should deal with the problems caused by the expected inflation during the period to which the decision is to relate. We also saw how decision makers should logically deal with the situation where there is a shortage of investment capital by modifying the basic NPV rule. Next we considered the relationship between corporate strategy and the use of NPV and saw that they are entirely compatible. We concluded the unit with a brief consideration of the process of identification, assessment, implementation and review of investment decisions.

Suggested solutions to self-assessment questions

Self-assessment question 1

Falco Ltd

Year	0	1	2	3	4
	£	£	£	£	£
Machinery	(100,000)				20,000
Sales revenue (note 1)		173,400	173,400	173,400	173,400
Labour		(51,000)	(51,000)	(51,000)	(51,000)
Component A (note 2)			(21,600)	(40,800)	(40,800)
Material B		(40,800)	(40,800)	(40,800)	(40,800)
Overheads		(20,000)	(20,000)	(20,000)	(20,000)
	(100,000)	61,600	40,000	20,800	40,800
Discount factor	1.00	0.87	0.76	0.66	0.57
Present value	(100,000)	53,592	30,400	13,728	23,256
ENPV	£20,976				

Since the ENPV is a significant, positive figure the project should be undertaken.

Note 1

Expected demand = $(8,000 \times 0.2) + (10,000 \times 0.5) + (12,000 \times 0.3) = 10,200$ units pa

Expected sales revenue = $10,200 \times £17 = £173,400$.

Note 2

Use of component A	Stock at year 0	15,000
	Usage in year 1 (from stock)	10,200
		4,800
	Usage in year 2 (from stock)	4,800
		zero

Therefore	year 2 purchase 5400 @ £4 each	21,600
	years 3 & 4 purchase 10,200 @ £4 each	40,800

Note 3

There is no reason why the NPV should not be calculated for each level of output and then the expected NPV deduced, though the above method is quicker.

Self-assessment question 2

Empall plc

Annual expected cash flows

Year	0	1	2	3
	£m	£m	£m	£m
Plant	(10.0)			
Redundancy pay (Note 1)	1.0			(1.0)
Supervision (Note 2)		(2.0)	(2.0)	(2.0)
Labour (Note 3)		(5.1)	(5.1)	(5.1)
Contract price				40.0
	(9.0)	(7.1)	(7.1)	31.9
PV Factor	1.000	0.870	0.756	0.658
Present value	(9.000)	(6.177)	(5.368)	20.990
Net present value	0.445	(positive)		

Though this is a positive figure, and it indicates that if the company is making its decisions on the basis of ENPV the contract should be accepted, it is not a large figure. The contract would probably be regarded as rather marginal, therefore.

Notes

1) This cost is relevant, even though the amounts are identical, because of the timing difference between the two payments.

2) The managers' salaries are relevant since they will only continue to be employed if the project goes ahead. The question was unclear as to whether the expenses were annual costs or just an initial one; either treatment was therefore acceptable.

3) The expected annual labour cost is:

$0.60[(0.75 \times 4.0) + (0.25 \times 5.0)] + 0.40[(0.75 \times 6.0) + (0.25 \times 7.5)] =$

$(0.6 \times 4.25) + (0.4 \times 6.375) = £5.1m$

(b) Annual cash flows

Year	0 £m	1 £m	2 £m	3 £m
Plant	(10.0)			
Redundancy pay (Note 1)	1.0			(1.0)
Supervision (Note 2)		(2.0)	(2.0)	(2.0)
Labour (Note 3)		(7.5)	(7.5)	(7.5)
Contract price				40.0
	(9.0)	(9.5)	(9.5)	29.5
PV Factor	1.000	0.870	0.756	0.658
Present value	(9.000)	(8.265)	(7.182)	19.411
Net present value	5.036	(negative)		

Probability of occurrence $0.4 \times 0.25 \times 0.25 \times 0.25 = 0.00625$

ie about 6 chances in 1000 of occurring.

In the unlikely event that the worst possible set of circumstances were to occur, a significant adverse outcome would arise, despite the positive ENPV of the contract.

(c) In order to know more about the range of outcomes either all of them (16 in total) would need to be assessed or some measure of spread (eg standard deviation) would have to be calculated. Probably it would be reasonable to deduce the NPV and probability of occurrence of each possible outcome. This would enable the company to assess, for example, the total probability that the contract would actually be favourable.

Other investment appraisal techniques, particularly payback period, could be calculated.

Note that these suggestions involve 'available data' as specified by the question.

Additional exercises

Exercise 1

The directors of Red River Mining Company are considering purchasing and extending a disused mine. The purchase price of the mine will be £150,000 payable immediately. Experience of mining in the geographical area suggests that the total amount of extractable tin depends on the type of rock found and that there are three possibilities for this:

Rock type	Total tin output	Probability
A	120 tonnes	0.4
B	72 tonnes	0.4
C	48 tonnes	0.2

If the company buys the mine it will spend the first year making the mine usable and installing extraction plant etc. This will cost £95,000 payable at the end of that year. The extraction will start at the beginning of the second year and proceed at a steady rate of 2 tonnes each month until the mine is exhausted.

Throughout the period of extraction the selling price of tin is expected to be £9,900 per tonne and the total annual extraction costs will be £105,000. These cash flows are expected to occur at the end of the year in which they arise.

Special mining equipment will be purchased at the start of the first year of extraction at a cost of £48,000. It will be sold at the end of the period of extraction for a price equal to its cost to the company less £200 for every tonne of tin extracted during its life.

Disposal proceeds of the mine and other equipment are expected to be negligible irrespective of the mine's closure date. The company uses a discount rate of 15% to assess such projects.

You are required to calculate the NPV of reopening the mine for each of the three possible rock types found and to use this information to deduce an expected NPV for the project. Comment on your results.

Exercise 2

Jimbo Ltd is contemplating an investment in a labour saving device. The cost would be £18,000 payable immediately. The machine can only last for 4 years, but the extent to which it will save labour in each year is not certain. Estimates of potential savings during each of the 4 years and of their probability of occurrence are as follows:

	£	Probability
Year 1	7,000	0.4
	8,000	0.5
	9,000	0.1
Year 2	6,000	0.3
	7,000	0.5
	8,000	0.2
Year 3	5,000	0.1
	6,000	0.6
	7,000	0.3
Year 4	4,000	0.2
	5,000	0.5
	6,000	0.3

The firm's cost of finance is 15%.

You are required:

(a) to calculate the 'expected' labour saving in each of the 4 years.

(b) to calculate the 'expected' net present value (NPV) of the investment.

(c) to calculate the NPV and the probability of occurrence of the worst possible case (ie the lowest level of labour saving in each year).

(d) to discuss briefly the advantages and disadvantages of using 'expected' NPV as a basis of investment decision making.

Exercise 3

Jalian plc is assessing whether or not to make an investment in a project. This will require an immediate cash outlay of £650,000 and is expected to give rise to net cash inflows at the end of each of the following two years. The amounts of these net cash inflows and their likelihood of occurring are as follows:

Net cash inflows

Year 1

Cash flow	Probability
£	
150,000	0.20
350,000	0.60
600,000	0.20
	1.00

The outcome from the second year depends on what happens in the first year as follows:

Year 2

If the net cash inflow for year 1 is:	there is a probability of:	that the net cash inflow in year 2 will be:
150,000	0.20	Zero
	0.60	200,000
	0.20	300,000
	1.00	
350,000	0.20	150,000
	0.60	500,000
	0.20	600,000
	1.00	
600,000	0.20	500,000
	0.60	600,000
	0.20	750,000
	1.00	

All of the above cash flows (except the initial investment) should be assumed to occur at the relevant year end.

Jalian has two sites on which it could operate the project, the North site or the South site. The choice of site will not in any way affect the above cash flows and probabilities. If the company chooses the South site, however, there is the opportunity to abandon the project at the end of the first year and to sell the uncompleted project to an interested purchaser for £250,000 payable immediately (ie at the end of the first year).

The company's management has decided that, were it to be undertaken on the South site, the project would be abandoned and sold at the end of Year 1 if its expected value at that point in time were less than the £250,000 disposal value.

The company has a cost of finance for projects like this one of 10%.

You are required:

(a) to calculate the NPV of the project on North site.

(b) to explain (using your calculations) the precise circumstances under which the company would choose to abandon the project on the South site.

(c) to calculate the NPV of the project on the South site taking account of the abandonment opportunity.

(d) to state the value as at year 0 of being able to use the South site and therefore to have the abandonment opportunity.

Exercise 4

Cooke Ltd is assessing the viability of manufacturing and marketing a new product. A market research survey has been undertaken, which has indicated an appropriate sales price to be £20 per unit of the product. At this price demand is estimated at 20,000 units of the product per annum. The uncertainty of the market raises doubts about how long the demand will last. The market survey estimates that there is a 0.3 probability that the market will last exactly 3 years, 0.4 probability of exactly 4 years and 0.3 probability that the market will last exactly 5 years. The cost of the market survey is £25,000, an amount which has yet to be paid.

To make the new product would require the company to buy some special equipment for £480,000, payable immediately. This equipment could cope with the production of the new product up to a maximum of 20,000 units per annum. The supplier of the equipment estimates that its effective productive life will be exactly 4 years (0.5 probability) or exactly 5 years (0.5 probability). The equipment is so specialised that it can be used for no purpose other than manufacture of the new product, so whenever the market ends the equipment will have zero sales value at that time.

The relevant cost of making the product is estimated at £10 per unit.

Cooke Ltd's cost of finance to support this project is 20% per annum.

The cost of the machine is payable immediately; other receipts and payments are expected to arise annually in arrears.

Ignore taxation.

You are required:

(a) to identify the possible outcomes for production in terms of the length of the project and the probabilities of each outcome

(b) to calculate the NPV for each outcome

(c) to calculate the ENPV of the project.

Solutions to additional examples

Exercise 1: Red River Mining Company

Rock type A (120/24 = 5 year life)

Year 0	Purchase price	(150,000)	× 1.000	(150,000)
Year 1	Extension work etc	(95,000)		
	Special equipment	(48,000)		
		(143,000)	× 0.870	(124,410)
Year 2	Sales (£9,900 × 24)	237,600		
	Annual costs	(105,000)		
		132,600	× 0.756	100,246
Year 3	ditto	132,600	× 0.658	87,251
Year 4	ditto	132,600	× 0.572	75,847
Year 5	ditto	132,600	× 0.497	65,902
Year 6	ditto	132,600		
	Special equipment	24,000		
	(48,000 - (200 × 120))			
		156,600	× 0.432	67,651

Net present value 122,487

Rock type B (72/24 = 3 year life)

NPV of rock type A (5 year life)		122,487		
Less	Final 2 years	(133,553)		
		(11,066)		(11,066)
Add	Special equipment	33,600	× 0.572	19,219
	(48,000 - (200 × 72)			
Net present value				8,153

Rock type C (48/24 = 2 year life)

NPV of rock type A (5 year life)		122,487		
Less	Final 3 years	(209,400)		
		(86,913)		(86,913)
Add	Special equipment	38,400	× 0.658	25,267
	(48,000 - (200 × 48)			
Net present value				(61,646)

Totals

Expected net present value	122,487	× 0.4	48,995
	8,153	× 0.4	3,261
	(61,646)	× 0.2	(12,329)
Expected net present value			39,927

On the basis of the ENPV the project to reopen the mine should go ahead because the figure is significant and positive. However it should be noted that there is a very real chance (one in five) that the project will result in a large adverse outcome. Moreover, it is not possible to find the expected value for the period of extraction and carry out just one calculation to find the ENPV. This is because the discount factors are non-linear.

Exercise 2: Jimbo

a)

		£
Year 1	7,000 × 0.4	2,800
	8,000 × 0.5	4,000
	9,000 × 0.1	900
		7,700

		£
Year 2	6,000 × 0.3	1,800
	7,000 × 0.5	3,500
	8,000 × 0.2	1,600
		6,900

		£
Year 3	5,000 × 0.1	500
	6,000 × 0.6	3,600
	7,000 × 0.3	2,100
		6,200

		£
Year 4	4,000 × 0.2	800
	5,000 × 0.5	2,500
	6,000 × 0.3	1,800
		5,100

(b) Net present value

Year	£	discount factor	£
0	(18,000)	1.000	(18,000)
1	7,700	0.870	6,699
2	6,900	0.756	5,216
3	6,200	0.658	4,080
4	5,100	0.572	2,917
Expected NPV			912

(c) Worst possible case

Year	£	discount factor	£
0	(18,000)	1.000	(18,000)
1	7,000	0.870	6,090
2	6,000	0.756	4,536
3	5,000	0.658	3,290
4	4,000	0.572	2,288
NPV			(1,796)

Probability $0.4 \times 0.3 \times 0.1 \times 0.2 = 0.0024$ (ie 24 in 10000)

(d) Advantages

- Convenient way of dealing with risk
- Gives a clear usable result

Disadvantages

- Difficulty in ascribing probabilities
- Loss of information inherent in the averaging process
- The fact that the expected result may be incapable of occurring.

Exercise 3: Jalian plc

(a) Expected value of the cash inflows: Year 2

If year 1 cash flow is:				Year 2 £
£150,000	0.20	×	zero	zero
	0.60	×	200,000	120,000
	0.20	×	300,000	60,000
				£180,000
or				
£350,000	0.20	×	150,000	30,000
	0.60	×	500,000	300,000
	0.20	×	600,000	120,000
				£450,000
or				
£600,000	0.20	×	500,000	100,000
	0.60	×	600,000	360,000
	0.20	×	750,000	150,000
				£610,000

If the North site is used

Expected NPV =

$$-650,000 + 0.20[(150,000/1.10) + (180,000/1.10^2)] + 0.60[(350,000/1.10) + (450,000/1.10^2)] + 0.20[(600,000/1.10) + (610,000/1.10^2)]$$

$$= £31,020 \text{ (positive)}$$

(b) At the end of year 1, the expected PV of the year 2 cash inflows would be:

If year 1 = £150,000 Year 2 = £180,000/1.10 =   £163,636
If year 1 = £350,000 Year 2 = £450,000/1.10 =   £409,091
If year 1 = £600,000 Year 2 = £610.000/1.10 =   £554,545

Thus at the end of year 1, the PV of the expected year 2 inflows will be greater than the abandonment value (£250,000) in the latter two cases, but less than the abandonment value in the first case. Therefore the project should be continue *unless* the year 1 cash inflow proves to be £150,000.

(c) If the South site is used

Expected NPV =

$$-650,000 + 0.20(150,000 + 250,000)/1.10) + 0.60[(350,000/1.10) + (450,000/1.10^2) + 0.20[(600,000/1.10) + (610,000/1.10^2)]$$

$$= £46,694 \text{ (positive)}$$

Note that if the first year cash inflow is £150,000, the project will be abandoned which will give rise to an additional year 1 cash inflow of £250,000.

(d) The value of having the choice of using the South site is £15,674 (ie £46,694 - 31,020). This is because the (expected) value of the project is greater on the South site than on the North site.

Exercise 4: Cooke Ltd

(a) The calculation requires the construction of a decision tree showing possible demand and sales, and the related probabilities:

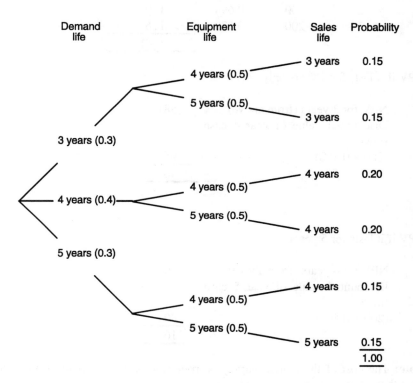

Demand life	Equipment life	Sales life	Probability
	4 years (0.5) →	3 years	0.15
3 years (0.3)	5 years (0.5) →	3 years	0.15
4 years (0.4)	4 years (0.5) →	4 years	0.20
	5 years (0.5) →	4 years	0.20
5 years (0.3)	4 years (0.5) →	4 years	0.15
	5 years (0.5) →	5 years	0.15
			1.00

Summary

       3 years: 0.30
       4 years: 0.55
       5 years: 0.15

(b)   Contribution per unit:

	£
Sales revenue	20
Relevant cost	10
Contribution	10

Contribution per year's sales is 20,000 × £10 = £200,000

Net present value (NPV) of project if it lasts for 3 years only

Year	Cash flows £000	Factor	Discounted £000
0	(480)	1.000	(480)
1	200	0.833	167
2	200	0.694	139
3	200	0.579	116
			(58)

NPV if it lasts for 4 years only

NPV for 3 years (from above)	(58)
Discounted value of year 4 cash flows	
(200×0.482)	96
	36

NPV if it lasts for 5 years

NPV for 4 years (from above)	36
Discounted value of year 5 cash flows	
(200×0.402)	80
	116

Note: The cost of the market survey is irrelevant as it has already been incurred even though not yet paid for (ie it is a sunk cost)

(c) 'Expected' NPV of project

$$= (0.30 \times (58)) + (0.55 \times 36) + (0.15 \times 116)$$

$$= 19.80 \text{ (ie £19,800)}$$

UNIT 5

COST–VOLUME–PROFIT ANALYSIS

IN THIS SECTION WE will consider the relationship between costs, volume and profit. We will see how an understanding of this relationship is useful for planning purposes. The relationship has particular relevance when managers are making short-term tactical decisions concerning such matters as whether to make or buy a particular product, whether to accept or reject a proposed contract and how to allocate scarce resources. Having completed this unit you should be able to:

- deduce fixed and variable cost elements from relevant data

- construct a break-even chart and profit-volume chart and deduce the break-even point of some activity.

- explain the meaning of contribution and use contribution analysis in the resolution of problems involving pricing, allocation of scarce resources and make or buy decisions

- discuss the deficiencies of the contribution analysis approach.

Outline of the unit

THE UNIT STARTS BY pointing out that the costs associated with pursuing any particular activity can broadly be classified into those which are:

- Fixed, relative to the volume of activity (level of output); and

- Variable, relative to the volume of activity.

To a business making wooden chairs, the cost of the timber used in the chairs would be a variable cost. The rent of the workshop in which the chairs are made would be a fixed cost. This is because the total cost of the timber used will increase as the number of chairs increases, whereas the rent of the workshop will be the same whether one chair or 100 chairs are made each week.

Note carefully that these classifications are relative to the volume of output. That a cost is fixed does not mean that you only have to pay it once in the life of the business. Neither does it mean that the cost does not alter over time as a result of changing price levels. The rent of the workshop is fixed because it is not affected by changes in the level of volume. The rent still has to be paid each month or quarter (depending on the terms of the lease) and it may well increase over time, to reflect inflation.

The great advantage of being able to separate the fixed and variable elements of the costs is that it then becomes possible to make predictions as to what the total cost will be at various output levels.

For example, say that you know that the total fixed cost of running your car for a month (including depreciation, insurance, road tax) is £100. You also know that the cost per mile (including petrol, servicing and additional depreciation due to usage) is 12 pence. You can now work out the total cost and average cost per mile for any chosen number of miles travelled in a month. Perhaps it is not the sort of calculation that you would do in non-business circumstances, but suppose that the car were a taxi from which you made your living. Knowledge of the total cost for a particular estimated future monthly mileage could enable you to work out how much profit you might make at some particular charge per mile to your passengers. Alternatively you could calculate what price per mile you would need to charge in order to be able to make a particular level of profit.

We tend to deduce the amount of future costs, whether fixed or variable, on the basis of either our own or other peoples experience of the past, adjusted for any possible changes in the environment, eg price increases.

A clear understanding of which costs vary, and by how much, with the level of output is vital to trying to identify the cash flows which will result from any particular level of predicted output. This is very important in decision making and planning as we have already seen in first four units of this course.

Some costs are clearly recognisable as being either fixed or variable. Motor car insurance is a fixed cost (relative to the mileage). Insurance companies do not even ask motorists how many miles they intend to drive next year, before setting the premium. Petrol is clearly a cost of running a car which varies with the number of miles driven. Costs like these are easy to classify, but what about the depreciation of the car? We know that cars normally depreciate due to the passage of time alone. We also know that the annual depreciation of a car increases as the mileage increases. In order to make predictions of the total cost of running a car at a particular mileage level, we need to be able to separate out the fixed from the variable element of the depreciation. To do this we probably need to look at prices of a range of second-hand cars all of the same age, but with different mileages. Then we could try to fit a straight line to the data to reach a conclusion on the depreciation rate per mile (variable) and the monthly depreciation (fixed), which together make up total depreciation.

Our knowledge of cost–volume relationships can be used to work out the total cost for any chosen volume of output. Since we can also easily work out the total sales revenues for that same level of volume, we can see what profit or loss is likely to be made from the activity at our chosen volume of output. Particularly important is the fact that we can also deduce the level of output at which the activity makes no profit or loss. This is the point at which total cost and total sales revenue are equal. This zero profit point is known as the *break-even point*. This can be done graphically, which has the advantage of making the cost–profit relationships more obvious, particularly to non-experts. Perhaps more accurately and practically, the break-even point can also be calculated quite easily.

The section explains how businesses can have different strategies concerning the balance between fixed and variable costs. It is sometimes possible to produce a good or a service with relatively low total fixed costs, but with high variable costs per unit of output. Alternatively the balance may be the other way round. Where there is a preponderance of fixed costs, the business is particularly vulnerable to significant reductions in profit for relatively insignificant reductions in sales output. This point is quite well illustrated in Activity 6. Here a provider of language courses has the choice of two strategies on the balance between fixed and variable costs. When you reach this activity you should bear this point in mind.

The section also shows how the break-even point can be calculated for any particular activity, provided that variable cost per unit, fixed cost per period and sales price per unit are all known. The calculation is usually done on the assumption that all of the relationships are linear, ie that fixed costs remain fixed, that both the variable cost per unit and the sales price per unit are the same irrespective of how many are produced and sold.

The underlying logic of the break-even calculation is as follows:

● Each additional unit of output produced and sold leads to the business generating the additional sales revenue associated with one unit.

● Each additional unit of output produced and sold leads to the business incurring the additional variable cost associated with one unit.

● The fixed costs (by definition) are not affected by additional units of output produced and sold.

● Thus the net effect on the business of producing and selling one additional unit of output is the sales revenue per unit less the variable cost per unit. This measure is known as the *contribution*.

● Provided that the sales revenue per unit is greater than the variable cost per unit, the contribution will be positive and therefore each unit of additional output will benefit the business by the amount of the contribution per unit.

● If we divide the fixed costs for the period by the contribution per unit of output, we discover the number of contributions, and therefore units of output, necessary to cover the fixed costs and to break even.

You should carefully note that the break-even point is calculated by reference to the fixed costs for a period (eg a week, a month, a year), therefore the break-even point also relates to a period. So when we say that a particular activity has a break-even point of 145 units, we must add the period during which these must be produced in order to break-even, eg 145 units per week. You should also note that no business would be prepared to accept negative contributions, except in very unusual circumstances. Faced with the prospect the business would shut down, limiting the losses to the amount of the fixed costs.

One of the advantages of knowing the break-even point for some activity is that it enables us to make some judgement about how far, below the planned level of output, actual output can fall before the activity fails to break even. It may occur to you that this is quite similar to sensitivity analysis which we met in section 4, in which case you are right. Comparing the break-even point with the planned level of output is another example of sensitivity analysis. In fact, this is probably the major benefit of knowing the break-even point, since no business will wish to operate at break-even point, in normal circumstances.

The section goes on to highlight the fact that the basic break-even chart and break-even analysis can be difficult under some circumstances. These are:

● Where some of the relationships are not linear. The basic approach which we have taken so far assumes that fixed costs remain fixed, that both the variable cost per unit and the sales price per unit are the same, irrespective of how many are produced and sold.

● Where the business produces more than one product or service. This is particularly problematical where more than activity uses the same production facilities. The problem really stems from the difficulty of separating the fixed costs of one activity from those of another activity. Unfortunately, it is almost always a matter of judgement, rather than of fact, as to how much of a cost like rent relates to each type of activity.

● The difficulty of separating out fixed and variable costs. In theory this is easy to do. In practice this is often rather less true.

Though these limitations must be taken fully into account when using break-even analysis, it would be wrong to write-off break-even because it is less than perfect. It can still be a useful approach provided that users are aware of the problems.

The section seeks to identify and reconcile the differences between the accountants' and the economists' approach to break even. Basically the difference lies in the fact that accountants tend to assume linear cost and revenue lines in the break-even chart. Economists, quite reasonably, make the point that, for example, as the level of output increases the price which can be demanded for each unit of output will probably fall. Similarly the cost function is not linear because, as output increases, economies of scale will come into play until their limit is reached. Though the economists are probably more correct theoretically, it should be borne in mind that, to the accountant, the main use of break even is for decision making and planning purposes. As soon as we start to deal with the future we are faced with many uncertainties. Thus it is probably more practical to deal with things on a simple basis and accept that this is as close as we are likely to get to the real outcome.

As we have already seen, one of the ingredients of break-even analysis is *contribution*. In the unit we consider how this factor can be applied in various ways.

We begin by considering the profit–volume chart. This chart is so arranged that the profit (or loss), at various levels of output, can be read directly from the chart, as can the break-even point. You should be very clear that the profit–volume chart and the break-even chart are basically the same. Thus, they rely on the same assumptions and principles. They are also limited in their usefulness by the same factors.

The section explains that fixed costs can sometimes be ignored when making decisions, thus taking account only of variable costs and revenues. This is because in the short-term, fixed costs cannot usually be abandoned so they cannot be affected by the decision. Similarly where the decision will not have far reaching effects, eg a small increase or decrease in activity, fixed costs may not be affected.

You should recall from Unit 2 that where a particular cost will not be affected by the outcome of a particular decision, it is irrelevant. Thus where fixed costs cannot be altered by the outcome of particular decisions they are all irrelevant. Only contribution is relevant.

We shall take a look at four areas where we can ignore the fixed costs in our decision making. The first of these concerns the problem of *spare capacity*. Sometimes, a business can use spare capacity to increase profit even though additional output can be sold at very low prices. For example, if an aeroplane is about to take off with a spare seat, the airline can sell this seat for a very small price indeed, yet the airline will, nevertheless, be more profitable as a result. This is because the variable cost of taking an additional passenger is tiny. Virtually all the costs of running a particular flight are fixed relative to the number of passengers travelling on it. However, care must be taken when adopting this 'marginal' approach to pricing. As is explained in this unit, even though in the short term a particular price may yield positive contributions, charging the marginal price may have adverse effects.

The idea of contribution can also be used in making the most of *scarce resources*. It will be explained that where there is a shortage a some factor of production, and where fixed costs will be unaffected by the decision, the use of the scarce resource which maximises the contribution for each unit of the scarce resource will be the most effective use of the scarce factor. However, we must be careful not to encourage a passive approach to coping with the shortage, rather than seeking ways to overcome the problem.

Another problem facing management is whether to *buy-in some goods or service, or to produce it internally*. The decision should be made on the basis of whether the relevant cost of buying is greater or less than that of producing it internally. Clearly the relevant cost of buying is the price which must be paid to the supplier. In the short-term, where the business has spare capacity, the relevant cost of producing is only the variable cost, because the fixed costs will not be affected. Where there is not spare capacity, so making internally is only possible by displacing some other activity, there is also an opportunity cost of the contributions lost from the displaced activity. Thus the relevant cost is the variable cost of making plus the opportunity cost just referred to.

A further area for contribution analysis is *where a business, or a particular activity within a business, may be unprofitable.* It may seem logical to close down the business or the activity, at least in the short term. However, where the business or activity yields a positive contribution, unless the fixed costs can be abandoned, it will be more profitable to continue than to close down. As with all areas of contribution analysis, we must be careful not to lose sight of the longer term position. The fact that it may be worth keeping a division running in the short-term, because it is not possible to abandon the fixed costs in the short-term, should not be used as a justification for keeping on an activity which is unprofitable in the long-term.

Now that you have a broad idea of what this section is about, you can make start on the detail.

The behaviour of costs

IN ORDER TO UNDERSTAND the relationship between costs volume and profit it is useful to understand how different costs behave in response to changes in output. It is often useful to classify costs as being either *variable* or *fixed* in nature. A variable cost can be described as one which varies directly and proportionately with output.

Activity 1

Can you think of any costs relating to a business which could be described as variable?

The following business costs may be described as variable:

● Raw materials used in a manufacturing business, for example, if material to make 1 vase is £3, then to make 2 vases the material cost will be £6 and to make 100 vases gives rise to a material cost of £300 etc

● The power used to operate machinery. The more the machinery is used the more power is required

● Wages of workers will be a variable cost where payment is directly related to output e.g where workers are paid only according to what they produce during a period.

● Petrol used by the lorries of a haulage business. The greater the distance travelled, the greater the consumption of petrol.

If we were to graph variable costs against the level of output we would see that variable costs rise as output rises giving the following linear relationship (see figure 1 below):

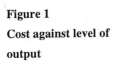

Figure 1

Cost against level of

output

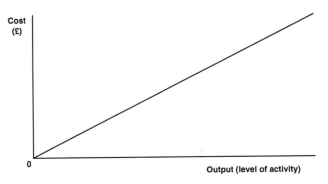

The relationship between costs and output can be expressed in the simple equation:

$$y = bx$$

Where:

y = the total expected cost
b = the cost per unit (which is constant)
x = level of output

Thus, given a variable cost of £10 per unit and an output level of 1,000 units, the total expected variable cost will be £10 × 1,000 = £10,000.

Activity 2

What is the total variable cost where the cost per unit is £5 and the expected level of output is 200 units?

Using the formula above the answer is:

$$y = £5 \times 200$$
$$= \underline{£1,000}$$

Fixed costs are those costs which remain constant whatever the level of output. Thus, they are not influenced by the particular level of activity of the business.

Activity 3

Can you think of any costs relating to a business which can be described as fixed?

The following, are examples of costs which are usually fixed in nature:

- rent

- rates

- managers' salaries

- insurance

In each of the above examples , the cost incurred will remain the same irrespective of the level of output.

If we were to graph fixed costs against the level of output we would obtain the following linear relationship (see figure 2):

Figure 2

Cost against level of output

This function can be expressed as follows:

$$y = a$$

Where

y = total expected cost
a = constant figure

The total costs for an activity will comprise the variable and the fixed costs. If we were to combine both types of cost we would obtain the following graph (see figure 3 overleaf):

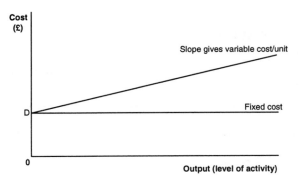

Figure 3

Cost against level of output

We can see that the total costs will touch the vertical line at point D which represents the fixed cost element of the business. Thus, at a zero level of output the total costs will be equal to the fixed costs of the business. The slope of the graph portrays the changes in total costs arising from changes in output.

The total costs of a business can be represented by the following equation:

$$y = a + bx$$

This equation, of course, simply combines the two earlier equations. Thus, a business with fixed costs of £2,000 for a particular period and variable costs of £8 per unit would, at an output of 1,000 units, have a total cost of:

$$y = £2,000 + (£8 \times 1,000)$$
$$= £\underline{10,000}$$

Semi-variable costs

AT THIS POINT YOU may feel that there are certain costs which cannot be easily classified as either fixed or variable. For example, maintenance costs may have a fixed element but may also increase with the level of activity. Telephone costs may also have these characteristics. The salaries of managers were described earlier as a fixed cost, however, where there is a system of performance related pay in operation the salaries would then have both a fixed element and a variable element. These types of cost are referred to as either *semi-variable* or *semi-fixed* costs.

Semi-variable costs, however, may be broken down into their fixed and variable elements. To discover how much of a particular cost is fixed and how much is variable various techniques are available. One technique is to compare the amount of the cost at a point when output is low with the cost incurred when output is high.

Example 1

Details of production of product x and related heating and lighting costs are shown below for two months. The first month provides data when output is low and the second month provides data when output is high:

	Low month	High month
Units produced	500	550
Heat and light	£2,750	£2,950

The difference between the heat and light figures between the two months must be due to the variable cost element relating to the additional 50 units of output. Thus:

		£
Heat and light	- month 2	2,950
	- month 1	2,750
Variable cost for 50 units		200
Variable cost per unit 200/50		= £4

Fixed element of month 1 total cost $= £2,750 - (500 \times £4)$

$$= £2750 - 2000$$

$$= £750$$

This technique is fairly simple to employ, however, it only uses two extreme observations relating to the particular cost (ie when output is low and when output is high). A more accurate measure may be produced if the actual heat and light costs are identified for a number of monthly periods for which the level of output is known. Then, either graphically or using regression analysis (least squares), we can separate out the fixed and variable elements.

Cost–volume–profit (CVP) analysis

IN THE PRECEDING SECTION we have examined the relationship between costs and volume (output). In this section we will consider the relationship between costs, volume and profit. To understand the relationship between these three variables it is useful to prepare a cost–volume–profit graph – or break-even chart as it is frequently called. This graph, or chart, is simply an extension of the total cost graph set out in figure 3 above. The cost–volume–profit graph simply takes the total cost graph and impose on it an additional line to represent the sales revenue at the various levels of activity. This line will start at 0 and rise steadily with the level of activity (see figure 4).

Figure 4

Break-even chart

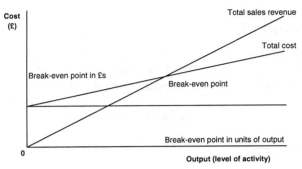

Break-even chart

The graph is known as a break-even chart because it identifies the break-even point for the activity. Where the total cost and total revenue lines intersect the activity will break even, ie make neither a profit nor a loss. The break-even point (BEP) can be read, either in terms of costs (revenues) or physical volume. Note that the total cost of the activity at various levels can be read from the graph as the vertical distance between the horizontal axis and the total cost line. Also the profit (loss) at any level of activity is the vertical distance between the total cost and total revenue lines. (A loss occurs at levels of activity below the BEP and a profit occurs above the BEP.)

This graphical representation is of particular value to users who have little understanding of accounting. It is fairly easy to understand and clearly illustrates the effect of output on the profitability of the business.

Activity 4

Dickens Ltd is involved in the manufacture of electronic games. The fixed costs of the operation are £1,000 per month, the selling price of each game is £30 and the variable cost per unit is £10.

Required:

Draw a break-even chart for the company and use it to deduce the break-even point (per month). Prepare the chart using the blank graph below.

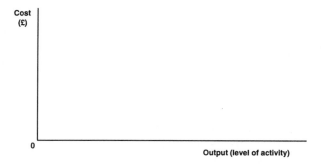

The chart you produce in answer to this activity should look like the one in figure 4 above. The break-even point should be 50 units per month (or £1,500 per month in sales revenue). You can check the accuracy of your chart by using the BEP equation shown above.

The effect of different cost structures

BY PREPARING A BREAK-EVEN chart, we can see clearly the effect of different cost structures on profitability. In figure 5 below, two different cost structures are portrayed. In the first example, the fixed costs are low and the variable costs are high relative to total costs. This type of cost structure can occur where a business employs a large number of manual workers and has a fairly low investment in fixed assets (and therefore low depreciation charges). You can see that the total cost line rises quite steeply as output rises. In the second example the fixed costs are high and the variable costs are low relative to total costs. This type of cost structure can occur where a business is capital intensive (ie it relies heavily on the use of capital equipment in order to produce goods or services). You can see that the total cost line does not rise as steeply compared to the first example.

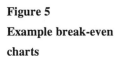

Figure 5

Example break-even

charts

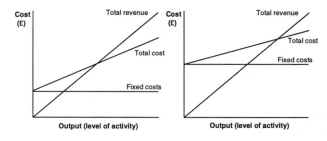

The angle at which the total cost line and total revenue line intersects on the break-even chart is referred to as the 'angle of incidence'. Where fixed costs are high in relation to total costs the angle of incidence can be large. The significance of this angle is that it provides an indication of the change in levels of profit (loss) which will occur given a change in output. Where the angle of incidence is large, a given change in output can lead to a much greater change in profit (loss) than where the angle is small. Thus, an understanding of the structure of the costs of the business can be very useful to managers when assessing the likely impact on profit of a given change in output.

The sensitivity of changes in profit to changes in output can be an important factor in assessing the degree of risk which relates to the business. A high level of fixed costs increases the risk associated with the business as these costs have to be incurred irrespective of the level of output. However, the benefit of taking on a high proportion of fixed costs in relation to total costs is that, beyond the break-even point, the profits can be high.

Calculating the break-even point

DEDUCING THE BREAK-EVEN POINT graphically is a useful exercise in helping you to appreciate the relationship between cost, volume and profit. However, it can be a time consuming, and potentially inaccurate approach. It is, in fact, fairly easy to calculate the break-even point by using the simple formula mentioned above.

To demonstrate the logic of this approach we can start by stating that:

Total sales revenue   = Sales revenue per unit (r) × number
of units sold (x)

The break-even point can be defined as the point at which:

Total revenue (rx)   = Total cost (y)

We saw earlier that:

Total cost (y)   = Fixed costs (a) + Variable costs (bx)

Similarly, we can state that, *at the break-even point*:

Total revenue (rx)   = Fixed costs (a) + Variable costs (bx)

By applying this formula to the data in Activity 4 (ie the fixed costs are £1,000, selling price per unit £30 and variable costs per unit £10) we can see that at the break-even point :

30x   = 1,000 + 10x

By rearranging we have:

$$30x - 10x \quad = 1,000$$

Thus:

$$20x \qquad = 1,000$$
$$x \qquad = \underline{50 \ (\text{units})}$$

To express the break-even point in terms of sales revenue we simply multiply the number of units by the sales revenue per unit (i.e 50 × £30 = £1,500).

The above formula can be extended to determine other points on the break-even chart. We may wish to know, for example, how many units need to be sold in order to make a particular profit. To deduce this we simply use the formula:

Sales revenue (rx) = Fixed costs (a) + Variable costs (bx) + Target profit

---

Activity 5

Using the data in the previous activity (ie fixed costs £1,000 selling price per unit £30 and variable costs per unit £10), determine how many units need to be sold in order to make a target profit of £900.

The answer to this activity is:

$$30x \qquad = 1,000 + 10x + 900$$
$$30x - 10x \quad = 1,900$$
$$x \qquad = \underline{95 \ (\text{units})}$$

Margin of safety

THE MARGIN OF SAFETY represents the difference between the planned level of output and the break-even point. This measure can be used to help assess the level of risk associated with a particular activity. An activity which has a planned output of 1,000 units per month and a break-even point of 700 units a month will have a margin of safety of 300 units . This may be regarded as less risky than one where the planned volume is 1,000 units per month and the break-even point is 900 units – a margin of safety of 100 units. The margin of safety can be expressed in terms of sales revenue as well as physical output.

Activity 6

Cervantes Ltd offer short, intensive tuition in the Spanish language for people going on holiday to Spain. Market research reveals that, at a price to the student of £80 for each course, the annual demand would be 2,500 students while at £100, the annual demand would drop to 1,500 students.

At the higher demand there would be justification for introducing more language laboratory facilities giving rise to savings in staff costs. The effect of this would be that, at the higher demand, the total fixed costs would be £35,000 pa and variable costs £50 per student, while at the lower demand fixed costs would be £20,000 pa and variable costs £60 per student.

Required:

What advice would you give Cervantes Ltd on which of these two prices to charge and why?

Your answer to this activity should involve calculation of the annual profit, break-even point and margin of safety for each option:

	High Volume £	Low Volume £
Sales	200,000	150,000
Variable costs	(125,000)	(90,000)
Fixed costs	(35,000)	(20,000
Annual profit	40,000	40,000
Number of students	2,500	1,500
Break-even point		
$(80x = 35,000 + 50x)$	1,167	
$(100x = 20,000 + 60x)$		500
Margin of safety	1,333	1,000
Margin of safety as % of planned volume	53.3%	66.7%

We can see that there is nothing to chose between the two schemes on the basis of profit but they have different margins of safety. There are no clear rules on how to interpret the margin of safety figures, but assessing them in relation to planned volume of output seems sensible, in which case the low volume scheme looks slightly safer.

Where a break-even chart is prepared, the margin of safety can be seen by measuring the distance between the break-even point and the planned level of output.

Limitations of the break-even chart

THE BREAK-EVEN CHART IS based on certain simplifying assumptions which may not hold in the real world. The major assumptions are discussed below.

LINEARITY

A major assumption concerns the linearity of costs and sales revenue. It was mentioned above that fixed costs remain the same irrespective of the level of output. A moments reflection will tell us that such costs are rare indeed. For example, rent (which was mentioned as an example of a fixed cost) may not fall within the strict definition of a fixed cost. Whilst the rent, say, of a factory may remain fixed there will be a limit to the level of production which can take place within it. If that level is exceeded, additional factory space will need to be rented giving a 'step' in the graph (see figure 6).

Figure 6

'Stepped' activity break-even chart

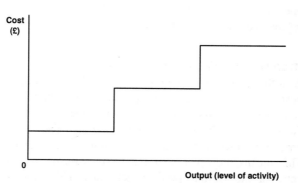

Graph of rent cost (with 'steps')/level of activity

Most fixed costs will have 'steps' in this way, though typically the range of output between steps will be large, perhaps very large.

In practice, it may be that variable costs do not rise in a perfectly linear fashion as portrayed by the break-even chart. For example, when stocks are being purchased in increasing quantities there may be discounts given for bulk purchases. This may have the effect of producing a curvilinear line as shown in figure 7 overleaf:

Figure 7

Curvi-linear break-even

chart

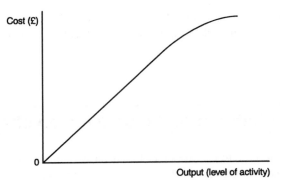

The sales revenue line may also be curvilinear. Beyond a certain point it may be necessary to offer discounts or to reduce the selling price in order to increase sales further.

Although the simplifying assumptions of linearity will result in an inaccurate representation of costs and profit over the whole range of possible output, it may be that, within the normal range of output for the business, the assumptions of linearity will hold. Thus, whilst at the extremes of output it would be unwise to assume linearity of costs and revenue, for the 'relevant range' of the business costs and revenue behaviour may follow a linear pattern.

MULTI-PRODUCT BUSINESSES

A further problem with the break-even chart is that it is difficult to employ where a business has more than one type of product/activity in its range. It is unrealistic to combine the results of different products/activities unless the 'mix' of sales remains the same over the whole range of output. The alternative approach for a multi-product business is to draw up a separate break-even chart for each product/activity. This means, however, that the fixed costs of the business must be apportioned between the various products/activities. This may prove a difficult task where equipment and facilities are being shared.

SEPARATION OF FIXED AND VARIABLE COSTS

In practice, it may be extremely difficult to separate out the fixed and variable elements of semi-variable costs. Although statistical techniques such as regression analysis may be used they may not produce satisfactory results. However, for decision making purposes, an accurate separation of the two elements may be important.

The economists' break-even chart

THE ASSUMPTIONS OF LINEARITY etc employed by accountants for planning purposes are not normally employed by economists when seeking to explain the behaviour of businesses. It is interesting, therefore, to compare the accountants view of the relationship between cost, volume and profit with that of the economist. In the case of perfect markets, the economist will portray the total revenue line as being linear and so will be in agreement with the accountants view. However, in the case of imperfect markets, the revenue line is portrayed by the economist as being curvilinear. In order to increase sales it will be necessary for a business to reduce the selling price per unit of the goods sold. Thus, the total revenue of the business will not increase in direct proportion to output. Indeed, beyond a certain point, the total revenue of the business will begin to decrease with increases in output because of the effect of reductions in the selling price per unit.

The economist will also normally portray the total cost line as being curvilinear. The total costs will rise quite steeply at first. This is largely due to the fact that the average variable cost per unit will be relatively high at low levels of output. However, the average variable cost per unit will decrease as output begins to rise due to economies of scale such as discounts on bulk purchases, more productive use of the workforce, etc. This decline in the average variable cost per unit will result in a levelling out of the total cost line. However, beyond a certain level of output, the average variable costs will begin to rise once more causing the total cost line to rise more steeply again. This increase in the average variable cost line will arise because the efficient range of operating capacity is being exceeded. The business may experience operating inefficiencies at higher levels of output because to plant breakdowns, difficulties in production scheduling etc.

The economists view of the relationship between cost volume and profit is shown in figure 8. Note that the total revenue and total cost lines intersect at two points, ie there are two break-even points.

Figure 8

Break-even chart with two break-even points

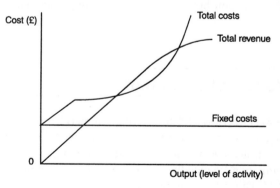

CVP analysis and the contribution margin

WHEN USING CVP ANALYSIS for decision making purposes, it is often useful to employ the concept of the 'contribution margin'. The contribution margin is simply the difference between the sales revenue and the variable costs. The contribution margin can be measured for both an individual item or the total output of the business. In effect, it represents the surplus on the sale(s) before taking account of any fixed costs. The surplus will be used to cover fixed costs in the first instance and after these have been covered will represent profit.

This surplus of sales value over variable costs can be used to provide another way of calculating the break-even point of a business. The number of sales required to cover the fixed costs will be determined by the contribution margin of each sale. Hence:

Break-even point   = $\dfrac{\text{Total fixed costs}}{\text{Contribution per unit}}$

Using the information in the activity relating to Dickens Ltd we can calculate the break-even point of the company as follows:

$$= \quad \frac{1,000}{30 - 10}$$

$$= \quad \underline{50 \text{ units}}$$

The break-even point is, of course, the same as calculated before. This is because the equation used is simply a rearrangement of the equation used earlier. The concept of contribution, however, is an important one as we shall see below.

Profit–volume charts

ONE APPLICATION OF THE contribution margin concept is in the preparation of profit –volume charts. Sometimes, we may wish to simply portray the relationship between just two variables – profit and volume. This may be of particular value in helping non-financially oriented employees appreciate the impact of output on profits. This relationship can be shown by means of a profit/volume (P/V) chart. To prepare this chart we simply plot the contribution margin directly against volume to produce a graph which shows profit (loss) at any level of activity. An example of a profit/volume chart is shown in figure 9:

Figure 9

Profit–volume chart

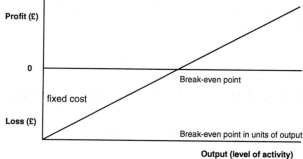

Profit / volume (PV) chart

Note that at zero level of activity there will be a loss equal to the fixed costs. As the volume increases, provided there are positive contributions (ie sales revenue per unit > variable cost per unit), the fixed costs will be eaten into until at the break-even point there are sufficient total contributions to equal fixed costs. Beyond this point profit will occur.

You should be clear that the P/V chart provides no further information than the break-even chart, nor is it based on different assumptions. It simply represents a slightly different version of the same approach.

Activity 7

Prepare a profit/volume chart for Dickens Ltd using the information contained in Activity 4 on page 154. Prepare this chart using the graph set out below.

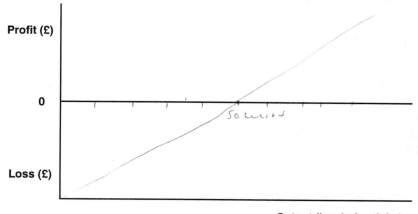

Profit / volume (PV) chart

The profit–volume chart should look like the one shown in figure 9 above. The break-even point should again be 50 units.

Tactical decisions and the contribution margin

TACTICAL DECISIONS INVOLVE THE following:

- short periods of time: and/or

- relatively minor changes from existing activity.

This contrasts with the longer-term, strategic type of decision which we considered in earlier units and for which NPV seems to be the most logical approach.

We have already seen that maximising the value of a business implies maximisation of positive net cash flows. If we are dealing with decisions where the fixed costs will not alter with the decision we can further reduce the objective to maximising positive contributions (sales revenue – variable costs). We shall now consider the contribution margin approach to tactical decision making in three separate areas.

Acceptance/rejection of short-term contracts

SOMETIMES A BUSINESS WILL be offered a short-term contract which would not normally be acceptable. However, if the business has spare capacity, the decision rule will be to accept such contracts which yield a positive contribution.

Example 2

Hardy Ltd has spare production facilities and has been offered a contract to supply 100 brass brackets at a price of £10 each. The following data are available:

Existing monthly production	400 brackets
Normal sales price per unit	£20
Variable cost per unit	£8
Fixed costs per month	£4,000

The cost per unit (based on 400 units of output) is £4,000 + (400 × £8) divided by 400 = £18. It may appear therefore, that the price offered of £10 per unit is too low. However, if we look at the existing level of profitability and compare this with the profitability if the contract is accepted we find the following:

		Existing production level (400 units) £	New production level (500 units) £
Sales revenue	400 @ £20	8,000	8,000
	100 @ £10		1,000
Variable costs	400 @ £8	(3,200)	
	500 @ £8		(4,000)
Fixed costs		(4,000)	(4,000)
Profit for month		£800	£1,000

Thus, the business is £200 better off by accepting the contract since each additional bracket will give rise to a £2 (ie £10 - 8) contribution and there are 100 of them. Taking a 'full costing' approach (identifying a £18 per bracket cost) is misleading in this context, because the fixed costs are irrelevant since they do not vary with the decision.

Activity 8

Orwell Ltd is heading for a loss this month as it only has orders for its sole product of 1,000 for a price of £2 per unit. The variable cost totals £1.20 per unit and the fixed costs for the month will be £1,000. The business has been offered a new order which must be fulfilled during the month for 200 units at a price of £1 each. There is sufficient spare capacity to meet the extra production without increasing fixed costs.

Should the order be accepted?

In this case the order should not be accepted as the variable cost per unit exceeds the offer price per unit. The variable cost per unit is £1.20 whereas the offer price is £1. As a result, the business will make an even bigger loss by accepting this order. The fact that the business is already heading for a loss is irrelevant, as is the amount of the monthly overheads.

Potential problems of the marginal cost approach to decision making

THERE IS A NUMBER of potential problems associated with the adoption of this 'marginal' approach to short-term decision making. These include:

● Rather than use spare capacity for marginally priced output, it may be more advantageous (in NPV terms) to relinquish spare capacity. This might involve selling surplus machinery, subletting factory space, etc.

● Selling at different prices in the same market might cause a loss of customer goodwill. Customers paying the full price might feel that they are being adversely discriminated against by a supplier if they discover that other customers are being supplied at cheaper prices. For this reason, the supplier may only be prepared to contemplate marginal pricing of output to be supplied to customers overseas. This is sometimes critically referred to as 'dumping'.

● Using spare capacity for marginally priced output may prevent it being used for normal priced output. Thus, for example, airline companies should try that for customers who are prepared to pay normal prices before any spare capacity is sold to 'bucket shops' at heavily discounted prices. At what point in time the supplier decides that the output cannot be sold at normal prices and begins to accept marginally price contracts is obviously a matter of judgement.

● The fact that output yielding a positive contribution will make the supplier better off, all other things being equal, should not encourage loss of sight of the fact that, for the business to prosper, its total sales revenue must cover its total costs (i.e variable costs plus fixed costs).

Activity 9

A business makes a single product. Production and sales are running at 1,000 units a month. The selling price per unit is £11 and the 'full' cost is £9. The monthly fixed costs are £4,000. There is considerable spare capacity.

Required:

(a) Should the business accept a special order this month for 200 units at £7.50 per unit; and

(b) What would be the effect on profit for this month of accepting the special order?

The full cost per unit is made up of £4 per unit (ie £4,000/1,000) for fixed costs and therefore £5 per unit for variable costs (making £9 per unit in total). Since the offer price of £7.50 per unit exceeds the variable cost per unit, the special order should be accepted, all other things being equal.

Accepting the order will increase profit as shown below:

	Existing production level		Acceptance of new contract	
	£	£	£	£
Sales (£11 × 1,000)		11,000		
(£11 × 1,000 + £7.50 × 200)				12,500
Less Variable costs	5,000		6,000	
Fixed costs	4,000	9,000	4,000	10,000
Profit		2,000		2,500

Allocation of scarce resources and production scheduling

THERE MAY BE SITUATIONS in which a business has a limited amount of a particular resource such as labour, materials etc. Where this occurs the scarce resource must be deployed in the most profitable way possible. The decision rule is to undertake the activity which maximises the contribution per unit of the scarce resource.

Example 3

A business make two products, Apex and Vortex, each of which requires the use of labour, material X (both of which are in plentiful supply) and material Y (which is in short supply). Summarised data relating to the two products are as follows:

		Per unit		
		Apex		Vortex
		£		£
Selling price		20		10
Variable costs				
Labour		(8)		(3)
Material X	(1.5 kg)	(3)	(1 kg)	(2)
Material Y	(2 kg)	(6)	(1 kg)	(3)
Contribution		3		2

Which product should the business make and sell, assuming that it is possible to sell a limitless amount of either product and fixed costs are unaffected by the decision?

At first sight we might be inclined to think that Apex is to be preferred since it yields the higher contribution per unit. However, this might be an incorrect judgement if any of the inputs are in short supply. In these circumstances we need to rank the products by dividing the contribution per unit by the amount of the scarce resource (ie material Y) which is required by each one. The preferred option will be the one which maximises the contribution per unit of resource. Thus,

Apex	£3/2 kg	= £1.50/kg
Vortex	£2/1 kg	= £2.00/kg

We can see that Vortex maximises the contribution per unit of the scarce resource and should therefore be selected. Only if the demand for this product is exhausted before the supply of material Y is exhausted should Apex be made.

If you doubt whether the above approach is logical, imagine some maximum amount of material Y which is available to the business and ask yourself how many of Apex and how many of Vortex can be produced with that amount of material and what the total contribution will be under each alternative.

Activity 10

Simat Engineering Ltd makes three products. Data relating to each product are as follows:

	Alpha £	Beta £	Gamma £
Selling price per unit	24	32	30
Variable costs per unit:			
Materials	(4)	(7)	(9)
Labour: Turning dept	(6)	(9)	(3)
Assembly dept	(7)	(7)	(14)

The labour rates for the turning and assembly departments are £3 and £0.50 per hour respectively.

The sales forecast for the forthcoming year indicates that demand for all three products is likely to be greater than the production capacity, which is limited by the capacity of the turning department.

Required:

Which product should the business regard as the most profitable, assuming that fixed costs will not be affected by the decision?

Your answer to this activity should be along the lines shown below:

	Alpha £	Beta £	Gamma £
Selling price per unit	24	32	30
Total variable costs per unit	17	23	26
Contribution per unit	7	9	4

The number of labour hours required by each product in the turning dept is:

labour cost per product (turning)	£6	£9	£3
Rate per hour (turning)	£3	£3	£3
Number of hours per product	2	3	1
Contribution per hour in turning	£7/2 £3.50	£9/3 £3.00	£4/1 £4.00
Ranking	2	3	1

In order to maximise the use of production capacity, the business should produce only Gamma. This product provides the highest contribution per hour from the turning department. If some of the production capacity of this department was used to produce other products the overall profit of the business would be reduced.

Activity 11

Can you think of any reason why the business may decide to make Alpha or Beta products despite the calculations shown above?

The business may feel that its long term viability and profitability requires a range of products being available to its customers. The business may be concerned that it will lose the goodwill of its customers if it does not attempt to meet the demand for Alpha and Beta products as well as Gamma.

Where there is more than one scarce resource to deal with the problem may be solved using the mathematical technique of linear programming. This technique is beyond the scope of this accounting unit but should be dealt with in your study of quantitative methods.

Weaknesses of the marginal approach to the allocation of scarce resources

WE SAW IN THE answer to Activity 11 that decisions concerning the allocation of scarce resources may require a broader perspective to be adopted. It may not be enough simply to provide calculations showing the highest contribution per unit of scarce resource (even though this will be a valuable input to the allocation decision). The business must also consider the likely effect of the decision on its future viability.

Over the longer term it might be in the best interests of the business (ie it will result in a higher NPV) if an attempt is made to overcome the scarcity problem rather than simply accepting it. For example, it may be possible to change the design of the product so as to reduce the amount of the scarce resource required. Alternatively, it may be possible to find a new source of supply.

Make or buy decisions

A BUSINESS MAY FIND that, for a short period, one of the following situations may arise:

● It has *spare capacity* which enables it to consider undertaking work which it normally has done elsewhere;

● It has a *shortage of capacity* which causes it to consider subcontracting work which it normally undertakes itself.

Where such situations arise, the decision rule is to take the option (other things being equal) which will maximise contributions. It should be borne in mind that making an item internally may use capacity which could be used for another activity. Hence, there may be an opportunity cost incurred. Similarly, buying-in an item may release capacity for another purpose.

Let us consider an example of a make or buy problem.

Example 4

A toy takes 20 hours to make on a particular machine. The toy has a selling price of £100 each and variable costs of £60. A component used in the manufacture of another item – trinkets – can be made on the same machine in three hours for a variable cost of £5. The component could be purchased for £10 each. Assuming a shortage of capacity on the machine, should the business make or buy the component?

The cost of *buying* the component is	£10
	£
The cost of *making* the component is:	
Variable costs	5
Opportunity costs:	
Lost contributions from toy output:	
$\dfrac{(£100 - £60) \times 3 \text{ hours}}{20 \text{ hours}}$	6
	£11

Thus we can see there is a net advantage in buying rather than making the component of £1 (ie £10 - £11). Contributions will be maximised if the component is bought-in.

Weaknesses in the marginal approach to make or buy decisions

IN PRACTICE, A MAKE or buy decision must consider other relevant factors. For example, there may be problems associated with relying on sub-contractors. The quality of the component being supplied may have to be checked thereby incurring additional cost for the business. Supplies of the component may sometimes be delayed or interrupted because of production problems experienced by the suppliers. Reliance on a particular supplier may make the business vulnerable to increases in the price of the component supplied etc.

In addition, capacity problems may be resolved over the longer term. It may be possible over the longer term to either reduce spare capacity (and the associated fixed costs) or increase capacity on a permanent basis.

Now try the self-assessment question overleaf. This is intended to give you the opportunity to see whether you have grasped the material so far. You should probably be able to complete this in half an hour. Don't worry if it takes you longer. The main point is that, once you have completed it, you are clear on all of the points which it involves. It is not really helpful to look at the answer to this until you have completed your answer.

Self-assessment question

The accountant of Helat Ltd has estimated that the full unit cost of making a component used in its main activity is as follows:

	£
Direct materials	12
Direct labour (3 hours)	9
Variable overheads	2
Fixed overheads	15
	38

(The direct costs are both variable)

The main activity is assembling a standard model of industrial mixerator. These are sold for £200 each and have unit variable costs of £80 for direct materials, £36 (ie 12 hours) for direct labour and £12 for variable overheads. The fixed overheads are £60 per unit.

Continued over . . .

The component could be bought in for £30 each.

Required:

Should the component be bought in assuming:

(a) there is spare capacity; and
(b) there is no spare capacity, ie the component can only be made internally by reducing the output of mixerators?

(The answer to this self-assessment question can be found at the end of the unit.)

Reading

You should now read Reader Article 5.1 'Make or buy decisions: a simpler approach' by Gordon Ellis.

This article points out that the conventional approach to make or buy decisions may produce sub-optimal results where it is necessary to make good shortfalls in production by buying in. It is argued that the conventional approach stresses the production aspects of the problem and takes insufficient account of the buying aspects. The author advocates an advantage-in-making approach which involves a series of steps. This approach requires calculation of the advantage gained in making a product rather than buying-in. The product with the greatest advantage is made first, then the product with the next best advantage in making is made and so on until internal production capacity is exhausted. When this occurs the product with the least advantage in making should be purchased from an outside supplier first.

Points to consider:

How does this approach differ from the conventional approach outlined earlier? How would opportunity costs be dealt with using this approach? How might the conventional approach lead to sub-optimal results?

Close down/continuation decisions

THE CONCEPT OF THE contribution margin can be useful when deciding whether or not to continue with a particular operating activity. In order to illustrate the usefulness of the contribution margin in this situation let us consider the following activity:

Example 5

House of Helen (Fashions) Ltd operates two large retail outlets in the south west of England. The performance of each outlet for the forthcoming year is estimated as follows:

	Bristol		Plymouth	
	£000	£000	£000	£000
Sales		682		896
Less cost of sales		481		632
		201		364
Operating expenses	182		311	
Share of warehouse fixed expenses	15		15	
Share of office fixed expenses	18	215	18	344
Net profit		(14)		20

The company is considering closing down the Bristol outlet because of its poor performance. By so doing, the company will no longer incur the operating expenses of this outlet. However, the company will still incur the fixed expenses of both the warehouse and the office.

Required:

Should the company close down the Bristol outlet?

At present, the company as a whole is making a small profit of £6,000 (ie £20,000 – £14,000). However, the effect of closing down Bristol outlet will be to turn this small profit into a loss. This is because the company must still bear the fixed warehouse and office expenses. Following closure of Bristol, these expenses will be borne entirely by the Plymouth outlet. Thus, the revised forecast profit and loss account for the company following closure will be as follows.

Revised profit and loss account	£000	£000
Sales		896
Less cost of sales		632
Gross profit		364
Operating expenses	311	
Warehouse fixed expenses	30	
Share of office fixed expenses	36	377
Net profit/(loss)		(13)

At present, Bristol outlet is making a contribution towards the fixed costs of the warehouse and the office. As mentioned earlier, these common costs are unavoidable and will have to be borne by the Plymouth outlet in the event of closure. The amount of the contribution made by each outlet can be seen by presenting the forecast profit and loss accounts relating to each outlet in a slightly different way:

Forecast profit and loss account	Bristol		Plymouth	
	£000	£000	£000	£000
Sales		682		896
Less cost of sales		481		632
		201		364
Operating expenses		182		311
Contribution to common fixed costs		19		53
Share of warehouse fixed expenses	15		15	
Share of office fixed expenses	18	33	18	33
Net profit		(14)		20

We can now see that the effect of closing down the Bristol outlet will be to lose a contribution to common fixed costs of £19,000 in the forthcoming year.

Other considerations in the close down/ continuation decision

WHEN MAKING DECISIONS CONCERNING closure it is important to consider the long run profitability of each activity. The fact that a particular activity or business segment makes a loss in one period may not be sufficient justification for closure. The business must also consider the effect of closure on sales generated by other activities. It may be wrong to treat a particular activity as being quite separate from other activities. There may be some interdependency of sales between the various business activities. The business must also consider whether the facilities considered for closure might be put to some more profitable use.

Activity 12

A medium sized resort hotel operates its financial year from May 19x8 to April 19x9. For the purposes of managing the seasonal features of this industry it is customary to consider May to October inclusive as summer season and November to April inclusive as winter season.

The budget for 19x8-x9 is as follows:

	Summer		Winter		Total	
	£000	£000	£000	£000	£000	£000
Sales		300		100		400
Variable costs	100		40		140	
Fixed costs	80	180	80	120	160	300
Profit/(loss)		120		(20)		100

From information currently to hand, the business is able to confidently predict that up to and including August 19x8, sales will be £180,000 and variable costs £60,000: the two remaining summer months is expected to produce a total of £60,000 in sales. The whole winter season is showing an expected sales level of £50,000.

Two strategies have been proposed to improve the situation:

(i) close for the winter season and transfer all business to nearby establishments. On average 20% commission would be received for this, based on existing reservations.

(ii) with a little extra work on sales promotion and special offers costing £10,000, sales could rise to £90,000 in total for September and October. The winter season sales would rise to £80,000.

Required:

Evaluate the present position and the two strategies put forward by preparing appropriate profit projections.

Comment on the evaluation and any other matters which should be considered by the hotel management.

The revised profit projection for the year is as follows:

	Summer £000	£000	Winter £000	Total £000
Sales	180	60	50	290
Variable costs*	60	20	20	100
Contribution	120	40	30	190
Fixed costs				160
Profit/(loss)				30

Profit projections for each option are as follows:

Option (i) – Close down in winter

	Summer £000	£000	Winter £000	Total £000
Sales	180	60	10	250
Variable costs*	60	20	–	80
Contribution	120	40	10	170
Fixed costs				160
Profit/(loss)				10

Option (ii) – Continue through the winter

	Summer £000	£000	Winter £000	Total £000
Sales	180	90	80	350
Variable costs*	60	30	32	122
Fixed costs**				170
Profit/(loss)				58

* Variable costs are assumed to vary with sales in the same proportion as the original budget (ie 100/300 = 333% for the summer season and 40/100 = 40% for the winter season)

** Fixed costs include an additional £10,000 in respect of sales promotion.

The revised profit projection for the business reveals that summer sales are 20% below the original forecast and winter sales are 50% below the original forecast. Overall, sales are 27.5% below forecast. The effect of this fall in sales is to reduce the forecast profit for the year from £100,000 to £30,000.

The option of closing for the winter season has little to commend it. Although a contribution to fixed costs will still be made during the winter from the commissions received, the amount of the contribution will be much lower than by not closing. In addition, the hotel management must consider the effect of closure on future sales. For example, some customers may wish to use the hotel throughout the year and may switch hotels if this facility is not available. By closing down it may be necessary to lay off valuable staff who may then find other, more secure, jobs. This will mean employing new staff at the beginning of the summer season.

The option of staying open and at the same time seeking to stimulate sales provides the highest level of profit. The contribution during both the summer and winter seasons will be increased by pursuing this option. The contribution to sales ratio (ie sales – variable costs/sales × 100) during the summer is 70% and during the winter season is 60%. This means that a relatively large proportion of any additional sales generated will contribute towards the profits of the business rather than be consumed by additional expenses.

Reading

You should now read Reader Article 5.2 'Considering the time value of money in breakeven analysis' by Mark Freeman and Kerrie Freeman.

In this article, the authors demonstrate the inconsistency which can occur between investment appraisal based on NPV analysis (which discounts future cash flows) and operating decisions using break-even analysis which is based on operating profits. By means of a simple example they show that operating at the break-even point can actually reduce the value of the business in NPV terms. This is because breaking even in terms of operating profit is not the same as breaking even in NPV terms.

Points for consideration:

Is break-even analysis a useful technique for managers when making operating decisions? Could conventional break-even analysis be improved in any way to overcome the problem outlined?

Cost information for decision making in practice

THE ACCA SURVEY (see Unit 1) sought to discover which different types of cost are used for decision making purposes. The replies from companies indicated that most use a combination of different cost methods. When asked the extent to which different costs were used for decision making, companies overall revealed a preference for using manufacturing rather than total cost (ie including non-manufacturing costs). Variable manufacturing cost was most popular with 52% of companies often or always using this method. Total manufacturing cost is often or always used by 46% of companies. 34% of companies often or always use total variable cost and only 31% of companies often or always use total cost.

The survey also revealed some difference in the popularity of cost methods according to the size of the company. The ranking of different costs often or always used by companies is as follows:

	Smaller Companies	Larger Companies	All Companies
Variable manufacturing cost	2	1	1
Total manufacturing cost	1	3	2
Total variable cost	4	2	3
Total cost	3	4	4

We can see that larger companies show a greater preference for variable costing than smaller companies.

It is interesting that the separation of costs between fixed and variable elements appears to be a fairly rough and ready process in most companies. The majority of companies (58%) classified costs according to subjective judgements made by managers. A further 27% simply equated variable costs with direct costs and fixed costs with indirect costs. Only 2% of companies used statistical regression techniques to separate fixed and variable elements of cost.

Summary

In this unit we have examined the relationship between cost, volume and profit and have seen the relevance of this relationship in areas such as profit planning, determining a suitable cost structure for the business and the measurement of risk. We have also examined the break-even chart which expresses the relationship between cost, volume and profit. The break-even chart provides a useful means of portraying the relationship between costs, volume and profit, particularly for those who are not financially oriented and who may feel less comfortable when this information is provided in numerical form. Although the assumptions underpinning the break-even chart are simplistic, they may well hold for the limited range of output which is relevant to the business for decision making purposes.

We have also considered the concept of the contribution margin and its relevance to tactical decision making. We have seen that maximising positive contributions is important when decisions concerning short time-periods and/or relatively minor changes from existing activities are being considered. However, we have also seen that it is often important for managers to take a broader perspective and, by so doing, take account of other factors before making a final decision.

Additional exercises

Exercise 1

Delta Ltd manufactures three products, *Regular*, *Super* and *De Luxe*, the variable costs of whose manufacture are planned to be as follows:

		Regular	Super	De Luxe
		£	£	£
Materials		21	14	21
Labour:	Machinists (hourly rate £3)	3	9	6
	Assemblers (hourly rate £2)	2	4	3

The company's fixed overheads for the forthcoming year are planned to be £200,000.

The marketing director has estimated that the demand for the products during the forthcoming year will be:

Regular	8,000 at a selling price of £40 each
Super	10,000 at a selling price of £45 each
De Luxe	6,000 at a selling price of £50 each

The production director has pointed out that machine capacity will be limited during the forthcoming year such that 44,000 hours of machinists' time can be worked.

The production director is currently trying to negotiate an arrangement for an outside firm to undertake some machining on a subcontract basis.

You are required:

To suggest what production should take place during the forthcoming year, assuming that no subcontract arrangement can be made, *and* to calculate the resultant profit;

To suggest the theoretical maximum figure which Delta should be prepared to pay for the subcontract machine work during the forthcoming year and to explain your figure;

To discuss briefly any factors beyond the immediately quantifiable which are likely to bear on the decision to subcontract or not.

Exercise 2

Andrews Ltd is involved in the manufacture of one standard product. During two consecutive months recently their output, sales revenues and costs were as follows:

	November	December
Sales (in units)	150	165
Total sales revenue	£7,500	£8,250
Total costs	£5,350	£5,800

Over the two months there had been no changes in unit selling price nor in the costs.

You are required to calculate the break even point for the company's activity.

Exercise 3

Manufacturers plc makes a product, the Digit, which requires the incorporation of a component, the Gadget, which the firm also makes. Jobbers Ltd, a local engineering company, has offered to produce Gadgets and to supply them to Manufacturers plc for £20 each. Jobbers has done a lot of work for Manufacturers in the past and is regarded as a reliable supplier.

Manufacturers' accountant has produced the following costing for an internally made Gadget:

	£	
Direct material	10	
Direct labour (1 hour)	4	
Variable overheads	2	
Fixed overheads		
(1 hour at £6 per hour)	6	
	£22	per Gadget

Manufacturers also makes another product, the Trinket, for which there is a heavy, unsatisfied demand. An attraction of buying-in Gadgets is that the labour released from Gadget work might be able to be used in Trinket manufacture.

Trinkets sell for £10 each and the cost is as follows:

	£
Direct material	2
Direct labour (1/2 hour)	2
Variable overheads	1
Fixed overheads	
(1/2 hour at £6 per hour)	3
	£8

Fixed overheads are apportioned to all work on a direct labour hour basis. Direct costs are strictly variable.

You are required:

To state, with reasons, whether Manufacturers should make or buy Gadgets, assuming that it **would not** be possible to transfer labour to Trinket manufacture.

To state, with reasons, whether Manufacturers should make or buy Gadgets, assuming that it **would** be possible to transfer labour to Trinket manufacture; and

To react to the assertion of Manufacturers' Products Manager that 'Gadget production must continue because the company had only recently invested £50,000 in a highly specialised machine which can only be used in making Gadgets and so has no resale value, since no one wants to buy it (not even Jobbers Ltd)'.

Exercise 4

Phillips Ltd has only one product. Brief data on trading over each of the last two months were as follows:

	April £	May £
Sales revenue	2,000	2,500
Costs	1,700	2,050
Net profit	300	450
Volume of sales	200 units	250 units

You are required:

To calculate the break-even point for the company's activity, stating any assumption which you need to make.

To outline the limitations of break-even analysis for decision making purposes.

Exercise 5

Farmer Giles farms a 150 acre arable farm which for this year is being employed as follows:

	Wheat	Barley	Sprouts	Cabbage
Acres	20	60	40	30
Yield per acre, in tonnes	8	8	10	10
Selling price, per tonne	110	130	120	120
Variable costs, per acre:				
Fertiliser	25	20	30	20
Seeds	20	20	30	25
Pesticides	15	10	20	25
Direct wages	400	380	500	500

The fixed overheads run at £70,000 per annum.

You are required:

To compute the anticipated profit for the current year.

To specify which of the above crops would be most beneficial to produce next year. (It may be assumed that any part of the farm may be used for any crop).

To calculate the break-even point in £s of sales of the crop identified in (b).

To calculate the maximum profit for the forthcoming year subject to Farmer Giles' desire to produce at least 80 tonnes of each crop.

(Ignore the time value of money).

Exercise 6

Speedybuild Ltd produces iron and steel building components. Several of these could be made externally though the main product, a steel shaft, can only be made internally. Details of the internal manufacturing cost of the components which could be made externally are:

Component	A1	A2	A3	A4
	£	£	£	£
Variable materials	1.00	2.00	10.00	4.00
Variable labour	1.50	1.00	5.00	2.50
Fixed overheads	1.50	1.00	5.00	2.50
Total costs	4.00	4.00	20.00	9.00
Product hours per component	4	2	1	4

The capacity of the company to manufacture these components is limited to 500,000 machine hours per year, 80% of which are required for the steel shaft manufacture.

The demand and external price for the other units is as follows:

Component	Annual quantity required (units)	External price (unit)
A.1	100,000	£3.00
A.2	80,000	£3.60
A.3	15,000	£21.00
A.4	100,000	£7.00

You are required to show how many of each of the four components the company should make, explaining all your workings.

Exercise 7

Southern Ltd manufactures and sells three products whose data are given below:

Product	Annual Output	Selling Price	Variable Cost (£)
X	5,000	20	17
Y	10,000	12	6
Z	15,000	30	23

The fixed costs of production are £150,000 pa which, because each product requires equal production time, is charged equally to each job. The factory is working at full capacity.

The production manager has just produced a report which suggests that product X is unprofitable as shown by his statement:

Product X	£	£
Selling price per unit		20
Variable cost per unit	17	
Fixed cost per unit	5	22
Loss per unit		(2)

He recommended dropping the product.

You are required:

To say whether product X should be dropped if there is no alternative use for the production capacity.

To say whether product X should be dropped if the released production capacity could be fully used to make a new product W each unit of which would sell at £20, give rise to variable costs of £15 and take twice as long to produce as the other products.

If it is believed that the market for product Y could be expanded by dropping the price for the entire production of Y, what minimum price could be accepted for product Y assuming that the production capacity to meet the increased demand could only come from abandoning product X?

To discuss the following statement: 'Provided that selling price exceeds variable costs a contract should always be accepted.'

Answer to self-assessment question

(a) The variable (avoidable costs) of internal manufacture are £23 per unit (ie £12 + 9 + 2). Since this is less than the buying-in price of £30 the component should be made internally.

(b) With no spare capacity the only way that the component could be produced internally is by diverting labour from mixerator assembly, thus losing contributions from that activity. The value of the contribution per mixerator is £72 (ie £200 - 80 - 36 -12). This is £6 (ie £72/12) per hour. Thus the relevant cost (outlay + opportunity cost) for each component is £23 (from above) plus £18 (ie 3 hours lost contribution @ £6 per hour). Since the component can be bought for £30, an effective £11 per component saving will be made by buying.

Answers to additional exercises

Exercise 1

	Regular £	Super £	De Luxe £
Sales revenue per unit	40	45	50
Variable cost per unit	26	27	30
Contribution per unit	£14	£18	£20
Hours of machinists' time per unit.	1	3	2
Contribution per hour of machinists' time	£14	£6	£10
Order of priority	1	3	2

Therefore:

(a) Produce

8000 Regulars using	8000	hours contributing	8000 × £14	£112,000
6000 De Luxes using	12000	hours contributing	6000 × £20	£120,000
8000 Supers using	24000	hours contributing	8000 × £18	£144,000
	44000			£376,000
	Less: Fixed cost			£200,000
	Net Profit			£176,000

(b) The only unsatisfied market demand is for Supers. These produce a contribution per unit of £18 after paying £9 per unit to machinists. If the subcontractor would machine a super for £27 (ie £18 + 9), this would reduce the contribution per Super to zero. Logically any subcontract price less than £27 would make the company more profitable.

(c) Factors would include:

- Loss of control
- Loss of independence
- Potential problems with quality of workmanship

Exercise 2

Increase over the month

Sales (units)	15 (ie 165 - 150)
Sales revenue	£750 (ie £8250 - 7500)
Total costs	£450 (ie £5800 - 5350)

Therefore:

Sales revenue per unit   =   £750/15 = £50

Variable cost per unit   =   £450/15 = £30

(Since prices have not altered, the increase must result from the increased volume ie variable cost.)

Fixed costs per month   =   £5350 - (150 × £30) = £850 (November)
OR
£5800 - (165 × £30) = £850 (December)

Breakeven point (in units)
per month   = $$\frac{\text{Fixed costs}}{(\text{sales revenue per unit - variable cost per unit})}$$

=   £850/(£50 - 30) = 42.5 units.

Thus the company will need to make and to sell 43 units per month in order to break even.

Exercise 3

(a) As presumably the fixed overheads would be unaffected by a decision to buy-in Gadgets, the comparison is between the variable costs of manufacture (£16) and the buying-in price of £20. Clearly making is to be preferred to buying.

(b) If labour can be transferred there is an opportunity cost of manufacture. This is £10-5 = £5 per 1/2 hour of labour time, ie £10 per hour. As a gadget takes an hour to produce the internal relevant cost goes up to £26. Thus it is better to buy-in than to manufacture.

(c) If the machine has no resale value its existence, however and whenever acquired, is not relevant to this decision. Manufacturers plc might well address itself to the question as to why it had made a decision to buy an expensive machine without first assessing alternative ways of acquiring Gadgets.

Exercise 4

$$\text{Variable cost/unit} = \frac{£2050 - 1700}{250 - 200}$$

$$= £7/\text{unit}$$

$$\text{Fixed cost per month} = £1700 - (£7 \times 200)$$

$$£300$$

$$(\text{or } £2050 - (£7 \times 250)) = £300)$$

$$\text{BE Point} = \frac{300}{(£10 - 7)}$$
$$= 100 \text{ units per month}$$

Assumptions

No change in fixed costs between months
No change in variable cost/unit between months

(b)

Simplistic
Difficult for multi-product firms
Assumes linear relationships
Ignores business objectives

Exercise 5

(a) Contribution per acre

	Wheat	Barley	Sprouts	Cabbage
Sales revenue per acre	880	1040	1200	1200
Variable cost per acre	460	430	580	570
Contribution per acre	420	610	620	630
Total contribution	8,400	36,600	24,800	18,900

Total		£88,700
Less fixed costs		£70,000
Net profit		£18,700

(b) Given the restriction on the size of the farm, cabbage is the most profitable crop (highest contribution per acre).

(c) BE point of cabbage - £70,000/630 - 111.11 acres × 120 × 10
= £133,333 of cabbage sales.

(d)

	Acres	Contribution £
Wheat	10	4,200
Barley	10	6,100
Sprout	8	4,960
Cabbage	122	76,860
	150	92,120
Less fixed costs		70,000
Net profit		22,120

Exercise 6

Available hours 20% × 500,000 = 100,000

	A1	A2	A3	A4
External price (£)	3.00	3.60	21.00	7.00
Variable Costs (£)(internal)	2.50	3.00	15.00	6.50
Effective Contribution	0.50	0.60	6.00	0.50
Contribution/hour	0.50	0.15	1.50	0.25
Order of preference	2	4	1	3

Therefore make   15,000 A3s = 60,000 hours
                           40,000 A1s = 40,000 hours

Exercise 7

(a) Product X should not be dropped since to do so would lose a £3 contribution (20-17) for each less X produced, without it is presumed reducing the total fixed costs.

(b)

	X	W
Selling price	£20	£20
Variable costs	17	15
	£3	£5

Let t mins be time taken to make one product X, then the contributions per minute are:

$$\frac{3}{t} \qquad \frac{5}{2t}$$

Clearly X's yield higher total contributions in the restricted time available.

(c)   Present contributions from Xs and Ys

$[5000 \times (20\text{-}17)] + [10000 \times (12\text{-}6)] = £75000$

To yield similar contributions the price of Y would need to be at least Y where:

$(Y - 6) \times 15000$ $= 75000$

$Y - 6$ $= \dfrac{75000}{150000}$

Y $= \underline{£11}$

UNIT 6

FULL (TOTAL) COSTING

IN THIS UNIT WE examine the methods employed to deduce the 'full' or 'total' cost of pursuing a particular activity. We will begin by examining the way in which the full cost can be deduced in a simple uni-product operation and then go on to examine the more complex problem of a multi-product operation. We also consider the usefulness of this approach and contrast it with the marginal approach to costing which was discussed in Unit 5.

On completion of this unit you should be able to:

● explain what is meant by the term 'full cost' and deduce the full cost of a unit of output in a uni-product operation (process costing) and a multi-product operation

● distinguish between 'direct' and 'indirect' costs

● discuss the various bases of indirect apportionment of indirect costs and be able to apply them

● discuss the usefulness and limitations of full cost information

● explain the difference between the full costing and marginal costing approaches when measuring profit for a period

● discuss the major principles underlying activity based costing.

Outline of the unit

THE UNIT STARTS WITH a definition of full cost, making the point that all of the costs involved with what is being costed are included here, no distinction being made between fixed and variable costs.

In order to understand the basic principles we begin by looking at a simple uni-product business. Where all of the production is identical, the full cost per unit of output is simply the total costs incurred for a period, divided by the number of units of production for that period. In practice, there is the problem of partially completed production, at the beginning and end of the period (work-in-progress), which needs to be addressed. Where the work-in-progress is such that it is complete to different degrees, eg fully complete as regards materials, but only half complete regarding other costs, a further minor complication is added.

The unit then goes on to look at a multi-product business. Where the output is not identical each unit of output of the product or service needs to be treated individually. Doing this requires separate identification of two types of cost relating to the each unit of output. These two types of cost are:

● Direct costs, ie those which can be objectively measured in respect of the job

● Indirect costs (or overheads), ie those which do not relate directly to the job being costed and which must, therefore, be apportioned to each job on some subjective basis

You must clearly understand the distinction between these two types of cost.

The unit makes three points about direct and indirect costs, about which it is important that you are clear. These are:

● Indirect costs are very important in amount in most real-life contexts

● Indirect costs should not be seen as things which a well managed business can easily do without. In some organisations money is wasted on unnecessary overheads or on poor management of overheads, but the same is also true of direct costs.

● The concept of direct and indirect costs is not related to the concept of fixed and variable costs. You should be careful not to confuse them.

The unit goes on to explain how knowledge of the direct and indirect costs enables them to be added together to deduce the full cost of a particular job. You should note particularly that the way in which the indirect costs are applied to a job is, inevitably, arbitrary. What the accountant must try to do in this context is to use a basis of application, which is reasonably logical, and is seen by those who will be affected by the resultant figures as being fair.

The section also makes the point that, irrespective of how overheads are applied to jobs, the total overheads applied must be the same. Activity 5 should make this point clear to you.

The unit also explains how job costing can be extended where production is of batches of products or services, where each item in the batch is identical, but where the items are different from one batch to the next.

In practice, collecting and applying overheads to jobs or batches is often done on a departmental basis, identifying different overhead recovery rates for each department. This, its advocates claim, will lead to more reliable and fairer costs. This section explains the nature of departmentalising overheads. It also makes clear that it is only in quite restricted circumstances that dealing with overheads on this basis, rather than on a business-wide basis, will make any significant difference to the job costs which result.

The unit shows how departmental overheads are derived in practice. You should be clear as to the distinction between a product cost centre and a service cost centre, also why it is important to make this distinction.

Note that general costs (eg rent of the entire premises and central administration costs) should be apportioned to each product cost centre, according to the relative level of benefit or service which the product cost centre derives from the general costs. Sometimes this can be done fairly objectively. For example, a maintenance department's costs can be apportioned to product cost centre according to how many hours of maintenance workers' time is spent in each product cost centre. With an overhead like the costs of operating the personnel department, it is more likely to be done fairly arbitrary, eg by apportioning the costs according to the number of employees in each product cost centre.

You should carefully work through Example 8, making sure that you are clear as to the reason for each step taken.

The unit identifies and discusses three areas where full cost information is used. These are:

- Financial accounting (income measurement)

- Measuring relative profitability between departments

- Pricing the output of the business.

The unit then goes on to discuss the doubtfulness of the value of full cost information and the reason for this. You should particularly note that, despite the doubts about the value of the information gained, full costing is extremely widely practised by all sorts of organisations.

The unit draws attention to the different philosophies underlying the full cost and marginal approaches to costing. (Remember that we considered marginal costing in detail in a previous unit.) The basic difference is that the full costing approach sees all costs, (fixed or variable, direct or indirect), as attaching to each unit of output, whereas marginal costing sees fixed costs as costs relating to the period, rather than to particular units of output. As we shall see, this difference can result in different measures of profit between years.

The unit also considers the question of cost which are controllable and non-controllable by departmental managers. This an important area. There is little point in a business generating accounting reports, showing departmental costs, as a means of controlling those departments, if the departmental managers have no real control over the costs, because of decisions made at a higher level of responsibility.

The last section of the unit deals with activity based costing. This is a relatively recent management accounting development. It seeks to provide a less arbitrary and, therefore, more fair and potentially more useful basis for relating overheads to output in a job or batch costing environment. Note in the batch costing example, given in this section, how the traditional approach gives a completely different, and less valid, application of overheads to jobs than does activity based costing. You should also note the reservations expressed about this new form of costing.

Now that you have a broad idea as to what this unit is about you can make a start on the detail.

What is full cost?

FULL COST CAN BE defined as the total amount of resources involved with pursuing a particular objective. Such an objective might be to produce a tin of peas, to carry out a car repair, or to build a channel tunnel. Broadly, the purpose of full costing is to be able to answer the question 'How much did it (will it) cost?' Why we may wish to answer such a question we shall discuss in detail later in this unit, but one such purpose might well be so that the producer of (say) a tin of peas will know the price to charge to customers to ensure that all costs are covered and an acceptable level of profit is made.

In the previous unit we saw how the distinction between variable costs and fixed costs was important for certain types of decisions. However, with the full costing approach this distinction between variable and fixed costs is not made. Instead, all costs relevant to achieving the particular objective, whether fixed or variable, are taken into account.

Full costing in a uni-product business

WHERE A BUSINESS PRODUCES units of output which are identical it is a relatively straightforward process to determine the full cost per unit of output. This is done by simply taking the total costs of production for a period and dividing this amount by the number of units of output during that period.

Example 1

Total cost (fixed and variable) for July	£1,750
Total output for July	100 units
Cost per unit = £1,750/100	= <u>£17.50</u>

For this purpose the length of the period is a matter of judgement of those requiring the information and/or preparing the information. Similarly whether the information is historically based (eg what was the full cost per unit of output during last month?) or based on future plans (what will be the full cost per unit of output next month?) is a matter of judgement and depends on the purpose for which the information is required.

Deducing the unit cost in a uni-product setting is usually referred as *process costing*.

Activity 1

During September, a business which produces only one product, the gadget, incurred the following costs:

Raw materials	£4,500
Labour	3,200
Rent and other costs	2,400

Records show that 6,300 gadgets were produced during the month.

What was the full cost per gadget?

The full cost per gadget is determined by taking the total cost of operations and dividing by the number of gadgets produced:

$$\text{Cost per gadget} = \frac{4,500 + 3,200 + 2,400}{6,300}$$

$$= \underline{£1.60}$$

Process costing and the problem of work in progress

THE SIMPLICITY OF DEDUCING unit full costs in a uni-product setting is often slightly complicated in reality by the existence, at the start and end of the period, of partially completed production known as *work in progress* (WIP). The complication which WIP causes is that WIP at the start of the period will probably be completed during the period and some items started during the current period will become finished production of the next period.

Example 2

The total cost incurred during June in the manufacture of a product was £25,000. During the month 10,000 units were completed. There were 1,000 units partially completed at the end of June.

What is the full cost per unit of the product ?

The answer to this question is *not* £25,000/10,000 = £2.50 since the £25,000 was incurred in producing more than the 10,000 units which were actually completed during the month. Similarly, the answer is *not* £25,000/11,000 = £2.27 because the £25,000 did not give rise to 11,000 completed units.

In fact without some more information about the 1000 units of WIP we cannot answer the question. We shall pick up this information and answer the question shortly.

There are three basic approaches which could be taken to solving the problem of WIP in process costing:

● Where the WIP is insignificant in amount it could be ignored;

● Where the WIP is similar at the start and at the end of the period, it can be ignored because the costs put into the production which is not completed by the end of the period is matched by the production brought forward from the previous period;

● Where the WIP is significant in value and dissimilar at the start and end of the period, WIP can be converted into an *equivalent number of completed units*.

This third approach requires further explanation. Perhaps the best way is to illustrate the approach using a simple example.

Example 2 (continued)

Taking the data above, let us add the information that the 1,000 units of WIP have on average had half of the cost of a completed unit applied to them ie they are, in cost terms, half-complete.

It is now reasonable to take the view that the effective output for the month was 10,000 units + (1/2 × 1,000) = 10,500.

Thus the unit cost was £25000/10500 = £2.38.

Activity 2

During December £15,000 was spent on production of trinkets; 1,200 completed trinkets came off the end of the production line and there were 300 partially completed trinkets at the end of the month. It was estimated that on average the 300 were 75% complete. There was no WIP at the start of the month.

What was the full cost per trinket?

The equivalent output for the month will be:

$$1,200 + (300 \times 75\%) \qquad = 1,425 \text{ trinkets}$$

Cost per unit $\qquad\qquad\qquad = £15,000/1,425$

$$= £\underline{10.53}$$

In practice it is unlikely to be the case that the WIP will be equally complete in respect of all elements, eg the WIP may be 50% complete as regards labour but 100% complete as regards materials. Here the cost of the production and hence the unit cost must be identified element by element.

Example 3

Jay Ltd produces a single product and the costs incurred for the month of January for process 1 are as follows:

	£
Materials	4,000
Labour	1,800
Other costs	1,700
	7,500

Units completed and transferred in January   800 units

Work in progress at 31 January   200 units.

The costing department estimates that the degree of completion of the units in progress is:

1. Materials – fully complete

2. Labour – half complete

3. Other costs – quarter complete

There were no uncompleted units in progress at the beginning of the month.

You are required to calculate the full cost/unit of completed production.

The cost per unit can be seen as being made up of three elements, the equivalent units of output for which of each are different.

| *Materials* | Equivalent units | $800 + (100\% \times 200)$ | = 1,000. |
| | Cost per unit | £4000/1000 | = £$\underline{4.00}$ |

| *Labour* | Equivalent units | $800 + (50\% \times 200)$ | = 900. |
| | Cost/unit | £1800/900 | = £$\underline{2.00}$ |

Other costs   Equivalent units   800 + (25% × 200)   = 850.
                 Cost/unit   £1700/850   = £2.00

Thus full cost per unit is:
                 £4.00 + £2.00 + £2.00   = £8.00

Activity 3

Formula QRS is a chemical product formed by subjecting the three ingredients Q, R and S to a patented process.

At the beginning of week 4 the following materials were drawn from the bulk stock and put into the process:

Q	5,000 kg	cost 40p per kg
R	4,000 kg	cost 50p per kg
S	1,000 kg	cost 80p per kg

During week 4, 8,400 kg of Formula QRS was processed: there was no work in progress at the beginning of the week and the process does not give rise to gains or losses in weight.

The wages of the process operatives amounted to £768 for the week and the process is to be charged with £1,152 for other costs.

The firm's chemist estimated that the work in progress at the end of week 4 was 75% complete as regards wages and other costs.

You are required to prepare a statement showing:

(a) the cost per kg of Formula QRS;

(b) the cost of production of the completed Formula QRS; and

(c) the value of the work in progress at the end of week 4.

If 10,000 kg of raw materials were put into the process, there were no losses, 8,400 kg of completed output occurred and there was no WIP at the start of the month, there must be 1,600 kg (ie 10,000 - 8,400) of WIP at the end of week 4.

Total cost per kg

Materials: Equivalent units 8,400 + (100% × 1,600)   = 10,000 kg
(Note that all raw material is put into the process at the start)

			£
Cost	Q	5,000 @ 40p	2,000
	R	4,000 @ 50p	2,000
	S	1,000 @ 80p	800
			4,800

Cost per kg
$$= £4,800/10,000$$
$$= £0.48$$

Wages and other costs:

Equivalent units $8,400 + (75\% \times 1,600)$ $= 9,600$ kg
Cost per kg $£(768 + 1,152)/9,600$ $= £0.20$

Total cost per kg $£(0.48 + 0.20)$ $= £0.68$

Value of completed output $(8,400 \times 0.68)$ $= £5,712$

Value of closing WIP

		£
Materials	1,600 @ 48p	768
Wages etc	1,200 @ 20p	240
		1,008

Full costing in a multi-product operation – direct and indirect costs

QUITE OFTEN IT WILL be the case that the units to be costed are not identical one with another. Examples would include repairs carried out by a garage, audits carried out by a firm of Chartered Accountants and new houses constructed by a builder. One approach to identifying the total cost of such units would be to ignore the difference between one job and the next and to use a process costing approach. This might be an acceptable expedient where the jobs are not strictly identical but where the difference, for costing purposes, is regarded as insignificant. For example, a garment manufacturer making a garment in different sizes might well decide for costing purposes (and therefore perhaps for pricing purposes), to treat the garments as being identical.

Where it is considered inappropriate to treat dissimilar units as if they are identical it will be necessary to take an entirely different approach. It is necessary to build up the costs which have gone into the particular unit to be costed. For this purpose costs must be divided into two categories:

● *Direct costs* Those which can be traced to a particular cost unit and can be measured with respect to it.

● *Indirect costs* Those which are incurred in pursuance of the activity being costed but which cannot be directly related to or measured in respect of it. These are also known as overheads or oncosts.

An example of a direct cost in respect of a car repair will be the cost of the labour of the mechanic who worked on the job. This is a direct cost because it is possible directly to measure how long the person worked on the repair and, by knowing the rate of pay, the cost can be deduced. How long the person worked on the repair and how much he/she is paid per hour are not judgements but matters of fact. Incidentally, it is common practice in operations such as garages for direct workers to record the time spent on each job.

Rent of the premises is an example of an indirect cost of a garage repair. The cost of occupying the premises is clearly part of the cost of each car repair carried out, but in respect of a particular repair it is not a directly measurable cost. It is not a matter of fact as to how much of the rent should be included in the cost of a particular repair, though judgement could be used to apportion part of it to each repair as we shall see later.

Activity 4

State with reasons whether each of the following are direct or indirect with regard to a particular car repair in a garage:

(a) the salary of the garage's accountant;

(b) the cost of heating the garage;

(c) engine oil used in the repair;

(d) a smear of grease used in the repair;

(e) the wages of the mechanic carrying out the repair;

(f) the wages of the supervisor supervising the mechanic carrying out the repair.

Your solution to this activity should be along the following lines:

(a) The salary of the accountant would be an indirect cost. This amount cannot be traced directly to the product. The accountant will not work directly on the cars being repaired.

(b) Heating costs will be indirect. Although the heating may be necessary to the efficient functioning of the garage, the effect of heating cannot be traced directly to a particular repair.

(c) The amount of engine oil could and usually would be measured and costed to a particular repair job.

(d) A smear of grease would be, strictly speaking, a direct cost. It would be possible to measure the approximate amount of grease used and cost it to the particular job. However, the amounts involved would almost certainly not justify the effort and so for the sake of expediency, it would be better to treat the item as an indirect cost.

(e) The wages of the mechanic, as we saw earlier, would be treated as a direct cost.

(f) The supervisor does not usually work on particular repairs. He/she has a supervisory role. This means that his/her contribution to a particular job cannot be directly measured and costed.

Direct and indirect costs: some further points

THERE ARE THREE POINTS which should be noted about direct and indirect costs. Firstly, direct costs are not necessarily more important in size, nor more worthy than indirect costs. With increasing sophistication of manufacturing processes etc, overheads (indirect costs) are tending to account for a large proportion of total cost, and, in some cases, they represent the larger part. Secondly, overheads are just as important and worthy as direct costs; the rent of the garage is just as essential to a particular repair as is the mechanic. Unless the rent is paid the mechanic has nowhere to work and the customer has no identifiable place to take the car to be repaired.

Finally, though direct costs are often variable with the level of output and indirect costs tend to be fixed you should be clear in your mind that the words variable and direct on the one hand and fixed and indirect on the other are not interchangeable. In other words, direct costs are not necessarily variable and indirect costs are not always fixed. For example, the direct labour costs incurred in making a product will be a fixed cost to the business if the direct workers are paid irrespective of the level of output. Similarly, an indirect cost such as indirect materials (oil for machinery etc) may vary directly with the level of output.

Variable and fixed relate to the behaviour of cost whilst direct and indirect relate to whether or not costs can be measured directly with respect to the thing being costed. These are completely different concepts and should not be confused.

Deducing the full cost of a job in a multi-product setting (job costing)

THE IMPORTANCE OF THE distinction between direct and indirect cost becomes apparent when we have to cost a particular item which is being produced by a multi-product business. The full cost of the item will be made up of the direct costs associated with the product plus a 'fair share' of the indirect costs of production.

Deducing the full cost of a particular product will involve two steps:

● Measure the cost of direct elements relating to a particular job (these are typically direct labour and materials). In principle, this is a simple matter and only requires that reasonable records are maintained.

● Total the indirect costs for a period and apportion part of this total to the particular job.

The sum of the figures from these two steps is the full cost for the job or cost unit.

The key question is, of course, on what basis do we apportion a share of the overheads to the job being costed? Perhaps the first idea to come to mind is to give each job undertaken during the period an equal share of the indirect costs. This may well be a reasonable solution, particularly where the jobs are not too dissimilar and/or where the overheads are relatively insignificant.

If sharing the overheads equally between jobs is not thought to be appropriate, the person doing the costing must ask, 'What is it about a particular job which makes him or her feel that it should have more or less overheads apportioned to it?'

Example 4

Two consecutive repairs carried out by a garage had the following direct costs:

	Job A		Job B	
		£		£
Direct labour	(16 hours)	48	(2 hours)	6
Parts		20		1
		68		7

Should these two jobs have equal shares of the business's overheads apportioned to them?

Most people would feel that they should not, on the basis that Job A was bigger than Job B. A fairly logical way to measure size of jobs in this context might be by reference to the direct labour hours worked, and in fact this is a very popular approach. One way or another, if sharing overheads equally between jobs is not felt to be appropriate, something measurable about the jobs must provide the basis for apportionment.

It must be emphasised here that there is no correct way of apportioning overheads. By definition, indirect costs do not directly relate to particular jobs and so any basis of apportionment must be arbitrary. However, provided that those who might be affected by the basis on which overheads are apportioned (eg, a customer of a garage which bases prices on total cost) find the basis acceptable, it may be considered an appropriate basis.

The following example illustrates how we can apportion overheads by reference to the direct labour hours relating to a particular job.

Example 5

Gafa Ltd, a firm of jobbing engineers, has just completed a piece of work for which the direct costs (also known as prime cost) were:

		£
Direct labour	(10 hours @ 2.70 /hour)	27
Direct materials		12
		£39

During the month that the work took place the total overheads of the business amounted to £5,000 and there was a total of 2,000 hours of direct labour worked. If Gafa Ltd apportions overheads on the basis of direct labour hours, how much should be added to the prime cost by way of overheads?

The rate at which overheads must be applied to jobs is:

£5,000/2,000 = £2.50 per direct labour hour.

OVERHEAD ABSORPTION RATE

This rate is frequently referred to as the *overhead recovery rate* or the *overhead absorption rate*.

The overheads for the job in question are therefore £2.50 × 10 = £25, giving a full cost for the job of £64 which is made up as follows:

	£
Direct labour	27
Direct materials	12
Share of overheads	25
	£64

Activity 5

Renotruck Ltd carries out major overhauls on heavy lorries. During November the business started and completed just three jobs. The prime cost (ie the total of direct costs) relating to each job were as follows:

	Lorry X £	Lorry Y £	Lorry Z £
Direct labour	600 (200 hrs)	450 (150 hrs)	720 (240 hrs)
Direct materials	420	60	340
Prime cost	£1020	£510	£1060

(Note that these three jobs represent the entire output of work for November.)

The overheads for the month were £2,300.

You are required to deduce overhead recovery rates on each of the following bases for each of the three jobs and use them to deduce the total cost for each job:

(a) per direct labour hour;
(b) per £ of prime cost.

Your answer to the above activity should be as follows:

(a) Rate per direct labour hour

$$= \frac{\text{overheads for month}}{\text{total direct labour hours for month}}$$

$$= \frac{£2,300}{(200 + 150 + 240)}$$

$$= £3.90$$

(b) Rate per £ of prime cost

$$= \frac{\text{overheads per month}}{\text{total prime cost for month}}$$

$$= \frac{£2,300}{(1020 + 510 + 1060)}$$

$$= £0.89$$

We can see overleaf that the total cost attributable to each lorry will vary according to the method of apportionment used:

Direct labour hour method

Lorry	Hours (@£3.90)	X £	Hours (@£3.90)	Y £	Hours (@£3.90)	Z £
Prime cost		1,020		510		1,060
Overheads	200	780	150	585	240	935
		1,800		1,095		1,995

'Per £ of prime cost' method

Lorry	£ (@£0.89)	X £	£ (@£0.89)	Y £	£ (@£0.89)	Z £
Prime cost		1,020		510		1,060
Overheads	1,020	906	510	453	1,060	941
		1,926		963		2,001

It can be seen that, although the total overheads are the same under both methods (ie £2,300), the apportionment of these overheads between the lorries is different. This results in a different total cost figure for each lorry depending on the method used. The prime cost, which is capable of direct measurement, will be the same whichever method of overhead apportionment is used.

The objective of overhead apportionment is merely to attribute a slice of the total indirect costs to each cost unit in what, under the circumstances, is the most reasonable manner, given the purpose for which the full cost figure is required.

The direct labour hour basis seems to be the most popular one in practice and, possibly, it is the most logical. Most overheads – rent, managerial salaries, heat and light, depreciation, etc – are time based ie the rent for two months is exactly twice that for one month. If overheads are to be apportioned to jobs then it seems reasonable to do so on the basis of the length of time that they benefit from the overheads rather than on some other basis. However it cannot be overemphasised that apportioning overheads on a direct labour hour basis is not the *only* way to do it; there is more than one way. In a business which is capital intensive the direct labour hours spent on the product may not be a valid method of overhead apportionment. The number of hours spent on a particular piece of equipment may be more appropriate.

Other methods which may be used to apportion overheads include:

● Machine hours (ie total overheads/no. of machine hours worked)

● Direct material cost (ie total overheads/direct material cost consumed)

● Products produced (ie total overheads/ no. of units produced).

Batch costing

IN SOME TYPES OF commercial or industrial activities the output consists of a batch of identical products or services, though each batch is different from the next. For example a particular title produced by a publisher is likely to be different in nature and cost from the other titles published by the business, but each copy of the particular title is identical. Other examples might include a garment manufacturer in respect of a particular line of clothing and a theatre in respect of a particular production.

The usual approach taken to finding the full cost per unit (eg per copy of a book, per garment, per seat in the theatre) is to cost the batch (eg the title, the run of the particular garment, the theatrical production) along job costing lines and then to divide the cost for the batch by the number of units in the batch.

Departmental overheads

FREQUENTLY FOR PURPOSES OF management and control, businesses are divided into sections or departments. Usually to promote control and accountability of departmental managers, the costs of running each department are identified. This is done by collecting direct departmental costs, eg wages and salaries of those who work exclusively in one department. To these direct departmental costs are added a share of more general costs which cover more than one department or perhaps the business as a whole, for example rent of the entire premises. Where costs are identified on a departmental basis, the department is known as a *cost centre*. Cost centres are simply aspects of the business for which costs are identified, they are not necessarily departments, but they frequently are. Where costs are collected on a departmental basis, more useful job costing information may result if overheads are apportioned to jobs according to how long the job spends in each department (assuming a direct labour hour or machine hour basis of apportionment) rather than the total time in the business as a whole. It will only make a significant difference to the outcome where:

● Jobs vary significantly from one another in the proportion of the total time they spend in different departments; *and*

● The overhead recovery rate varies significantly from one department to another.

Note that it will only make a difference where *both* of these conditions apply simultaneously.

Example 6

Ace Ltd has two departments, some data concerning which are as follows:

	Department	
	Processing	*Finishing*
Monthly overheads	£10,000	£4,000
Monthly direct labour hours	4,000	4,000

During the month, among other work, the business carried out Job A which took 3 hours in the processing department and 1 hour in the finishing department and Job B which took 1 hour being processed and 3 hours being finished.

How much overheads should be applied to each job if overheads are applied:

(a) on a departmental basis; and
(b) on a business-wide basis,

assuming that overheads are apportioned on a direct labour hour basis?

Solution

The first step is to calculate the *overhead recovery rates*. These represent the rates at which the overheads should be apportioned to a particular job. Using a direct labour hour basis of apportionment the rates are as follows:

Processing dept recovery rate   = £10,000/4,000   = £2.50 per D.L.H.

Finishing dept recovery rate   = £4,000/4,000   = £1.00 per D.L.H.

Business-wide recovery rate

$$= (£10,000 + 4,000)/(4,000 + 4,000) \qquad = £1.75 \text{ per D.L.H.}$$

(a)

	Job	
	A	B
	£	£
Processing dept (£2.50/hour)	7.50	2.50
Finishing dept (£1.00/hour)	1.00	3.00
	8.50	5.50

(b)

	Business Wide	
	£	£
[(3+1) × £1.75]	7.00	
[(1+3) × £1.75]		7.00

Of course the overhead figure would be added to the direct cost for each job.

Note that if *all* jobs spent roughly the same proportion of the total time in each department, (this would imply half in each department since they both had 4,000 hours for the month), the overheads applied to each job would be the same irrespective of whether overheads were applied departmentally or not. Obviously if overheads were at similar levels (compared with direct labour hours) from one department to the next ie similar recovery rates, again it would make no difference how overheads were applied.

Apportioning overheads between departments

IF THE DEPARTMENTAL ROUTE towards job costing is to be followed, it is necessary to identify the overheads for each department through which the cost units actually pass, this includes a share of the overheads of the departments through which cost units do not actually pass. Such cost centres are known as *service cost centres*, so called because they render a service to the *product cost centres*. Service cost centres would include such things as raw materials stores, canteen, personnel departments and general administration.

A worked example can be used to explain the process of apportioning overheads between departments.

Example 7

JPE Ltd is divided into five departments which are also cost centres. These are departments A, B and C (through which cost units physically pass), an administrative department and a canteen.

Some details of the business are as follows:

	A	B	C	Canteen	Admin
Floor area (sq ft)	5000	5000	4000	4000	2000
Personnel (persons)	10	18	8	4	4
Hours worked per month					
direct	1280	2400	1120	–	–
indirect	320	480	160	320	420
Remuneration per month					
direct	1920	3600	2240	–	–
indirect	360	480	240	320	870

Direct materials consumed (£)	5500	250	400		
Machine hours per month	600	2400	200	–	–
Power costs per month (£)	50	500	20	80	–
General overheads per month (£)	1000	2000	1200	650	1230

The following additional material is available:

The monthly rent of the company's premises is £6,000.

The monthly takings of the canteen are £600, food bills totalled £470. None of the administrative staff use the canteen.

The monthly electricity charge for heat and light is £1,000.

The administration costs are made up mainly of personnel related costs.

Calculate an overhead absorption rate for each product cost centre.

To deal with this problem we must undertake a series of steps. These are as follows:

STEP 1
The first step is to apportion the overheads to both product and service cost centres. The basis of apportionment should be reasonable, although it has already been stated above, that there is no single correct way of doing this.

STEP 2
Having apportioned the overheads to the various cost centres, the service cost centres must be apportioned between the product cost centres using some reasonable basis. Such a basis should take account of the level of service rendered by the service cost centre to the production cost centre (see notes 3 and 4 below).

STEP 3
Finally, the total amount for each product cost centre must be divided by some measure of activity (such as direct labour hours) in order to derive the overhead absorption, or overhead recovery rate.

The calculations are:

	A £	B £	C £	Canteen £	Admin. £
Indirect labour	360	480	240	320	870
Power cost	50	500	20	80	–
General overheads	1000	2000	1200	650	1230
Rent (Note 1)	1500	1500	1200	1200	600
Canteen takings	–	–	–	(600)	–
Food				470	
Electricity (Note 2)	250	250	200	200	100
	3160	4730	2860	2320	2800
Apportionment of admin. dept costs (Note 3)	700	1260	560	280	(2800)
	3860	5990	3420	2600	–
Apportionment of canteen costs (Notes 4 and 5)	722	1300	578	(2600)	–
	4582	7290	3998	–	–
Overhead absorption rate (per DLH) (Notes 6 and 7)	£3.58	£3.04	£3.57		

Notes

1. Rent was apportioned on the basis of floor area occupied by each department.

2. Electricity was apportioned on the basis of floor area since heating and lighting were assumed to accrue on that basis.

3. Administration department costs were apportioned before canteen costs since it renders a service to the canteen but not vice versa. Administration costs were apportioned on the basis of the number of employees in the other four departments since they are mainly personnel related.

4. Canteen costs (net of takings) were apportioned on the basis of the number of employees since it is presumed that the other departments benefited from the canteen according to the number of staff, ie the larger the number of employees in each cost centre, the larger the service it is presumed to have received from the service cost centre.

5. Service cost centre costs must ultimately be apportioned to the product cost centres otherwise there is no mechanism for incorporating service cost centre costs in the cost of units of output of the business, despite the fact that the cost of administration and of the canteen are very real costs of production.

6. The overhead absorption rates are calculated by dividing the total overheads for each product cost centre by the direct labour hours. Provided that all of the hours of

direct labour are actually worked, all of the overheads will find their way into the cost of the jobs done.

7. It is usual to deduce overhead recovery rates for the immediate future (perhaps a year at a time) by use of planned or budgeted overheads and direct labour hours (if D.L.H. is to be the basis of apportionment of indirect costs), rather than wait until actual costs are known, by which time the value of the information may be reduced.

Now try this self-assessment question. This is intended to give you the opportunity to see whether you have grasped the material so far. You should probably be able to complete this in three quarters of an hour. Don't worry if it takes you longer. The main point is that, once you have completed it, you are clear on all of the points which it involves. It is not really helpful to look at the answer to this until you have completed your answer.

Self-assessment question

Barclay Engineering has three product cost centres and two service cost centres. The company has budgeted its overheads for a period as follows:

	£
Rent and rates	6,000
Heating	3,000
Power	10,000
Depreciation of machinery	10,000
Indirect labour cost	18,000
Miscellaneous costs	3,000

The following information is available about the cost centres:

	Total	Production cost centres			Service cost centres	
		Cutting dept	Machining dept	Finishing dept	Maint'ce dept	Personnel dept
Floor space (sq ft)	8000	2000	2000	2000	1000	1000
Cubic capacity (cu ft)	70000	20000	20000	15000	8000	7000
Machine power (hp)	300	60	150	30	50	10
Machine book value (£000)	250	50	130	20	30	20
Direct labour hours	9000	2000	3000	2000	1000	1000

You are required:

(a) to apportion the overhead costs between the five cost centres and then between the three product cost centres using whatever basis seems appropriate to each type of cost.

(b) to calculate an overhead absorption rate for each of the three product cost centres on the basis of direct labour hours and use them to calculate the overheads that should be applied to a job that is worked on by direct labour as follows:

Cutting dept	2 hours
Machining dept	3 hours
Finishing dept	1 hour.

(The answer to this self-assessment question is at the back of the unit.)

Having now spent some time in finding out how to calculate the full cost of a product you might well ask why do we need such information? In the following section we consider the possible uses of full cost information.

Uses of full cost information

THREE USES ARE TYPICALLY identified for full cost information:

● *For financial accounting purposes.* Where it is necessary to identify the cost of production and hence the cost of sales to compare with the sales figure to arrive at gross profit. It is standard practice to include overheads in the cost of production. (This point is discussed in more detail below.)

● *To measure relative profitability of departments, divisions etc.* If some attempt is to be made to compare the unit cost of the output of some department with the outside purchase price, it will usually be necessary to use full cost information.

● *For pricing purposes .* Where it may be considered necessary or useful to base the price on the full cost.

For all three purposes, the arbitrary nature of the apportionment of overheads in the case of job costing must call the value of total cost information into question.

Though some businesses in particular industries may be able to base their selling prices on incurred costs, ie they are *price makers*, most businesses are, in fact *price takers* who must accept the market price for the goods or services they supply. However, full cost information is not necessarily useless to price takers since knowledge of the full cost will enable them to make a judgement on whether or not to enter or to remain in a particular market given the price dictated by that market.

Though the usefulness of full costing can be questioned, it is probably fair to say that the majority of businesses engaged in manufacturing, or in the provision of services, and other organisations such as hospitals and universities use full costing to arrive at a cost for their output.

Full/marginal costing systems and profit measurement

IN A PREVIOUS UNIT it was seen that marginal costing can be very useful for short-term decision making. Under this costing system only *variable costs* will be charged to the particular cost units. Fixed costs are not apportioned but are written off against the contribution (ie sales – variable costs) for the period. Under the full costing system, however, both *fixed and variable costs* are allotted to the cost units.

This difference in the treatment of fixed costs between the two methods will lead to a difference in the way in which stocks are valued and this, in turn, will lead to a difference in the measurement of profit. An example may be used to illustrate the difference in reported profit which may arise under the two systems.

Example 8

A business commences production of a single product on 1 January. The following information relates to the first two months of production:

| | No. of units | |
	January	*February*
Opening stock	-	2,000
Production of finished goods	12,000	12,000
Sales	10,000	11,000
Closing stock	2,000	3,000

Each unit is sold for £25. The variable cost per unit is £8 and the fixed production costs are £72,000 per month. There was no work in progress at the end of either month.

The gross profit under the full costing and marginal costing systems will be as follows:

Full costing

	January		February	
	£	£	£	£
Sales		250,000		275,000
Opening stock (see note)	–		28,000	
Cost of production	168,000		168,000	
	168,000		196,000	
Closing stock	28,000	140,000	42,000	154,000
Gross profit		110,000		121,000

Note

The overhead recovery rate for each month will be £72,000/12,000 = £6 per unit. The total cost per unit will therefore be £8 + £6 = £14. The closing stock at the end of January is therefore 2,000 × £14 = £28,000.

Marginal costing

	January		February	
	£	£	£	£
Sales		250,000		275,000
Opening stock (see note)	–		16,000	
Cost of production	96,000		96,000	
	96,000		112,000	
Closing stock	16,000	80,000	24,000	88,000
Contribution		170,000		187,000
Less fixed costs		72,000		72,000
Gross profit		98,000		115,000

Note

Only the variable costs of £8 will be charged to the units produced. The closing stock at the end of January is therefore 2,000 × £8 = £16,000.

As stated earlier, the difference in profit between the two systems arises because of the different treatment of fixed production costs. Under the marginal costing approach all fixed costs incurred during the period will be written off even though some of the goods produced during the period remain unsold at the end of the period. Under the full costing approach those fixed costs apportioned to unsold stock will be carried forward and charged against the future period in which the stock is sold.

Those who support the marginal costing approach argue that fixed production costs will be incurred in making the particular item and it would therefore be prudent to write off these costs during the production period rather than during the sales period which may be later. Those who support the full costing approach, on the other hand, argue that it would be excessively prudent to write off fixed production overheads in the period of production irrespective of when the sale of the items occur. By apportioning fixed production overheads to units produced, it is possible to achieve a better matching of sales and associated expenses during a particular period and therefore a more realistic measure of profit.

It should be noted that Statement of Standard Accounting Practice 9 issued by the accountancy profession and which deals with the accounting treatment of stocks and work in progress, supports the latter approach when preparing published accounts for limited companies. However, it would still be possible for a company to employ a marginal costing approach for internal management purposes.

Over the full life of the product the *total* profit (ie total sales less total variable and total fixed costs) will be the same whichever costing system is employed. However, *between periods*, as we have seen above, there can be significant differences in reported profits arising under each system.

Cost centres and responsibility accounting

WE HAVE SEEN ABOVE that the traditional full costing approach is based on the idea of allocating and apportioning overhead costs to cost centres, reapportioning service centre costs to production centres and then ensuring that costs are absorbed by the cost units which pass through the production cost centres. Where a system of *responsibility accounting* is employed, each cost centre may be seen as being under the control of a particular manager. This will mean that the manager is accountable for expenses incurred within the cost centre. In order to be able to evaluate the performance of a manager responsible for a particular cost centre, it is important to distinguish between *controllable* and *non-controllable* costs.

CONTROLLABLE AND NON-CONTROLLABLE COSTS
Controllable costs are those costs incurred by the cost centre which the cost centre manager has the authority to regulate. Non-controllable costs are those costs which the cost centre manager does not have the authority to regulate. Which costs are regarded as controllable and which are regarded as non-controllable will vary according to the level of management. It may be that certain costs relating to a cost centre have been authorised by a higher level of management. For example, a higher level manager may decide to rent premises for a particular cost centre. Where this occurs, the rent payable may be regarded as a controllable cost for the higher management level even though it represents an uncontrollable cost for the cost centre manager. It is important to recognise, however, that all costs can be regarded as controllable by some level of management.

Activity-based costing

We have seen that the traditional full costing system relies on subjective judgement concerning the basis of apportionment of overheads to cost centres. To a greater or lesser extent, all methods of apportionment employed are arbitrary in nature. Where overheads form a relatively low proportion of the total costs of a business, the arbitrary nature of overhead apportionment may not be a serious issue. However, a significant feature of many modern businesses is the relatively high level of overhead costs in relation to total costs. In this situation, the traditional full costing system can create a problem for management seeking to accurately identify unit costs and exert control over these costs. This problem has particular significance given the highly competitive environment faced by many businesses.

ACTIVITY-BASED COSTING

Activity based costing (ABC) provides an alternative to the traditional method of determining full cost. The objective of this method is to establish a better means of relating overheads to output. It is claimed that the ABC method provides managers with a better basis for both cost control and for the analysis of profitability.

Example 9

In order to illustrate one of the drawbacks of the traditional method of full costing, consider the example of a business which sells 20,000 coffee mugs per year which is divided between large mugs (10,000), medium-size mugs (8,000) and small mugs (2,000). Let us assume the time spent on each mug by direct labour is the same for each mug and the time spent on the machines is also the same for each mug. This will mean that, using either the direct labour hour method or the machine hour method of apportionment, the overheads apportioned to each mug will be the same. Thus, assuming the total overheads are £15,000, each mug will bear £0.75 (ie £15,000/20,000) of the total overheads.

Overall, the large mugs will absorb 50% of the total overheads (ie 10,000/20,000), the medium-size mugs will absorb 40% of the total overheads (ie 8,000/20,000) and the small mugs will absorb 10% (ie 2,000/20,000). However, this may not be an equitable apportionment of overhead costs. For example, where there are high set-up costs or there are demanding requirements concerning a particular product, the volume of output may be an unreliable guide to the time and effort expended by the service departments on each product. It may be that each type of mug produced places equal demands on the support departments such as administration, distribution, packaging, etc. If this situation occurs, it can be argued that the large mugs and medium size mugs, which are the higher volume items, will bear too high a proportion of the total overheads and the small mugs, which have a lower volume of output, will bear too low a proportion of the total overheads if the traditional approach is followed.

Activity 6

Assume each type of mug made equal demands on the support departments. Can you devise a more equitable method of apportioning overhead costs to the products than the conventional approach?

If each type of mug places equal demands on the support departments then, it can be argued, they should each bear an equal amount of the total overheads, ie £5,000 each. The overheads borne by each type of mug will then be as follows:

Large	£5,000/10,000	= £0.50
Medium-size	£5,000/8,000	= £0.625
Small	£5,000/2,000	= £2.50

Thus, the higher volume mugs (large and medium size) will have a lower overhead cost per unit assigned to them whereas the small mugs will have a higher overhead cost per unit.

The reapportionment of overhead costs in this way, so as to recognise the benefits received by each product, is consistent with the ABC method. In essence, ABC is concerned with identifying the nature and cause of overhead costs and then defining their relationship with each product according to the benefits received.

ABC recognises that costs arise as a result of the activities engaged in by the business. These activities eventually result in the production of goods or services by the business. The type of activities engaged in will vary according to the nature of the business but may include such things as the placing of stock orders, the receipt of raw material, the transportation of goods, packaging, etc. The first step in ABC is to identify these activities. Once this has been done, the next step is to identify the 'cost drivers', ie the factors which have a significant influence on the cost of the activities undertaken. Activity costs can be assigned to products according to how much of the cost is 'driven' by the particular product during a period. For example, the cost of the purchasing department may be largely determined by the number of orders placed. The frequency of orders placed will be the cost driver and this can be used as a basis for apportioning costs. This should result in each product receiving a fairer share of total overheads.

In order to control costs it is necessary to control the factors which produce the costs incurred. Thus, the efficient management of costs requires identification of the 'cost drivers'. By identifying the 'cost drivers' it may be possible for management to exert some influence on these and this, in turn, should reduce unit costs.

Although the ABC method has received a great deal of attention in recent years, it has been criticised as being time-consuming and costly. Some commentators are not convinced that the benefits of this method outweigh the costs of using it. It has also been criticised as being less useful for decision making purposes than the relevant costing approach considered in an earlier unit. It may be some time before we know whether or not this method will really be accepted by managers and take root in businesses and other organisations.

Reading

You should now read the following Reader Articles concerning ABC:

Reader Article 6.1 'ABC in retail financial services' by Colin Drury and David Pettifer;
Reader Article 6.2 'ABC: The right approach for you?' by Robin Cooper;
Reader Article 6.3 'ABC in the UK – a status report' by Brent Nicholls.

The first article sets out the various stages in designing an ABC system for a business and then demonstrates how these stages would be undertaken in the retail financial services sector. This is an interesting application of the ABC approach; much of the literature on this topic is concerned with the manufacturing sector. The article goes on to discuss the ways in which ABC should be of benefit to managers in managing the business.

Points to consider:

How should ABC help managers control costs?
ABC employs sunk costs and ignores opportunity costs. Can it really be a useful basis for decision making?
Should ABC be a substitute for, or a supplement to, the traditional approach?

The second article examines the factors to consider when deciding whether or not it is worthwhile introducing ABC into a business. It is important to determine whether the benefits to be gained from ABC outweigh the costs of implementing the system.

The author argues that there are three important factors to be considered: the sophistication of the company's information systems, the cost of errors and the diversity of the company's products.

Points to consider:

To what extent can the factors identified be measured?
What costs of implementing a new costing system were identified by the author? Can you think of any other costs?

Continued over . . .

The third article provides us with survey information concerning the extent to which ABC is being employed in the UK. The survey also provided information concerning the perceived benefits and problems of implementing ABC.

Points to consider:

The survey findings reveal that 90% of respondent companies were considering ABC and 10% had implemented this approach. Why might these findings not be representative of UK companies as a whole?
What problems and pitfalls were identified by respondents? To what extent do they relate to the points made in the preceding article concerning factors to consider in implementing ABC?

Measuring costs in practice

THE ACCA SURVEY asked companies which method of overhead recovery they normally used. 26% indicated that there was a single overhead rate for the plant, 31% indicated there were separate overhead rates for each department and 38% indicated there were separate overhead rates for each work centre, or group of work centres, within a department (5% indicated other methods were used). The extent to which a single plant-wide rate is being employed is rather surprising given the limitations of this method discussed earlier. In a multi-product business there is a strong likelihood that product costs will be distorted as a result of adopting this approach.

The survey asked companies to indicate how many cost overhead absorption rates a typical manufacturing plant employs. It was revealed that 37% of companies responding indicated that there were 11 or more (with 20% indicating there were more than 20). By far the most popular method of allocating overheads proved to be the direct labour hour method. 73% of companies use this method (to some extent at least) for non-automated production activities and 68% use it for automated production activities. This latter finding is again rather surprising. It is hard to believe that direct labour hours is a major element of product cost where automated production facilities are employed.

Summary

IN THIS UNIT WE HAVE examined the methods used to derive the full or total cost of a product. We have seen how overhead costs may be apportioned and the problems which this process involves. We have discussed both the usefulness and the limitations of full cost information. We have also contrasted the full costing approach with the marginal costing approach for measuring and reporting profits for a period.

Although the full cost system has been the subject of much criticism, it remains in widespread use. However, in recent years there has been a demand from businesses for more accurate identification of, and greater control over, unit costs as a result of an increasingly competitive environment. This, in turn, has led to the development of activity based costing(ABC). It is not yet clear whether ABC will gain widespread acceptance and provide benefits to businesses in excess of the costs involved in implementing such a system.

Additional exercises

Exercise 1

Mixers Ltd produces only one product, 'Gusto', on a continuing basis.

During May, when 2,700 tonnes of Gusto were completed, £1,400 was spent on direct labour, £920 of materials were put into production and overheads of £1,250 were incurred.

There was work in progress at both the beginning and end of May, details of which are as follows:

	At 1 May	At 31 May
Tonnes of WIP	350	420
Degree of completion:		
Labour	75%	80%
Materials	100%	100%
Overheads	87.5%	90%

All costs have remained steady over recent months.

You are required:

a) to deduce the production cost per tonne of Gusto.
b) to value the closing work in progress.
c) to discuss briefly the circumstances where the above approach to costing production would be inappropriate.

Exercise 2

A new process has been started, the costs for which for the first month were as follows:

Material A: 400 kg at £1.25/kg
Material B: 2000 kg at £0.90/kg

(All materials enter the process at the start)

Labour   1000 hours at £3.00/hour
Overheads   £2000

During the month, finished production of 2,000 kg was taken into stock. The process gives rise to neither weight loss or weight gain. It is estimated that the work in progress (WIP) at the month end was 75% complete as regards labour and 80% complete regarding overheads.

You are required:

a) to value the completed production during the month and the WIP at the month end;
b) to discuss the circumstances under which 'process' rather than 'job' costing would be employed to discover the full cost of production.
c) to identify the uses to which full cost information can be put.

Exercise 3

Industry plc is a manufacturing firm with three production and two service departments.

The budgeted costs for the forthcoming year are as follows:

| | Production departments | | | Service departments | | |
| | Mach'ing | Assembly | Finishing | Personnel | Maint'nce | Total |
	£000	£000	£000	£000	£000	£000
Direct Materials	10,000	3,000	1,000			14,000
Direct Labour	3,000	4,000	2,000			9,000
Indirect Materials	1,500	1,000	500	100	400	3,500
Indirect Labour	1,000	1,000	500	200	300	3,000
Power	5,000	1,000	1,000	200	800	8,000
Rent and Rates	3610	4820	1200	240	120	10,000
Production Administration and supervision	4068	5808	1740	144	228	12,000
Machine Insurance	2307	462	231			3,000

The following additional information is also available:

	Machining dept	Assembly dept	Finishing dept	Personnel dept	Maint'nce dept	Total
Floor area (sq m)	15,000	20,000	5,000	1,000	500	41,500
Machine Hours	1,500,000	300,000	200,000	-	-	2,000,000
Direct Labour hours	1,200,000	1,600,000	500,000	-	-	3,300,000
Number of Employees	700	1,000	300	25	40	2,065
Value of Machinery	£5.0m	£1.0m	£0.5m	-	-	£6.5m

The Maintenance department renders no service to the Personnel department.

You are required:

a) to deduce overhead absorption rates for each production department on the direct labour hour basis.
b) to explain why the direct labour basis seems to be popular in practice.
c) to comment on the usefulness of apportioning overheads to individual cost units.

Exercise 4

Uniproduct Ltd makes one standard product. During May, 50 units were completed and a further 25 units were partially completed. The partially completed units were estimated to be 50% complete as regards materials and 30% complete as regards labour and overheads.

Production costs incurred during May totalled:

	£
Materials	5350
Labour	2940
Overheads	4720

There were no uncompleted units at the start of May.

You are required:

to deduce the full cost per unit of the company's product.

Exercise 5

Greg's Garage carries out repairs on motor cars. Greg bases his charges to customers on the full cost (labour, materials and overheads) plus 20%.

Next month Greg expects that he and his one employee, also a mechanic, will work 300 hours between them. He pays his mechanic £4 an hour and he charges his own time at the same rate. Greg estimates that his other costs for the month will be as follows:

	£
Rent and rates	250
Electricity and power	100
Depreciation of tools etc	50
Insurance	20
Sundries	20

You are required:

to suggest a price for a repair carried out next month which will take the employee 10 hours, plus 6 hours of Greg's time and will involve spares and parts costing £125. You should explain why you have taken the approach which you have chosen to take in deducing this price.

Exercise 6

Symi Ltd manufactures three products in two production departments, a machine shop and a fitting section; it also has two service departments, a canteen and a machine maintenance section. Shown below are next year's budgeted production data and manufacturing costs for the company:

Product	A	B	C
Production	4,200 units	6,900 units	1,700 units
Prime Cost:			
Direct Materials	£11 per unit	£14 per unit	£17 per unit
Direct Labour –			
Machine Shop	£6 per unit	£4 per unit	£2 per unit
Fitting Section	£12 per unit	£3 per unit	£21 per unit
Machine Hours, per unit	6 hrs per unit	3 hrs per unit	4 hrs per unit

Budgeted Overheads:	Machine Shop	Fitting Section	Canteen	Machine Maint'nce Section	Total
	£	£	£	£	£
Allocated Overheads	27,660	19,470	16,600	26,650	90,380
Rent, Rates, Heat and Light					17,000
Depreciation and Insurance of Equipment					25,000

Additional data:

	Machine Shop	Fitting Section	Canteen	Machine Maint'nce Section
Gross Book Value of Equipment	£150,000	£75,000	£30,000	£45,000
Number of Employees	18	14	4	4
Floor Space Occupied – Square Metres	3,600	1,400	1,000	800

It has been estimated that approximately 70% of the Machine Maintenance Section's costs are incurred servicing the Machine Shop and the remainder incurred servicing the Fitting Section.

You are required:

a) to calculate the following budgeted overhead absorption rates: A machine hour rate for the Machine Shop. A rate expressed as a percentage of direct wages for the Fitting Section. (All workings and assumptions should be clearly shown.)

b) to calculate the budgeted manufacturing overhead cost per unit of Product A.

c) The production director of Symi Ltd has suggested that, 'as the actual overheads incurred and units produced are usually different from that budgeted and as a consequence profits at each month end are distorted by over/under absorbed overheads, it would be more accurate to calculate the actual overhead cost per unit each month end by dividing the total number of all units actually produced during the month into the actual overheads incurred'. Critically examine the production director's suggestion.

Answer to self-assessment question

Barclay Engineering Co

Cost	Basis	Cutting £	M'ing £	Fin'g £	M'tce £	Pers. £
R and R	Area	1500	1500	1500	750	750
Heating	Cu.cap.	857	857	64	343	300
Power	M/c power	2000	5000	1000	1667	333
Dep'n	book val	2000	5200	800	1200	800
Ind. lab.}						
Misc. }	D.L.hours	4667	7000	4667	2333	2333
		11024	19557	8610	6293	4516
Pers.	-ditto-	1129	1694	1129	564	(4516)
M'tce	M/c power	1714	4286	857	(6857)	
		£13867	£25537	£10596		

(b) Overhead absorption rates:

Cutting	= £13867/2000	= £6.93/DLH
Machining	= £25537/3000	= £8.51/DLH
Finishing	= £10596/2000	= £5.30/DLH

Overheads for the job = $(2 \times £6.93) + (3 \times £8.51) + (1 \times £5.30)$
= £44.69

Answers to additional exercises

Exercise 1

$$\text{Cost per tonne} = \frac{\text{Total cost}}{\text{Completed output (tonnes)} + \text{C/WIP(tonnes)} - \text{O/WIP(tonnes)}}$$

Since the elements of WIP are not homogeneous in their degree of completion, the cost per tonne must be deduced on an element by element basis.

(a) Labour cost/tonne = $\dfrac{£1,400}{2,700 + (420 \times 80\%) - (350 \times 75\%)}$ = £0.505

Material cost/tonne = $\dfrac{£920}{2,700 + (420 \times 100\%) - (350 \times 100\%)}$ = £0.332

Overhead cost/tonne = $\dfrac{£1,250}{2,700 + (420 \times 90\%) - (350 \times 87.5\%)}$ = £0.451

Total cost/tonne = £1.288

(b) Closing WIP $= 420 \times [0.505 \times 80\%) + (0.332 \times 100\%) + (0.451 \times 90\%)$

$= 420 \times (0.404 + 0.332 + 0.406)$

$= £479.64$

(c) The process costing approach is not appropriate where there are significant differences from one cost unit to the next. It is a matter of managerial judgement as to the definition of the word 'significant'. The ease of calculating total cost per cost unit might encourage a process costing approach even where it is not strictly valid since the resultant figures would tend to be adequate for the purposes to which full cost information is typically put.

Exercise 2

(a)

$$\text{Materials/kg} = \frac{(400 \times 1.25) + 2000 \times 0.90)}{2400}$$

$$= \underline{£0.958/kg}$$

$$\text{Labour/kg} = \frac{(1000 \times 3.00)}{2000 + (75\% \times 400)} = \frac{3000}{2300}$$

$$= \underline{£1.304/kg}$$

$$\text{Overheads/kg} = \frac{£2000}{2000 + (80\% \times 400)} = \frac{2000}{2320}$$

$$= \underline{£0.862/kg}$$

Cost per kg of completed production

$$= \underline{£3.124} \text{ or } \underline{£6248} \text{ in total}$$

WIP is worth $0.958 + (75\% \times 1.304) + (80\% \times 0862)$

ie £2.626/ kg or £1050 in total

(Strictly, completed production and WIP should total £7300, the £2 difference is due to a rounding error.)

(b) Process costing tends to be used where production is of identical units rather than output which varies from unit to unit. Expedience/and cost/benefit are important factors here.

(c) Total costs can be used for:

    (1) Pricing
    (2) Measures of efficiency
    (3) Financial Accounting

Exercise 3

(a) Overhead apportionment

Overhead Cost	Basis of Appor'ment	Mach'ing Dept	Assembly Dept	Finishing Dept	Personnel Dept	Maint'nce Dept	Total
		£000	£000	£000	£000	£000	£000
Indirect materials	-	1500	1000	500	100	400	3500
Indirect labour	-	1000	1000	500	200	300	3000
Power	-	5000	1000	1000	200	800	8000
Rent and Rates	Floor area	3614	4819	1205	241	121	10000
Production admin	Number of employees	4200	6000	1800	--	–	12000
Machine insurance	Value of machinery	2308	462	230	–	–	3000
		17622	14281	5235	741	1621	39,500
Personnel dept costs	Number of employees	254	363	109	(741)	15	
					–	1636	
Maint'ance dept. costs	Machine hours	1227	245	164		(1636)	
		£19,103	£14,889	£5,508		–	

Direct labour rate:

    Machining dept   = $\dfrac{19103000}{1200000}$ = £15.92

    Assembly dept   = $\dfrac{14,889,000}{1,600,000}$ = £9.31

    Finishing dept   = $\dfrac{5508000}{500000}$ = £11.02

(b) It is something measurable about a cost unit, it is time based as are most overheads, it usually is regarded as a fair measure of overhead apportionment.

(c) The areas of usefulness are:

    (i)   in pricing
    (ii)   in valuing WIP and finished stock for financial accounting purposes
    (iii)   in assessing relative efficiency etc.

It is necessary for (ii) arising from the SSAP9. For purposes (i) and (iii) it is rather less valid, few firms are in a position independently to set prices, full cost information, relying as it does on arbitrary bases of apportionment, can be a misleading means of assessing efficiency etc.

Exercise 4

(a) Equivalent completed units:

Materials	$50 + (25 \times 50\%)$	=	62.5 units
Labour & Overheads	$50 + (25 \times 30\%)$	=	57.5 units

Cost per unit

Materials	$\dfrac{£5350}{62.5}$	=	£85.60
Labour	$\dfrac{£2940}{57.5}$	=	51.13
Overheads	$\dfrac{£4720}{57.5}$	=	82.09
Full cost/unit			£218.82

Exercise 5

(b)

Total overheads   £440

Overhead recovery rate/DLH = $\dfrac{£440}{300}$ = £1.47

Cost of job

	£
Labour 16 hours at £4/hour	64.00
Materials	125.00
Overheads 16 hours at £1.47/hour	23.52
	212.52
Loading 20% × £212.52	42.50
Price for the job	255.02

Exercise 6

(a)

	Machine Shop £	Fitting £	Canteen £	Maint'nce £
Allocated overheads	27,660	19,470	16,600	26,650
Rent, Rates etc (sq m)	9,000	3,500	2,500	2,000
Depreciation etc (Book value)	12,500	6,250	2,500	3,750
	49,160	29,220	21,600	32,400
Canteen (No. of Employees)	10,800	8,400	(21,600)	2,400
	59,960	37,620	–	34,800
Maintenance (70/30)	24,360	10,440		(34,800)
	£84,320	£48,060	–	–

M/c hour rate (for Machine Shop)

Hours	6 × 4200	=	25,200
	3 × 6900	=	20,700
	4 × 1700	=	6,800
			52,700 hours

Rate = $\dfrac{84320}{52700}$ =   £1.60/hour

DL Wages Rate (for Fitting Department)

£

Wages	12 × 4200	=	50,400
	3 × 6900	=	20,700
	21 × 1700	=	35,700
			£106,800

Rate $\dfrac{£48,060}{£106,800}$ =   £0.45/£

(b)   Product A

£

6 × £1.60	=	9.60
12 × £0.45	=	5.40
		£15.00

(c) The principal objection to the PD's suggestion is that it would not be possible to price a job until well after the end of each month, by which time all overheads for the month would be known.

A further objection is that the PD's suggestion could lead to fluctuations in cost from month to month which could lead to uncertainty, particularly regarding pricing policy.

UNIT 7

BUDGETS AND BUDGETARY CONTROL

THIS UNIT IS CONCERNED with the nature and purpose of budgets. The unit also deals with the way in which budgets are prepared and the impact of budgets on attitudes and behaviour within an organisation. On completion of this unit you should be able to:

- define a budget and explain the relationship between budgets, corporate objectives and long-term plans

- construct a budget from relevant data and explain the inter-relationship of the various budgets within an organisation

- outline the major benefits of preparing budgets and discuss the effect of budgets on attitudes and behaviour within an organisation

- explain the nature and purpose of zero-base budgets.

Outline of the unit

THIS UNIT BEGINS BY establishing budgeting within the decision making and planning process of all organisations or, at least, all organisations which are successful in the long term.

The unit shows how the broad objective or objectives of the organisation are converted into long-term strategic plans, and then into short-term plans of action. You should be clear that the budget target for sales output for a particular business for a particular month is, ultimately, working towards the achievement of the overall objectives for that business.

A good example of the relationship between objectives, long-term plans and short-term plans is a government, either national or local. The political party has its overall, almost permanent, policies. For example those of the British Conservative Party probably include strong military defence, effective policing and a vigorous economic private sector, among other things. These are part of the party's philosophy and do not alter over time. These are included in the objectives of any conservative government. In the run up to an election, the party will put forward its plans for the next period of government, should the party win the election. This is the long-term plan, putting flesh on the bones of objectives. If the party wins the election, it must then start to set short-term plans or budgets. These will include detailed plans on raising finance, tax rates, etc. They will also include detailed plans for spending on various projects and services for which governments are responsible.

The unit makes the point that long-term planning and budgeting is the job of managers generally. Accountants should have technical expertise, which make them useful to their management colleagues in these tasks, but it is not the accountants who make the budgeting decisions.

The unit then goes on to consider possible planning horizons. These are normally three to five years for long-term plans and one year for the more detailed budget. Typically, budgets are broken down into shorter (eg one month) control periods.

In many organisations, setting budgets is a large scale annual operation which occurs shortly before the start of the new financial year. Other organisations set budgets on a more continual basis. The advantages of this latter approach, *rolling budgeting*, are discussed in the unit.

The unit makes clear the relationship between budgets and forecast. You should be in no doubt that a budget states what management **intends** to achieve in various areas.

The unit outlines the four generally accepted advantages of having a sound system of budgeting. These are:

● Promotion of forward thinking

● Promotion of co-ordination between all of the various facets of the organisation

● Motivation of managers

● Provision of the basis for exercising control over the organisation.

It is probably not unreasonable to say that all successful organisations (businesses, governments, charities), of any size larger than tiny, have sound budgetary system. Budgeting is extremely widely practised.

The unit goes on to explain how budgets can be useful in helping to exercise control, that is making things happen according what was meant to happen, rather than randomly. We shall consider, in some detail, the issue of control in the next unit.

The unit explains how budgets can be used to achieve co-ordination between departments. This is necessary to try to ensure that what the sales department is selling is being produced by the production department. It is easy to imagine the problems, financial and otherwise, which are likely to ensue if goods, which do not exists, are being promised to customers or where the personnel department has taken on more production workers than production and sales plans make necessary.

Figure 3 (see page 243) shows how the various budgets all link together.

If budgets are to be derived which can provide the benefits outlined earlier in the unit, there must be some formal process for preparing budgets. This process is outlined in this unit and should be studied carefully.

Until about 25 years ago, most organisations carried out most of their accounting and budgeting by hand, or by rather unsophisticated mechanical methods. This meant that the process of budget setting was often a nightmare. The co-ordinating aspect of budgeting means that all aspects of the organisation must dovetail together. This usually means that some form of iterative (trial and error) approach is necessary, before a set of budgets can emerge, which all fit together.

Now that we have cheap computers, budgeting is a much simpler task, with most of the clerical drudgery taken out of the process. This probably means that we now tend to have much better and more sophisticated budgeting within organisations.

In this unit the process of preparing a particular budget is explained and illustrated. This includes some discussion of a suitable layout for the budget. You will see that a cash budget has been chosen for the illustration and the reason for this choice is given. You should not lose sight of the fact, however, that the cash budget will be just one of a large number of budgets, all of which must fit together. You should follow carefully through the example.

We also examine some of the other budgets (besides the cash budget). Activity 9 gives you the opportunity to prepare three budgets for a business.

When budgets are first prepared, they are intended to be plans to be achieved. In the period between the preparation of the budget and the particular period to which it relates circumstances may change, however. If they change in such a way as to render the original plan unreasonable, it is pointless to pretend that such a change has not occurred. In these circumstances it will probably be useful to revise or 'flex' the budget to reflect the changed circumstances. Since budgets must inter-link with one another, flexing one budget is likely to mean that other targets will also need to be adjusted.

In the next unit, we shall see that when using budgets for control purposes it is usually necessary to flex the budget. We shall also see that the reason for the need to flex the budget is carefully considered and that attempts are usually made to identify the manager accountable for this need.

It might be useful to remind ourselves that the only purpose of all branches of accounting is to affect peoples' behaviour. Accounting is all about providing information to help people to make decisions and to exercise control. Decision making and control involve people taking actions of some description or another. Accounting information should indicate, to those people, what are the bests actions to take. Accounting has no other purpose. If it cannot affect peoples' behaviour it is a complete waste of time and money. In view of this, it is highly pertinent to try to assess how accounting effects behaviour.

The unit undertakes a brief consideration of the effects of budgets on peoples' behaviour. It specifically considers questions of the motivational effects of budgets, ie are managers more effective when they are working towards targets than when this is not the case. The question of the desirability of managers being involved in their own target setting is also considered. The unit goes on to consider the problem that, if managers have influence in the targets set in the budget, they may deliberately seek targets which are not in the best interests of the organisation.

The unit also addresses the problem of trying to assess managerial performance through budgets. Particular problems include:

● Outcomes are not always within the influence of managers.

● Managers can sometimes influence the way in which events are accounted for, so as to show themselves in a better light than the real events justify.

● The danger that managers may make bad long-term decisions in order to boost short-term performance, eg not investing in research and development.

The last section of the unit looks at zero-base budgets (ZBB). This is an approach to setting budgets, where all items in each budget must be justified as if they were being proposed for the first time. They are particularly appropriate to central and local governments, where many of the budgets are concerned with the amount of money to be spent on each service provided by the authority. Here it would not be assumed that if £X million was spent on, say, providing nursery schools for children under five last year, that amount would automatically be the starting point for negotiating this year's budget. Instead the whole question of providing nursery education at all, and, perhaps, alternative approaches to its provision would be addressed, in conjunction with the accompanying costs. ZBB has some obvious benefits and defects, as well as some not so obvious ones. These are considered in this section.

Now that you have some broad idea of what the unit is about let us consider the detail.

Business objectives, long-term plans and budgets

IN A PREVIOUS UNIT we saw how important it is for businesses to define clearly what they are ultimately seeking to achieve. To survive and prosper over the longer term, a business must possess a clear sense of direction and must gear its activities to the achievement of specified objectives. This implies the need for a systematic approach to both the setting of objectives and to planning for the future.

Planning within an organisation is often a two-stage process. In the first stage a business will produce a long-term plan. This plan will set out the objectives to be pursued and the broad direction of the business over the longer term. This long-term plan will often cover a five-year period although, as we shall see below, the planning horizon can vary between businesses. The long term plan represents a major exercise for the management of a business and requires them to begin by defining clearly their objectives.

Having reached agreement on objectives for the business, the managers may then identify a number of possible courses of action which could be pursued and which are consistent with the objectives which have been formulated. Information regarding each course of action must be collected and should then be properly evaluated. The evaluation process will consider the likely impact of each course of action on the future financial health of the business. It will involve preparation of profit and cash flow projections as well as projections of future financial position. Following this detailed evaluation the most suitable course of action will be selected.

The long-term plan will reflect the course of action which has been selected and will usually set out:

- capital investments to be made

- profitability and cash flow requirements

- the products or services the business will offer

- the market which the business will seek to serve

- the labour requirements

- the raw material requirements.

Having set out the objectives of the business and the broad direction to be pursued the second stage of planning can begin. This second stage operates within the framework of the long-term plan and seeks to produce a detailed short-term plan for the business. This short-term plan is referred to as the *budget*. A budget can be formally defined as a financial plan for a future period of time. 'Financial' in this context implies that the budget is stated in monetary terms. Although managers may start the budgeting process by dealing with non-monetary measures such as number of items produced and sold, number of workers employed and quantities of material to be purchased these will ultimately be expressed in monetary terms.

The budget will provide details for the forthcoming year of such things as:

- sales, expenses and profits (losses)

- cash receipts and payments

- debtors and creditors

- levels of stock held.

The sequence involved in the planning process can be shown diagrammatically as follows overleaf:

It can be seen that objectives, long-term plans and budgets are related elements of the planning process. The objectives provide the sense of direction for the business and, once set, may remain the same for a long-time (although changes can and do occur). The long-term plan provides a means of pursuing the objectives which have been set and the budgets produced indicate how the long-term objectives will be achieved.

Figure 1

The sequence of the planning

process

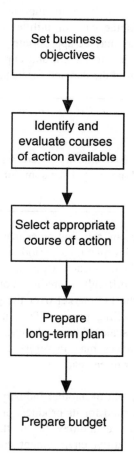

Set business objectives

Identify and evaluate courses of action available

Select appropriate course of action

Prepare long-term plan

Prepare budget

Derivation of long-term plans and budgets

IT MUST BE EMPHASISED that setting out the long-term plans and budgets for a business is the task of management. Although budgets set out the planned activities of the business in monetary terms it is *not* the function of the accountant to produce budgets for each area of activity. Indeed, the accountant is rarely in a position to produce sensible budgets for most areas of the business. In the case of sales, for example, it is the general sales manager who, in consultation with district sales managers and marketing colleagues, will usually be able to produce the most realistic measure of what is achievable. The role of the accountant in the budgeting process is to help in the co-ordination of the various budgets and to provide additional data (eg past sales performance) to help managers in deciding on the appropriate targets that should be set.

It was mentioned above that a typical long term planning horizon is five years. However, this need no necessarily be the case. The type of industry within which the business operates will be an important factor in deciding on the appropriate planning period. In the case of utilities (gas, water, electricity, etc) a planning horizon of five years may be appropriate as demand for the products or services is not likely to be subject to violent and unpredictable fluctuations. Similarly, a food manufacturer may find the demand for its products is fairly predictable over time.

Activity 1

Can you think of an industry where a planning period of five years may be considered too long by at least some of the businesses within it? Why is this the case?

A business involved in, say, computer manufacturing may decide that five years is an unrealistically long planning period since the environment and technology can change dramatically over such a period. Moreover, the nature and extent of the change will be too difficult to predict. You need only think of the changes which have occurred in the PC market over the past five years (widespread use of PCs, rapid falls in the selling price of PCs, massive increases in their capability) to appreciate that the scale of these changes are a planner's nightmare! A computer manufacturing business may therefore adopt a planning period which is much shorter – say, two or three years.

You may have thought of another industry which is equally valid because it has a highly unstable demand for its products or services. This instability may be due to possible changes in technology (as in the example above), or due to possible changes in the competitive environment, consumer tastes, government policies, etc.

The budget usually covers a full year and is usually broken down into monthly periods in order to establish monthly targets. In many cases the annual budget will, in any case, be built up from projected monthly figures. However, in some types of business it may be very difficult to establish, at the beginning of the budget period, the detailed financial targets for each of the 12 months comprising the budget. In such a situation, a business may decide to set financial targets for (say) each quarter and provide only a detailed monthly breakdown for the first quarter of the year. Towards the end of the first quarter it may be possible to produce detailed monthly targets for the second quarter and so on. Thus, managers will establish detailed monthly targets only as the year unfolds.

A budget may be an annual exercise for the business. This will mean that towards the end of the year a new budget for the forthcoming twelve-month period will be produced. Alternatively, the budget can be continually extended. For example, each month the budget for the same month in the following year is set. This will mean there will always be fairly detailed plans for a full 12 months into the future. This type of budget is referred to as a 'rolling' budget.

Activity 2

What do you see as the advantages of 'rolling' budgets as compared with annual budget setting?

Rolling budgets have the following advantages over annual budgets:

- fairly detailed plans are available for usually a full year into the future at any given moment. In the case of annual budgets, the availability of detailed future plans will depend on the particular point in the budget cycle

- looking to the future becomes a constant management activity rather than simply an annual exercise

- potential problems (eg a cash shortage) which the budget identifies is brought to the attention of managers a full year before the event thereby allowing time for plans to be revised in order to overcome the problem.

The relationship between budgets and forecasts

IT WAS MENTIONED ABOVE that a budget is a financial *plan* for a period. This is not the same as a forecast.

Activity 3

What do you think is the major difference between a budget and a forecast?

As mentioned above a budget is a plan rather than a forecast. The word plan implies an intention to achieve whereas a forecast implies what is expected to happen; a much more passive approach.

In making their plans businesses will obviously need to take account of forecasts of such things as the economic environment, size of the market, etc in much the same way as a person may take account of the weather forecast when making plans for some outdoor activity, eg spending a day at the beach. However, the budget is what the business intends to happen, not merely what it expects will happen.

The benefits of budgets

BUDGETS ARE GENERALLY REGARDED as providing the following benefits to a business:

> ● *they can promote forward thinking.* This can result in the early identification of short-term problems which may, in turn, allow managers time to overcome them.

> ● *they can promote co-ordination between various aspects of the business.* It is vital that all aspects of the business are pulling in the same direction. For example, if sales and production are unco-ordinated sales may be made for goods which cannot be delivered, or goods may be produced for which there is no market. Both of these possibilities are unhealthy for the business.

> ● *they can motivate managers.* Under a system of budgeting managers are given a clearly defined task (eg to achieve £x000 of sales) which can be directly related to the overall objectives of the business. Some believe that this clear definition of what is required, and the relationship between the task and the overall objectives of the business, can help motivate managers.

> It was mentioned above that budgeting is a management exercise and therefore managers should participate in the setting of budget targets. It is sometimes argued that where a manager has contributed to the setting of his/her own budget there will be a greater sense of 'ownership' which will result in the manager trying harder to achieve the targets set.

> ● *they can provide a basis for a system of control.* In order for senior management to monitor performance of subordinates and to exercise control over the business it requires a benchmark against which to assess performance. The logical benchmark to employ is the one which it has itself established as the target i.e the budget. In fact, a general definition of control is compelling events to conform to a plan. It is impossible to control something other than in relation to some predetermined plan or standard. Even when we talk about controlling a motor car, we mean making the car behave in a manner which the driver planned, even though that plan may have been made only a second earlier.

If information is available concerning the actual performance for a defined period this can be compared to earlier planned performance. This comparison of actual performance against planned performance provides the basis for control. The control process can be shown as follows overleaf:

Figure 2

The budgetary control

process

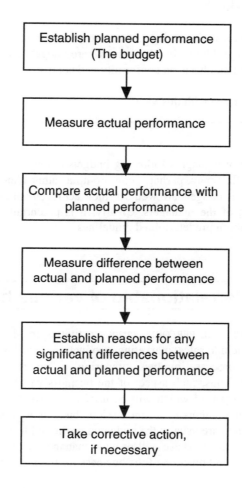

By establishing a system of control such as described above, we permit *management by exception* principles to operate. This is a technique which aims to ensure senior managers spend their time in an efficient and effective manner. A major function of senior management is to develop plans for the future. We have seen above that it is important to anticipate future threats and opportunities and to develop appropriate plans to deal with these. Providing senior managers receive information concerning actual information relating to performance which correspond to earlier planned performance they need not become closely involved in the day-to-day running of the business. Their time may be better spent on forward planning. It is only when there is a significant divergence between planned and actual performance that senior managers need become involved and deal with those areas of the business where the budget is not being achieved. Thus, senior managers need only concern themselves with the exceptional cases of things going wrong rather than the normal case of things going according to plan.

Activity 4

'Budgets restrain managers from exercising intuition and flair in dealing with business problems. In a business where budgets are given importance there is too much emphasis on conformity and control.'

Do you agree with this view?

The notion of managers following budgets rather than following their intuition and exercising flair may, perhaps, conjure up a rather bland view of the manager's job. In practice, if budgets are well set, their achievement can still require skill and flair on the part of the managers. Clearly, it is potentially disastrous for manager's to operate without predetermined guidelines.

The interrelationship of various budgets

A BUSINESS WILL PERFORM various activities in pursuit of its objectives. These activities include sales, marketing, production, distribution, administration, etc. The budgeting process involves preparing a separate budget for each activity undertaken. Thus, each aspect of the business will be set targets to achieve in the forthcoming period which will be used as a basis for performance evaluation and control. The contents of all the various budgets will be summarised in the *master budgets* which are usually the budgeted profit and loss account, cash flow statement and balance sheet. These will provide managers with an overview of the expected performance and position of the business for the forthcoming period.

Figure 3 reveals the relationship between the individual budgets and the master budgets. In this case, a trading business, ie a business which purchases goods in their completed state and then resells them, is used for illustration purposes.

The figure indicates the individual budgets which may be prepared by the trading business. As stated earlier, these individual budgets are then used to draw up the master budgets for the business. The links between the various individual budgets and the master budgets are denoted by a continuous line. Thus, the sales budget will provide information for the budgeted profit and loss account and the cash budget of the trading business, the capital expenditure budget will provide information for the cash budget and the budgeted balance sheet etc.

Figure 3

Relationship between budgets

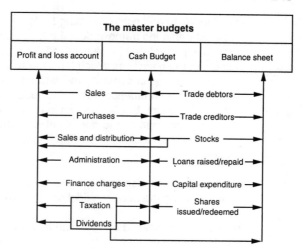

In addition, to the relationship between the individual budgets and the master budgets, there are also interrelationships between the individual budgets. For example, there is a strong and direct link between sales and the trade debtors budget, between purchases and the trade creditors budget and between finance charges and loans raised. In addition the level of sales will be an important determinant of the level of purchases, sales and distribution costs, capital expenditure, etc. These interrelationships are numerous and will vary in strength. For the sake of clarity they are excluded from the diagram above, however, you must be aware of there existence.

Preparing budgets

ORGANISATIONS WILL TEND TO adopt budget preparation procedures which are most appropriate to their needs. Hence, there are likely to be differences between organisations in the way in which budgets are prepared. Nevertheless, the preparation of budgets normally involves a series of stages that have to be followed. An illustration of the kind of stages that occur in the budgeting process is as follows:

> ● *establish a budget committee.* A committee consisting of members of the board of directors and managers in key functional areas will often be formed to take responsibility for the preparation of the final budgets. They will have a responsibility to communicate relevant information to those involved in the budgeting process. They will also have the responsibility for co-ordinating and finally agreeing the various budgets which are prepared and for preparing the master budgets. A budget officer, usually an accountant, will often be appointed to assist the budget committee in carrying out its tasks.

● *establishing and communicating budget guidelines.* Budgets are prepared within the framework of the long-term plan of the business and it is important that those involved in preparing budgets take account of the objectives which have been set. Similarly any long-term programmes or commitments which have been agreed and which span, or commence within, the budget period must also be taken into account. Likely changes in the environment such as changes in the market, the rate of inflation, the degree of competition etc should also be communicated to preparers of budgets.

The budget committee should be responsible for establishing and communicating the budget guidelines to relevant managers.

In larger businesses, a *budget manual* will be available to help managers prepare their budgets. The budget manual will outline the stages in the budgeting process and the responsibilities of each manager. It will also usually provide a recommended format for budgets to be presented and a timetable for the preparation of draft budgets and agreement of the final budgets.

● *identify key factor (limiting factor).* It is important that the key factor, or limiting factor, for the business is identified at the outset. The key factor will set limits to the growth of the business and will determine its level of activity or output during the budget period. This key factor will provide the starting point for preparation of the various budgets. Only when the key factor budget is prepared will it be possible to prepare sensible budgets for other areas. For many businesses the key factor will be its sales. The degree of competition or the size of the market may well determine the level of sales which are possible. Thus, many businesses will begin the budgeting process by preparing a sales budget. Other budgets can then be prepared based on the level of sales expected during the budget period.

Activity 5

What other factors, besides sales, might act as a limiting factor for a business?

A business may have limited production capacity in the short-term and so this factor may determine the budget level of output. The availability of skilled workers or raw materials may also limit the output of the business.

● *prepare draft budgets for other areas.* Draft budgets can be developed in other areas using either a 'bottom up' or 'top down' approach. The former approach will ensure a high level of participation in the budgeting process as budgets will be developed, in the first instance, by lower levels of management.

To illustrate the 'bottom up' approach it may be useful to consider the preparation of a sales budget for a nationwide business. In this case, each district sales manager would submit a draft budget for his/her particular district to a regional sales manager who has overall responsibility for a number of districts within the region. Each district sales manager would have to defend his/her budget and amendments to the budget may take place after discussions and negotiation with the regional sales manager. Having gone through this process with each district sales manager and compiling a sales budget for the region, the regional sales manager will now submit the regional budget to the national sales manager who has overall responsibility for a number of regions. The regional sales manager will be required to defend his/her budget and, once again, amendments may take place following discussions and negotiations with the national sales manager. Thus, we can see that, at each level of management, budgets are discussed and refined before passing on to the next, higher, level.

Activity 6

How do you think the 'top down' approach to preparing budgets would differ from the 'bottom up approach'?

With the 'top down' approach budgets originate at the higher levels of management and targets are communicated to the lower levels of management for their particular area of responsibility. Although some form of consultation may take place, both before and after the setting of the budgets, the lower levels of management do not participate as fully under this approach as in the 'bottom up' approach.

- *co-ordinating the budgets which have been prepared.* The budget committee will have a responsibility to ensure that the various budgets prepared are in harmony with each other and with the overall objectives of the business.

- *preparing the master budgets.* The budgeted profit and loss account, cash flow statement and balance sheet can now be prepared from the various budgets. These master budgets will be prepared by the budget committee and will summarise the targets which have been set for the budget period.

Budgets and the computer

IN A BUSINESS OF any size, the preparation of budgets will rely heavily on the use of computers. There are available numerous spreadsheet models which can be used in preparing budgets and which can be of great value in the manipulation of budget data. You will already be aware from your earlier studies that a spreadsheet is, in essence, a worksheet consisting of rows and columns which can be used to display both textual and numerical material and which can undertake mathematical calculations. Many spreadsheet models also now provide facilities for graphical display, statistical calculations and for database functions.

The spreadsheet is an ideal tool for preparing budgets. The various budgets, including the master budgets, can be assembled onto a spreadsheet for manipulation purposes. Budgeting is often an iterative process. It is extremely useful, therefore, to be able to change one budget and to then see the consequences of this change on other budgets quickly and without too much effort. Where spreadsheets are employed this kind of adjustment can be carried out very quickly and accurately. Figures, sub-totals and totals are automatically adjusted to take account of changed inputs.

When budgets are being prepared managers will often wish to examine and evaluate a number of possible scenarios. For example, they may wish to examine the likely impact on profits given (i) a 4% rise (ii) an 8% rise and (iii) a 10% rise in the price of its products. This kind of 'what if' analysis can also be carried out on a spreadsheet quickly and accurately.

Preparing budgets – a worked example

IN THIS SECTION WE will work through an example involving the preparation of a budget. The particular budget to be prepared is a cash budget. This has been chosen because most economic aspects of an organisation reflect themselves in cash sooner or later and so the cash budget reflects the whole business.

There is no required format for any budget. Budgets are documents used within the business by managers and, as such, their style and content need only reflect the requirements of the managers. However, there are certain features which would typically be encountered in the cash budget of most businesses. These include:

(i) month by month data

(ii) the budget being set out in columns, one column for each month

(iii) monthly receipts of cash, item by item, also showing total receipts

(iv) monthly payments of cash, item by item, also showing total payments

(v) a monthly net receipts or net payments figure ie (iii) - (iv). This is sometimes referred to as the 'net cash flow'.

(vi) a cash balance for the end of each month. This is derived by taking the opening cash balance and adding the net cash flow for the month (ie item (v) above)

Let us now look at an example of a cash budget.

Example

George Cook and Co, retailers, plans to have £2,000 in its current account in the bank on 1 January. The budgeted income statement for the following six months is as follows:

	Jan £	Feb £	Mar £	Apr £	May £	June £
Sales (all for cash)	5,000	5,000	5,500	5,500	6,000	6,000
Cost of goods sold	3,000	3,000	3,300	3,300	3,600	3,600
Wages	320	320	320	320	320	320
Electricity	200	200	200	150	100	100
Stationery etc	60	60	60	60	60	60
Depreciation	150	150	150	150	150	150
Total expenses	3,730	3,730	4,030	3,980	4,230	4,230
Net profit	1,270	1,270	1,470	1,520	1,770	1,770

The business plans to increase its stock in trade by £500 worth in each of the months February to April (inclusive). Purchases of stock are paid for one month after purchase (the December purchases were £3,500). Wages and stationery etc are paid in the month concerned. Electricity is paid quarterly in arrears in March and June. New electronic cash registers will be bought (and paid for) in March for £3,000. The proprietors of the business plan to take out £1,000 each month as drawings.

You are required to show the firm's cash budget for the six-months ending 30 June.

Solution

Cash budget for the six months ended 30 June

	Jan £	Feb £	Mar £	Apr £	May £	June £
Receipts (inflows)						
Sales	5,000	5,000	5,500	5,500	6,000	6,000
Payments (outflows)						
Purchases	3,500	3,000	3,500	3,800	3,800	3,600
Wages	320	320	320	320	320	320
Electricity			600			350
Stationery	60	60	60	60	60	60
Cash registers			3,000			
Drawings	1,000	1,000	1,000	1,000	1,000	1,000
Total payments	4,880	4,380	8,480	5,180	5,180	5,330
Net receipts/ (payments)	120	620	(2,980)	320	820	670
Opening balance	2,000	2120	2,740	(240)	80	900
Closing balance	2,120	2,740	(240)	80	900	1,570

Notes to the solution

(a) Purchases for each month must be sufficient to replace the stock sold during that month plus any increase in stock during that month.

(b) Depreciation has been ignored because it is not related to cash.

The cash budget would tell the business, amongst other things, that unless it alters its plans it will suffer a cash shortage during the month of March, ie a short-term problem has been identified which could not have come to light other than through some form of cash budget.

Activity 7

How might the management of George Cook and Co go about solving the problem of the cash shortage during March?

There is a number of possible ways to overcome the temporary cash shortage, although each option is likely to have its drawbacks. These options include the following:

- delaying until April the March payment to creditors for purchases. (However, the possible loss of goodwill by suppliers must be taken into account)

- delaying the payment of the electricity bill until April. (However, this might lead to the supply being cut off)

- expanding activities more gradually, since the rapid expansion is a major cause of the problem. (However, the possible loss of customer goodwill must be taken into account)

- delaying acquisition and/or payment of the cash registers. (However, this may be inconvenient or create problems with a supplier)

- delaying part of the March drawings. (However, this may be necessary to live on)

- seeking overdraft facilities from the bank. (However, interest will be incurred).

Some combination of options may provide the most feasible solution, eg reduction in drawings plus a small overdraft at the bank.

Activity 8

'Managers are really only interested in the "bottom line" ie the final cash balance figure when looking at the cash budget'.

Do you agree with this view?

Although the final cash balance is important to managers, it is also important for managers to understand how that final figure was derived. Thus, managers will carefully analyse the nature and amounts of cash receipts and payments during each month and the effect of these on monthly cash flows. Once a draft cash budget has been prepared it may be necessary for managers to try and influence the timing of particular budgeted inflows and outflows in order to improve the cash flow position of the business.

Preparing budgets – some further points

IN ACTIVITY 9 BELOW you are given the opportunity to prepare some budgets from information provided. In this activity you are required to produce a stock budget for a trading business and a budgeted profit and loss account in addition to a cash budget for a period. These additional budgets should not pose any real problems providing you understand the form and content of each budget.

The stock budget will record the expected stock inflows and outflows of stock for a period and will adjust for opening stocks held in order to derive the closing balance of stocks. A stock budget, like a cash budget, may be prepared to show the monthly balances. A format for a stock budget of a trading business is set out below:

Stock budget for three months to 31 March 19x4

	January £000	February £000	March £000
Opening stock	120	140	120
Stock purchased	200	240	270
	320	380	390
Cost of stock sold	180	260	330
Closing stock	140	120	60

When preparing a budgeted profit and loss account, the format and content will be basically the same as when you prepared these statements on a historic basis in your earlier studies. The only real difference is that the budgeted profit and loss account uses projected information rather than past information. In practice, the budgeted profit and loss account may be broken down into monthly periods in order to show expected levels of performance for each month. However, accounting exercises for students often only require preparation of a profit and loss account for the whole budget period.

Activity 9

Changes Ltd owns a chain of 8 shops selling fashion goods. In the past the company maintained a healthy cash balance. However, this has fallen in recent months and at the end of September 19x6 it had an overdraft of £70,000. In view of this, its managing director has asked you to prepare a cash budget for the next six months. You have collected the following data:

	Oct £000	Nov £000	Dec £000	Jan £000	Feb £000	Mar £000
Sales	140	180	260	60	100	120
Purchases	160	180	140	50	50	50
Wages and salaries	30	30	40	30	30	32
Rent			60			
Rates						40
Other expenses	20	20	20	20	20	20
Refurbishing shops				80		

Stock at 1 October amounted to £170,000 and creditors were £70,000. The purchases in October, November and December are contractually committed and those in January, February and March, the minimum necessary to restock with spring fashions. Cost of sales is 50% of sales and suppliers allow one month's credit on purchases. Taxation of £90,000 is due on 1 January. The rates payment is a charge for a whole year and other expenses includes depreciation of £10,000 per month.

Required:

(a) Prepare a cash budget for the six months to 31 March 19x7 showing the cash balance at the end of each month.

(b) Prepare a stock budget for the six months to 31 March 19x7 showing the stock levels at the end of each month.

(c) Prepare a budgeted profit and loss account for the six months ended 31 March 19x7.

(d) What problems might Changes face in the next six months and how would you attempt to overcome them?

The cash budget for Changes Ltd will be as follows:

Cash budget for the six months ended 31 March 19x7

	Oct £000	Nov £000	Dec £000	Jan £000	Feb £000	Mar. £000
Receipts						
Cash sales	140	180	260	60	100	120
Payments						
Stock purchases	70	160	180	140	50	50
Wages	30	30	40	30	30	32
Rent			60			
Rates						40
Shop refurbishment				80		
Tax payment				90		
Other expenses	10	10	10	10	10	10
	110	200	290	350	90	132
Cash flow	30	(20)	(30)	(290)	10	(12)
Opening Balance	(70)	(40)	(60)	(90)	(380)	(370)
Closing Balance	(40)	(60)	(90)	(380)	(370)	(382)

The stock budget for Changes Ltd will be as follows:

	Oct £000	Nov £000	Dec £000	Jan £000	Feb £000	Mar £000
Opening Stock	170	260	350	360	380	380
Stock purchased	160	180	140	50	50	50
	330	440	490	410	430	430
Cost of stock sold	70	90	130	30	50	60
Closing stock	260	350	360	380	380	370

The budgeted profit and loss account for Changes will be as follows:

Budgeted profit and loss account for the six months ended 31 March 19x7

	£000	£000
Sales		860
Less cost of goods sold (50%)		430
Gross profit		430
Wages and salaries	192	
Rent	60	
Rates	20	
Other expenses	120	392
Net profit*		38

*Shop refurbishment has been treated as capital expenditure and will not therefore appear in the budgeted profit and loss account.

The cash budget reveals a significant rise in the bank overdraft in the final three months of the period. This is largely due to the fact that the purchase commitments are high in relation to anticipated sales. We are told in the question that there are contractual commitments for October, November and December purchases and that January, February and March purchases are considered the minimum necessary to restock with spring fashions. These factors place severe constraints on management's room to manoeuvre. The company may try and negotiate a higher overdraft facility for the business in order to deal with the cash flow problem. If this is not feasible, other sources of finance such as a share issue may be considered. The company may also try to reduce its financing requirements during the period by postponing the shop refurbishment programme.

Now try this self-assessment question. This is intended to give you the opportunity to see whether you have grasped the material so far. You should probably be able to complete this in a half to three quarters of an hour. Don't worry if it takes you longer. The main point is that, once you have completed it, you are clear on all of the points which it involves. It is not really helpful to look at the answer to this until you have completed your answer.

Self-assessment question

Linpet was incorporated on 1 June 19x9. The opening balance sheet of the company was as follows:

	£
Assets	
Cash at bank	60,000
Share capital	
£1 ordinary shares	60,000

During June the company intends to make payments of £40,000 for a freehold property, £10,000 for equipment and £6,000 for a motor vehicle. The company will also purchase initial trading stock costing £22,000 on credit.

The company has produced the following estimates:

(i) Sales for June will be £8,000 and will increase at the rate of £3,000 per month until September. In October, sales will rise to £22,000 and in subsequent months sales will be maintained at this figure.

(ii) The gross profit percentage on goods sold will be 25%.

Continued over . . .

(iii) There is a risk that supplies of trading stock will be interrupted towards the end of the accounting year. The company, therefore, intends to build up its initial level of stock (ie £22,000) by purchasing £1,000 of stock each month in addition to the monthly purchases necessary to satisfy monthly sales. All purchases of stock (including the initial stock) will be on one month's credit.

(iv) Sales will be divided equally between cash and credit sales. Credit customers are expected to pay two months after the sale is agreed.

(v) Wages and salaries will be £900 per month. Other overheads will be £500 per month for the first four months and £650 thereafter. Both types of expense will be payable when incurred.

(vi) 80% of sales will be generated by salesmen who will receive 5% commission on sales. The commission is payable one month after the sale is agreed.

(vii) The company intends to purchase further equipment in November 19x9 for £7,000 cash.

(viii) Depreciation is to be provided at the rate of 5% per annum on freehold property and 20% per annum on equipment. (Depreciation has not been included in the overheads mentioned in (v) above.)

Required:

Prepare a cash budget for Linpet Ltd for the six month period to 30 November 19x9

(The answer to this self-assessment question is at the back of the unit.)

Fixed and flexible budgets

IT IS USEFUL TO distinguish between fixed and flexible budgets. A fixed budget will remain the same whatever the level of activity of the business. A flexible budget, on the other hand, will change according to the level of activity which the business is expected to achieve. In order to prepare flexible budgets it is necessary to separate costs into their fixed and variable elements. We can then estimate future levels of expenditure for each possible level of activity. This form of budgeting is useful where it is difficult to predict the level of activity for the budget period.

In effect, flexible budgeting requires the preparation of a number of budgets rather than a single budget. For example, a series of production budgets may be prepared to cover a range of possible levels of output. At the end of the budget period we can then compare the expenditure incurred for the actual level of output with the expected expenditure for that level of output.

In practice, a business may use fixed budgets for certain areas of the business (eg accounts and administration) where there is a very large fixed cost element. Flexible budgets will be used in areas where costs are more sensitive to changes in the level of activity (eg sales and production.)

Reading

You should now read Reader Article 7.1 'Budgeting and cost management: a route to continuous improvement' by Robin Bellis-Jones.

In this article the author argues that, in practice, conventional budgeting is too often seen as a costly and burdensome routine which reinforces bad practice and hinders response to changes in the business environment. He then cites a number of reasons why budgets fail in their ability to effectively control the organisation. Having considered the problems, the author then sets out the initial steps required to deal with them and the benefits which should flow.

Points to consider:

Can you think of other potential problems with conventional budgeting? Will the solutions proposed overcome all of the problems cited by the author?

Budgets as targets – some behavioural issues

BUDGETS CANNOT BE VIEWED simply as a set of financial statements. The way in which they are prepared and used can have a significant effect on management attitudes and behaviour. This, in turn can have an effect on the performance of the business.

It was mentioned above that budgets can be used to motivate managers. There is ample evidence from research studies in psychology that the setting of clearly defined targets (rather than simply urging people to do well or saying nothing at all) can lead to improved performance. Moreover, there is also evidence that increasing the degree of difficulty in the targets set can lead to improved performance. However, targets must not be set at an unrealistically high level. Where the degree of difficulty is seen as being too great, no real effort will be made to achieve the targets set. Performance may, therefore, be lower than if targets were regarded by participants as being achievable. It is often argued that, when setting budget targets, they should be challenging but achievable. What is regarded as being achievable, however, is likely to vary between individual managers. This suggests that target setting should take account of the characteristics of the particular managers responsible for achieving the budgets.

Where budget targets are accepted by those managers responsible for their achievement, a higher level of performance is likely to result. The implications of this seem to be that managers should participate in the setting of their own targets as this is likely to increase their level of acceptance. Managers may feel more committed to a budget target which they have helped to establish themselves. This idea seems to be supported by certain studies which have shown that both management performance and job satisfaction can be improved where a business adopts a participative approach to the setting of budgets.

Activity 10

Can you think of any problems that may arise as a result of increasing the level of participation in budgeting?

Whilst participation in budgeting can have a beneficial effect on performance there are possible dangers. Managers may seek to reduce the degree of difficulty in the budget targets in order to make them more easily achievable. This is particularly true where the performance of the manager is being evaluated by reference to the budget target. In some cases, managers may seek to build some 'slack' into the budget in order for it to be used at a later date when the manager is faced with a difficult environment. Thus, participation must be used carefully and must not be allowed to enable some managers to avoid taking on challenging tasks.

Where there are significant variances from budget standards, senior managers must investigate *why* they have occurred. There may be a number of possible reasons why a particular variance has occurred. In some cases it may be that the budget targets have been set at an unrealistic level. In other cases it may be that certain managers have under-performed.

Activity 11

Assume you are a senior manager within a business.

How would you deal with a subordinate manager who has failed to meet the budget targets which have been set?

Where it is found that junior managers have failed to meet the budget targets it is important that this is dealt with in a positive manner. Strong criticism of a junior managers may simply reduce their level of motivation and this, in turn, may further reduce their level of performance in the future. Criticism may spur the junior managers to greater efforts and may lead to the reporting of smaller variances in future periods. However, the methods involved in achieving those smaller variances may have undesirable effects on the long-term prospects of the business. For example, a divisional manager may reduce the expenditure on training and developing employees in order to boost short-term profits. However, this policy may harm the competitive position and profits over the longer term. A more useful approach than simply criticising managers may be to talk the problems through with them in order to find out the problems experienced and to establish more effective ways of achieving the tasks which have been set.

Budget bias

IT WAS MENTIONED ABOVE that managers may seek to build 'slack' into budgets in order to make the budget targets easier to achieve and thus make their performance appear to be good or at least acceptable. Where the performance of managers is being evaluated by reference to budget targets this kind of behaviour can lead to manager rewards which may not be deserved. It can also undermine the purpose of budgets and lead to under performance of the business.

Other types of management behaviour can also lead to budget bias and, in some cases, the bias may be in the other direction. For example, a manager who is seeking promotion may put forward an extremely difficult budget in the expectation that he/she will be promoted before the budget targets have to be achieved. Similarly, a manager who has under-performed in the past may put forward an optimistic budget target in order to gain approval from senior managers. This kind of behaviour, however, can lead to problems for the manager when the results of the budget period are finally reported.

Budgets and performance appraisal

BUSINESSES WILL NORMALLY WISH to use budget performance as a standard by which to judge management performance. Moreover, budget performance may also be used as a basis for rewarding managers. However, the use of budgets in these ways must be considered carefully. The fact that a part of the business has performed well or badly may not be a sufficient basis for rewarding or criticising the relevant managers. The performance of a particular element of a business is not solely determined by the performance of its manager. There may be a number of critical factors affecting performance of a business element which are beyond the control of the relevant managers.

In practice, it is often difficult to assess the degree of control which managers actually have over certain internal or external factors. Some managers may try to take credit for favourable outcomes over which they have had little influence. Similarly, some managers may blame factors beyond their control for poor outcomes even though they should have anticipated and dealt with those factors.

Senior managers must somehow come to an independent judgement concerning the ability of the subordinates to predict the conditions with which they are faced and the adequacy of the response to those conditions when considering performance-related rewards to staff.

The use of budgets as a means of appraising managers may sometimes have unintended consequences. Where managers are evaluated by reference to budget performance they may try to influence the way in which certain items are accounted for in the budget in order to produce more favourable accounting numbers, eg costs may be allocated in a different manner in order to boost the profits of a particular division. In addition, as we have seen earlier, managers may also try to build 'slack' into budget targets in order to ensure that the targets can be achieved.

Managers may also make budget decisions which boost short-term profits at the expense of long-term profits. This may be done in the expectation that the manager will be promoted before the long-term consequences are felt by the organisation. An example of this type of behaviour would be to cut back on discretionary expenditure such as staff training or research and development. This will increase profits in the short-term but may have serious long-term consequences.

Reading

You should now read Reader Article 7.2 'Evaluating performance' by Dr Graham Morgan.

This short article examines three ways of using budgets to evaluate managerial performance: the budget constrained style, the profit-conscious style and the non-accounting style. The views of a group of managing directors of companies were then solicited to see which style of evaluation they preferred also the style by which they believed they were being assessed.

Points to consider:

Do you think the different styles of using budgets to evaluate managerial performance are valid? Which particular style, if any, do you prefer and why? What is your evaluation of the responses given by the managing directors?

Zero-base budgets

IN RECENT YEARS THERE has been some interest in the zero-base approach to budgeting. This has been in response to problems recognised in the conventional approach to budgeting. Under the conventional approach budgets are developed on an incremental basis. This means that figures for the previous year will be taken as the starting point for the development of the budget. The new budget will often reflect the previous years results after allowing for changes in demand, inflation, etc.

Activity 12

What do you think are the problems of using an incremental approach?

The major problem of the incremental approach is that there is no real attempt to justify the use of the previous year as a starting point for the current year. It may be that the budget in past periods was too high, in which case the incremental approach will perpetuate the inefficient use of resources. It may even be that, due to changes in the environment, a budget for a particular area is no longer really necessary. An incremental budgeting approach does not encourage a questioning attitude amongst managers and, as a result, they may not easily identify changes quickly.

Zero base budgeting requires that managers adopt an inquisitorial attitude to existing budget activities. The approach rests on the assumption that existing budget activities need not exist and should therefore incur zero costs to the business. Thus, in order to justify incurring costs for a particular activity the relevant managers must provide a clear rationale for its existence. It must be shown that the activity is consistent with the objectives of the business and that there are not more suitable ways of providing the particular activity. It must also be shown that the level of costs required are commensurate with the level of benefits produced.

Under a system of zero-base budgeting the various budget activities will be evaluated by senior managers and ranked in order of priority. The rankings will largely reflect the expected cost/benefit relationship of the activities. Resources will then be allocated on the basis of these rankings.

A number of benefits have been claimed for the zero-base budgeting approach. These include the following:

● it helps to ensure the efficient and effective use of resources. Resources are allocated on the basis of clearly justified need and wasteful practices are identified and eliminated

● it helps managers focus more sharply on the overall objectives of the business and the role of their particular areas of responsibility in achieving those objectives

● it can create a climate within the business which is more inclined towards acceptance of change

● it can lead to new ideas and practices being developed

● it can increase manager involvement in the business.

Activity 13

Can you think of any possible problems with adopting this kind of approach within a business?

Possible problems with this approach include the following:

- it can be extremely time-consuming. In a business of any size it would not be feasible to have a thoroughgoing review of each activity at the commencement of each budget period. However, it is possible to apply zero-base budgeting on a selective basis.

- employees and managers may feel their jobs are under threat particularly where the activity is of marginal importance to the business

- it may be difficult to quantify the benefits (and costs) relating to a particular activity. As a result the ranking of activities may be difficult.

When applied on a selective basis, zero-base budgeting does not replace incremental budgeting. Rather it is used in conjunction with the conventional approach to help ensure 'value for money' when allocating resources.

Reading

You should now read Reader Article 7.3 'Activity-based budgeting' by Mike Harvey.

In this article the author argues that conventional budgets, which are organised on a departmental basis, provide information which is often lacking in relevance for decision making purposes. He suggests that budgets would be more effective if they were organised in a way which focused on activities of the business instead. The concept of activity-based budgeting can be seen as an extension of activity-based costing which was considered in an earlier unit. Mike Harvey sets out a number of benefits which should flow from adopting an activity-based budgeting approach. He also identifies some of the disadvantages and problems associated with this approach.

Points to consider:

Should activity-based budgeting supplement or replace the conventional budgeting approach? What are the key differences between the activity-based approach and the conventional approach to budgeting?

Budgets in practice

THE ACCA SURVEY examined various aspects of budgeting. It revealed that 58% of companies do not employ flexible budgets when comparing actual with planned performance. This finding is consistent with earlier studies in this area. The survey also found that, where flexible budgeting is used, it tends to be larger rather than smaller companies which adopt the technique.

The use of budgets in evaluating management performance has been discussed earlier. The survey found that 67% felt that variances from budgets occurring within their company were either above average importance or vitally important in evaluating managerial performance.

Summary

In this unit we have considered the nature and purpose of budgets. We have seen how budgets are prepared and what benefits they provide to the business. We have also seen that the way in which budgets are prepared and applied can have a significant effect on the behaviour and attitudes of managers. Senior managers must be aware of the possible impact of budgets on staff motivation and morale.

Zero-base budgeting is concerned with achieving 'value for money' within a business. It is based on a questioning approach to the activities of the business and can help prevent the wasteful use of resources. However, it can be a time-consuming process.

Additional exercises

Exercise 1

Ortan Co is to launch a new product in the market on 1 February with production commencing in January.

The variable cost per unit of the product will be:

	£
Direct Materials	1.5
Direct Labour	1.3
Overheads	1.0
	£3.8

Fixed costs are expected to be £2,200 each month from January. This figure includes £1,000 for depreciation.

The planned sales of the product are (in units):

February	5,000
March	5,200
April	5,200
May	5,400
June	5,600
July	5,400
August	5,400

The units will sell for £4.50 each.

The following policies are to be followed:

1. Stocks of finished goods at the end of each month are to be equal to 50% of the following month's sales.

2. Direct material stocks at the end of each month are to be equal to 50% of the following months production requirements. All raw material stock used in January will be purchased in January.

3. Direct wages are to be paid in the month worked.

4. Variable overheads are to be paid 40% in the month of usage the balance to be paid the following month.

5. Fixed overheads, other than depreciation, are to be paid one-third in the month concerned, the other two-thirds in the following month.

6. Creditors for raw materials are to be paid in the month following purchase.

7. Debtors are expected to pay 30% in the months of sale, which will be subject to a 2% cash discount, 50% in the following month and 15% in the second month after sale. The balance of 5% will probably prove to be irrecoverable.

You are required to produce the following, in columnar form (a column for each month), for the six months to 30 June:

    (a) the finished stock budget (in units); **
    (b) the raw materials stock budget (in units); ** and
    (c) the cash budget (in £, assuming a nil cash balance at 1 January).

Work to the nearest £

** The two stock budgets should take the following form:

Opening stock	X
plus: Purchases (or production)	X
	X
less: Issues to production (or sales)	X
Closing stock	X

Exercise 2

Richard Cliff Ltd makes and sells one product, the budgeted sales for which are:

	units
March	180,000
April	240,000
May	250,000
June	230,000

The selling price is £2 per unit. 50% of the sales are paid for during the month of sale and the customers deduct a 5% discount from these payments in accordance with the company's terms of trade; 49% are paid in the following month and 1% become bad.

Stocks of finished goods were 36,000 units on 1 March. The company's stock-holding policy is that its finished stock at the end of each month should represent 20% of the following month's sales. There is no work-in-progress.

Stocks of raw material were 45,600 kg on 1 March. Here the company's policy is that 40% of the following month's production requirements of raw materials should be held in stock at each month end. This policy should be established as soon as possible.

The standard variable production cost of the product is:

	Cost per unit £
Direct materials (1 kg)	0.50
Direct labour	0.40
Variable overheads	0.20
	£1.10

Fixed overheads (including £8,000 per month for depreciation) total £53,000 per month.

Payments for raw materials are made in the month following that of purchase. All other payments are made in the month in which they are incurred.

The cash balance at 1 April will be £12,000.

You are required to prepare:

   (a) the finished stock budget (in units) for March, April and May.
   (b) the raw materials stock budget (in units) for March and April.
   (c) the cash budget for April.

Exercise 3

Northern Products Ltd is a manufacturing company which is in the process of compiling its budgets for the months of July, August and September 19x9.

All budgets except the cash budget have been prepared and show the following:

	May £000	June £000	July £000	August £000	Sept. £000
Sales	40	60	80	60	40
Raw materials usage	15	35	30	20	20
Labour	10	10	20	12	10
Overheads	10	10	20	10	10
Capital expenditure			15		

The following information is available:

(a) Sales are usually 50% for cash (immediate payment), 25% on credit, with customers paying one month after the sale, and 25% to a special customer who pays two months after the sale.
(b) The company has for many months maintained a base stock of £5,000 which it intends to maintain until July. During August the company plans to increase it to a permanent base stock of £10,000.
(c) Materials purchased during one month are paid for in the following month.
(d) Labour (wages) is paid one-half during the month in the month incurred and the remainder in the following month.
(e) Overheads are paid in the month following their being incurred.
(f) The company will have fixed assets which originally cost £100,000 in operation at 1 July. The capital expenditure of £15,000 relates to the purchase of a machine which will be delivered and paid for in July. It is the company's practice to depreciate its fixed assets at 20% (of cost) per annum.
(g) The balance at bank on 30 June is planned to be £2,000 in funds.

You are required:

   (a) to prepare a cash budget, in columnar form, for the period 1 July to 30 September showing the cash requirements each month.
   (b) to comment on the cash budget and to suggest what action, if any, management should take as a result of what it shows.
   (c) to suggest to what purpose the management of the company might put the cash budget.

Exercise 4

Microco Ltd wholesales a particular model of microcomputer. Sales have been running at a steady rate of 50 each month for some time, but the company is dissatisfied with this level of sales and from next month, July 19x8, intends to advertise actively. This is expected to increase sales by 10 units per month from July to November inclusive after which it will remain steady at 100 units per month.

Each microcomputer costs £1500 and sells for £2000. All purchases are on one month's credit and sales on two month's credit. The company feels that, to give a good service to customers, it must have sufficient stock at the end of each month to meet the whole of the following month's sales.

Additional fixed assets (a delivery van to help cope with the increased sales) will be bought and paid for in August at a cost of £15,000. Corporation tax of £25,000 is due for payment on 1 September. The balance of cash at 30 June 19x8 is planned to be £30,000.

Operating costs will give rise to cash payments totalling £10,000 each month. The advertising will cost £20,000 in July and £10,000 for each month from August to October inclusive, payable one month in arrears.

The finance director has not yet had a cash budget prepared for the rest of the year, but he feels that the sales expansion plans are likely to lead to cash flow problems. Suggestions have been made that, if his fears are justified, it might be possible to overcome the problem by increasing the creditor payment period to two months and buying stock as it is used (ie zero stock at month ends).

You are required:

(a) to prepare a cash budget for Microco Ltd for the six months ending 31 December 19x8, showing the planned cash position at the end of each month; on the basis of the original planned credit and stockholding periods.
(b) to redraft your cash budget to reflect the suggested alterations to these planned periods.
(c) to suggest what other aspects Microco Ltd should consider to solve the expected cash flow problem, should the suggested solution be unachievable.

Solution to self-assessment question

Cash budget for the six months to 30 November 19x9

	June £	July £	Aug £	Sept £	Oct £	Nov £
Cash inflows						
Credit sales	-	-	4,000	5,500	7,000	8,500
Cash sales	4,000	5,500	7,000	8,500	11,000	11,000
	4,000	5,500	11,000	14,000	18,000	19,500
Cash outflows						
Motor vehicles	6,000					
Equipment	10,000					7,000
Freehold premises	40,000					
Purchases	-	29,000	9,250	11,500	13,750	17,500
Wages/salaries	900	900	900	900	900	900
Commission	-	320	440	560	680	880
Overheads	500	500	500	500	650	650
	57,400	30,720	11,090	13,460	15,980	26,930
Net Cash flow	(53,400)	(25,220)	(90)	540	2,020	(7,430)
Opening balance	60,000	6,600	(18,620)	(18,710)	(18,170)	(16,150)
Closing balance	6,600	(18,620)	(18,710)	(18,170)	(16,150)	(23,580)

Answers to additional exercises

Exercise 1

(a) Finished stock budget for the six months to 30 June (in units)

	January	February	March	April	May	June
Opening stock	0	2,500	2,600	2,600	2,700	2,800
Production	2,500	5,100	5,200	5,300	5,500	5,500
	2,500	7,600	7,800	7,900	8,200	8,300
Less: Sales	0	5,000	5,200	5,200	5,400	5,600
Closing stock	2,500	2,600	2,600	2,700	2,800	2,700

(b)   Raw materials stock budget for the six months to 30 June (in units)

	January	February	March	April	May	June
Opening stock	0	2,550	2,600	2,650	2,750	2,750
Purchases	5,050	5,150	5,250	5,400	5,500	5,450
	5,050	7,700	7,850	8,050	8,250	8,200
Less: Issues to production	2,500	5,100	5,200	5,300	5,500	5,500
Closing stock	2,550	2,600	2,650	2,750	2,750	2,700

(c)   Cash budget for the six months to 30 June (in £)

	January £	February £	March £	April £	May £	June £
Inflows:						
Debtors:						
Current month	–	6,615	6,880	6,880	7,144	7,409
Previous month	–	–	11,250	11,700	11,700	12,150
Pre-previous month	–	–	–	3,375	3,510	3,510
Total inflows	–	6,615	18,130	21,955	22,354	23,069
Outflows:						
Creditors	–	7,575	7,725	7,875	8,100	8,250
Direct labour	3,250	6,630	6,760	6,890	7,150	7,150
Variable overheads	1,000	3,540	5,140	5,240	5,380	5,500
Fixed overheads	400	1,200	1,200	1,200	1,200	1,200
	4,650	18,945	20,825	21,205	21,830	22,100
Surplus/(deficit) for the month	(4,650)	(12,330)	(2,695)	750	524	969
Cumulative surplus/(deficit)	(4,650)	(16,980)	(19,675)	(18,925)	(18,401)	(17,432)

Exercise 2

Finished stock budget (units)

	March	April	May
Opening balance	36,000	48,000	50,000
Production	192,000	242,000	246,000
	228,000	290,000	296,000
Sales	180,000	240,000	250,000
Closing balance	48,000	50,000	46,000

Raw materials stock budget (units)

	March	April
Opening balance	45,600	96,800
Purchases	243,200	243,600
	288,800	340,400
Issues to production	192,000	242,000
Closing balance	96,800	98,400

(These figures should be 40% of the following month's production figures.)

Cash Budget

		April £
Inflows: Debtors		
March sales:	49% × £360000	176,400
April sales:	47.5% × £480000	228,000
Total inflows		404,400
Outflows: Purchases		121,600
Labour		96,800
Variable overheads		48,400
Fixed overheads		45,000
Total outflows		311,800
Surplus for the month		92,600
Balance as at 30 April		104,600

Exercise 3

(a) Cash budget for the period 1 July to 30 September 19x9

	July £000	August £000	Sept £000
Inflows			
Cash sales	40	30	20
General credit sales	15	20	15
Special customer	10	15	20
	65	65	55
Outflows			
Materials	35	30	25
Wages: Current month	10	6	5
Previous month	5	10	6
Overheads	10	20	10
Fixed assets	15		
	75	66	46
Surplus/(deficit) for the month	(10)	(1)	9
Cumulative balance	(8)	(9)	Nil

(b) Clearly this shows that, principally as a result of the large expenditure on fixed assets in July, there will be a need to finance a cash deficit for July and August.

Measures which could be considered as ways of overcoming this problem include the following:

● delay the acquisition of and/or the payment for the fixed assets (note that delaying payment until September would overcome the problem)
● seek to lease the fixed assets rather than buying them outright
● attempt to collect debts more quickly
● reduce stock levels

Obviously trying to negotiate overdraft facilities with the bank remains a possibility, but perhaps a relatively expensive one.

(c) A cash budget like any other budget can be useful in the following ways:

● it can be used as a co-ordinating device
● it can be useful to communicate plans
● it can help to motivate managerial performance, in this case the performance of the cash controller or treasurer
● it can provide a control device in that actual performance can be compared with budget targets, to see whether plans are being met or not

A good answer would relate these points specifically to a cash budget.

Exercise 4

(a)

	July £000	Aug £000	Sept £000	Oct £000	Nov £000	Dec £000
Receipts						
Debtors	100	100	120	140	160	180
Payments						
Creditors	90	105	120	135	150	150
Van		15				
Corporation Tax			25			
Operating costs	10	10	10	10	10	10
Advertising		20	10	10	10	
	100	150	165	155	170	160
Monthly net cash flow	Nil	(50)	(45)	(15)	(10)	20
Monthly cash balance	30	(20)	(65)	(80)	(90)	(70)

(b)

	July £000	Aug £000	Sept £000	Oct £000	Nov £000	Dec £000
Receipts	100	100	120	140	160	180
Payments						
Creditors	75	75	90	105	120	135
Van		15				
Corporation Tax			25			
Operating costs	10	10	10	10	10	10
Advertising		20	10	10	10	
	85	120	135	125	140	145
Monthly net cash flow	15	(20)	(15)	15	20	35
Monthly cash balance	45	25	10	25	45	80

UNIT 8

CONTROL THROUGH VARIANCES

THIS UNIT IS CONCERNED with control of industrial and commercial types of activity.

On completion of this unit you should be able to:

- explain the nature of control and explain the way in which decentralisation and central control can be reconciled.

- discuss the nature of variance analysis and standards

- explain why the annual budget is inadequate for control purposes and describe and carry out the process of flexing the budget

- calculate variances and use them to reconcile budgeted and actual profit figures

- discuss the factors in the decision to investigate variances and possible reasons for variances of all types

Outline of the unit

THIS UNIT FOLLOWS ON from the previous unit dealing with budgets. In this unit we shall consider some of the inadequacies of the normal budget in the context of control and how the budget can be revised to become a more effective tool for control purposes. After this, we shall consider how comparison of the revised budget with measures of actual performance can provide valuable insights into what, if anything, is at variance from the plan and, therefore, out of control. We shall also consider some of the prerequisites of effective budgetary control and how effective budgetary control is likely to be in practice.

There are five steps in the control process. These are:

- establish the plan or standard;

- perform;

- provide feedback data on actual performance;

- compare actual performance with budgeted or standard performance;

- take appropriate action to exercise control.

The last step is really the most important of all. The accounting statements produced can tell managers that things are not going according to plan but this will only be useful to the organisation if managers then take corrective action.

Accounting information can be used to show managers where actual performance differs from planned performance. The process of identifying where costs and revenues differ from earlier plans is known as *variance analysis*. We shall see that the variances arising from various costs and revenues can be highlighted and the sum of these variances will represent the difference between the budgeted profit and the actual profit.

Before considering variances in detail the idea of standards is introduced. A *standard* in the context of accounting for control, is simply the target cost, usage, etc relating to a single unit of production. Standards are closely related to the budgeting process. A standard represents a financial plan for one unit of output whereas a budget represents a financial plan for total output over a period of time. In effect, standards are the building blocks of budgets.

We shall explore how standards are prepared and how they are used for control purposes. In addition, we shall see that standards have uses other than purely for control.

Direct comparison of the original budget with actual performance does not really tell us very much. This is because there is often a difference between the budgeted level of output and the actual level of output. It is useful for control purposes to 'flex' the budget, ie to draw up the budget based on the actual level of output. In this way managers can gain a much better appreciation of where variances between planned and actual costs and revenues arise.

As managers rarely have perfect foresight, some difference between planned and actual performance will usually occur. However, this does not mean that a particular variance is worthy of investigation. In practice, managers must decide whether or not the reasons for a variance should be investigated. We shall consider the issues involved with decisions about investigation of variances.

There are both advantages and disadvantages in decentralising and delegating authority. Thus, when an organisation decides to decentralise and to delegate it must seek to gain the associated advantages whilst trying to minimise the potential disadvantages. Budgets and standards can play an important role in achieving this aim.

When seeking to gain the advantages of decentralised decision making and responsibility, it is vital that an effective and efficient reporting and control system should be established.

It is important to appreciate that variance analysis, although widely practised, is not without its problems. Some of these problems are highlighted in the unit.

The nature of control

WE SAW IN THE previous unit that control is compelling events to conform to a plan. This implies that the steps in the control process are as shown overleaf.

You should particularly note that the last step is the vital one. Information does not exercise control, it merely provides a tool which can be used by management to exercise control. It is people, by taking action, who control; it is not accounting statements which do it. This process is known as 'feedback control'.

Of course, there is nothing that can be done about that which went wrong last month. What can be done, however, is to find out as much as possible about what went wrong last month and try to correct things for the future. In other words, having discovered, by comparing the budgeted and actual results for last month, that the operations of the business were to some extent out of control (not going according to plan), management will be eager to identify as precisely as possible where in the business things went wrong and to try to ensure that things are put right for this month.

Figure 1

The steps in the control process

Establish the plan or standard

Perform

Provide feedback on actual performance

Compare actual performance with budgeted or standard performance

Take appropriate action to exercise control

Unfortunately, direct comparison of the actual and budget figures is going to tell us little about how things went wrong. In fact, no accounting statement can ever tell us how things went wrong. What sensible use of accounting statements can achieve is to tell us how much of, say, a profit shortfall, relative to budgeted profit, was caused by each particular aspect of the business being out of control. Accounting can provide an analysis of the profit shortfall, apportioning parts of the shortfall to the relevant areas of managerial responsibility. If this can be done, senior management can identify where significant loss of control is occurring, take steps to discover the cause of it and seek means to get things back under control.

Activity 1

From what you have seen so far, what do you feel is the first step which senior management needs to take when it sees things going out of control?

Jot you answer down a piece of paper.

From the above it can be seen that one of the objectives of the post-performance review must be to identify which manager should be held accountable for a failure (relative to the budget) of a particular aspect which has gone out of control. It is only after the relevant manager can be identified, that steps can be taken by that manager, perhaps with the assistance of his or her senior manager, to get things back on course for subsequent periods. Thus senior management's first step in seeking to deal with some loss of control is to identify the manager concerned.

Variance analysis

THE PROCESS OF IDENTIFYING where and how costs and revenue differed from what they were planned to be is known as *variance analysis*. Each individual variance should be seen as the effect of differences caused by the particular aspect under review (and only by that aspect), on the budgeted profit for the period.

Thus | **Budgeted profit**
plus or minus | **Algebraic sum of all the variances**
equals | **Actual profit**

This means that the failure of a business to reach its profit target during a period can be analysed between the various causes, eg failure to sell as many of the product as was planned, overspending on overheads, excess usage of raw materials, etc.

Standards

BEFORE WE GO ON to consider variances in greater detail, it might be useful to introduce the idea of standards.

Whereas the budget represents a total for a period of time, it is useful to identify target costs, usages, etc, for each unit of output (or input). The title given to these is *standard*.

Thus we can to say the following in respect of a particular product or service:

The standard direct labour time	=	2.0 hours
The standard rate of the direct labour	=	£5.00/hour
The standard direct labour cost (per unit of the		
product or service) =		£10.00

Thus a standard is a financial plan for *one unit* of output (or input) whereas a budget is a financial plan for a *period of time*. In effect, standards are the building blocks of the budgets.

Activity 2

A business has a budgeted sales output for a particular product of 10,000 units for next year. The budgeted sales revenue is £35,000. The budgeted variable costs total £17,000.

See if you can work out each of the following for the particular product:

The standard selling price; the standard variable costs; the standard contribution margin.

The standard is the cost, usage, etc for one unit of output or input.

Thus for this product :

> Standard selling price is £3.50 (ie £35,000/10,000)
> Standard variable cost is £1.70 (ie £17,000/10,000)
> Standard contribution margin is £1.80 (ie £3.50 - 1.70) – remember that
> contribution is selling price less variable cost.

Standards are established using judgement as to what represents a reasonable target for relevant aspects of input or output. For example, the standard direct labour time (ie how long it should take to make one unit of output) would be established originally on the basis of pre-production trials. Standard material prices would be established from knowledge of the market.

It must be recognised that a badly set standard is always going to be a possible reason why a variance could occur in a particular case. Obviously, if the yardstick by which performance is being measured is flawed, the whole process of seeking to exercise control through standards is going to be, at best, a waste of time and money. In such circumstances, managers will soon start to ignore the variance reports and to be unenthusiastic about attempts to use variance analysis. It is, therefore, essential that standards are reasonable and seen as such by those whose performance will be assessed by reference to them.

Standards are not set in stone for all time. If a standard is found to be unreasonable (in either direction) it should be revised. Thus the standard direct labour time may be revised in the light of practical experience. Similarly raw material price standards would normally be revised annually in the light of changing expectations of the market for the particular material concerned.

Standards have uses other than purely for control purposes. These include:

● *Decision making.* If some decision needs to be made which requires knowledge of costs of an existing activity, the established and tested standard costs are obvious inputs into the analysis.

● *Speed-up record keeping.* There are occasions where it is useful to have accounting records written up to date (eg stock accounts), but where the actual information may not yet be available. As a temporary measure the standard costs can be used, subsequently to be adjusted if there are variances from actual.

Limitations in the use of budgets for control purposes

BUDGETS MAY NOT ALWAYS be very useful for exercising control over many aspects of the business.

Example 1

Smokey Ltd makes just one product, the 'Atomet', by taking a single raw material and working on it by hand using only one grade of labour.

The actual performance and the budget for last month are as follows overleaf:

	Actual		Budget	
Units made and sold	9,000		10,000	
	£		£	
Sales revenue	86,000		100,000	
Direct materials	36,400	(17,500 kg)	40,000	(20,000 kg)
Direct labour	17,400	(4,600 hr)	20,000	(5,000 hr)
Fixed overheads	9,500		10,000	
	63,300		70,000	
Net operating profit	£22,700		£30,000	

The bracketed figures following the *actual* direct materials and labour figures are the physical amounts of those commodities actually used in production during the month. Those following the corresponding *budget* figures are the planned physical quantities. The budgeted figures imply that each Atomet requires 2 kg of raw material (ie 20,000/10,000) costing £2.00 per kg (ie 40,000/20,000) and 0.5 hours of labour (ie 5,000/10,000) at £4.00 per hour (ie 20,000/5,000).

Comparing the actual with the budget columns reveals two crucial things:

- Actual output and sales were 10% below budget.

- Actual profit was £7,300 below budget.

Since the company's primary objective is likely to be to increase its own value and, bearing in mind that profit is the net increase in value for the period, management is likely to be rather concerned about the significant (24%) profit shortfall.

Activity 3

Is the profit shortfall caused only by the 10% sales volume shortfall?

What other factors may have caused it?

The answer would appear to be 'no' because, for example, actual direct material cost is higher than would have been expected given the actual level of output (90% × £40,000 = £36,000). So there was not only a shortfall in the output but at least one other aspect did not go according to plan either.

'Flexing' the budget to identify variances

AS WE HAVE ALREADY seen, direct comparison of the original budget with the statement of actual performance will not tell us very much. For example, in Example 1 the budgeted material cost was £40,000, but the actual cost turned out to be £36,400. Does this mean that the manager responsible for managing production (production manager) should be congratulated for efficient use of materials? Does it mean that the manager responsible for buying materials (the purchasing manager) should be congratulated for some shrewd buying at below the standard price for the material? On the other hand production was 10% below budget, so should not material cost have been 10% below budget? In fact material cost turned out to be more than would have been expected given the production shortfall, so was there a loss of control of the use of materials or was there a loss of control in purchasing, or both of these?

In order to come to some sensible conclusions we need to 'flex' or adjust the budget to show what the budget would have shown had it been drawn up on the assumption that 9,000 Atomets would be made and sold. To flex the budget it is necessary to know the relationship between the various revenues and expenses and the volume of activity. In other words, we need to know the extent to which various factors vary with the level of activity.

In this example we shall assume that sales revenue, direct materials usage and labour hours vary directly with the volume of activity, ie they are 'variable' in the context of cost behaviour. We shall also assume that the fixed overheads remain fixed over the range of activity concerned (remember that 'fixed' costs are not usually fixed over large volume changes). In practice, all of these assumptions are likely to be reasonable, except that direct labour is often not directly variable with output. Obviously in a particular practical situation, the precise relationship between the activity level and the various revenues and costs will need to be clearly established, both to draw up the original budget and to flex it to help exercise control.

Thus the actual performance, the original budget and the flexed budget for last month are as follows:

	Actual	Original budget	Flexed budget
Units made and sold	9,000	10,000	9,000

	£	£	£
Sales revenue	86,000	100,000	90,000
Direct materials	36,400 17,500 kg	40,000 20,000 kg	36,000 18,000 kg
Direct labour	17,400 4,600 hr	20,000 5,000 hr	18,000 4,500 hr
Fixed overheads	9,500	10,000	10,000
	63,300	70,000	64,000
Net operating profit	22,700	30,000	26,000

Having established the flexed budget we shall now proceed to analyse the variance between the budgeted and actual profit, in as much detail as the information will allow. We shall now review the mechanical process of analysing profit variances. At the same time we shall consider who is likely to be the accountable manager for each analysed variance and likely reasons for particular variances.

Sales volume (contribution) variance

IT MAY HAVE STRUCK you that by flexing the budget to reflect the actual volume of output we were, in effect, saying that the difference between the actual and original budgeted volume of sales was of no consequence. Nothing could be further from the truth. A 10% shortfall in sales volume would normally have a profound effect on the profit of any organisation, so the size of this effect needs to be quantified. In fact, quantifying this effect on profit is very easy to do because it is simply the difference between the profit figures shown by the original and the flexed budgets. This is because the only difference between these two versions of the budget is the sales volume. The variance is therefore:

£30,000 - 26,000 = £4,000 (adverse)

It is adverse because the shortfall in sales volume has the effect of causing actual profit to be *less* than the budgeted figure.

The sales volume (contribution) variance can be defined as (budgeted sales volume – actual sales volume) × standard contribution.

The standard contribution is £4 (ie £10 - 4 - 2). Thus, if the number of Atomets sold is 1,000 less than budgeted, the profit will be less by £4,000 (ie £4 × 1,000).

Activity 4

Upon what assumption does this last statement rely?

Can you suggest why it is useful to make this assumption?

Saying that if the number of Atomets sold is 1,000 less than budgeted, the profit will be less by £4,000, relies on the assumption that all other aspects go according to plan. Volume is not the only thing which could differ from budget, nor is it the only one which actually does in this case; in fact everything which could differ from budget does so. Thus it is not true to say that profit will actually be £4,000 less than was budgeted because many things have an effect on profit.

It is useful to make the assumption, when considering the volume variance, that everything else goes precisely according to plan. The objective of variance analysis is to identify the effect on budgeted profit of the particular aspect under review at that point (volume of sales in this case), as if it is the only factor which varies from budget.

We know, from a glance at the figures, that the actual sales price was not £10 per unit, nor was the material cost £4 per unit, nor was the labour cost £2 per unit. However, the profit variances to which these differences give rise will be separately identified.

To do other than to make the assumption that everything but the particular factor under review went according to plan, would mean that it would be impossible to identify how much of the overall difference between budgeted and actual profit was caused by particular factors being out of control.

Activity 5

ABC Ltd had a budgeted sales output last month of 2,000 hours of its service, which is sold for £15 per hour. The actual output was 2,100 hours all of which were charged at £15 per hour.

Does this mean that there was a favourable sales volume variance of £1,500 (ie 100 @ £15) for the month?

The answer is **no**. It is important to recognise that a sales volume difference will **not** affect profit by the volume difference multiplied by the sales revenue per unit. This is because though sales revenue will be different as a result of a difference in volume, so will variable production costs. What, in effect, is lost through a shortfall in sales volume is the potential profit on that shortfall. For this reason sales variances are only concerned with contribution margins.

Activity 6

Which manager would normally be asked to account for Smokey Ltd's adverse sales volume variance?

Do you think that the variance is necessarily caused by that manager's failings?

Irrespective of the cause of this variance, the sales/marketing manager should be able to provide clear reasons for it. The sheer size of the variance (13% of budgeted profit) makes it a highly significant figure. It would, therefore, be unreasonable for the person responsible for the company's marketing not to be able to explain the reason for this variance.

The reasons could be very wide-ranging.

Activity 7

What possible reasons can you suggest for the existence of the adverse sales volume variance?

Possibilities include, among a large number of reasons, the following:

1. Failures by marketing staff.
2. An unexpectedly low demand.
3. Production failures, leading to output not being available to sell.
4. Raw material stock shortages, causing dislocations in production.
5. Labour shortages, leading to dislocations in production.

Note that only reason 1 is the direct failure of matters under the control of the marketing/sales manager. Reason 2 is quite possibly outside of the control of the business. Reasons 3, 4 and 5 are likely to be the responsibility of the production, purchasing and personnel managers, respectively. These managers should be held accountable for any failings in their sphere of responsibility.

Had this variance been favourable, implying a higher than budgeted volume of sales for the month, the reasons for it would be likely to be the opposite of the reasons suggested above for the actual adverse variance. These would include:

1. Above average performance by the marketing staff.
2. An unexpectedly high demand.
3. Levels of production higher than planned, making more stock available for sale.

Having identified and quantified the **full** profit difference caused by the shortfall in sales volume, we can now continue to calculate other variances without concerning ourselves with the volume difference. We can now simply say, given that the volume was 9,000 sales units, what **should** the sales revenue, material cost, labour cost, etc have been and what was it actually? In other words we can now concentrate on differences between the actual results and the flexed budget.

You should make sure that you understand the calculation of each variance and analysis and what the resultant figure means. "Rote" learning formulae is not a good idea in this context. The calculation of each variance follows a simple logic. If you can understand this logic you will find it easy to remember how to calculate the variance.

Sales price variance

THIS IS THE DIFFERENCE between the price for which the actual volume should have been sold and the actual sales revenue achieved. Looking at the accounting statements (on page 279), we can see that this is £4,000 (A) (ie £90,000 - 86,000). (A and F are the normal abbreviations for adverse and favourable variances, respectively). It is adverse because it is £4,000 less than it was planned to be, given the actual level of output. Thus there will be an adverse effect on profit.

The sales price variance can be defined as (standard selling price × actual sales volume) – actual total sales revenue.

Activity 8

Which manager would normally be asked to account for Smokey Ltd's adverse sales price variance?

Suggest possible reasons for the adverse variance.

Once again it is the marketing/sales manager who would be asked to account for the lower than planned sales prices earned. The reasons for this variance could include:

1. Failings of the marketing staff.
2. An unexpectedly difficult/competitive market.

Had the variance been favourable, the reasons for it would include the opposite to these reasons, ie particularly good performance by marketing staff, or an unexpectedly favourable market.

Direct material variances

THE £400 DIFFERENCE BETWEEN the flexed budget figure (£36,000) and the actual figure (£36,400) for direct material cost is the *total direct material variance* for the month. It is adverse (as opposed to favourable) because the actual cost is more than the flexed budget figure. All other things being as budgeted, the profit of the business for the month would be £400 less than budgeted. As was mentioned above, a variance is the effect of the particular aspect under consideration on the budgeted profit.

The total direct material variance (TDMV) can be defined as:

Budgeted raw material cost of actual outputs (ie standard cost x actual output) less actual cost.

Where actual is greater than budgeted cost the variance is said to be *adverse*, where savings are made the variance is said to be *favourable*.

Unfortunately the TDMV is rather limited as a control devise. This is because it encompasses differences of usage, as well as those of price, and these are probably the responsibility of different managers. Usage is the responsibility of a production manager and price is the responsibility of the buyer. If senior management sought to hold either of these two managers responsible for the £400 adverse variance, each one could easily avoid being held accountable by arguing that it was the other one's responsibility. Clearly this cannot be a basis for a reasonable system of control.

It is therefore useful and, fortunately, it is also easy to analyse the TDMV into its component parts.

The direct materials usage variance (DMUV) is the difference between the standard usage (for the actual output) and the actual usage. This is then priced at the standard price per kg.

ie $(18,000 - 17,500) \times £2.00 = £1,000$ (F)

The variance is favourable since the actual usage is less than the standard one. All other things being equal, this is the extent to which the profit would be higher than budgeted, as a result of efficient use of materials.

The *direct materials price variance* (DMPV) is the difference between the standard price for the actual material used and the actual price paid for it.

ie $(17,500 \times £2.00) - £36,400 = £1,400$ (A)

The variance is adverse because the material was bought for more than the standard price.

Since the DMUV and the DMPV are both analyses of the TDMV, they should always add algebraically to it, as they do in this case. Thus the TDMV provides an arithmetical check, which is probably its main use.

It may have occurred to you that there seems to be no particular reason why the direct material price variance should include all of the material used, when more or less of it was used than was planned to be used (ie non-standard usage). For instance, why should the price variance relate to 17,500 kg when the standard usage for the output was 18,000 kg?

In practice, it is usually done this way because price variances are normally calculated when materials are bought, not when they are used. We shall continue to adopt this widely-used convention when calculating variances.

Figure 2

Smokey Ltd's direct material

variances

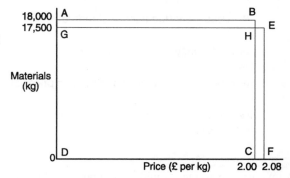

Figure 2 is a graphical representation of the direct materials flexed budget, the actuals and the variances (not drawn to scale). The rectangle ABCD is the flexed budget for direct materials cost and its area is £36,000 (ie 18,000 kg × £2.00/kg). The rectangle GEFD represents the actual materials cost. The area is £36,400 (ie 17,500 kg × £2.08). (Note that the actual cost per kg is £2.08 (ie £36,400/17,500).) Thus the differences between the flexed budget and the actual are represented by the two narrow strips.

HEFC represents the price variance and its area is £1,400 (ie (£2.08 - £2.00) × 17,500). This is adverse because the strip lies outside the flexed budget rectangle, ie actual is larger than flexed budget.

The usage variance is represented by the strip ABHG. The area of this strip is £1,000 (ie (18,000 - 17,500) × £2.00). It is favourable because it lies inside the flexed budget rectangle, ie actual is less than flexed budget.

Reasons for the favourable materials **usage** variance include:

● A badly set (too loose a) standard

● Better than standard efficiency at using materials

● Higher than standard quality of materials being used, leading to lower than standard levels of material waste and/or rejected output.

Clearly an adverse variance would have implied opposite reasons to these, namely:

● Too tight a standard

● Sloppy usage of materials

● Lower than standard quality of materials being used, leading to higher than standard levels of material waste and/or rejected output.

Variances regarding usage of materials must be the responsibility, though not necessarily the fault of, the production manager.

Reasons for the adverse materials **price** variance include:

● A badly set (too tight a) standard

● Inefficiency in buying materials

● Higher than standard quality (and price) of materials being used

● An unexpected increase in market prices of raw materials purchased

A favourable variance would tend to be caused by such factors as:

● Too low a standard price

● An unexpected decrease in market prices, relative to the standard, of raw materials purchased

It would normally be the buying manager who would be held accountable for materials price variances. Of course, some of these reasons may not be the buyer's fault.

Note that when standards are set for production factors, particularly materials and labour, a particular grade or quality will be part of the standard and specified. For example, if the standard for direct materials includes 1 kg of material X, the standard must specify the grade of this material which is to be used, assuming that X comes in more than one grade. Similarly the grade of labour needs to be specified. The job may be envisaged as capable of being performed satisfactorily by an unskilled worker, and the standard direct labour cost will reflect this. If a higher grade of labour is employed on the work, the actual labour cost will tend to be higher, which will manifest itself in adverse labour cost variances.

In many practical cases, output requires the use of more than one type of material or labour (Smokey Ltd's product uses only one type of each). Where this is the situation it is necessary, if material and labour variances are to be useful to managers, to deal with each type of grade of material and labour separately.

Activity 9

Some people have advocated reporting the DMUV to the manager responsible for usage in physical quantities (in the case of the above example as 15 kg (A)), rather than as a financial figure.

Why do you think that this is the case and what is the counter argument?

The reason put forward for reporting such a variance in physical, rather than financial, terms is simply that the manager responsible for it deals with physical factors (eg quantities of the material) rather than with money.

The counter argument is that, in order for the manager responsible to assess the full implications of the failure to meet the target, the variance needs to be stated in financial terms. This is particularly important since the organisation's objectives are likely to be dominated by financial ones. In practice, it is probably a good idea to report both physical quantities and financial effects.

Activity 10

Hangups Ltd makes plastic coated wire clothes hangers. It buys the wire in lengths, which it cuts and shapes and then dips in molten plastic. The standard direct material cost of a clothes hanger is £0.38, made up as follows:

	£
1 metre of wire (@ £0.35/metre)	0.35
30 grams of plastic (@ £1.00/kg)	0.03
	£0.38

During January, 2,600 hangers were completed with the following direct material usage and cost:

2,700 metres of wire at cost of	£922
85 kg of plastic at cost of	£78

Have a try at calculating the total variance for each direct material, and to analysing it into its constituents. (Hint: You will need to do this separately for each material – wire and plastic.)

Hangups Ltd direct materials variances

Wire

TDMV	= (2600 × £0.35) - £922 =	£12 (A)
DMUV	= [(2600 × 1m) - 2700] × £0.35 =	£35 (A)
DMPV	= (2,700m × £0.35) - £922 =	£23 (F)

Plastic

TDMV	= (2600 × £0.03) - £78 =		ZERO
DMUV	= [(2600 × 0.03 kg) - 85] × £1.00 =		£7 (A)
DMDV	= £(85 × 1.00) - £78 =		£7 (F)

Note that, despite the fact that the TDMV for plastic is zero, there are nevertheless equal and opposite variances for the other two. Also note that there is a similar point with the wire, ie a small TDMV masking two larger figures.

Note also that the calculation of the two total variances is, in effect, flexing the budget.

Direct labour variances

THESE ARE QUITE SIMILAR to those for direct materials. The names given to the labour variances are different from those used for materials, however.

The *total direct labour variance* (TDLV) is the standard labour cost for the actual output, less the actual labour cost. In the case of our example, this figure can be read directly from the accounting statements, as the difference between the actual and flexed budget figures. This is £600 (F) (ie £18,000 - 17,400). It is favourable because the actual cost was £600 less than the budget 'allowance'. All things being equal, this would have led to an actual profit £600 greater than had been budgeted.

The *direct labour efficiency variance* (DLEV) (equivalent to DMUV) is the standard labour time for the actual output, less the actual labour time, costed at the standard labour rate. For Smokey Ltd last month, this would have been:

(4,500 - 4,600) × £4.00   = £400 (A)

This variance is unfavourable. This is because using more labour hours than are allowed for in the budget, given the level of output, lead to less profit than was budgeted. Obviously there may be other variances which will affect the relationship between the actual and the budgeted profit figures, but the direct labour efficiency taken alone will have an adverse effect on the budgeted profit.

The *direct labour rate variance* (DLRV) (equivalent to DMPV) is the standard rate for the actual hours less the actual labour cost.

ie (4,600 × £4.00) - £17,400   = £1,000 (F)

This is favourable because the actual amount paid for labour was less than the budget allowed, given the number of hours worked.

Activity 11

The standard direct labour cost of making a plastic coated wire clothes hanger at Hangups Ltd is £0.25, since the standard direct labour hour rate is £2.50 and the standard time to make a hanger is 6 minutes. In January, when the output was 2,600 hangers, the total labour cost was £725 and the hours worked were 280.

Have a go at calculating the total direct labour variance and analysing it between the direct labour efficiency and rate variances.

Hangups Ltd direct labour variances

TDLV	= (£0.25 × 2600) - £725 =	£75 (A)
DLEV	= [(2600 × 6/60 - 280] × £2.50 =	£50 (A)
DLRV	= (£2.50 × 280) - £725 =	£25 (A)

Activity 12

Which manager would normally be asked to account for Smokey Ltd's adverse labour efficiency variance?

Can you suggest possible reasons for a labour efficiency variance?

Do you think that the variance is likely to be that manager's fault? Why?

It is the production manager who would normally be responsible for managing direct labour, so it is this person who would be asked to account for efficiency variances in that area.

Possible reasons for an adverse direct labour **efficiency** variance include:

1. An unreasonably set standard.
2. A lower than planned grade of labour doing the work, leading to slowness.
3. A lower than planned grade of material being used, leading to more than standard levels of rejected work.
4. Generally poor management of the labour.

Since reasons 2 and 3 may not be within the control of the production manager, the adverse variances are not that person's fault, but he or she should be able to explain the reason for the variance.

Reason 4 is clearly under the direct control of the production manager.

A favourable direct labour efficiency variance could be caused by one or more of the following:

1. Too loose a standard.
2. A higher than planned grade of labour doing the work, leading to higher speed of working.
3. A higher than planned grade of material being used, leading to less than standard levels of rejected work.

Of course, reasons 2 and 3 are not necessarily reasons for rejoicing. Higher grades of labour and materials cost more. Thus, favourable efficiency variances are likely to be offset by higher rate and price variances. We shall return to the topic of the 'trade-off' of variances later in this unit.

Activity 13

What possible reasons are there for either favourable or an adverse direct labour rate variance?

A favourable direct labour **rate** variance could be caused by one or more of the following:

1. Too loose a standard.
2. A lower than planned grade of labour doing the work, leading to a lower rate of pay.
3. An unexpected reduction in the market rate of pay, relative to the standard.
4. A lower than planned level of production leading to lower than planned premium-rated overtime working.

Possible reasons for an adverse direct labour **rate** variance include:

1. An unreasonably set standard.
2. A higher than planned grade of labour doing the work, leading to a higher rate of pay.
3. An unexpected increase in the market rate of pay, relative to the standard.
4. A higher than planned level of production, leading to higher than planned premium-rated overtime working.
5. Poor management of labour costs.

Normally the personnel officer is the manager who would, in the first instance, be tackled about labour rate variances. Many of the reasons suggested above for such variances are, of course, not necessarily that managers fault. For example, these probably include reasons 3 and 4 for the adverse variances.

Fixed overhead variance

THIS IS SIMPLY THE difference between the budgeted and actual expense for fixed overheads. Since, by definition, fixed overheads do not vary with quantity, it does not matter whether we compare actual with the original budget or with the flexed one.

For Smokey Ltd the fixed overhead variance is:

£10,000 - 9,500 = £500 (F)

It is favourable because £500 less expense was incurred than had been allowed for in the budget, so all other things being as budgeted, the actual profit will be higher than budget by £500.

Possible reasons for fixed overhead variances could include a vast range of factors. This is because, unlike a cost such as direct labour, fixed overheads encompasses a very large number of different costs. These could include managerial salaries, depreciation of plant and machinery, rent of the premises. Probably we can summarise the situation by saying that favourable fixed overhead variances occur when less than the budgeted amount is spent on fixed overheads. Overspending, relative to the budget, will lead to adverse variances.

Such is the diverse nature of fixed costs that it would normally be unrealistic to seek to control all aspects through one single variance. Similarly, managerial responsibility for fixed costs is also likely to be fragmented. For example, it is unlikely that the manager who controls electricity usage is the same person who is responsible for the costs of employing cleaners, yet both of these costs are likely to be fixed, relative to the level of output.

Overheads are notoriously difficult to control. How, for example, can the person responsible for electricity usage exercise control? The business could insist that all lights, heaters or electrically powered equipment can only be switched on by, or on the express instructions of the person responsible. This would almost certainly be impossible, and undesirable, to achieve in practical terms. Probably the best that can be done here is for electricity costs to be managed on a departmental basis and for a general need to be careful with the use of electricity to be emphasised to staff.

The introduction of new technologies involving greater automation and lower direct labour input has tended to make fixed costs an increasingly large part of total costs for many businesses. This has probably meant that cost control is increasingly difficult.

Reconciling budgeted and actual profit

WE HAVE NOW IDENTIFIED and quantified all of the variances which occurred at Smokey Ltd last month. Since a variance can be defined as the extent to which actual profit will differ from budget in respect of the particular item under review, we should now be able to produce a statement reconciling the actual profit with the budgeted profit through the variances which we have just calculated.

This reconciliation would be as follows:

	Variances		
	Favourable	Adverse	
	£	£	£
Budget operating profit			£30,000
Sales volume variance		4,000	
Sales price variance		4,000	
Direct material usage variance	1,000		
Direct material price variance		1,400	
Direct labour efficiency variance		400	
Direct labour rate variance	1,000		
Fixed overhead variance	500		
	2,500	9,800	
		2,500	
Net adverse variance			7,300
Actual operating profit			£22,700

From this statement it is possible to see, in a reasonable amount of detail, how various factors have contributed to the extent to which the activities of Smokey Ltd went out of control last month. We can use this information to try to identify the manager who can be held accountable for each particular failure to perform to, or better than, budget. This is not to say that the manager concerned should be held to blame for failures to meet the budget, merely that there should normally be an identifiable individual who should be capable of pinpointing the reason or reasons for the failure. This will provide the first step towards the possibility of putting things right for the future. It is essential that in any well managed organisation there is an identifiable individual who is responsible for each aspect of the organisation's activities. This responsibility should include being aware of how and why there are significant variances between budgeted and actual performance in the area concerned. Later in this unit we shall consider the various features which need to be in place, if a system of control through variances is going to be able to work effectively.

The point was made in Unit 7 that one of the advantages claimed for budgets is their value as a motivating device. It seems reasonable to presume that knowing that explanations will need to be provided for failures to meet budget, will tend to encourage managers to take steps to try to ensure that budget totals are met. Put another way, it seems likely that accountability will tend to motivate performance.

Self-assessment question 1

Johnson Ltd makes one product, the gadget, the standard cost for which are as follows:

	£
Sales revenue	25
Direct labour (2.5 hours)	(10)
Direct material (1 kg)	(4)
Fixed overheads	(4)
Net profit	£7

During February, when the manufacturing and sales output were each budgeted at 1,000 gadgets, the actual output and sales were 900 gadgets sold for £22,100. The fixed overheads expenditure during the month was £3,740. The direct labour cost was £8,800 for 2200 hours work. The direct material consumed in production was 930 kg which was bought at a cost of £3,940.

Calculate all of the variances which we have covered so far in this unit and use them to reconcile the budgeted and the actual profit for the month.

Self-assessment question 2

Rupert Ltd makes one product, the trinket, for which the standard is as follows:

	£
Sales revenue	12
Direct material (3 kg)	(3)
Direct labour (2 hours)	(5)
Fixed overheads	(2)
Net profit	£2

The business carries no stocks of raw material, nor of completed goods. During January when the budgeted manufacturing and sales output was 2000 trinkets, the following took place:

Continued over . . .

> £
>
> | | | |
> |---|---|---|
> | Sales | 2,100 units | 26,500 |
> | Materials used | 6,400 kg | 6,520 |
> | Labour | 4,300 hours | 11,100 |
> | Fixed overheads | | 4,200 |
>
> Calculate all of the variances which we have covered so far in this unit and use them to reconcile the budgeted and the actual profit for the month.

Compensating variances – trade off of variances

SOMETIMES VARIANCES MIGHT BE related to other another, in such a way that an adverse variance on one aspect might give rise to a favourable one elsewhere. For example, a raw material buyer may be presented with the opportunity to buy some required raw material at a price lower than the standard price, because it is of lower than standard quality. The buyer may judge that, although this will engender adverse usage variances, these will be more than compensated for by favourable price variances.

Activity 14

Should the buyer follow his or her judgement in these circumstances? Can you think of possible reasons why trading off variances may not be a good idea here?

Whilst it is clearly a very restrictive and narrow approach to say that trading-off variances is never acceptable, it must nevertheless be approached with caution. The buyer should make sure that the scheme is acceptable to the production manager(s) concerned since substandard materials may have ramifications which go beyond usage and price of materials. Such materials may give rise to excessive direct labour time and/or substandard output each of which may have profound adverse effects on the business.

Other profit variances

THERE ARE MANY OTHER variances and sub-variances which can be calculated and can be useful in particular contexts. In this unit we have looked at the mainstream variances used in manufacturing industry. Once you have grasped the basic principles involved with variance analysis, you should find little difficulty with the others.

Variances not directly related to profit

WE HAVE SO FAR only considered departures from budgets, to the extent that these have a direct effect on profit. Organisations also make plans in areas other than sales and costs, however. There will, for example, be a cash budget. When an organisation is drawing up its plans for the forthcoming period, it will set out its projected cash receipts, payments and the resultant balance, probably on a month-to-month basis. An individual, a funds manager, will be given the responsibility for the management of the cash. Failure to follow the cash budget will not lead to a profit difference in the same way as will a failure to follow the sales budget. However, a cash shortage may well lead to the organisation being unable to follow its plans in other areas. For example, a lack of cash available to pay staff could mean that the organisation will have to scale down its level of output relative to that which was planned and depicted in the budget. This will have a real effect on profit, if only because to overcome the cash shortage, the organisation may have to borrow money and pay interest on it. Where borrowing is not an option, for example because the organisation does not have a sufficient credit rating, the cost of a cash shortage could be much greater than the cost of the interest which would have been payable.

If those charged with managing assets like cash are to be held accountable for what happens within their area of responsibility, there needs to be some way of quantifying the effects on profit of any departures from budget. This can be difficult because it is likely to involve some judgement as to the precise effect on profit of a particular difference between the actual and the budgeted cash balances. Nevertheless, it is important that there is proper accountability by all managers, so some means of confronting managers with the effects of their actions needs to be available.

As is often the case in management, a shortfall in performance of the manager responsible for cash management is not necessarily that manager's fault. If the credit controller, the manager responsible for managing trade debtors, fails to collect debts according to the trade debtor's budget, the ability of the cashier to meet the cash budget will be seriously impaired. Since, sooner or later, virtually every facet of the organisation will affect cash, the cashier may not be at fault if the cash budget is not met. The funds manager should however be in a position to explain where the problem lies.

There are other types of variance which are not directly related to profit. These relate to qualitative factors such as quality of product or service, customer satisfaction and staff turnover. Most organisations find it useful to set standards for the level of quality of its output of goods or services. Many also set standards for the level of customer satisfaction and for staff turnover. The actual level for these factors can be compared with the standard and the relevant managers held accountable for differences. As with areas like cash management, failures to achieve targets may not have direct effects on profits, but they can have profound indirect effects. Effective management probably requires that attempts are made to quantify these qualitative factors.

Organisations providing services, rather than producing goods, might find qualitative factors more useful control devices than variances which are concerned with purely financial matters. This is probably equally true of profit seeking businesses, like an advertising agency, as it would be for a non-profit seeking organisation, like a hospital.

Investigation of variances

VARIANCES TELL US THE location (within the organisation) and the extent of differences between planned and actual performance. The question arises as to what a manager should do when an area, within that manager's sphere of responsibility, shows a variance. As we have seen, variances simply highlight differences between plans and actual results. They do not tell us the cause. Sometimes the cause will be obvious, but often when there is a variance, work needs to be done to find its precise cause. This work costs money.

Not all variances should lead to senior management action. Many will be too trivial. If a manager is responsible for staff who, between them work 6,000 hours during a control period, should he or she be required to account to a superior if there has been an adverse labour efficiency variance of 10 hours, costing £50?

The reason for a small variance like this one could be very difficult and, therefore, expensive to trace. Taking any notice of it at all could well be highly prejudicial to staff morale. It might show senior management to be petty and unreasonable. Variances are not, in practice, expected to be zero in any particular control period. On the other hand there is a point at which a particular variance needs to be investigated. Most of us would agree that 10 hours in 6,000 is not a significant variance, but would 60 hours be significant? Would 600 hours be significant?

It is important to remember that the only logical purpose for calculating variances is to inform managers as to whether changes in behaviour will be necessary in order to meet future targets. Whether past targets have been met is somewhat academic, but a failure in one control period may imply that something is going wrong on a continuing and systematic basis. Obviously things may go wrong due to chance factors, ie factors which are unlikely ever to occur again. If these factors are the sole cause of variances for a particular aspect of the organisation, we should expect to find that, over a reasonable number of control periods, the cumulative sum of the variances will be zero. This is because chance factors, which adversely affect outcomes in one period, will be cancelled by other chance factors, of a favourable nature, in subsequent periods. This, of course, presupposes that the standards are sensibly set because, if this is the case, achievement of the targets will be 'normal' and failures 'abnormal'. It is worth noting that badly set standards are of themselves systematic failures, which must be corrected.

What we can probably say about investigating variances is:

● Where a variance is considered to be significant, it should always be investigated. A judgement may need to be made as to how far to take the investigation. The cost of investigation will need to be balanced against the potential benefits, in terms of being in a position to take steps to avoid repetitions of the same errors. Frequently a threshold level is preset, eg that all variances greater than 5% of the budgeted figure will cause some action to be taken.

● Even where a particular variance is deemed not to be significant enough to justify investigation, it is useful to look at the cumulative picture for that variance over a number of control periods. (Typically a control period is one month.)

Delegation and decentralisation of decision making

A COMMON FEATURE OF nearly all successful organisations is a fairly high degree of allowing junior managers to make decisions about, and take responsibility for, their own area of the business. Many people would argue that failure to do this is inconsistent with the best interests of the organisation, except in the short-term. This implies that businesses which are tightly managed by one dominant character do not succeed as well as do firms where there is delegation. There are powerful arguments in favour of decentralisation and these are reviewed in Unit 9. There are also powerful arguments for retaining a significant element of central control, however.

Reconciling the advantages and problems of delegation and decentralisation of decision making

FORTUNATELY THERE IS A technique for going much of the way to reconciling the obvious and profound benefits of delegation with its severe defects. This is by central control of budgets and standards. By defining the junior managers' terms of reference in the budget and then holding them accountable for failures to meet targets at regular and fairly frequent intervals, the junior manager can be left to manage, but within centrally agreed guidelines.

For example, an arable farmer employs a worker. Each day the farmer and the worker agree the day's task, say, on a particular day to plough a specific area of land. The farmer can now leave the worker to get on with the task and to make whatever decision might be necessary in doing the job. This seems a desirable state of affairs for both parties.

The job can be organised as the worker sees fit. The worker can work without a break until the job is finished and then go home early. The worker can take a long lunch break and finish late. The farmer is not breathing down the worker's neck all day. The worker is to some extent his or her own boss with the satisfaction that this is likely to engender. All that is required is that the specified area is ploughed during the day.

The farmer can spend the day doing other work, leaving the worker unsupervised. At the end of the day the farmer can physically inspect the land and judge whether or not the job has been done adequately. Even if things go wrong, perhaps because the worker takes this approach as an opportunity to take a day off, only one day has been wasted before this comes clearly to light. Bearing in mind that the alternative is much closer supervision, a time consuming activity particularly if the farmer would prefer to do some work some distance from the land to be ploughed, the risk of a lost day seems not too high a price to pay. This is particularly true where a sensible farmer would only apply this approach to a worker who was regarded as being reasonably responsible.

In this example/analogy the farmer is the senior manager, the worker the junior manager and the specified day's work is the budget (or perhaps the standard).

Control through budgets and standards

IN ORDER THAT THE benefits of centralised control can be combined with those of decentralised decision making and responsibility the following points must be considered:

● *Clearly defined areas of responsibility* must be identified or established. If a manager is to be held accountable for some aspect of the business, that manager, and every other interested person, should know clearly where the demarcation lines of responsibility lie. Situations where more than one manager has authority in an area should be avoided.

● Budget holding should go down to the *lowest practical managerial level*, so that as many people as reasonable are making their own decisions and being responsible for them. There is no reason for the advantages of delegation to be limited, except by the lack of suitability of the people involved to take decisions. In practice, there probably are not many individuals, however unskilled they may be, who would not perform better if they felt more involved in the decision making process, at however low a level.

Managers should *participate* in setting their own targets. The evidence is conflicting on this topic, which is perhaps not surprising in view of the difficulty of assessing motivation. However, it seems likely that the farm worker in our example would be more motivated to achieve a target, in the setting of which he or she has been involved, than one imposed. There is the obvious danger that managers will deliberately attempt to establish easy targets for themselves. However, people do not seem to do this in most aspects of life and if a particular manager is of such a character that he or she seeks to do so, it raises the question as to whether that person should have been made a manager in the first place.

● *Routine post-performance reporting systems* should be established. These should be part of the routine work of the accounts department, not a special exercise to be undertaken on odd occasions. These would be equivalent of the farmer's inspection of the ploughed land. The reports should show the actual performance (output, costs, etc), the budgeted performance and variances.

● Reporting periods should be *fairly short.* A month is a popular span for such reports. This is because it is judged that a month is sufficiently long a period to make a sensible assessment, without chance factors affecting the outcomes too much. It is also judged short enough for things not to be able to go out of control for too long before this fact is recognised, and corrective action taken. The amount of reports generated is inversely related to the length of the period, thus short periods lead to much generation of paper work. Generally people react adversely to having to read too many reports.

● Reports should be *designed specifically* for the manager concerned. Reports should restrict themselves to matters within the control of the particular manager. For example, a production supervisor should receive a report dealing only with material usage and labour efficiency within his or her domain. The production manager (the supervisor's immediate superior) should receive a report on the performance of each of the supervisors within production, perhaps in the form of a copy of each supervisor's report plus a report on matters which are the direct responsibility of the production manager, for example production overheads. The managing director (the production manager's immediate supervisor) should receive a summary of the production manager's report.

Individual reports designed for specific managers seems to imply a lot of work for the accounting staff. In fact, in these days of cheap computers and software, production of individual, tailor-made reports is not necessarily time consuming nor expensive.

● Reports should arrive *shortly after* the end of the reporting period to which they relate. The longer after the end of the reporting period that the report emerges, the less use it has. If the report on what happened in June does not appear until September the opportunity to use the June information quickly to correct anything going out of control is lost. In fact things could have been going wrong for over three months before there is any clue that this is the case.

Provided that the information on actual performance (for example, labour hours, wage payments, materials used and price paid, etc) can be identified closely following the end of the month, there seems little reason why a computer, already primed with the information on budgets and standards, should not be able to produce appropriate reports very quickly.

● *Tolerance levels* for variances should be established and only variances above this level should be investigated. It seems illogical that a production supervisor should be required to justify why 1 hour (say costing £4) of direct labour has been worked in excess of the allowed time, given the level of production, when the total labour hours worked in that area of the business was, say, 500 for the month. It seems sensible that, if insignificant variances are to be ignored, some definition of insignificance should be established in advance, and applied systematically, until some decision is taken at a high level of management to redefine insignificance.

● *Reasons for* significant variances should be sought, both by the manager whose responsibility it is, and by that manager's immediate superior. It should be emphasised that, because there may happen to be an adverse variance on some aspect within an individual manager's sphere of responsibility, this does not necessarily mean that he or she is at fault.

For example, an adverse variance for raw material price is within the sphere of influence of the buyer. If that variance is significant, the buyer should be held accountable for it since he or she is the person who knows, or should know, what has gone wrong. In fact, what might have gone wrong is a large unexpected increase in the price of a particular commodity.

It is clearly reasonable to ask the buyer to account for the variance to the extent of expecting him or her to be able to identify the reason for it, but not necessarily to blame him or her.

● *Corrective action* for the future should be taken, where variances reveal *systematic* deviations from standard. Usually it will be too late to correct things that have gone wrong in the past, but corrective action may well be possible for the future. For example, if investigation into a significant adverse materials usage variance reveals that pilferage was the problem, it may be possible to tighten security to avoid future occurrences of the same thing.

● The whole process of target setting, reporting and control should be seen as *important to senior management*, otherwise it will not be taken seriously by anyone and expense, perhaps great expense, will be incurred for nothing.

● Though a primary objective of variance reporting etc is to facilitate 'management by exception', senior managers should be careful to *recognise consistently good performance* by their subordinates and to reward it where possible. The danger of any system which tends to highlight failure (for one reason or another) to achieve targets is that it might fail formally to recognise success in achieving targets.

● Variance reporting should not be used as part of a *reign of terror* by senior management, but as a means of identifying junior managers who may well need some assistance and support from senior management.

Footnote to control through budgets and standards

IT MAY HAVE STRUCK you as you have worked through this unit that in learning management accounting through these units in an open learning environment you have been put in a very similar position to a junior manager in industry or commerce.

Activity 15

Go through the bullet points in the last section. With regard to each one, jot down the respects in which the way that you are working through this module follows the points.

We feel that the following is broadly true of Management Accounting.

● You have been given clearly defined tasks over which you had full control.

● You have had day to day control over your own work, you have not been told what to do, except as defined by the units and the study guide.

● There has not been participation in target setting for a number of reasons including the fact that the University insists on its own standards being imposed, not unreasonably. On the other hand, feedback on individual units will be taken up and alterations made for the future on such questions as insufficient activities etc.

● Routine past performance reporting has occurred in that, following each study period, a test or some other assessment has been set and the marked script returned to you.

● The study periods have all been relatively short, so there have been frequent assessments. It has not been possible for a student to fall far behind before this fact comes to light.

● You have had feedback on tests and other assessments specifically relating to your performance, rather than on the performance of others.

● Reports (marked assessments) have arrived shortly after the assessment was submitted (end of the particular study unit).

● Tolerance levels have been established. You have not been expected to achieve 100% for each test. It is accepted that though 100% may be possible, it is not reasonable to expect it more than occasionally.

● Reasons for poor performance have been sought in marking the tests and other assessments.

● Corrective action has been encouraged.

● Clearly the staff (senior management!?) have seen the whole process as important and have taken action to see people who seem to be having problems.

● Staff have tried to recognise good performance by comments on returned test scripts etc.

● Whether staff have used the whole process to indulge their sadistic tendencies by conducting a reign of terror, you are left to judge!

Reading

You should now read Reader Article 8.1 'Cost control: the manager's perspective' by C. Graham, D. Lyall and A. Puxty.

This article discusses some research finding on the views of managers on the effectiveness of cost control systems.

Points to consider as you read the article:

To what extent does standard costing/variance analysis seem to be used in UK companies?
Were managers pleased with the information which they received from the standard costing system?
How did the views of managers compare with those of accountants which were discovered in an earlier survey?

Problems with traditional variance analysis

THE USE OF VARIANCE analysis in an attempt to exercise control is widely practised, in all types of organisations. Clearly it is widely seen as a useful approach to management. The technique is not without its problems, some of which have had reference made to them already in this unit. The principal problem areas include the following:

- Large parts of the activities of most organisations cannot be controlled in the apparently neat, mathematical way which analysis of variances seems to imply. How, for example, should Shell control its expenditure on advertising, when there is no direct relationship between money spent and gallons of petrol sold? Such examples are not isolated or unusual, and probably such costs account for a significant proportion, easily more than 50% of all costs, in some cases. Costs like these are probably forming an increasing proportion of total costs.

- Standards become out of date. This is particularly a problem with standard prices. Unless steps are taken to keep them up-to-date their use can quickly bring the whole control process into disrepute. It is possible to link standard costs to some price index. This will only be satisfactory where the factor under consideration is changing in price at the same rate as the index used.

- The original budget may have become unachievable before a particular control period has even started. This will lead to variances which are caused by planning errors rather than operational problems. Unless variances arising from these two factors (planning and operations) are carefully separated, variances will be useless for control purposes.

- Lines of authority are not always capable of being as clear, in practice, as they should ideally be. Thus responsibility for some aspect of operations can fall into the area of responsibility of more than one manager.

Reading

You should now read Reader Article 8.2 'Feedforward control for competitive advantage: the Japanese approach' by Malcolm Morgan.

This article distinguishes between 'feedback' and 'feedforward' control, both of which have been discussed, but not in those precise terms, in this unit and in Unit 7. The point is made in the article that Japanese industry and commerce tends to pay rather more attention to feedforward control than we tend to do in other parts of the world.

Continued over . . .

Points to consider as you read the article:

What are the advantages of attaching particular importance to feedforward control?
Can an organisation use both feedback and feedforward control at the same time?

You should now read Reader Article 8.3 'Throughput accounting: the Garrett Automotive experience' by John Darlington, John Innes, Falconer Mitchell and John Woodward.

This article discusses the advantages which a UK company found from using throughput accounting (TA) techniques. TA tries to measure manufacturing performance in terms of the time taken to transform an order for goods into a shipment of those goods. Garrett Automotive's accountants estimated that they could vastly reduce manufacturing costs and, therefore, increase profit, if production time could be cut. They thus set out to provide management with reports which identified throughput times and areas of production where bottlenecks are occurring which slow down throughput time.

Points to consider as you read the article:

What problems did the company find with their previously produced detailed statements of variances?
Is TA incompatible with standard costing and variance analysis?

Control through variances in practice

THE ACCA SURVEY shows standard costing to be very widely used in UK manufacturing industry. 76% of all companies in the survey used the approach, with 83% of larger companies using it. This is consistent with the results of another survey mentioned in Reading 8.1. The ACCA survey showed that only 11% of the companies had ceased using standard costing in the previous 10 years.

In terms of what the companies used standard costs for, the following were found to be regarded as important uses to which standards were put:

	Percentage of companies
Cost control and performance evaluation (variance analysis etc)	72
Costing stock in trade	80
Deducing product costs	62
As an aid to budgeting	69
Data recording economies	43

The survey also showed that variances of the type which we considered in this unit are very widely used by UK manufacturers.

Some people have suggested that standard costing is less widely used in the non-manufacturing sectors. If this is true the results shown by the ACCA survey may not be entirely representative of all organisations.

Summary of the unit

THE UNIT STARTED BY considering the nature of control and the place of budgets and variance analysis in that context. The original budgets are, in practice, severely limited for control purposes. However if the budgets are revised to reflect actual levels of output, they can be valuable to help exercise control. Flexing the original budget requires a clear understanding of the relationships between costs, revenues and volumes. Comparison of the flexed budget and the actual performance enables us to identify areas of the business which are contributing to any failure of the business, as a whole, to meet its profit target. Thus variances can help to identify those managers who need to be held accountable for the variances. In order that any system of control through standards can work, certain practical steps must be taken regarding the administrative structure and culture of the business. The unit concluded with a brief discussion of the problems of trying to exercise control through variance analysis and a recognition that some of these problems are, in many practical situations, impossible to overcome.

Additional exercises

Exercise 1

Kellow Ltd manufactures one product which involves combining the bought-in components (one of each component per finished product) and carrying out some finishing work. All of the labour is of the same grade.

The standard for the product is as follows:

Original

	per unit £
Sales revenue	10.00
Direct labour (15 minutes)	(1.00)
Direct materials:	
component A	(2.00)
component B	(2.00)
Fixed overheads (based on output of 1000 units per month)	3.00)
Standard profit	2.00

During May, when the budgeted level of output was 1000 units, the following actual results occurred:

Actual

	£
Sales (980 units)	9,900
Direct labour (245 hours)	(990)
Direct materials:	
component A (985 used)	(2,010)
component B (980 used)	(1,950)
Fixed overheads	(2,850)
Actual profit	£2,100

You are required to calculate and analyse all the variances between planned and actual outcomes for May, and show how the planned and actual profit can be reconciled.

Exercise 2

The Elvery Manufacturing Company produces only one product. The budget and actual figures for the month of May were as follows:

	Budget	Actual
Sales (units)	1,000	1,050
	£	£
Sales revenue	12,500	12,600
Direct material cost	(2,200)	(2,500)
Direct labour cost	(6,000)	(6,250)
Fixed overhead cost	(3,000)	(2,800)
Profit	£1,300	£1,050

The following additional information is available:

i) There was an unexpected increase in the direct material cost of 10% of the budgeted figure. All of the material used during May was bought at the higher price.

ii) Each unit has a budgeted direct labour requirement of 2 hours. The actual total direct labour hours for May was 2,100.

You are required to calculate all of the variances and use them to reconcile the budgeted and actual profit figures.

Note This question is not quite the same as the other variance analysis problems which you have met so far in this unit. However, the question does contain sufficient information for you to be able to provide a full answer. It may require you to think about the problem just a bit more.

Solutions to self-assessment questions

Self-assessment question 1

Johnson Ltd

First it is necessary to flex the budget. The actual performance, the original budget and the flexed budget for February are as follows:

	Actual	Original Budget	Flexed Budget
Units made and sold	900	1,000	900
	£	£	£
Sales revenue	22,100	25,000	22,500
Direct materials	3,940 (930 kg)	4,000 (1,000 kg)	3,600 (900 kg)
Direct labour	8,800 (2,200 hr)	10,000 (2,500 hr)	9,000 (2,250 hr)
Fixed overheads	3,740	4,000 (see below)	4,000
	16,480	18,000	16,600
Net operating profit	5,620	7,000	5,900

The standard fixed overhead figure (£4) would originally have been deduced by taking the budgeted figure and dividing it by the budgeted output. To deduce the budgeted figure from the standard therefore is simply the reversal of that calculation. The flexed budget figure for fixed overheads will be the same as the original budget one since, by definition, fixed overheads do not vary with the level of output.

From the flexed budget we can go on to deduce the individual variances.

Sales volume variance

This is the difference between the original and flexed budgeted profit figures, ie £7,000 - 5,900 = £1,100 (A)

Sales price variance

This is the difference between the actual and flexed budget sales figures, ie £22,500 - 22,100 = £400 (A)

Direct labour efficiency variance

This is the difference between the flexed budget and actual hours of labour worked, priced at the standard rate per hour, ie (2,250 - 2,200) × £4 = £200 (F)

Direct labour rate variance

This is the difference between the actual wages paid and the amount which would have been paid had the rate been the standard one, ie £8,800 - (2,200 × £4) = zero

Direct material usage variance

This is the difference between the flexed budget and actual usage of the material, priced at the standard price per kg, ie (930 - 900) × £4 = £120 (A)

Direct material price variance

This is the difference between the actual amount paid for the material, and the amount which would have been paid had the price been the standard price, ie £3,940 - (930 × £4) = £220 (A)

Fixed overhead variance

This is simply the difference between the actual and budgeted overhead expense, ie £4,000 - 3,740 = £260 (F)

This reconciliation would be as follows:

	Variances		
	Favourable	Adverse	
	£	£	£
Budget operating profit			£7,000
Sales volume variance		1,100	
Sales price variance		400	
Direct material usage variance		120	
Direct material price variance		220	
Direct labour efficiency variance	200		
Direct labour rate variance			
Fixed overhead variance	260		
	460	1,840	
		460	
Net adverse variance			1,380
Actual operating profit			£5,620

Self-assessment question 2

Rupert Ltd

First flex the budget. The actual performance, the original budget and the flexed budget for February are as follows:

	Actual	Original Budget	Flexed Budget
Units made and sold	2,100	2,000	2,100
	£	£	£
Sales revenue	26,500	24,000	25,200
Direct materials	6,520 (6,400 kg)	6,000 (6,000 kg)	6,300 (6,300 kg)
Direct labour	11,100 (4,300 hr)	10,000 (4,000 hr)	10,500 (4,200 hr)
Fixed overheads	4,200	4,000	4,000
	21,820	20,000	20,800
Net operating profit	4,680	4,000	4,400

From the flexed budget we can deduce the following variances:

Sales volume variance

This is the difference between the original and flexed budgeted profit figures, ie £4,400 - 4,000 = **£400 (F)**

Sales price variance

This is the difference between the actual and flexed budget sales figures, ie £26,500 - 25,200= **£1,300 (F)**

Direct material usage variance

This is the difference between the flexed budget and actual usage of the material, priced at the standard price per kg, ie (6,400 - 6,300) × £1 = **£100 (A)**

Direct material price variance

This is the difference between the actual amount paid for the material and the amount which would have been paid, had the price been the standard price, ie £6,520 - (6,400 × £1) = **£120 (A)**

Direct labour efficiency variance

This is the difference between the flexed budget and actual hours of labour worked, priced at the standard rate per hour, ie (4,300 - 4,200) × £2.50 = **£250 (A)**

Direct labour rate variance

This is the difference between the actual wages paid and the amount which would have been paid, had the rate been the standard one, ie £11,100 - (4,300 × £2.50) = **£350 (A)**

Fixed overhead variance

This is the difference between the actual and budgeted overhead expense, ie £4,200 - 4,000 = **£200 (A)**

This reconciliation would be as follows:

Variances

	Favourable £	Adverse £	£
Budget operating profit			4,000
Sales volume variance	400		
Sales price variance	1,300		
Direct material usage variance		100	
Direct material price variance		120	
Direct labour efficiency variance		250	
Direct labour rate variance		350	
Fixed overhead variance		200	
	1,700	1,020	
	1,020		
Net favourable variance			680
Actual operating profit			£4,680

Answers to additional exercises

Additional exercise 1

Kellow Ltd

The actual performance, the original budget and the flexed budget for May were as follows:

	Actual		Original Budget		Flexed Budget	
Units made and sold	980		1,000		980	
	£		£		£	
Sales revenue	9,900		10,000		9,800	
Direct labour	990	(245 hr)	1,000	(250 hr)	980	(245hr)
Direct material						
Component A	2,010	(985 un.)	2,000	(1,000 un.)	1,960	(980 un.)
Component B	1,950	(980 un.)	2,000	(1,000 un.)	1,960	(980 un.)
Fixed overheads	2,850		3,000		3,000	
	7,800		8,000		7,900	
Net operating profit	2,100		2,000		1,900	

From the flexed budget we can deduce the following variances:

Sales volume variance

This is the difference between the original and flexed budgeted profit figures, ie £2,000 - 1,900 = **£100 (A)**

Sales price variance

This is the difference between the actual and flexed budget sales figures, ie £9,900 - 9,800 = **£100 (F)**

Direct labour efficiency variance

This is the difference between the flexed budget and actual hours of labour worked, priced at the standard rate per hour, ie (245 - 245) × £4.00 = **zero**

Direct labour rate variance

This is the difference between the actual wages paid and the amount which would have been paid, had the rate been the standard one, ie £990 - (245 × £4.00) = **£10 (A)**

Direct material (component A) usage variance

This is the difference between the flexed budget and actual usage of the material, priced at the standard price per unit, ie (985 - 980) × £2 = **£10 (A)**

Direct material (component A) price variance

This is the difference between the actual amount paid for the material and the amount which would have been paid, had the price been the standard price, ie £2,010 - (985 × £2) = **£40 (A)**

Direct material (component B) usage variance

This is the difference between the flexed budget and actual usage of the material, priced at the standard price per unit, ie (980 - 980) × £2 = **zero**

Direct material (component B) price variance

This is the difference between the actual amount paid for the material and the amount which would have been paid, had the price been the standard price, ie £(980 × £2) - 1,950 = **£10 (F)**

Fixed overhead variance

This is the difference between the actual and budgeted overhead expense, ie £3,000
- 2,850 = **£150 (F)**

The reconciliation would be as follows:

	Variances		
	Favourable	Adverse	
	£	£	£
Budget operating profit			2,000
Sales volume variance		100	
Sales price variance	100		
Direct material (A) usage variance		10	
Direct material (A) price variance		40	
Direct material (B) usage variance			
Direct material (B) price variance	10		
Direct labour efficiency variance			
Direct labour rate variance		10	
Fixed overhead variance	150		
	260	160	
	160		
Net favourable variance			100
Actual operating profit			£2,100

Additional exercise 2

The Elvery Manufacturing Company

The actual performance, the original budget and the flexed budget for May are as follows:

	Actual		Original Budget		Flexed Budget	
Units made and sold	1,050		1,000		1,050	
	£		£		£	
Sales revenue	12,600		12,500		13,125	
Direct materials	2,500		2,200		2,310	
Direct labour	6,250	(2,100 hr)	6,000	(2,000 hr*)	6,300	(2,100 hr*)
Fixed overheads	2,800		3,000		3,000	
	11,550		11,200		11,610	
Net operating profit	1,050		1,300		1,515	

* The original and flexed budget figures for labour hours are deduced from the fact that the standard time for each unit of output is 2 hours.

From the flexed budget we can deduce the following variances:

Sales volume variance

This is the difference between the original and flexed budgeted profit figures, ie £1,515 - 1,300 = £215 (F)

Sales price variance

This is the difference between the actual and flexed budget sales figures, ie £13,125 - 12,600 = £525 (A)

Direct material price variance

All of the material was bought for 10% more than the standard cost. This means that 10/110 of the total cost of materials is the adverse materials price variance, ie 10/110 × £2,500 = £227 (A)

Direct material usage variance

From the information provided it is not possible to calculate this variance directly. However, we know the total direct materials variance is the difference between the actual and flexed budget figure for direct materials ie £190 (A) (ie £2,500 - 2,310). This is the algebraic sum of the price and usage variances. Thus the usage variance must be £227 - 190, ie £37 (F).

Direct labour efficiency variance

This is the difference between the flexed budget and actual hours of labour worked, priced at the standard rate per hour, ie (2,100 - 2,100) × £3 = zero.

Direct labour rate variance

This is the difference between the actual wages paid and the amount which would have been paid had the rate been the standard one, ie (2,100 × £3) - 6,250 = £50 (F)

Fixed overhead variance

This is the difference between the actual and budgeted overhead expense, ie £3,000 - 2,800 = £200 (F)

This reconciliation would be as follows:

	Variances		
	Favourable	Adverse	
	£	£	£
Budget operating profit			1,300
Sales volume variance	215		
Sales price variance		525	
Direct material usage variance	37		
Direct material price variance		227	
Direct labour efficiency variance			
Direct labour rate variance	50		
Fixed overhead variance	200		
	502	752	
		502	
Net adverse variance			250
Actual operating profit			£1,050

UNIT 9

DIVISIONAL PERFORMANCE MEASUREMENT AND CONTROL

IN THIS UNIT WE will consider the problems and issues associated with the measurement of performance and the control of businesses which are organised into operating divisions. We will discuss the methods used for measuring and controlling divisional performance and we will examine the issue of pricing goods and services transferred between operating divisions within the same business entity.

Having completed this unit you should be able to:

● outline the main features of a divisional structure within a business

● identify and discuss the advantages and disadvantages of a divisional structure within a business

● calculate return on investment (ROI) and residual income for an operating division and discuss the strengths and weaknesses of the ROI and residual income methods

● explain the main objectives of a transfer pricing system and discuss the advantages and disadvantages of the main methods of setting a transfer price for goods and services.

Outline of the unit

MOST ORGANISATIONS, WHICH EMPLOY more than a very small number of people, are managed on a divisional or departmental basis. That is to say that these organisations consist of a number of sub-units, which are usually known as divisions or departments. Divisionalisation is so common that we may not even consider whether it is a good idea or not. This unit starts by pointing out that to try to manage a business as a single unit will be virtually impossible, unless that business is very small.

The unit goes on to discuss the varying levels of autonomy which divisions tend to have, in practice. In some cases control, and much decision making, is held at the central senior management level. Only the day-to-day operating decisions, concerning the division, are made by divisional managers. In other cases the divisions are almost completely independent businesses, where virtually all of the decisions, concerning the division, are made at divisional level. How any particular business is organised, in this respect, is a matter of the judgement of the senior management of the business (eg the board of directors). This judgement will reflect the particular circumstances involved, as well as the attitudes of senior managers.

The unit assesses the advantages and disadvantages of divisionalisation. The advantages are partly concerned with the smoother running of the division; speedier decision making etc. You should note, however, that there are also more general advantages to the business; freeing senior management time, developing junior management talent, etc. The disadvantages of divisionalisation should be noted. To some extent these can be mitigated, but there will inevitably be some disadvantages, with which the divisionalised business will have to live. One potential disadvantage of delegation of decision making is a loss of control of the organisation by senior management. We saw in previous units, however, that a sound system of budgetary control can overcome this problem to a great extent.

Much of the unit is concerned with yardsticks by which a division's performance can be assessed. When budgets are being set for and by divisions, some overriding measure of performance will be established, at which the divisional management will aim. This is exactly the same as the position for the business as a whole, ie it will also have such a target. This 'profit' target will be incorporated in the divisional budgets, in exactly the same way as the budgets for the whole business will incorporate such a target. It is against the target (ie the budgets) that the division's actual performance will be assessed. Two profit-type targets are frequently used as divisional performance measures.

The first of the two popular divisional performance measures is return on investment (ROI). This is basically a return on capital employed measure, similar to that which is sometimes used by analysts to assess overall business performance. This compatibility with a measure used to assess the whole business is regarded as a major strength of ROI for assessing a division. There are problems with using ROI and these are discussed in the unit and illustrated in Activity 3.

The second divisional performance measure discussed in this unit is residual income (RI). RI is essentially the profit of the division, after making an allowance for the financing cost of the assets tied up in the division. One advantage which RI has over ROI is that it not a ratio. Ratios can mislead. Activity 5 highlights differences between the two measures of performance.

This unit also discusses the more general problems of assessing divisional performance and makes the point that neither ROI, nor RI, is the perfect answer. It goes on to explain that there are other measures, not all of them financial, which can be used.

The unit also introduces the subject of transfer pricing. It is very common for one division of a business to sell some part, perhaps all, of its output to another division. Where the business is a conglomerate, it may just happen to be the case that one division uses a product or a service which another division could provide. With vertically integrated businesses, a division may exist expressly to supply another division.

If the performance of individual divisions are to be separately assessed, transfer pricing becomes a problem. If a high price is charged, the supplying division will make a high profit on the output transferred. At the same time the receiving division will be less profitable as a result of being charged the high price. Obviously where the receiving department is selling its output externally there is a limit to how much of the high transfer price it can pass on to customers. Where divisional managers are assessed on some measure of divisional profit, this situation will lead to conflict. The problem does not really arise with transfers between two independent businesses, because the discipline of the market place and the likely existence of other suppliers, in a competitive market, will establish the price. This discipline will not really exist for internal transfers between divisions.

You should note carefully the objectives which are pursued when setting a transfer price, explained in the section. These should be uppermost in the mind of managers when faced with the problem. As we shall see in later sections, it is often impossible to reconcile two or more of these and some compromise must be reached.

The main methods of setting transfer prices are reviewed in this unit. You should note that, where there is an external market, into which a supplier division can sell and from which a receiver division can buy, the best transfer price is the market price. This is because the market price represents the opportunity cost of making the internal transfer to both divisions. Put another way, both divisions will be just as happy to deal with one another, as they would be to deal with an outside customer or supplier because it is equally profitable for them to do so.

Unfortunately such markets do not always exist, in which case a price needs to be generated within the business.

Now that you have a broad idea of what the unit is about let us consider the detail.

Divisionalised businesses

LARGE BUSINESSES OFTEN ENGAGE in a variety of business activities which can result in a wide range of goods and services being supplied to customers. Where this occurs, the day-to-day operations of the various activities can become extremely difficult to manage. In order to deal with the scale and complexity of a large business it is common to divide the business into operating segments or divisions. Each division is, in essence, a business within a business and will operate, to a large extent, as a separate entity. The managers of a division will take responsibility for a particular product/service or group of products/services. They will usually be given the authority to make decisions concerning the pricing and mix of these products/services and the level of output required. As the divisional managers are given a considerable amount of autonomy in their decision making, they will also normally be held accountable for the level of sales performance, costs and profit performance of their division.

In practice, the extent to which large businesses operate a divisionalised structure will vary. Some large businesses may have certain functions such as administration, personnel and public relations remaining the responsibility of central management. These central functions will usually support all the divisions operating within the business. The degree of autonomy permitted at the divisional level will also vary. Some businesses will give divisional managers the authority to make capital expenditure decisions in addition to decisions concerning revenues and costs. Where this level of autonomy is allowed the division is referred to as an *investment centre*. Other businesses, however, will require capital expenditure decisions relating to a division to be sanctioned by central management. Managers at the divisional level will be responsible only for the profit performance of the division based on the assets assigned to it by central management. In this, case, the division is referred to as a *profit centre*.

Advantages and disadvantages of divisionalisation

DIVIDING A BUSINESS INTO operating divisions has both advantages and disadvantages. The managers of the business must therefore evaluate the potential advantages and disadvantages in order to decide whether a divisionalised structure is appropriate to their particular business.

Activity 1

Can you think of any advantages which may accrue to a business which operates a divisional structure rather than a structure where central management makes decisions?

A number of advantages may accrue to a business from the operation of a divisional structure. These include the following:

Forward planning In a divisional structure, decisions concerning day-to-day operations are delegated to divisional managers. This should allow the central managers more time to consider the future direction of the business. They should have more opportunity to anticipate future threats and problems and to develop appropriate policies to deal with these.

Responsiveness to market conditions Where operating decisions are made by central management there may be delays in making decisions as information passes through the chain of command. This may make the business less able to respond quickly to changes in market conditions.

Local knowledge Managers of operating divisions usually have an intimate knowledge of the issues and problems associated with the products for which they have responsibility. This detailed knowledge should improve the quality of decisions made.

Motivation A divisional structure permits managers greater autonomy in their decision making. This can improve the level of motivation and commitment of managers which may, in turn, improve their performance.

Management development Managing an operating division provides managers a taste of the problems of running a business. This should provide useful experience for managers and should help prepare them for a more senior position within a business.

Although there are advantages associated with a divisional structure there may also be disadvantages.

Activity 2

Can you think of any disadvantages of having a divisionalised structure for a business?

Some possible disadvantages include:

Economies of scale The organisation may be less able to benefit from economies of scale such as the benefits of bulk buying or administration savings if operating decisions are being made at the divisional level.

Conflicts of interest Operating divisions may compete with each other particularly where they are operating in the same markets. The gains enjoyed by one division may be at the expense of another division within the same business. This competition between divisions may hinder the sharing of resources and information within the business as a whole. This could mean that profits for the total business entity are adversely affected.

Risk avoidance At the level of the business as a whole, the risks of a project opportunity in a particular division may be reduced by other project opportunities in other divisions. In addition, shareholders may hold a portfolio of shares in different companies thereby further reducing their exposure to risk from the project. This may mean that shareholders will be prepared to accept a high risk project within a particular division. The divisional manager, however, may be less willing to take on a high risk project as his/her exposure to the risk of the project failing may be much higher. This may lead to a decision by the divisional manager to abandon the project which may not be in the interests of the owners of the business.

Increasing costs It may be difficult for central management to monitor closely the way in which divisional managers operate. As a result, there is a risk that divisional managers will act in a way which increases their own welfare at the expense of the owners of the business. For, example, divisional managers may award themselves various perquisites ('perks') which are not really necessary to retain their services. They may also try to increase the size of their division simply in order to increase their status and power within the business and to enhance their prospects of promotion.

It is necessary for central management to be aware of the potential disadvantages associated with divisionalisation. Some of the problems can be eliminated or reduced by careful monitoring or by ensuring that divisional managers are given appropriate incentives to act in the interest of owners.

Measures of performance

IT IS IMPORTANT FOR central management to monitor the performance of operating divisions within their business. Central management will require regular performance reports in order to:

● assess the profit generated by the resources invested in each division.

● assess the methods and policies employed to achieve the profits generated.

● assess the performance of the divisional managers.

Two measures of performance used by divisionalised businesses to help make such assessments are return on investment (ROI) and residual income. Both of these measures are considered in detail below.

Return on investment (ROI)

THIS IS A WIDELY used ratio and represents a fundamental measure of profitability. ROI relates the profits generated to the assets employed (investment). For an operating division, the ratio is calculated as follows:

$$ROI = \frac{\text{Divisional profit}}{\text{Divisional investment}} \times 100$$

This ratio may be broken down into its two main elements as follows:

$$ROI = \frac{\text{Divisional profit}}{\text{Divisional sales}} \times \frac{\text{Divisional sales}}{\text{Divisional investment}}$$

This breakdown reveals that ROI is determined both by the net profit margin on sales generated and the productivity of the investment base in generating sales.

The ratio measures *relative* performance rather than *absolute* performance. This means it can be used to compare the performance of divisions of differing size within a business.

Example 1

Consider the data relating to two separate divisions within the same business:

	Melford division £	Hexbury division £
Divisional profit for the year	100,000	200,000
Divisional investment	400,000	2,000,000

Melford division generating a profit of £100,000 with assets employed of £400,000 will generate a ROI of 25% and Hexbury division generating a profit of £200,000 with assets employed of £2 million will generate a ROI of 10%. Although Hexbury division has made twice the profits of Melford division in absolute terms, it has a much lower ROI. This may be due to a lower profit margin, lower productivity of assets employed, or both of these.

It can be argued that, as ROI is a widely used measure of performance for the business as a whole, the use of this measure for the divisions within the business is, therefore, appropriate. However, the use of ROI for operating divisions does raise certain issues and problems. Some of the more important are as follows:

Defining ROI There is a problem in deciding how divisional profit and divisional investment should be defined. Measuring divisional revenues and expenses may be difficult, particularly where sales and purchases of goods and services are made between divisions within the same business. (This issue is discussed in detail later in this unit.) The term 'divisional investment' is also rather vague. It may be defined in terms of either net assets (ie assets net of liabilities) or total assets employed. In addition, divisional assets may be valued either at historic cost or by using some form of current value.

Controllable items In the unit which dealt with full costing, we saw that, in order to be able to evaluate the performance of a manager, it is important to distinguish between *controllable* and *non-controllable* items. Controllable items are those items incurred by the division which the divisional manager has the authority to regulate. Non-controllable items are those items which the divisional manager does not have the authority to regulate. Only controllable items should be used when evaluating the performance of the divisional manager. Thus, when employing ROI as a measure of managerial performance, only *controllable profit* and *controllable investment* should be taken into account. Controllable profit will normally be equal to sales less variable costs and controllable fixed costs. Any allocations of central costs to the divisions should be excluded as they will be the responsibility of another manager. The level of controllable investment will depend on the extent to which the divisional manager has authority over investment in fixed assets stocks and debtors etc.

Behavioural problems In the unit which dealt with budgets we saw that, where budget targets are set for managers to reach, they may try to manipulate accounting numbers in order to achieve the desired result. If divisional ROI is used as a basis for managerial performance evaluation there is a danger that similar problems will occur.

Sub-optimal performance If ROI is used to evaluate managerial performance, there is a danger that this will result in divisional managers rejecting profitable opportunities. To illustrate this point consider the following activity.

Activity 3

The chemical division of ICP plc made a profit of £5m for last year on assets invested of £20m. The divisional manager has an opportunity to exploit a new product which will require an additional investment of £8m and will generate an additional profit of £1.5m.

The cost of capital of ICP plc is 15%.

Required:

Explain why this new product opportunity may create a dilemma for the divisional manager.

A dilemma may be created because the effect of taking the opportunity to exploit the new product could lower the ROI of the division. For last year the ROI was 25% (£5m/£20m). However, other things being equal, the ROI will be reduced to approximately 23% (£6.5m/£28m) if this opportunity is taken. This reduction in ROI may reflect badly on the divisional manager and may make him/her reluctant to pursue the new opportunity. Note that the cost of capital of the company is 15%. As this is below the expected return of 23%, the wealth of the shareholders would be enhanced by taking this opportunity. The manager may, therefore, have to decide between what may appear to be in his/her own best interests and what will be in the best interests of the shareholders.

It is also possible to have a converse situation arising. Suppose the investment base for the division in the above activity was £45m and all other information remained the same. The ROI for last year would then be approximately 11% (£5m/£45m) and the ROI would increase to more than 12% if the project is undertaken. The improved ROI, however, is still well below the cost of capital of the business. Thus, by deciding to undertake the project, the ROI of the division will be improved although this investment may not be in the best interests of the shareholders.

Residual income

THIS SECOND MEASURE OF divisional performance is designed to avoid some of the problems mentioned above. Residual income may be defined as the income of the division after deducting a capital charge for the cost of the divisional investment. The cost of capital is used as the basis for deriving the capital charge to be deducted. The cost of capital will be applied to the divisional investment in order to calculate the appropriate capital charge. Consider the following example.

Example 2

Hydra Controls Ltd has a paint manufacturing division which recently reported operating profits of £80,000. The division has assets employed of £320,000 and the company has a cost of capital of 10%.

What is the residual income of the division?

The residual income is calculated as follows:

	£
Operating profit	80,000
Less capital charge (10% × £320,000)	32,000
Residual income	48,000

Activity 4

Refer to the information in Activity 3 above.

Required:

(a) Calculate the residual income for the chemical division of ICP plc:
(i) for last year, and
(ii) for the current year assuming the new product opportunity is taken.

(b) Explain how this measure of divisional performance may result in a different view being taken by the divisional manager towards the new product opportunity.

The residual income of the chemical division is calculated as follows:

	Last year £m	Current year £m
Divisional income	5.0	6.5
Less		
Capital charge (15% × £20m)	3.0	
Capital charge (15% × £28m)		4.2
Residual income	2.0	2.3

We can see that the residual income of the chemical division will increase by taking on the new product opportunity. There is an incremental benefit of £0.3m (£2.3m - £2.0m) arising. Residual income will always increase if new opportunities generate a return which is in excess of the cost of capital. This increase in residual income should result in a different decision to that made if ROI is used in this situation.

The use of this measure should eliminate the sort of problem where the interests of the division may be in conflict with the interests of the business as a whole. The measure should facilitate goal congruence, ie a situation where the objectives of the divisional manager and the owners are in harmony. An increase in residual income will reflect an improvement in divisional performance and will also increase the returns of the owners.

We have seen that residual income is an absolute measure and does not provide a ratio of profitability. One advantage of a ratio, as discussed earlier, is that differences in size between divisions can be dealt with more easily. Consider the following activity.

Activity 5

Amalgamated Consolidated plc has two operating divisions. Maintenance division has assets of £1.0m and Building division has assets of £20.0m. The ROI of each division for the current year is 20% and 15% respectively. The company has a cost of capital of 10%.

Required:

(a) Calculate the residual income of each division for the current year.

(b) What return on investment ROI would Maintenance division require in order to achieve the residual income of Building division?

(c) Comment on your findings.

---

a) The residual income of each division may be calculated as follows:

	Maint'nce £m	Building £m
Divisional income		
20% × £1.0m	0.2	
15% × £20.0m		3.0
Cost of capital		
10% × £1.0m	0.1	
10% × £20.0m		2.0
Residual income	0.1	1.0

b and c) We can see that the residual income of Maintenance division is much lower than Division. However, the ROI calculation shows that it is producing a better return on divisional investment.

It is easier for Building division to generate a high residual income than Maintenance division. In order to achieve the same residual income as Building division, it would be necessary for Maintenance division to achieve a ROI of 110% (1.0 + 0.1/1.0).

When comparing the performance of different divisions it is, therefore, desirable to take account of the assets employed by each division.

Measurement issues

WE HAVE SEEN ABOVE that both of the major measures of divisional performance have their drawbacks. In reality, there is no single measure of performance that can portray the performance of an operating division and its management adequately. By focusing on a single measure there is a risk that the measure itself will become more important than the underlying performance of the division which it attempts to reflect. This may lead divisional managers to undertake actions which are not in the best interests of the business as a whole (see Activity 3 above) or to manipulate the measure in order to achieve the desired result.

Wherever possible, the performance of a division should be compared to some external yardstick, such as the performance of a business offering the same range of goods and services as the division. The fact that a division has outperformed other divisions within a particular business may not be very significant if it is operating in a market which produces high returns and other divisions within the business are operating in markets which produce low returns. It is the returns of the division *relative to similar businesses* which are important for evaluation purposes. Similarly, the fact that divisional performance has improved over previous periods may not be cause for satisfaction if the division has a much lower level of performance than similar businesses in the same industry.

Where divisions within a business have quite different risk characteristics it may be appropriate to apply different costs of capital when measuring residual income or when making comparisons between ROI and the cost of capital. Thus, a high risk business may have a risk premium added to its cost of capital in order to make a proper assessment of its performance.

An excessive concern for ROI or residual income measures can create a short-term perspective among divisional managers. This may lead them to make decisions which will improve the particular measure in the short-term even though this may be harmful to long-term profitability. For example, it may be possible to increase profits in the short-term by reducing staff training, or by cutting back on R&D even though these factors may be important to the long-term success of the business. This kind of tension between short-term and long-term profits is not, of course, peculiar to divisions operating within a business. It can also occur in businesses which do not have a divisional structure where there is an excessive concern for short-term measures of profitability.

It is important for owners and managers to recognise that various factors contribute towards the success of a business and that short-term improvements in profits may be at the expense of long-term profits. This means that a variety of measures both financial and non-financial, and covering different time horizons, will be necessary to evaluate the performance of an operating division and its management. These measures may look at various aspects of performance such as **productivity, market position, customer satisfaction, employee satisfaction, social responsibilities of the business, investment in research and development, etc.**

Various measures are available for each aspect of performance identified above.

Activity 6

Consider a manufacturing business which has an operating division producing a single product.

Can you suggest how the senior managers might seek to measure the productivity of the operating division? Try and think of *three* possible measures.

You may have thought of some of the following:

    total output during an operating period
    output per employee
    profit per employee
    sales/assets employed
    profit/assets employed

This is not an exhaustive list. You may well have identified other measures of productivity you consider to be appropriate.

Note that the measures of productivity may be expressed in both financial and non-financial terms. The measures identified are not mutually exclusive. Each measure will help provide an insight into the productivity of the business. By using a number of measures the manager is likely to obtain a better 'feel' for the productivity of the division.

The various aspects of divisional performance identified earlier (ie market position, customer satisfaction, etc) are relevant to the manufacturing and service sectors alike. In the activity which follows, you are required to think about how financial and non-financial measures of performance might be used to evaluate a division of a service sector business. When answering this activity try and put yourself in the position of a senior manager of the business who is accountable for the results of the division.

Activity 7

Hoopers & Co is a large accountancy firm which has a management consultancy division.

Can you suggest *four* measures (two financial measures and two non-financial measures) which might be used to help evaluate the performance of the management consultancy division?

The measures you select can attempt to deal with any of the aspects of divisional performance identified above.

In answering this activity you may have thought of some of the following measures:

Financial

> market share
> % change on fee income
> fee income per consultant
> investment in staff training and development

Non-financial

> staff turnover
> number of new clients taken on
> level of client satisfaction

You may have thought of other measures which are equally valid.

Now try this self-assessment question. This is intended to give you the opportunity to see whether you have grasped the material so far. You should probably be able to complete this in three quarters of an hour. Don't worry if it takes you longer. The main point is that, once you have completed it, you are clear on all of the points which it involves. It is not really helpful to look at the answer to this until you have completed your answer.

Self-assessment question

Glasnost plc is a large group organised on divisional lines. Two typical divisions are East and West. They are engaged in broadly similar activities and, therefore, central management compares their results in order to make judgements on managerial performance. Both divisions are regarded as investment centres.

A summary for the current year's return of the two divisions is as follows:

	West		East	
	£000	£000	£000	£000
Capital employed		2,500		500
Sales		1,000		400
Manufacturing cost:				
Direct	300		212	
Indirect	220		48	
Selling and distribution cost	180	700	40	300
Divisional profit		300		100
Allocation of uncontrollable				
central overhead costs		50		20
Net profit		250		80

West division has recently incurred substantial expenditure on automated production lines and new equipment. East has quite old plant. Approximately 50% of the sales of East are inter-company transfers to other divisions within the group. These transfers are based on an unadjusted prevailing market price. the inter-company transfers of West are minimal.

Management of the group focus on return on investment as a major performance indicator. Their required minimum corporate rate of return and cost of capital is 10%.

Required:

a) Compute any ratios (or other measures) which you consider will help in an assessment of the costs and performance of the two divisions.

b) Comment upon this performance making reference to any matters which give cause for concern when comparing the divisions or in divisional performance generally.

(The answer to this self-assessment question is at the back of the unit.)

Reading

You should now read the Reader Article 9.1 'Bench-marking in divisionalised companies' by Roy Skinner.

In your previous studies you may have learnt that businesses often find it useful to compare their own performance with the performance of similar businesses in the same industry. Performance data of similar businesses, which are a form of 'bench-mark', may be available through an inter-firm comparison (IFC) scheme for the industry. However, where a business has divisions operating in different business sectors finding a similar business overall may be impossible. As a result, it is more useful for comparisons of performance to be made on a divisional basis. In this way you are more likely to be comparing like with like.

This article explores the benefits and problems associated with comparing the performance of divisions owned by different businesses. You will see that a major problem concerns the comparability of data. Different businesses may have different views on how to measure divisional profit and divisional investments.

Points for consideration:

What are the practical problems of setting up a divisional IFC scheme?
What do you think is the best way of measuring divisional profit and divisional investment?
What types of ratios could usefully be computed for divisionalised companies for comparison purposes?

Transfer prices

A DIVISION MAY SELL or buy goods and services from other divisions within the business. These goods and services may include raw materials, completed goods, transport services, technological 'know-how' or, indeed, anything that may be acquired in the external market. Where internal transfers of this nature occur, a question arises as to how much should be paid for the goods and services supplied? If a division is dealing with the external market, of course, the forces of supply and demand will determine the appropriate transaction price. However, for internal transfers of goods and services these forces do not apply in the same way.

The answer to the question of what is an appropriate internal transfer prices is far from straightforward. It will depend on the objectives which are being pursued. Transfer prices can be set in order to fulfil various objectives.

Some of the more important objectives of transfer prices are as follows:

● *Evaluating divisional performance* Prices can be set in order to arrive at a valid measure of divisional profit for performance evaluation purposes. This should be of value to central management in allocating resources between divisions.

● *Improving the quality of decisions* Transfer pricing may help divisional managers to make better decisions. Prices can be used to determine how much of a product or service a particular division is prepared to sell and how much a division is prepared to buy. This can aid the efficient use of resources within a division.

● *Promoting autonomy* Transfer pricing can help promote the autonomy of divisions. Divisional managers can make independent decisions concerning whether or not they wish to trade with other divisions based on the transfer prices which are quoted. This should help in supporting the policy of divisionalisation of the business.

● *Allocating profit* Transfer pricing can be used to allocate the profits of a multinational business to divisions operating in particular countries. The allocation process may be designed to minimise the liability of the business as a whole, to taxation and duties and/or to avoid restrictions on the transfer of profits abroad. A business may wish to report high levels of profit within a division which is situated in a country where taxes and duties are low and to report low levels of profit within a division where taxation and duties are high. This policy will enable the business, as a whole, to reduce its total liability to taxation. (It should be noted that some taxation authorities will object to this practice if they believe this is simply a tax avoidance measure.)

One problem of setting a transfer price is that a particular method of pricing which achieves one of the above objectives may be inappropriate for another.

Consider the following activity.

Activity 8

Universal Engineering Ltd has two plants – one in Ruritania and the other in Transylvania. The rate of corporation tax in each country is 60% and 40% respectively. The Ruritanian plant produces a single component for a range products made at the Transylvanian plant. The component costs £10 to make and sells on the open market at £15 per unit. The output of the Ruritanian plant is 100,000 units per year, all of which is transferred to the Transylvanian plant.

Continued over . . .

Required:

a) Calculate the tax implications to the company as a whole if the Ruritanian plant transferred its components to the Transylvanian plant at cost rather than at their market value.

b) If you were the manager of the Ruritanian plant how would you feel about this pricing system?

a) The effect of transferring the components at cost will mean that the Ruritanian plant will make no profit as the sales value of goods produced will equal the cost of those goods. The effective 'profit' made by the Ruritanian plant (ie the difference between the cost of producing the component and the market value of the component £15 - £10 = £5) will be transferred to the Transylvanian plant in the form of a cost saving.

This means that the Ruritanian plant will have no liability to taxation, as no profit has been made, whereas the Transylvanian plant will have an additional profit of £5 per component due to the cost saving. The total profit of the business will not be affected by this pricing policy. However, the liability to taxation on profits made for the business as a whole will be reduced. The effective profit generated by the Ruritanian plant (ie 100,000 components @ £5 each = £500,000) has been transferred to the Transylvanian plant where the rate of taxation is 40%. Thus, a tax liability of £200,000 (ie £500,000 @ 40%) will be incurred in Transylvania on the components made. This compares with a tax liability of £300,000 (ie £500,000 @ 60%) if the profit was recorded in Ruritania where the components originated.

b) Although a transfer pricing system can be employed to allocate profits between divisions to achieve this end, it may well be inappropriate as a basis for evaluating divisional performance. The manager of the Ruritanian plant may well feel the selling price is an artificial one and, therefore, does not reflect the profitability of the Ruritanian division.

Another problem is that a particular transfer pricing system, designed to meet one of the objectives identified above, may work to the advantage of one division but to the disadvantage of another. For example, central management may decide that, in setting a transfer price for goods and services the need for divisional autonomy should be taken into account. Thus, where there is a competitive outside market for the goods supplied, the divisional managers should be able to decide whether to purchase from within the business or from an outside supplier. However, this may create problems for a division which is dependent on the continuing custom of another division. A decision to purchase from outside by a division may result in spare capacity being created in another division. This may not be in the interests of the business as a whole. (Where there is no outside market for the goods being transferred, there will be much greater interdependence between divisions.)

The impact of a particular transfer pricing policy can be significant. Sometimes, a small change in the transfer price of goods and services can result in a large change in the reported profit of the division. This is a particularly relevant issue where there are a large volume of transfers between divisions.

Methods of setting transfer prices

WHEN SELECTING AN APPROPRIATE method of setting transfer prices the objectives for transfer pricing specified earlier should be borne in mind. In addition, the method of transfer pricing should not undermine the benefits of divisionalisation and should not create undue conflict within the business. Ideally, the method of transfer pricing should provide an incentive for the divisional manager to make decisions which are in best interests of the business as a whole as well as the best interests of the division.

The transfer price should also attempt to reflect the opportunity cost of the goods and services provided. The opportunity cost of goods and services represents the benefits foregone by both the purchasing and the supplying division. This measure is important to a business when making decisions which seek to maximise its wealth.

As we shall see below, the application of these principles is not always an easy task and there may well be problems when establishing transfer pricing policies. Central management must be sensitive to the conflicts and problems which can arise and must recognise that, for many situations, a perfect measure of transfer pricing does not exist.

Numerous possibilities exist when considering a method of setting transfer prices. Some of the more important of theses are set out below:

MARKET PRICES
Market prices Where there is an external market for the goods or services being provided, market prices may be employed. This allows the divisions to operate as independent units. In a competitive market, where the division supplying the goods or service can sell all its output in the market and the purchasing division can acquire the goods and services it requires from the market, this method of pricing is most suitable. This is because market price represents the *opportunity cost* of goods supplied for both the buying and the supplying division. In a competitive market, a market-based transfer pricing system will mean that profits of the business as a whole and profits of the supplying and purchasing divisions will be the same whether the goods or services are sold internally or externally.

Activity 9

Can you think of any problems which may arise in practice, when trying to employ this form of transfer pricing? Try and jot down on a piece of paper, two possible problems

---

Problems may arise in practice either because there may not be a market price for the goods or services being supplied or the market price may require some sort of adjustment. An adjustment may be required to reflect the cost savings arising from internal sales (eg commission may not be paid to salesmen for sales to another division within the business, there may be lower distribution expenses, etc). An adjustment may also be required if the purchasing division has different product specifications to those of the standard products being offered to the external market.

If, in the short-term, a supplying division has unused capacity, a market based transfer price may not be in the interests of the business as a whole. Where unused capacity exists, a supplying division should be able to use a contribution-based approach to pricing in order to become more competitive. (This form of pricing has been dealt with in an earlier unit.)

The following example should help to reinforce some of the points made above.

Example 3

Griznez Company has several divisions which include a computer services division (CSD) and an office equipment division (OED). CSD wishes to purchase some office equipment. This can be acquired either from OED or from other suppliers. OED supplies direct to independent retailers. The price which a retailer would normally charge to its customers for the equipment needed by CSD would be £80,000, and the retailer normally marks up office equipment supplied by OED by 60%. The sales management of OED has offered to sell the equipment to CSD for £75,000. This reduction of £5,000 represents savings which OED makes on costs of marketing, selling and credit management as a result of a sale inside the company. It is company policy to pass on these savings to the purchaser within the company.

OED itself subcontracts all manufacturing. OED's purchasing manager indicates that OED has a backlog of orders from the independent retailers which cannot currently be met due to a shortage of reliable supplies. She also indicates that the office equipment of the type required by CSD would cost OED £20,000 if it were delivered by subcontractors to OED's warehouse ready for dispatch to the independent retailers.

You are required to write a short memo to the general manager of CSD giving the following:

(i) a recommended transfer price for the office equipment;
(ii) the reason why you have chosen this price.

The question indicates that there is an external market for the equipment and there is no unused capacity in the supplying division. In addition, we are informed that the supplying division can sell as much equipment as it can obtain. In these circumstances, the appropriate transfer price should be based on the market price of the goods. However, the price quoted by OED is based on the price which the retailers sell to the market rather than the price which OED sells to the retailers The price of £80,000 is after adding a mark-up of 60%. The price at which OED sells to the market is therefore, 100/160 × £80,000 = £50,000. This is the market price which should be used as a basis for transfer pricing. The price, however, should be adjusted for £5,000 in cost savings on marketing etc. The appropriate transfer price should therefore be:

	£
Market price	50,000
Less: Cost savings	5,000
	45,000

The market price, in the circumstances described, will represent the opportunity cost of OED supplying the equipment to CSD rather than supplying to an independent retailer. This point can be illustrated as follows:

	£	£
Price to retailers		50,000
Less:		
Cost of equipment from subcontractors	20,000	
Marketing, selling and credit management costs	5,000	25,000
Contribution		25,000

The cost of the equipment (£20,000) plus the contribution (£25,000) = £45,000 and will represent the opportunity cost foregone if the equipment is sold to CSD rather than an independent retailer. This should therefore represent the price required from CSD.

COST-BASED PRICES
Cost-based prices Transfers can be made between divisions at their *full cost*. The full cost will normally be determined on some predetermined basis. The advantage of using a predetermined standard cost for goods or services rather than actual cost is that, in the short-term at least, operating inefficiencies of the supplying division will not be borne by the purchasing division. This may provide some incentive for the supplying division to keep down its costs. However, over the longer term, there is a risk that predetermined cost levels will be increased due to operating inefficiencies.

> ## Activity 10
>
> What do you think are the advantages and disadvantages of using full cost from the point of view of the divisional manager of the business?

The use of a full cost approach has the advantages that it is easy to calculate and simple to apply. However, transfers at full cost will not help in the evaluation of divisional performance. If goods are supplied to another division at cost, the budgeted profit on the transaction will be zero. In addition, transfers at full cost will not help managers in making decisions concerning such matters as output, investment and product mix as they will have no profitability measures to guide them.

Transfers may also be made between divisions at their marginal or incremental cost. We saw earlier that the use of a market price is suitable where a competitive market exists as it represents the opportunity cost of the goods or services supplied. Where there is no competitive market for the product or service being supplied the opportunity cost of the goods or services provided will be measured by reference to their marginal or incremental cost. To illustrate this point, let us first consider a situation where there is no competitive market for the final product and the goods and/or services supplied by the supplying division has no external market.

Example 4

Effel plc has two operating divisions. Acton division supplies a partly completed product to Barnet division which then makes it into a final product which is sold to the external market. Purchases of the intermediate product and sales of the final product are in batches of 1,000 units. There is no external market for the intermediate product and the external market for the final product is not perfectly competitive (ie demand relative to price is non-linear). The cost structure for Acton division is as follows:

Production	Marginal cost	Total cost
(units)	£	£
1,000	5,000	5,000
2,000	5,000	10,000
3,000	4,000	14,000
4,000	3,500	17,500
5,000	3,000	20,500
6,000	6,000	26,500
7,000	7,000	33,500
8,000	9,000	42,500

Barnet division provides the following information concerning production and forecast sales revenue:

Production	Marginal revenue less conversion cost of intermediate product	Total revenue less conversion cost of intermediate product
1,000	10,000	10,000
2,000	10,000	20,000
3,000	8,000	28,000
4,000	8,000	36,000
5,000	7,000	43,000
6,000	6,000	49,000
7,000	4,000	53,000
8,000	4,000	57,000

In order to maximise profits, both for the company as a whole and for the individual divisions, it would be desirable to set the transfer price at £6,000 per 1,000 units. This is the point at which the additional cost of producing the intermediate product will be equal to the marginal revenue of the final product (after deducting conversion costs incurred by Barnet division). Acton division will have an incentive to produce up to 6,000 units at the transfer price of £6,000 per 1,000. The table shows that, up to 6,000 units of production the transfer price will exceed the marginal costs of production. Hence, Acton division will benefit from each batch of units produced. Beyond 6,000 units of production, however, the marginal costs will exceed the transfer price. This will act as a strong disincentive for Acton division to increase production beyond this point.

Activity 11

What about Barnet division? Will this operating division have different incentives than Acton division?

Barnet division will also have a strong incentive to purchase the intermediate product up to a maximum of 6,000 units. Up until this point there is a profit on each batch of the final product sold. Beyond this level of output however, the marginal revenue from the final product (after deducting conversion costs incurred by Barnet division) will exceed the transfer price of the intermediate product. Thus, losses will be incurred on each batch of 1,000 units beyond an output of 6,000 units.

If there is a market for the intermediate product, the transfer price set should be at the point where the marginal cost of producing the intermediate product equals the marginal revenue from the external market and the marginal revenue (after deducting conversion costs) from the purchasing division.

Example 5

Let us now assume there is an external market for the intermediate product supplied by Acton division in the example above. Let us further assume the marginal revenue of each batch of 1,000 units from the external market is forecast to be as follows:

	Marginal revenue £
1,000	9,000
2,000	8,500
3,000	7,500
4,000	5,000
5,000	4,500
6,000	4,000
7,000	4,000
8,000	3,600

In order to maximise profits of the business as a whole, Acton division should sell the intermediate product according to where the highest marginal revenue lies. Thus, the first 1,000 units will be sold to Barnet division as this will generate the highest marginal revenue after deducting conversion costs, (ie £10,000). Similarly, the second batch of 1,000 units will be sold to Barnet division as this will generate the same marginal revenue. The third batch of 1,000 units will be sold to the external market as this will generate the third largest marginal revenue (£9,000) and so on.

Activity 12

Calculate the point up to which the Acton division should continue to produce the intermediate product. What is the appropriate transfer price for the intermediate product?

The point at which Acton division should continue to produce the intermediate product is 7,000 units. Up until this point the marginal revenue from the external market or from Barnet division (after deducting conversion costs) will exceed the additional costs of producing the intermediate product. Beyond that point, the marginal costs exceed the marginal benefits.

The transfer price should be set at 7,000 per 1,000 units as this will achieve an optimum output.

Although the marginal approach to transfer pricing has strong theoretical appeal there are problems in implementing this method. Where the marginal costs of production are not constant, the supplying division will have to prepare a table of marginal costs for different levels of output. However, the divisional manager may not have the necessary information to do this. Marginal costs over the whole range of output may be difficult to measure. The divisional manager may also believe it is in his/her own best interests to overstate the marginal costs of production in order to increase divisional profits.

This transfer pricing approach does not really treat the operating divisions as being autonomous profit centres. Divisions must supply goods and services in a way which considers, primarily, the potential benefits to the business as a whole rather than the potential benefits to the divisions.

COST PLUS PRICES

Cost plus prices Transfers may be made at *full cost plus a profit mark-up* for the division supplying the goods or services. Apart from its simplicity, this method of pricing has little to commend it. The supplying division may have the opportunity to pass on operating inefficiencies to the purchasing division in the form of higher prices. Where no predetermined cost is agreed between the divisions, this problem can arise in the short-term as well as the longer term. As the amount of profit for the supplying division is determined by the amount of cost incurred, this can lead to a situation where the division can actually increase its profit through greater inefficiency! The purchasing division must bear the burden of any increased costs in the supplying division and, unless these costs can be passed on to customers in the form of higher prices, profit of the purchasing division will be reduced. These potential problems make full cost plus pricing an unsatisfactory method to use when seeking to improve the quality of divisional managers' decisions or when evaluating divisional performance.

It is possible to transfer goods and services at their *marginal cost plus a fixed charge*. The fixed charge may be paid by the purchasing division at regular intervals and will enable the supplying division to cover its budgeted fixed costs and make a return on the capital invested in the division. This approach makes the purchasing division aware of the total cost of the goods or services supplied and allows the supplying division to make a profit on internal transfers, which will be useful in the evaluation of performance.

Although this approach has advantages, there are also problems associated with its use. One such problem concerns the effect of fluctuations in demand for the final product. Consider the following example:

Example 6

Titanium plc has two operating divisions. Boron division provides an intermediate product to the Silicon division at its incremental cost plus a fixed fee of £8,000 per quarter. Up to 10,000 units of production, the incremental cost is £10 per unit. For the current year the sales of the final product is expected to be 10,000 units. However, forecast sales for next year are only likely to be 5,000 units because of increased competition. The net revenue of the final product received by the Silicon division (ie selling price less conversion costs incurred by the Silicon division) is £16 per unit up to 10,000 units of output.

Required:

(a) Calculate the profit contribution of each division for the current year.

(b) Calculate the expected profit contribution for next year.

(c) Comment on your findings and make any suggestions you feel appropriate.

The profit contribution for the current year for each division will be:

	Boron £	Silicon £
Sales		
10,000 units @ £10 per unit	100,000	
10,000 units @ £16 per unit		160,000
Fixed fee	32,000	(32,000)
	132,000	
Cost of sales	(100,000)	(100,000)
Profit contribution/(loss)	32,000	(28,000)

The expected profit contribution for next year for each division will be:

	Boron £	Silicon £
Sales		
5,000 units @ £10 per unit	50,000	
5,000 units @ £16 per unit		80,000
Fixed fee	32,000	(32,000)
	82,000	
Cost of sales (5,000 @ £10 per unit)	(50,000)	(50,000)
Profit contribution/(loss)	32,000	(2,000)

The above example shows that the supplying division (Boron) will be unaffected by the change in demand for the final product whereas the purchasing division (Silicon) is expected to make a loss next year. Although Silicon sells the final product above its incremental cost, the fixed fee payable will lead to a loss being incurred. It can be seen that, it is the Silicon division which is bearing the brunt of the downturn in demand for the final product.

Activity 12

What action might be taken to avoid Silicon division bearing the brunt of the downturn in demand?

As both divisions contribute towards producing the final product and both share in the profits when demand is high, it would seem to be more equitable if both divisions shared in the fall in profits arising from the downturn in demand. Thus the fixed fee should be renegotiated for the next period to take account of the expected change in the market for the final product.

A further problem associated with both the marginal cost plus and the full cost plus approach is that the costs reported by the divisional managers which are used as a basis for transfer pricing may be 'enhanced' by the reporting managers in order to boost the profit performance of their particular divisions. Whilst this may serve the short-term interests of the divisional manager, it may hinder the efficient allocation of resources within the business as a whole.

NEGOTIATED PRICES

Negotiated prices A transfer price for goods and services may be established by negotiation between the relevant divisional managers. Under this system, divisional managers will seek to strike a price for the goods or services to be supplied which is acceptable to both the supplying and the purchasing divisions. If they are unable to reach agreement on a price, the divisional managers will be free to buy or sell the goods or services in the outside market. Occasionally, central management may be required to arbitrate in disputes between divisions. However, this arbitration process should respect the autonomy of the divisions. Normally, central management should not seek to impose a transfer price on a particular division. This policy of non-interference, however, can create a conflict for central management if the negotiated price is not in the interests of the business as a whole.

In order for a negotiated transfer price system to operate effectively the divisional managers should have the freedom to accept or reject offers which are made by another division. In addition, an outside market for the goods or services supplied should exist. The existence of an outside market helps to create a price framework within which negotiations can take place. This should help ensure the negotiated transfer price approximates to the opportunity cost of the goods or services supplied. The absence of an outside market can result in a wide difference in the relative bargaining strength of negotiating divisions. For example, a division may find itself in a monopoly position when negotiating with another division to either buy or sell goods. As a result, the final negotiated price may be extreme.

The use of negotiated transfer prices can result in serious disputes between divisions which may be harmful to the business as a whole. If this occurs, central management may be forced to intervene and this may be extremely time-consuming for them. It may also undermine the benefits of divisionalisation such as divisional autonomy and central management delegation of responsibilities. Under this system of transfer pricing, divisional performance will be influenced by the negotiating skills of the divisional managers. This can be a problem if divisional performance is too dependent on this particular attribute.

Activity 13

The following information applies to the planned operations of Turbo division of ABC Corporation for 19x9.

	£
Sales – 100,000 units at £12	1,200,000
Variable costs at £8 each	800,000
Fixed costs (including depreciation)	250,000
Turbo division investment (at original cost)	500,000

The minimum desired rate of return on investment is the cost of capital of 20%.

The company is highly profit conscious and delegates a considerable level of autonomy to divisional managers. As part of a procedure to review planned operations of Turbo division, a meeting has been convened to consider two options (shown below).

Option I
Turbo division may sell a further 20,000 units at £11 to customers outside ABC Corporation. Variable costs per unit will be the same as budgeted but to enable capacity to increase by 20,000 units, one piece of extra equipment will be required costing £80,000. The equipment will have a four year life and the company depreciates assets on a straight line basis. No extra cash fixed costs will occur.

Option II
Included in the current plan of operations of Turbo division is the sale of 20,000 units to Motor division also within ABC Corporation. A competitor of Turbo division, outside the group, has offered to supply Motor division at £10 per unit. Turbo division intends to adopt a strategy of matching the price quoted from outside the company to retain the order.

Continued over . . .

Required:

(a) Calculate for 19x9 for Turbo division the residual income of:

(i) the original planned operation,
(ii) Option I only added to the original plan,
(iii) Option II only added to the original plan, and briefly interpret the results of the options as they affect Turbo division.

(b) Assess the implications for Turbo division, Motor division and the Corporation as a whole of Option II, bearing in mind that if Turbo division does not compete on price it will lose the 20,000 units order from Motor division. Make any recommendations you consider appropriate.

The residual income for each of the three choices will be as follows:

	Option I	Option II	Original Plan
	£000	£000	£000
Sales	1,420	1,160	1,200
Less variable costs	960	800	800
Contribution	460	360	400
Less fixed costs	270	250	250
Net profit	190	110	150
Capital charge (20%)	116	100	100
Residual income	74	10	50

The figures above reveal that the original plan plus Option I provides the best return for Turbo division. The increased contribution from sales more than covers the additional fixed costs and capital charge arising from the purchase of extra equipment. Option II provides the lowest return. Although a positive residual income arises, it is considerably lower than the residual income under the original plan. The effect of competing on price for the Motor division order reduces sales revenue by £40,000. As there is no change in the costs incurred, this results in an equivalent fall in both profit and residual income.

Assuming the reliability and quality of supplies will be the same from both Turbo division and the outside supplier and the price will also be the same, Motor division is likely to be indifferent about the source of its supplies. The results of Motor division will be unaffected by the choice of supplier. However, Turbo division and the business as a whole will lose out if Motor division uses an outside supplier.

The revised results of Turbo division if it loses the sales to Motor division (but excluding Option I) will be as follows:

	£000
Sales	960
Variable costs	640
Contribution	320
Fixed costs	250
Net profit	70
Capital charge	100
Residual income	(30)

The results reveal a contribution of £40,000 less than the plan for Turbo division to compete on price. In addition the residual income is now negative. This loss of contribution will affect the profits of the business as a whole.

Pursuing Option I will mean no additional outlay on capital expenditure if Motor division uses an outside source of supplies. The additional sales generated will simply use up the spare capacity created in Turbo division by the loss of sales to Motor division.

The revised results of Turbo division if it loses the sales to Motor division (but including Option I) will be as follows:

		£000
Sales	80,000 @ £12	960
	20,000 @ £11	220
		1,180
Variable costs		800
Contribution		380
Fixed costs		250
Net profit		130
Capital charge		100
Residual income		30

These results are still not as good as those obtained by Turbo division when competing on price for Motor division sales and making additional outside sales.

Reading

You should now read Reader Article 9.2 'Transfer pricing comes to Barts' by Roger Halford.

This article points out that most of the accounting literature concerning transfer pricing is based upon business organisations seeking to maximise profits. However, this technique can also be applied within the public sector where profit maximisation is not the ultimate goal. Recent changes in the organisation of the health service in the UK has lead to the creation of autonomous units and this, in turn, creates an opportunity to introduce a transfer pricing mechanism.

Points for consideration

Which of the two transfer pricing approaches outlined do you prefer and why?
Could conflict arise between autonomous units under either of the transfer pricing approaches? If so, why?

Divisional performance measurement and transfer pricing in practice

THE ACCA SURVEY revealed that, in assessing the performance of divisional managers, a range of financial measures are often employed. The companies responding to the survey provided the following picture of measures used:

	%
Target return on capital employed established by the group (ROCE)	55
Target profit after charging interest on divisional capital employed (RI)	20
Target profit *before* charging interest on divisional capital employed	61
Target cash flow	43
Ability to stay within budget	57
Other	6

It is interesting to note that, despite the support in the literature for RI, this measure does not seem to enjoy widespread popularity in practice. ROI, on the other hand, is a much more popular measure. Various reasons have been put forward to explain this phenomenon. One reason is that, as ROI is a widely used measure of performance for the business as a whole by investors, central management want each segment of the business to perform in accordance with this measure. Another reason put forward is that ratios such as ROI facilitate inter-divisional comparisons. However, we have seen earlier that there are potential problems in adopting this measure.

Where ROI or RI was being used to assess performance, the overwhelming majority of respondent companies included fixed assets, stocks and debtors in their calculation of divisional capital employed. Cash and bank balances were less likely to be included. The vast majority of companies used historical cost (less depreciation) as their valuation base when applying the two performance measures.

The ACCA survey found that companies often use more than one method of transfer pricing between divisions. The following measures are employed with varying degrees of frequency by companies:

	%
Unit variable cost	18
Unit full cost	42
Unit variable cost plus fixed mark-up	31
Unit full cost plus fixed mark-up	52
Marginal cost (or incremental cost)	18
Market price/adjusted market price	52
Negotiated transfer price	70
Lump sum payment plus a cost per unit transferred	9
Other	6

We can see from the above that negotiated transfer price is the most popular transfer pricing method and that methods based on variable cost tend to be less popular than full cost methods.

Summary

IN THIS UNIT WE have examined various issues surrounding the measurement of divisional performance. We have considered the two most important methods of performance measurement – return on investment (ROI) and residual income (RI). We have seen that both methods have their advantages and disadvantages and that there is no clear choice of method. It was argued that in order to arrive at a proper assessment of divisional performance a variety of measures both financial and non-financial should be used.

A major issue in the measurement of divisional performance concerns the price at which goods and services are transferred between divisions. In this unit we have examined a number of bases for establishing a transfer price. Where a competitive market exists for the goods or services the market price provides an appropriate basis. However, where there is no competitive outside market other methods may be more suitable. The major principle to be applied is that the transfer price should attempt to reflect the opportunity cost of the goods or services supplied.

Additional exercises

Exercise 1

A large company is considering methods for improving its profitability by the creation of divisions. It is intended that the divisional managers should run their units on a commercial basis using guidelines laid down by the company's board of directors. A unit formerly responsible for all printing and stationery within the company is to be transformed into a division as an 'in-house' printing business. The former pricing policy was based on charging users for direct costs plus a proportion of fixed overheads.

You are required to draft a note for the board of directors which identifies and comments on some of the main issues which this change may raise.

Exercise 2

CBMC company is a computer bureau and a management consultancy practice. Each division offers its services separately although a considerable proportion of work is undertaken in collaboration.

The services of the computer bureau centre on the preparation and analysis of the final accounts of the client firms, usually small businesses. The management consultancy offers advice and consultancy which can be based on the final accounts produced by the bureau.

Charges to clients are standardised as follows:

(i) final accounts preparation only – £200 per client;

(ii) final accounts preparation and subsequent consultancy service – £300 per client.

An analysis of variable costs of each operation involving machine time, management time and special stationery reveals:

(i) final accounts preparation – £120 per client;

(ii) consultancy service (not including final accounts preparation) – £150 per client.

The owners, whilst keen to promote the profitability of the business as a whole, are seeking to focus also on the contribution made by each division. When a client has received both the final accounts and consultancy it has been the practice for the computer bureau management to charge the consultancy division with the full market rate for the final accounts preparation, ie £200 per client. The manager of the consultancy service objects to this charge, asserting 'when the two divisions collaborate I can never be profitable'.

Required:

(a) Summarise the data in a form which will either refute or confirm the assertion made by the manager of the consultancy division, and make brief comments.

(b) If the computer bureau is fully occupied should it undertake work for the consultancy division in preference to its own 'outside work'? What transfer charge per client should be adopted in such circumstances? Explain your reasoning.

(c) If the computer bureau is not fully occupied should it undertake work for the consultancy division? What transfer charge would be appropriate in such circumstances? Explain your reasoning.

Exercise 3

ABC plc is a large public company which is organised into autonomous divisions. For the purpose of managerial performance measurement, a return on investment (ROI) is calculated by relating net profit to gross investment. This company interprets gross investment as current assets plus fixed assets at original cost.

Extracts from the budgeted results of Division A and Division B for 19x7 are shown below:

	Division A £000	Division B £000
Net profit	200	64
Current assets	200	150
Fixed assets	800	650

There are two projects which are being considered by the division managers. Neither of them is included in the figures given above. They are:

(i) Project Alpha – in which Division A has the opportunity to increase annual sales by £200,000 by undertaking an annual advertising campaign which will have a fixed cost of £15,000. The sales increase will improve the divisions contribution by £30,000 but will require stock levels to be increased by £100,000 per annum on average.

(ii) Project Beta – in which Division B can invest in some new equipment costing £200,000 which will improve annual profits by £20,000 due to increased efficiency.

Required:

(a) Determine the budgeted return on investment (ROI) for each division:

(i) before the two projects are incorporated;
(ii) assuming the managers adopt the projects available to their division and incorporate them in their budgets.

(b) Determine the budgeted residual income (RI) for each division before and after the incorporation of the respective projects. The company has a cost of capital of 12% per annum.

(c) Contrast the results under (a) and (b) and consider to what extent they encourage the division managers to pursue corporate profit objectives whilst acting in their own best interests.

Exercise 4

A major motor dealership called Motorgo offers the usual range of garage services including new and used car sales, repairs and servicing. The general manager is keen to achieve a high level of co-operation and incentive in his managers' actions so a profit centre reporting system has recently been established. In addition to a basic salary, managers are paid a commission based on their performance against target profit levels.

A recent event has, however, caused some friction between the three profit centre managers and cast doubt in the general manager's mind. He provides you with the following information:

A new car which had a list price of £8,000 was in stock at a cost of £5,000. It had proved to be a difficult car to sell. A customer had approached the dealer about this car with a vehicle to trade in. The value of this vehicle according to a trade-in guide was £2,800. It would then retail from the used car section with a warranty for about £3,600.

The service department had carried out a brief inspection and estimated that repairs and servicing costing £600 would be required to prepare the vehicle for their own showroom. The service manager added that if similar repairs were to be carried out for an external customer the charge would be £900. Being aware of the above information, the new car sales manager had authorised a trade-in price of £3,500 against the new car.

Required:

(a) If all the transactions envisaged were completed at the values indicated, within one trading period, determine their impact on the profit of Motorgo and each of the three profit centres of the company.

(b) Explain how the results would change if the company elected to send the vehicle, which was traded in, to a cut-price auction for £1,700 without any warranty or repair work undertaken.

(c) Is the system of profit centres good for the company? Should it be preserved? Make some recommendations.

Exercise 5

Diamond Group plc, your employer, operates two divisions, one in food production, the other in catering and leisure. You do not yet have full information in relation to the last year's performance of the two divisions.

From various memoranda and conversations you have been able to extract the following:

The food production division made a profit of £12m, this represented an average margin of profit to sales of 10%. The rate of turnover of capital employed in sales during the last year was two.

The catering and leisure division achieved sales of £80m, the return on capital employed of the division was 32% achieved with a profit to sales ratio of 20%.

Diamond Group uses a cost of capital of 18% in all its calculations.

The in-tray of a colleague who deals with group purchases contains a letter, the abbreviated contents are:

'Included in the reported profit of the food production division is £4m made from inter-divisional sales of £22m to the catering and leisure division. An outside supplier is offering to undertake this supply in the future. Their price for supplies equivalent to the above would be £19m'. Capital employed would not be affected significantly by such an event.

Required:

(a) From the information on the last year's performance calculate other appropriate measures or ratios in order to determine which division you consider to be more profitable. Give your reasons and any qualifications you may have.

For the purpose of this part ignore all reference to the outside supplier.

(b) Briefly examine the implications for each division and the group of the outside supplier's offer. For any numerical illustration you should use the figures relating to last year assuming such a situation would otherwise be repeated in the current year.

Answer to self-assessment question

Glasnost plc

ROI and residual income measures for the two divisions are as follows:

	West	East
ROI using divisional profit		
$(300/2500) \times 100$	12%	
$(100/500) \times 100$		20%
ROI using net profit		
$(250/2500) \times 100$	10%	
$(80/500) \times 100$		16%
	£000	£000
Residual income using divisional profit		
$300 - (10\% \times 2500)$	50	
$100 - (10\% \times 500)$		50

Another profitability ratios is:

	West	East
Divisional profit/sales		
$(300/1000) \times 100$	30%	
$(100/400) \times 100$		25%

In addition to these profitability measures, various costs to sales ratios may be used to evaluate the performance of each division:

	West	East
Direct costs/Sales		
$(300/1000) \times 100$	30%	
$(212/400)$		53%
Indirect costs to sales		
$(220/1000) \times 100$	22%	
$(48/400) \times 100$		12%
Selling and distribution costs to sales		
$(180/1000) \times 100$	18%	
$(40/400) \times 100$		10%

As we are told that central management wishes to compare results in order to evaluate managerial performance, divisional profit which is controllable by the divisional managers should be used. Similarly, only divisional investments which are controllable by divisional managers should be used in the calculations. (It is assumed that all investment stated in the question is controllable investment.)

The ROI of West is substantially lower than that of East. However, we are informed that West division has recently incurred substantial capital expenditure whereas East operates with quite old plant. The fact that West will report its assets at near current values and East will report its assets at heavily written down values means that ROI comparisons between the divisions will be distorted. There is a danger that too much emphasis will be placed on the short-term ROI results. Over the longer term, divisional profits will be improved by shrewd capital expenditures. Thus, it may be useful to monitor ROI over a period of several years.

The residual income measures reveal that West and East have achieved an identical level of performance. However, this measure will also be distorted by the difference between the divisions in the timing of capital expenditure as the capital charge is based on the recorded asset values.

The results reveal that West has a better divisional profit to sales ratio than East. This is a valid comparison to make between the divisions as we are told that they are engaged in broadly similar activities. Inspection of the costs to sales ratios gives an insight into why there is a difference in the divisional profit margins. The direct costs to sales ratio is substantially lower for West although this benefit is partly offset by a higher indirect cost to sales ratio. This difference in manufacturing cost structure is probably due to the fact that West has invested in automated production lines recently.

West has a higher selling and distribution cost/sales ratio. This may be due, in part, to the fact that West has minimal inter-company sales whereas 50% of the sales of East are inter-company transfers to other divisions. This can result in substantial savings for East in sales commission, collection costs, etc. To take account of these cost savings, it may be more valid to make an adjustment to the market price of internal transfers. Such an adjustment could make a substantial difference to the reported profits of East division.

It is clear from the above that focusing on ROI will result in only a partial view of divisional performance and the other measures and ratios discussed should also be employed when evaluating performance.

Solutions to additional exercises

Exercise 1

When moving to a divisionalised structure the board of directors should give consideration to the following issues:

Transfer prices The price at which the goods or services are transferred between divisions should represent the opportunity cost of these items to the purchasing and supplying divisions. Where there is a perfectly competitive external market, this will be represented by the market price of the goods or services provided. Where no such market exists the marginal or incremental cost of the goods or services or some negotiated price should be used. The use of cost plus based pricing which has been used in the past is inappropriate for a divisionalised structure. The supplying division will be able to pass on operating inefficiencies to the supplying division.

Divisional autonomy In order to reap the benefits of divisionalisation, it is important for the divisional managers to be given a fair degree of autonomy. This should allow the business as a whole to be able to respond more quickly to market opportunities and to take full advantage of local knowledge. This, in turn, should lead to improved profit performance.

Sphere of control Divisional managers should be quite clear about the areas over which they have control and for which they will be accountable. The areas over which central management still wish to exercise control should be clearly demarcated. When evaluating management performance, only controllable profit should be used in computing measures of divisional performance such as residual income.

Exercise 2

The manager of the consultancy division has expressed concern as collaboration with the computer division will produce the following results for each division:

	Computer Bureau £	Consultancy Division £
Client charge for final accounts preparation and consultancy service		300
Internal charge for final accounts	200	
Variable cost of final accounts preparation	(120)	
Variable cost of consultancy		(150)
Computer bureau charge		(200)
Profit/(loss)	80	(50)

The method of transfer pricing will act as a disincentive for the consultancy division to collaborate with the computer bureau as it will incur a loss by so doing. However, the computer bureau will record a profit on any collaborative work. In addition, the business as a whole will benefit from such collaboration. The profit of the business as a whole will increase by £30 (£80 - £50) as a result of a client receiving the services of both divisions. There is, therefore, a conflict between the interests of the consultancy division and the interests of the business as a whole as a result of the transfer price system being operated.

If the computer bureau is fully occupied there is little incentive for the manager to agree to a transfer price which is not based on the market rate as this will represent the opportunity cost of the services provided. Some reduction in the full market rate, however, may be appropriate if there are cost savings arising as a result of dealing with the consultancy division rather than with outside organisations, (eg savings in advertising costs, etc).

If the computer bureau is not fully occupied, a price lower than the full market rate would be appropriate. In such circumstances, the full market price would not represent the opportunity cost of the services provided. As there is an external market for the computer bureau services, a *negotiated transfer price* system could be operated to determine the appropriate internal charge. The agreed price should lie somewhere between the variable cost of the computer bureau services and the full market price. Another possibility would be to use a *marginal cost plus* pricing approach. The advantages and disadvantages of each pricing method has been dealt with in the unit.

We are told that a considerable amount of collaborative work is undertaken. This indicates that many clients wish to receive *both* services provided. If the divisions are highly interdependent, the business as a whole may lose if either divisional manager rejects the offer of collaborative work as a result of the transfer price being unacceptable. We are not told the market rate for the work performed by the consultancy division, or whether an external market exists for such work. If the market rate is £100 (ie the difference between the price for both services provided and the price for the computer bureau service only), the consultancy division will never have any incentive to undertake such work as this is below the marginal cost of the work undertaken. However, the business as a whole may be prepared to offer the consultancy work at a price below its marginal cost in order to attract clients and make an overall profit on the collaborative work undertaken. Where this type of consultancy service represents a high proportion of the total work undertaken by the consultancy division, it would not be appropriate to regard the division as a separate profit or investment centre.

Exercise 3

Return on investment (ROI)	Division A	Division B
Before project incorporation		
(200/1,000) × 100	20%	
(64/800) × 100		8%
After project incorporation		
[(200 + 30 -15)/(1,000 +100)] × 100	19.5%	
[(64 + 20)/(800 + 200)] × 100		8.4%

Residual income (RI)	Division A £000	Division B £000
Before project incorporation		
Net profit	200	64
Less capital charge		
(1000 × 12%)	120	
(800 × 12%)		96
RI	80	(32)
After project incorporation		
Net profit	215	84
Less capital charge		
(1100 × 12%)	132	
(1000 × 12%)		120
RI	83	(36)

The above results reveal that Division A will suffer a slight decline in ROI as a result of taking on Project Alpha. This may make the divisional manager reluctant to take on the project as he/she may feel that a decline in ROI will reflect badly on his stewardship of the division. However, the ROI, after incorporating this project, exceeds the cost of capital of the company and should therefore be undertaken if the company wishes to maximise its profits. The RI of Division A reveals an increase as a result of taken on the project. The emphasis on this measure of performance will enable the manager to feel that his interests and the interests of the company as a whole will be served by undertaking this project.

The results above reveal that Division B will improve its ROI as a result of taking on Project Beta. This may make the divisional manager wish to take on this project. However, the ROI, after taking on the project, is still below the company's cost of capital and should therefore be rejected. The RI of Division B will decline as a result of taking on the project. Once again, emphasis on this measure should make the divisional manager feel that his interests, as well as the company's interests, will not be served by taking on this project.

Exercise 4

Profit for the period

	New car sales £	Used car sales £	Repairs £	Total £
New car sold	8,000			8,000
Used car sold		3,600		3,600
Repairs charged		(900)	900	–
New car cost	(5,000)			(5,000)
Price discount (3,500 - 2,800)	(700)*		(700)	
Used car cost		(2,800)		(2,800)
Repairs cost			(600)	(600)
Profit (loss) on transaction	2,300	(100)	300	2,500

* As the new car profit centre allowed a trade-in price in excess of the guide price, it should bear the additional cost. (It is also possible to argue a case for charging the repair cost to the new car profit centre.)

Assuming the trade-in car was sent to auction rather than sold, the profit for the business would be as follows:

	£	£
Sale of new car		8,000
Sale of used car		1,700
		9,700
Cost of new car	5,000	
Trade-in price	3,500	8,500
Profit		1,200

The above results reveal that it is more profitable for the business as a whole to sell the used car rather than send it to auction.

It is clear from the results obtained that the used car profit centre manager is likely to be displeased with the transaction. The transaction will result in a loss to the used car profit centre. If the manager of this centre does not have the right to refuse to accept the trade-in vehicle at the guide price, the reported loss is not really a matter over which he/she has control. However, refusal to accept the vehicle at the guide price may result in it being auctioned and this, in turn, will result in a lower profit for the business as a whole. The problem may be overcome by allowing the new car manager and used car manager to negotiate a transfer price for the used car. The price negotiated should induce the managers to arrive at a price which approximates to the opportunity cost of the vehicle. (This is likely to be somewhere between the auction price and the guide price.)

The repair manager should quote for any repairs to be undertaken before the used car manager accepts the car. If the quote is too high, the used car sale manager may decide not to accept the car or to look for a cheaper source of repairs. In order for the quote to be competitive, it should reflect the opportunity cost to the supplying and the purchasing centre of the repairs. It is not clear from the information provided how the repair quote was arrived at. A cost plus approach should not be used as this will provide the repair centre manager with an incentive to make repairs which are not strictly necessary.

The use of profit centres may be beneficial to the company if a system of transfer pricing can be established which properly reflects the efforts and achievements of the various centres and if any disputes which arise between profit centre managers can be resolved without too much acrimony or central management time being spent.

Exercise 5

The following ratios and measures can be used to assess the profitability of each division:

	Food production
Net profit/sales (as per question)	10%
Sales £12m/10%	£120m
Sales/capital employed (as per question)	2
Return on investment	20%
[(Net profit/sales) × (Sales/capital employed)] (10% × 2)	
Total capital employed (net profit/ROI) (£12m/20%)	£60m
Residual income [(£12m - (18% × £60m)]	£1.2m

	Catering and leisure
Net profit/sales (as per question)	20%
Sales (as per question)	£80m
Net profit(£80m × 20%)	£16m
ROI (as per question)	32%
Sales/capital employed (ROI/net profit/sales) = (32%/20%)	1.6
Total capital employed (£80m/1.6)	£50m
Residual income [£16m - (18% × £50m)]	£7m

The above ratios and measures reveal that Catering and leisure have a much higher ROI than Food production. Examination of the main components of ROI reveals that the net profit margin of Catering and leisure is double that of Food production while the sales to capital employed ratio is only slightly lower. The higher profit margins achieved by catering and leisure explain the higher ROI.

The difference in profit margin means that, whereas Catering and leisure sales of £80m are only two thirds of those of Food production, the profit achieved of £16m is one third greater than Food production.

The residual income of Catering and leisure is much higher than that of food production. However, the above calculations assume that the two divisions have similar risk characteristics. If the cost of capital were adjusted to take account of differences in the levels of risk associated with each division a different picture may emerge.

If Catering and leisure accept the supply of goods from an outside supplier a saving of £3m will be made by the division. Assuming there is no difference in the quality of the goods being supplied, it would pay the division to do this. The ROI of the division would increase to 38% and the residual income would increase to £10m.

If the Food production division is unable to sell the goods previously sold to Catering and leisure to an external market it will lose profits of £4m. This will mean an ROI of 13.3% and a negative residual income of £1.8m. This may cast doubt on the future viability of this division.

The business as a whole will be worse off if the goods are provided by an outside supplier. The gain of £3m by Catering and leisure must be offset by the loss of £4m by Food production. Hence, a reduced profit of £1m for the business as a whole will result. This situation should not be acceptable to central management. In addition to the short-term problems that this issue raises there may also be a longer term issue. The supplier may be offering to supply goods cheaply at first in order to gain the custom of the division. Once this has been done the price of supplies may rise over the longer term to a similar (or higher) figure to that of the Food production division.

A sensible solution would be for the Food production division to match the price offered by the outside supplier. This will mean that Food production still makes a profit on its supplies to Catering and leisure. In addition, the business as a whole will be no worse off. The £3m increased profit made by Catering and leisure will be offset by a £3m lower profit made by Food production.

Management Accounting

READER

CONTENTS

READER ARTICLE 1.1

'The link between management and management accounting'

Mark Inman

Reproduced from Students newsletter of the Chartered Association of Certified Accountants, ACCA.

November 1992

THE LINK BETWEEN MANAGEMENT
AND MANAGEMENT ACCOUNTING

A look at how large areas of papers 2.4 and 2.5B can link and overlap

By Mark Lee Inman

Examiners frequently complain that students "pigeon hole" all that they learn, and hence display a total inability to relate from one subject to another. This is particularly evident at Level 2 where students can compute and analyse but not explain and report, and contributes to the Level 3 failure rate where students fail to relate across from one subject to another. The purpose of this article is to demonstrate a link between the 2.4 Cost and Management II and the 2.5B Effective Management papers. Students need to be especially aware of such a link, since recent years have seen an increase in the number of textbooks that are aimed not at pure techniques, but at the overall organisational implications of management accounting and the subsequent reports.

A valuable starting point can be the essential elements of management as defined by Henri Fayol.(*) These were:

- To forecast and plan (French *prevoyance* — pre-seeing) examining the future and drawing up the plan of action.

- To organise : Building up the structure, material and human [resources], of the undertaking.

- To command: maintaining activity among personnel.

- To coordinate: binding together, unifying and harmonising all activity and effort.

- To control: seeing that everything occurs in conformity with established rule and expressed command.

To this can be brought the latest CIMA Terminology (1991) expanded definition of management accounting. First it is "an integral part of management concerned with identifying, presenting and interpreting information." It is perhaps noteworthy that the adjectives "accounting" and "financial" are both missing. This helps to reinforce the rather blurred distinction that has developed between MIS and management accounting. However, it is clearly felt by the Council of

CIMA, as it was by the American Accounting Association on numerous occasions since the 1950s, that management accounting uses non-financial data in its information process.

Secondly, such information is used for:

- formulating strategy (part of planning);

- planning and controlling activities (Fayol):

- decision making:

- optimising the use of resources;

- disclosure to shareholders and others external to the entity;

- disclosure to employees;

- safeguarding assets.

Thirdly, the above involves participation in management to ensure that there is effective:

- formulation of plans to meet objectives;

- formulation of short term operation plans;

- acquisition and use of finance;

- recording of transactions;

- communication of financial and operating information;

- corrective action to bring plans and results into line;

- reviewing and reporting on systems and operations.

It should be immediately evident to the student that some parts of this definition are very close to the pioneering ideas indeed, and to demonstrate the vital link, these similarities will be discussed.

1. To forecast and plan

We can immediately see that management accounting is intimately involved with this first essential component of management. Management accounting information is a vital part of the managerial process of formulating strategy and the plans to meet previously agreed objectives. It is worth adding that in this context, H A Simon (1960)

identified information that might be externally generated, such as market size and share. In addition it might be accurate in magnitude only, a summary rather than minute detail, have a long range time horizon, qualitative in many aspects, and be aimed at producing broad policies.

In the context of an organisational hierarchy, this information will be derived from staff very close to the top of any pyramid, and used by the senior executives at board level.

2. To organise

As we have already observed, Fayol saw this as the "building up of the structure, material and human [resources] of the undertaking." This can be interpreted as bringing together the essential resources in order to run the entity. Such action suggests the optimising activity implied by the CIMA definition can be related to the traditional factors of production — men, material and machines, or to the original Fayol function notion of the Financial (NB Not accounting) activities of searching for and the optimum use of capital.

Such an activity places the management accounting skills again very much towards the apex of the organisational pyramid, and involved at the beginning of the business. Lest students feel that this is subversive propaganda, they should remember that these skills will draw upon their valuable Level 3 knowledge. Optimising scarce capital and operating resources can involve fiscal as well as pure financial management.

3. To command

Accounting is a tool of management, and as such, those with accounting skills are not perceived as rising to the position of command, and are often resented when they do. A wider definition of command is thus required. Accounting skills bring with them a technical authority which should command a level of respect. Townsend advocated keeping accountants out of the "driving seat" but respected their advisory and navigational skills. He thus advocated that all plans should be shown to the accountants for their specialist advice and counsel.

4. To co-ordinate

Belkaoui quotes the 1972 American Accounting Association, assumptions on the nature of management accounting.

(i) "The role of managerial accounting encompasses the entire formalised information function of an organisation." This will inevitably include both financial and non-financial data.

(ii) "The accountant is the best candidate for a manager of this information system."

Thus initally, the management accounting role is perceived as being at the nerve centre of all information and data flows within an entity. All the data passes through the function in some form, and is readily available to be turned into relevant information.

The co-ordinating role is seen at its best in the budgeting process. In a participatory budgeting environment, the accountant brings together data on sales, purchases, operations and expenses to prepare the overall master budget and the control documents. To be sure, the managing director would ensure that the sales or marketing director would confirm with the operations director that there were the resources and facilities to enable him to meet his sales expectations, but all the data would find its way into the information process in the accounting function.

5. To control

Meaningful control requires four essential elements.

(a) There must be an agreed achievable objective/goal for any control to exist.

(b) The outputs of the operation must be measured in the same terms as the objectives being pursued. Not only is this conceptually consistent, but it permits meaningful comparisons.

(c) A predictive model of the operation must exist to enable analysis of deviations and any responsive action. The most obvious example of such a model is a budget.

(d) The facility to respond to the deviations must exist.

Students should note the deliberate choice of the word "deviation". Control is error-led and the perception of an error is that it equates with failure. In participating in the management control process, the management accountant must analyse and investigate the failures, but also explore the ways of capitalising on the successes.

Since the senior management accountant is often described as the "controller", this is perhaps the most obvious link between pure

Figure 1		
Level	Principal role	Nature of information
"Top" management (Financial manager)	Strategy/ planning	Information for forecasting
"Middle" (Controller)	A mix of planning and control against objectives.	Management control
"Lower" (Supervision) (Management accountant)*	Day to day operational	Agreed control measures

*Indicates possible title of person reporting the information . (From Wilson and Chua)

management and management accounting. Inevitably, the CIMA definition touches base with Fayol at several points. First, the management accountant will provide information for the planning and control of activities within the entity. However, an active role is expected in the formulation of plans to meet objectives, the formulation of short-term plans or budgets, communicating of financial and operational information and the suggesting of corrective action to bring back plans and results into line. As with strategic planning, H A Simon has identified the level of information requirements, dividing control into two levels, management control and operational control.

Management control information characteristics are:

● the information is mostly internally generated,

● accurate within the parameters previously established and agreed,

● moderately detailed data,

● regularly reported,

● has a medium range time horizon,

● is structured or formal and contains financial and non-financial data,

● is likely to concentrate upon exception reporting,

● is reporting on the achievement of organisational objectives in the same terms.

The last characteristic emphasises that this is still information within the realms of the apex of the organisational hierarchy, where management is more involved in strategy and planning, rather than day to day operational control.

By contrast, operational control infor-

mation characteristics are:

● again the information is internally generated, but exclusively so,

● there is a high degree of accuracy and detail,

● it is frequently reported even daily and certainly weekly and monthly,

● there will be a short time horizon because of the frequency of reporting,

● the information will be quantitative, largely financial and current, — this week's figures,

● it will be repetitive.

We can thus formulate a useful grid that relates the hierarchy to the management accounting information (see Figure 1 above).

If the student has been ticking off the ostensibly common points in the two definitions, he will now have observed that all the Fayol points have been covered. However, the CIMA list still has items outstanding. These points can now be discussed in turn, and related to management theory.

The impact of communication

From the second part of the definition comes the reference to the use of information for disclosure. In the third is communication of financial and operating information. Both can be dealt with under the important management heading of communication. Communication may occur at any level. The reports themselves are a form of structured, written and regular communication, and much effort is needed by the skilful management accountant to ensure that his information communicates correctly. Reports are prepared for some purpose, even if it is only as a measure of stewardship and scorekeeping and, as such, they must communicate correctly and effectively.

Chester I. Barnard (*) defines communication as an essential component of the formal organisation, linking the common purpose with those willing (required? motivated?) to co-operate in it. Communication is essential to translate purpose into action. Two forms of communication can be identifed. first through the written and spoken word, i.e. the reports and figures prepared by the management accountant, and "observational feeling". This latter item is very difficult for students, especially those doing full time courses, since it requires the experience that is derived from continuity of association.

In addition, Barnard sees communication having two components: the organisation scheme and the contributors.

Thus in this context, the management accountant must provide the information that is relevant to the position in the organisation. This may mean planning information towards the top, and control nearer the operations level. Also, this information must be further constrained by what the recipient needs to know and what he is responsible for. It is pointless preparing a detailed variance analysis statement for a manager who has no control over labour rates paid, or the price of materials. The scheme of organisation should clearly identify duties and responsibilities.

Horngren adds another important component to our understanding of effective communication of information. He identifies "attention directing ' information. Information must go beyond the notion of Fayol's statistics, pure stewardship and scorekeeping. Information must give rise to action. If it is control information, measuring and reporting deviations from control, then it must:

- highlight the deviations,

- measure the deviation,

- explain the deviation and possibly suggest a solution.

This places another important responsibility upon the communicator of information. The communication must be in a format that is readily understood by the recipient and not give rise to misinterpretation.

Recording transactions and safeguarding assets

These have been brought together because they are pure Fayol. It will be recalled that Fayol identified six functions existing in any entity. One of these was descr ibed as "Security activities" which implied the protection of property and persons. Undoubtedly Fayol who was a mining engineer, was

more concerned about the physical aspect of security. However, a more legalistic interpretation can also be applied to management's duty to be a faithful steward of all the assets entrusted to them. The control information the scorekeeping and statistics are all part of that process.

Recording transactions comes under Fayol's "Accounting activities." He saw this as embracing stocktaker and inventory control, the compliance with the needs for a balance sheet, recording of costs and maintaining statistics. It is tempting to dismiss this as mundane bookkeeping. However, it is the basis of the corporate data base, and even in Fayol's time, this is how it was expected to be used. Solomons (1968) reported the existence of crude unstructured product costs in the late Victorian era to at least record the use of material and direct labour. However, this was more in keeping with Fayol's statistics rather than attempting a useful data bank. Two things contributed to the change of attitude and a recognition of the importance and relevance of cost accounting as a management tool. First, the onset of increased competition and the need for better cost information to improve the quality of quotes for future business. Secondly, and ultimately more controversial, was the impact of more capita l intensive industrial operations which demanded consideration of the effective treatment of overheads.

It is for this reason that the AAA recognised that the accounting function was critical in that it had all the statistics available for it to be the centre of information. The much vaunted Vatter text emphasises from the outset the importance of accounting as a management tool and thus introduces management students to the various techniques of management accounting. However, the text devotes considerable space to basic accounting familiarisation so that the techniques are properly understood, and also that the user is aware of where the information is derived.

Reviewing and reporting on systems and operations

If information is to generate action, it must be accurate. Here, accuracy is not confined to the obvious limits of numerical accuracy, but whether the components of the information are correct and relevant to effective control against the objective. This is an area of considerable debate at present and is the basis of much of the argument in favour of Activity Based Costing. From basic costing, the student should be aware of the practice of apportioned and absorbed overheads. Apportionment means that overheads are shared on an equitable basis between departments and rates are then computed whereby these overheads, deemed an essential part of

the conversion process are absorbed into costs. No one will deny that overheads are a necessary part of any operation, and that many have to be shared. While this sharing process is adequate for inventory valuation, for other purposes it may be inaccurate and even misleading. The development of marginal costing, whereby all direct costs of a good or service is a response to this problem, and essentially all Activity Based Costing does is try to make as much of the traditional conversion or operational overhead part of the direct costs. This will, it is argued, improve the accuracy of costs and hence the quality of information. To comply with definition, therefore.,it behoves the accountant to look to see if the information being prepared for management is correct for what it is needed for. If it is not, then he must find methods of cost recording, collection, analysis and even synthesis that correctly respond to the need. An obvious example might be where a product relies on raw materials being supplied exclusively on a JIT (Just In Time) Inventory control basis. Such a product would have little use for the central stores and therefore take no apportionment of the cost, nor should any absorbed overhead include the stores. By the same token, equipment that is exclusively used, should be charged direct, rather than as depreciation incorporated into an apportionment. It should thus be apparent that the exclusion of the stores will decrease the cost, while the charging of exclusive equipment will have the opposite effect.

This bring us to the last item on the list, decision making.

Decision making

This is an important element of the management process, and it is perhaps curious that it was only implied in Fayol's pioneering formula. Perhaps Fayol perceived a manager as a decision maker, and equated management with decision making. Certainly since we have perceived the manager as the user of information presented by the management accountant, such a view has some validity. Curiously, Handy discovered that decisions were not a large part of the managerial process suggesting the possibility that Fayol anticipated Handy. Another view, and perhaps one that is not surprising is that of R S Kaplan (1989). He makes the distinction between financial accounting as providing information for external users, while management accounting information "should be designed to make decision making within the firm." This is a view that is supported by Wilson and Chua (1988). Inevitably, there are a variety of components involved, and we shall attempt to relate each of them to the role of management accounting.

Decision making itself can be defined as

dealing with:

- (problem identification, definition and diagnosis,
- (generating alternative solutions,
- (evaluating and selecting alternative solutions.

(Huber 1980)

The student should be able to envisage the scenario of the management accounting control process drawing attention to a problem. Management should be able to generate possible alternative solutions. From the data bank management accounting can evaluate these solutions and present a ranking of the feasible alternatives for final selection and implementation. This logical and largely quantitative approach is described by Lindblom(*) as a *synoptic approach*. Students should know from their 2.5B studies that this is a little remote from reality. Reality is what Lindblom describes as the strategy of disjointed incrementalism, a way of proceeding by successive limited comparison. This recognises that there are subjective constraints that thwart the synoptic approach. One obvious example is the amount of data. The conversion of data into meaningful information requires that the data be effectively filtered. To achieve this objectively requires considerable management accounting skills.

How the management accountant might be involved can be seen in the decision model of Vroom and Yetton(*). In a situation where there is likely to be more than one solution, and one is likely to be more rational than the alternative(s), the first question has to be. "Do I, as the manager, have sufficient information to make a high quality decision?" If the answer is a negative. then the first priority is to identify and obtain the relevant information required.

Programmed and non-programmed decisions

H. A. Simon identified these two types of decision, lying at each end of a spectrum. Programmed decisions: those which are repetitive, routine or a definite procedure has been developed to handle them. The routine control process of reports is a programmed decision, as is processing orders, computing sickness benefit and even capital asset appraisal. Much of the information flow within an entity makes programmed decisions possible. By contrast, a non-programmed decision is one that is new, unstructured and lacking any set procedure for solution. Such a decision might be the developing of a new product, moving into new markets, redundancies and re-location. The spectrum aspect can be recognised in that both types of decision spawn sub-decisions that may be of either kind.

The hierarchy may also have some impact on the frequency may also have some impact on the frequency or type of decision. At the risk of a dangerous generalisation, the student can consider that there are likely to be more non-programmed decisions at the top of the hierarchy, where the emphasis is on strategy and planning, and more programmed decisions at the bottom where the emphasis is on operations and control.

The behavioural school of both accounting and management focuses upon participation. An example of this is the System 4 of Rensis Likert.(*) In such a situation, management demands high performance goals, makes full use of group participation and there is a good communication flow. Decisions are made very much on the group basis. For this to work requires management accounting information to be communicated to all levels in a way that will be understood and meaningful to all levels. To avoid patronising the lower levels of supervision, training in the use and understanding of information is required. The perceptive student can see elements of the Japanese use of quality circles and consensus decision-making evident. Not only are Japanese employees encouraged to participate, they are trained to participate better. As accountants, we will obtain better results if we educate our users as well as present information in a way that is readily understandable.

The impact of the organisation

All accounting information, and management accounting information in particular, has to be prepared in the context of the organisation. This final section will consider briefly the organisational aspects, concluding with a comment on how the management accounting system may be a function of the particular type of organisation.

Beginning with organisational control, this is defined as "the process of ensuring that the organisation is pursuing courses of action that will enable it to achieve its purposes" (Otley and Berry 1980). This means following agreed routes towards objectives. and monitoring any deviations from the route. Such deviations will then have to be corrected, or incorporated into revised routes or even objectives, although depending upon the context, it will either be operational day-to-day control or strategic control monitoring progress towards a corporate goal or objective.

Organisational goals are apparently less easy to define. Indeed, there is some element of controversy. There is the micro-economic notion of maximising profit or the shareholders' return. This is seen as a single goal. This view is rejected by numerous authors, who

suggest that there is evidence that organisations strive to achieve a number of goals simultaneously. The writer favours the middle ground, accepting that there must be one overall objective, but there are a number of very highly rated ancillary objectives. Measuring performance against these goals is fairly straightforward. If the goal is 15% market share by December 1994, to be achieved in two $2^1/2\%$ steps from December 1992, then the control aspect is whether or not this has been achieved. To have a number of equally ranking goals is likely to confuse the objectives and make meaningful monitoring extremely difficult. What must be done, however, having agreed the goal, is to ensure that it is communicated, and that progress towards it is monitored and communicated. This is the measure of organisational effectiveness. In addition, the effect of achieving that goal must be communicated, because this will have a significant influence on the response and motivation of the people towards that goal. Such an approach will come close to complying with the slightly bizarre Wilson and Chua definition of "satisfying genuinely the needs of the essential members in the long run." Whatever definition is finally accepted, the management accountant will have a vital part to play in the communication process.

One final point is the impact of contingency theory on the design of management accounting systems. The student should be aware of the Mintzberg(*) view that managerial roles relate to the situation and the unstructured nature of events. Equally, Joan Woodward(*) concluded that the structure and control of an organisation depended very much upon its size and nature. The same can be said for the strucutre of the management accounting system. This will be a function of five criteria:

(a) the environment, i.e whether or not it is a tough, highly competitive one where results would be hard to come by, or one where it was relatively easy to make a profit.

(b) technology — this is very much the Joan Woodward[†] view of technology in that the management accounting system for a large complex mass producer such as a volume car manufacturer would be substantially different from that of a jobbing operator such as the garage which services them.

(c) size — since we have already observed the problem of large amounts of information causing serious difficulties in the decision-making process it is almost inevitable that a large organisation, even if it is only producing one product or service, will be broken down into some kind of sub-divisional structure for management and control purposes.

(d) orientation — this follows on from

size. Once it has been accepted that a large organisation must be sub-divided, the question remains, "How?" One obvious answer is on the basis of products, and the control systems report on product performance. Another option is on the basis of customer service. Yet others may be on a production or regional basis. The student may wish to look at his own organisation, or that of clients and see if he feels that the organisation is appropriate for control, reporting and perhaps most important, effective evaluation and decision-making purposes.

(e) organisational structure — this is a controversial factor. Some research has suggested that where there is a highly centralised organisation, management accounting imformation and budgetary control information in particular was deemed to be unhelpful by the users. By contrast, where there was a structure that encouraged participation, and the management style was flexible, budgets were regarded as helpful towards a more effective performance. Only two research projects have produced this conclusion. As a result, it has been largely disregarded.

Concluding remarks

Hopefully this article should begin to direct students' thoughts. With the onset of texts such as Emmanual, Otley and Merchant, and the earlier Ezzamel and Hart, there is a large area of the 2.4 syllabus which is likely to overlap albeit from a different angle with 2.5B. Thus a question impinging upon management accounting information in a behavioural or organisational context could come up on either paper. Experience shows that students will handle such a question well only when it appears on the "right paper". By identifying where management accounting techniques relate to their organisational context, progress has been made to addressing this problem for the future.

References and further reading

Belkaoui A, Management Accounting a Conceptual Basis, Reading, Mass. 1981.

Horngren C, Cost Accounting — a Managerial Emphasis, PHI Englewood Cliffs, NJ.

Huber G P, Managerial Decision Making, Scott Foresman Glenview, 1980.

Kaplan R S and Atkinson A A, Advanced Management Accounting, PHI Englewood Cliffs NJ. 1989.

Otley D and Berry A J, "Control, Organization and Acounting", *Accounting, Organizations and Society,* 1980.

Pugh D S (ed), Writers on Organizations, Penguin. A useful guide for all 2.5B students to key authors on management. (*)Reviewed in detail in this text.

Simon H A, The New Science of Management Decision, Harper & Row, New York 1960.

Solomons D (ed), Studies in Cost Analysis, London 1968.

Vatter W J, Managerial Accounting, PHI New York 1950.

Wilson R M S and Chua W F, Managerial Accounting Method and Meaning, VNR, Wokingham 1988.

Three core texts that adopt this approach to management accounting:

Emmanual C, Otley D and Merchant K, Accounting for Management Control, Chapman and Hall, London 1990.

Ezzamel M and Hart H, Advanced Management Accounting — an Organisational Emphasis, Cassell, London 1987.

Otley D, Accounting Control and Organisational Behaviour, Heinemann, Oxford 1987.

(†)See also:

Gordon L A and Miller D, "A contingency framework for the design of accounting information systems", *Accounting Organisations and Society,* 1976.

Edwards K A and Emmanuell C R, "Diverging views on the boundaries of Management Accounting", *Management Accounting Research,* 1990.

Mark Lee Inman BSc MPhil FCMA FCCA is the Professional Accounting Courses Tutor at the Polytechnic of North London and contributes regularly to the Newsletter.

READER ARTICLE 2.1

'Fixed costs and sunk costs in decision making'

Robert G. Luther

Reproduced from *Management Accounting*, Journal of the Chartered Institute of Management Accountants

January 1992

FIXED COSTS AND SUNK COSTS IN DECISION-MAKING

Robert G. Luther suggests that sunk costs, which are included in financial accounting, are not relevant to an organisational decision-maker except in a limited number of simplified situations. We must ensure that the classification of costs is always decision-specific.

It is well known that historical-cost accounting has major shortcomings when used as the input for managerial decision-making. But management accountants in their enthusiasm to run down conventional balance sheets and profit and loss accounts, are often guilty of misconceptions. Many, for example, might suggest that fixed costs, being those that do not vary in line with production or sales volumes, are *ipso facto* not relevant. It is even more commonly held that sunk costs are irrelevant. Jevons's (1911) saying, 'In commerce, bygones are forever bygones', is one that has stuck fast in many minds.

A cost or benefit is relevant, narrowly defined, to a decision-making situation if it is one that will be affected by the choice between alternative possible courses of action. Fixed costs *can* frequently be relevant costs. The monthly rental of a high-street shop is a fixed cost for a retail operation — it will not increase if sales volumes are doubled nor disappear if no sales are made. It remains, nevertheless, a cost over which management can exercise an option — it can be avoided by terminating the lease. That same rental charge could, however, be a non-relevant cost if a five-year agreement had been entered into, in which case the rentals would be a sunk cost and payable whatever course of action was taken.

An interesting situation in which costs which are both fixed and sunk may be relevant is pricing. Where they have created a valuable resource with alternative uses, the inclusion of such costs in product pricing may ensure that selling prices cover opportunity costs, i.e. the net benefit that could be derived by applying the resource to the next most profitable activity. A practical example of this approach is a luxury hotel allocating the building's fixed costs to their restaurants and other trading centres.

Marginal costing would indicate that the restaurant's prices should not be required to recover fixed costs that would be

Robert Luther is Lecturer in Accountancy at the University of Exeter and Branch Careers and Education Officer for the Institute's Devon and Cornwall Sub-Branch.

incurred anyway, but the critical point is that if they can't do so there is an indication that the space could be more profitably rented out to outsiders, e.g. a jeweller or hairdressing salon. This support for absorption costing based on fixed costs acting as a surrogate for opportunity costs was first made by Baxter and Oxenfeldt in 1961.

Sunk costs have been defined as those 'incurred in the past and unaffected by any future action and thus irrelevant to decision-making' (Parker 1984). If this were always so one could perhaps conclude that, for decision-making, no purpose is served by reporting sunk costs.

A nice example of such a sunk cost would be the expenditure incurred in digging an 800ft mineshaft. The decision of whether or not to extract ores should not be influenced by the cost of the hole. In addition, if there was an option to sell the hole, the market value would presumably be determined only by reference to the net incremental receipts that could be derived from its exploitation. So, the argument goes, for decision-making as opposed, perhaps, to stewardship, the sunk costs need not be reported.

Certainly managers are often faced with an excess of figures when they are required to make decisions and there is a natural and logical desire to eliminate those which will not be influenced by the choice to be made. Many fixed costs and overheads that find their way onto historical-cost profit and loss accounts are not relevant to a specific decision. Depreciation of machinery based on the passage of time is an obvious item for discarding. But care does need to be taken that sunk costs are not, as a matter of course, eliminated and 'buried'.

For strategic decision-making one's own irretrievably sunk costs may be critically relevant. First, they give one a good idea of the costs that potential competitors would have to incur to enter one's market. The past research and development costs of a new wonder-drug may be no longer incremental for our company but they would be incremental for another company considering competing. For this reason they have obvious implications as to how keenly one might need to trim the price in contestable markets.

In an indirect way this approach lends further support to the recovering of sunk costs in product pricing, i.e. full-cost pricing. If the costs that you have incurred in getting the product to its present condition and location are ones that competition would need to incur, then the full cost is an indication of how high the price can be set without inviting others to

contest one's niche of the market.

Furthermore, this has implications for financial reporting. One's own sunk costs, provided they have not been inefficiently or ineffectively incurred, represent barriers to entry. A case can therefore legitimately be made for treating them as assets. Strategically, costs that have been irretrievably sunk by one's own company, but which have yet to be incurred by competitors, can provide a strong card to play. In our pricing we can go down to a level which, for us, equates marginal revenue with marginal cost. It would only be worthwhile for competitors to contest the market if they could recover similar ongoing marginal costs *and* sink the requisite 'capital' costs. 'With this view, accountants should seek to provide information on sunk costs because of the strategic advantages they may bring to the enterprise which possesses them. This really requires a continual study of fixed costs because any given fixed cost may be expected to have a sunk component, at least over some short time period.' (Bromwich 1990).

A second aspect of the relevance of sunk costs is related to their behavioural significance. Weber (1968) questions the applicability of objective rationality and suggests that organisational behaviour is more influenced by subjective and positional rationality. In similar vein, it has been argued (e.g. Mepham 1987) that decision relevance is but one form of relevance which ignores the decision-maker and the environment in which he operates.

Several reasons for the ongoing recognition of past sunk costs come to mind. First, the elimination of sunk costs unambiguously signals an error in past decisions. Thus, in all but the strictly rational economic sense, the cost at which investment shares were bought *is* relevant to the sell-retain decision. There are numerous examples of projects that, like *Concorde*, have attracted an emotional commitment that may defy simple rationality. If there is any slim chance that future net revenues will be generated out of the sunk costs, those sunk costs will remain relevant.

Following our mining analogy, a different and unanticipated mineral ore may be discovered. This leads on to the second point, which is that once expenditure, whether it is an asset or not, is written off the custody over it is relaxed. The policy of rapid depreciation of equipment has often led to loss to companies of assets that have nil book value but significant real value.

Third, the record of what has happened may, in itself, be significant. The decision, *ex ante*, to sink costs will usually have been

Continued on page 42

Fixed and sunk costs

Continued from page 37

taken in expectation of net economic benefit and once the costs are sunk they may have lost their rational economic relevance but they still 'tell a story'. The failure of an expensive research plan to provide economic benefit may just indicate 'bad luck', i.e. 'you can't win them all'. It may also, however, indicate inadequate pre-decision information or indeed poor implementation.

Mistakes are often a useful learning experience. The track record of ongoing research by a chemical company may have relevance when application is made for government grants. Furthermore, as a practical matter, sunk costs may retain a purely economic relevance to the extent that they may retain tax significance.

The American Accounting Association defined accounting as 'the process of identifying, measuring and communicating economic information to permit informed judgments and decisions by users of the information' (AAA 1966).

This article has aimed to show that sunk costs, included in financial accounting, are not irrelevant to an organisational decision-maker except in a limited number of simplified situations. The argument, i.e.

'the costs whose variations are of significance for one decision will be of no significance for others' (Coase 1938), gives theoretical support to the eclectic approach actually used by decision-makers (J. M. Clark's dictum [1923] of 'different costs for different purposes'). In our disillusionment with conventional historical-cost accounting, or the current enthusiasm for ABC, we need to remember that the classification of costs has to be decision-specific. □

American Accounting Association (1966): *A Statement of Basic Accounting Theory.*

BAXTER, W. T. and OXENFELDT, A. R. (1961): 'Costing and pricing: the cost accountant versus the economist', *Business Horizons.*

BROMWICH, M. (1990): 'The case for strategic management accounting: the role of accounting information for strategy in competitive markets', *Accounting, Organisations and Society*, (Vol. 15).

CLARK, J. M. (1923): *Studies in the Economics of Overhead Costs*, University of Chicago Press.

COASE, R. H. (1938): 'Business organisation and the accountant', *The Accountant.*

JEVONS, W. S. (1911): *Theory of Political Economy.*

MEPHAM, M. J. (1987): 'The relevance of sunk costs' in *Management Accounting in Research and Practice: Expanding the Horizons*, COOPER, D., ARNOLD, J. and SCAPENS, R. (eds) (CIMA).

PARKER, R. H. (1984): *Dictionary of Accounting.*

READER ARTICLE 3.1

'Is there a "correct" method of investment appraisal?'

David Dugdale

Reproduced from *Management Accounting*, Journal of the Chartered Institute of Management Accountants

May 1992

Is there a 'correct' method of investment appraisal?

David Dugdale of Bristol Business School studies the different methods of investment appraisal and suggests that the management accountant should have a thorough understanding of all of them if they are to be wisely used.

Investment appraisal is a key element of management accounting and a thorough understanding of the techniques of investment appraisal is very important. Textbooks compare the techniques of accounting rate of return, payback, net present value and internal rate of return, recommending net present value as the soundest technique. Here the arguments will be reviewed and it will be concluded that the choice of technique in practice should not be as clear cut as is sometimes suggested.

Accounting rate of return

Accounting rate of return is calculated in basically the same way as 'return on investment' as:

$$\frac{\text{Profit}}{\text{Investment}}$$

but whether 'profit' is before or after interest charges and whether 'investment' is the initial outlay or is averaged over the life of the project is unclear.

This lack of clarity seems strange. The point of this technique is that it is based on the same principles as the published financial statements. Companies (and managers) are often evaluated by the 'return on investment' or 'return on capital employed' ratio derived from published profit and loss account and balance sheet. (The two ratios are identical, merely reflecting the two sides of the balance sheet; 'capital employed' reflects the financing of the business, 'investment' reflects the use of that finance. It is therefore logical that it should be calculated in a way which makes it comparable with these ratios. As the balance sheet contains written down asset values one would expect accounting rate of return to be calculated as:

$$\frac{\text{Profit}}{\text{Average (written down) investment}}$$

And this accords with common sense because if profit is after depreciation then one would expect that depreciation to affect the value of the investment. Following the same principle (that the numerator and denominator must be comparable) allows other difficulties to be resolved. If we are measuring management's performance the ratio would be:

$$\frac{\text{Profit before interest and tax}}{\text{Average (total) capital employed}}$$

but if we were measuring return to shareholders the ratio would be:

$$\frac{\text{Profit after interest and tax}}{\text{Shareholders' funds}}$$

We must compare 'return' with the funds (or investment) which generate that return.

The following simple example will be used to compare accounting rate of return with other techniques:

	£000
Investment	(100)
Cashflow — Year 1	20
2	30
3	40
4	40
5	10

Straight-line depreciation of £20,000 per year over the five year life of the asset would mean reported profits of:

	£000
Year 1	–
2	10
3	20
4	20
5	(10)

Average profit would be £8,000 per year. Average investment would be £50,000 (as the investment declines in value over the five years due to the depreciation charge) and accounting rate of return would be:

$$\frac{8,000}{50,000} = 16 \text{ per cent}$$

Payback

Payback is a simple investment-appraisal technique which involves determining how long will be needed before the initial investment is 'paid back'. Unlike accounting rate of return which is bound by accounting definitions of 'profit' and 'investment', payback concentrates on the specific *cashflows* which an investment will generate. (In this respect payback is superior to accounting rate of return because the management accounting theory of decision making is based on the simple concept that financial advice should be based on whether the wealth of the decision-maker will be increased if a particular decision is taken. The definitions and conventions of financial accounting should not be allowed to muddy the waters of this essentially simple problem.)

The well documented drawbacks of the payback technique are based on the fact that future cashflows, in themselves, do not indicate increased wealth. This is because a money flow in the future is not worth as much as the same money flow now. (Cash available now can be invested and so is worth more than the same cashflow at a later date.)

The disadvantages of payback:
- all cashflows within the payback period are given equal weight;
- cashflows outside the payback period are ignored.

Although one might expect payback to be little used because of these disadvantages, in practice, it is used extensively! Its simplicity probably explains its popularity:
- decision-makers understand information presented to them;
- calculations are straightforward and likely to be error-free;
- since data is itself unreliable (estimates of future cashflows) sophisticated analysis may not be justified.

Payback can also be recommended if the business requires liquid funds at some date in the future — a project which 'pays back' before this date would be preferable to one which needs to be funded for a longer period. A further advantage is the 'risk aversion' of payback and this will be discussed later.

Payback period in our example would be 3.25 years. If the stipulated payback period were longer than this the investment would be accepted, if not, it would be rejected.

Discounting techniques — net present value

The recommended approach is to calculate the 'net present value' of a proposed investment by 'discounting' future cashflows to present value and summing (or 'netting') them together. The present value of a future cashflow is calculated by multiplying it by the factor

$$\frac{1}{(1 + r)^n}$$

where r is the discount rate and n is the number of periods (usually years) in the future when the cashflow will take place. 'Discounting' is the opposite of 'compounding' and, remembering that a principal, P, will grow to an amount, A, after n years if invested at a rate of interest r, we have:

$$A = P(1 + r)^n$$

and

$$P = \frac{A}{(1 + r)^n}$$

We can say that P grows to A in n years or, equivalently, that the future cashflow A is worth P in *present value* terms. By discounting future cashflows the problem of the time value of money is eliminated and, if the net present value is positive (inflows in present-value terms exceed outflows in present-value terms) the project can be recommended.

In practice NPV calculations are easy because tables of discount factors are readily available. In our example, assuming a discount rate of 10 per cent per annum:

Year	Cashflow (£000)	Factor	Present value (£000)
0	(100)	1.000	(100)
1	20	0.909	18.2
2	30	0.826	24.8
3	40	0.751	30.0
4	40	0.683	27.3
5	10	0.621	6.2
			6.5

If the *cost of capital* were 10 per cent this project could be recommended because it generates a positive NPV of £6,500. One interpretation of NPV is that, if the project were financed by a loan at 10 per cent per annum, the interest on the loan and the original capital could be repaid out of project cashflows and this would eventually leave a cash balance at the end of the project worth £6,500 *in present value terms*.

The net present value technique is the academic recommendation and it is theoretically sound. However, its use in practice implies that the decision-maker must judge a project by an *absolute* number and while it is easy to give the 'rule' — any project generating positive NPV is acceptable — a decision maker will be interested not only in the final NPV 'payoff' but also in the size of the initial investment and the length of time before the project 'matures'.

Use of the NPV rule becomes problematic if capital is 'rationed', because not all projects can then be accepted. In this situation it becomes necessary to rank projects according to their 'earning power' — placing the project which generates the maximum NPV per pound invested at the top of the list. Conventionally the *profitability index* is calculated in order to rank projects, where:

$$\text{Profitability index} = \frac{\text{NPV of cash inflows}}{\text{Investment outflow}}$$

In our example:

$$\text{Profitability index} = \frac{106.5}{100} = 1.065$$

This project would rank behind a project with profitability index of 1.1 but ahead of a project with profitability index of 1.05.

A common source of confusion and misunderstanding in NPV calculations is the treatment of inflation. Typically, the discount rate is the *money* cost of capital, i.e. the rate payable on borrowed money (the source of funds may be a bank, debentures, equity or some combination of

sources). Such a rate *includes* an allowance for inflation in the sense that the lender cannot expect any more than the interest rate. (The lender may charge a 15 per cent rate assuming that inflation will be 8 per cent and so a 7 per cent 'real return' will be generated.)*

If a money cost of capital is employed then the cashflows on which the analysis is performed should also *include* any inflation which is expected. (And, if different rates of inflation are expected on revenues and costs then this should be reflected in the cashflows.)

In practice, cashflows are often projected in so called 'real' terms, i.e. excluding inflation. Given the uncertain nature of estimated future cashflows this is not surprising, inflating 'guesstimated' future cashflows may give even the most determined accountant pause for thought! And, since inflation might be expected to affect all companies equally, it can reasonably be assumed that, if there are unexpected inflationary pressures, they will be compensated by price adjustments.

There are therefore compelling reasons for the use of cashflows in 'real' terms in NPV analysis. However, it therefore follows that the discount rate should also be in 'real' terms.

Any inflation element in the cost of capital should be *excluded* from the discount rate before proceeding with the analysis. It would not be surprising if this important point were overlooked in practice and a survey by Carsberg and Hope (1976) showed that this was indeed the case.

Discounting techniques — internal rate of return

An alternative approach, still based on discounting principles, is the calculation of 'internal rate of return' — that discount rate at which the net present value of the project is zero. The decision rule now becomes — accept the project if its internal rate of return (IRR) is greater than the cost of capital, reject if the IRR is less than the cost of capital. If a decision has to be made about a single project with 'conventional' cashflows (i.e. a single outlay followed by a series of inflows) IRR will lead to the same decision as NPV. However, in more complex circumstances IRR and NPV can lead to different decisions and IRR generally receives a bad press for a number of reasons:

Calculation is complex
In our example the IRR might be calculated as follows — by trying a different discount rate — say 15 per cent:

Year	Cashflow (£000)	Factor	Present value (£000)
0	(100)	1.000	(100)
1	20	0.870	17.4
2	30	0.756	22.7
3	40	0.658	26.3
4	40	0.572	22.9
5	10	0.497	5.0
			(5.7)

And a linear approximation allows the discount rate where NPV is zero to be calculated:

$$IRR = 10\% + \frac{6.5}{12.2} \times 5\% = 12.7\%$$

The calculation appears both messy and approximate. Nevertheless neither of these criticisms is fair. The existence of powerful spreadsheets such as Lotus 1-2-3 and Excel allows IRR to be calculated instantly and accurately by using the relevant function.

There may be multiple IRRs
If project cashflows reverse during the life of the project — there may, for example, be an initial outflow followed by several inflows before another major outflow (as plant undergoes major refurbishment, for example) — there may be more than one IRR. A graph of discount rate versus NPV might appear as follows:

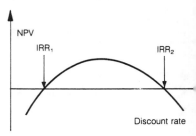

In such an example the IRR decision rule (accept if cost of capital is less than IRR) is misleading because the project should only be accepted if cost of capital is *between* IRR_1 and IRR_2.

To explain this result it is necessary to understand the *re-investment assumptions* implicit in the NPV and IRR calculations. All NPV calculations assume that incoming cash can be re-invested at the rate which is used in the NPV calculations. This means that the calculation of IRR_1 assumes re-investment at IRR_1 while the calculation of IRR_2 assumes re-investment at IRR_2. Only at rates between IRR_1 and IRR_2 can the incoming cash be reinvested at a rate which is sufficient to offset both the initial cash outflow and the eventual second cash outflow. This analysis is perfectly sound and, arguably, the project is only acceptable if the cost of capital lies between IRR_1 and IRR_2. Unfortunately, however, it means that the IRR decision rule — accept if cost of capital is less than IRR — can only be applied to projects having conventional cashflows.

The NPV approach avoids this problem quite simply. By using the cost of capital as the discount rate in the NPV formula a negative NPV is generated if cost of capital

---

* Strictly the 'money' cost of capital is given by

$$(1 + r)(1 + I) - 1$$

where r is the 'real' cost of capital and I the rate of inflation. If inflation is assumed to be 8 per cent then a 'money' cost of capital of 15 per cent implies a real return of 6.5 per cent.

is less than IRR$_1$, a positive NPV is obtained if cost of capital is between IRR$_1$ and IRR$_2$, and the NPV is negative again if cost of capital is greater than IRR$_2$.

The possibility of multiple IRRs is cited as a disadvantage of the IRR technique. However, the problem can be overcome. Multiple IRRs arise only when cashflows reverse more than once. In these circumstances it is only necessary to identify the (possibly) several IRRs (some calculators will draw the graph of NPV versus discount rate in a few seconds) and draw the correct conclusions.

IRR is inappropriate if projects are mutually exclusive

The third problem concerns the selection of a favoured project from two or more projects which are 'mutually exclusive' (i.e. if one is chosen the others are automatically ruled out). Suppose that, instead of our project (A) being a simple accept/reject decision we have to choose between it and another project (B) which can be compared with project A as follows:

	Project A	Project B
Initial investment (£000)	100	50
Net present value (£000)	6.5	5.0
Internal rate of return (%)	12.7	18.0

The internal rate of return approach would favour project B (18.0 per cent compared with 12.7 per cent), however, provided funds are freely available project A would maximise wealth because, if chosen, it could generate £6,500 NPV compared with project B's £5,000. In essence, IRR can mislead because it may select a lower investment with higher 'earning potential', when it may be preferable to invest a greater sum which generates a lower 'return' but (because of its scale) produces a greater sum in the end.

The last objection does mean that IRR must be used with caution if a choice has to be made between mutually exclusive projects. And NPV is usually recommended in preference to IRR because of the three objections discussed above and a much more subtle point concerning the re-investment assumptions implicit in the two methods.

Whilst the IRR technique assumes that cashflows can be re-invested at the IRR, the NPV technique assumes that cashflows can be re-invested at the cost of capital used in the discounting process. This difference has two repercussions:

1 Even if mutually exclusive projects have the *same initial investment* (so the third objection raised against IRR does not apply) NPV and IRR can give conflicting results. IRR may prefer a project with high early cashflows (assumed re-invested at the IRR) whilst NPV may prefer a different project — with higher flows later.
2 If IRR is used to rank projects in a capital-rationing situation the ranking may be different from that obtained used profitability index because IRR will favour early cash inflows (assuming re-investment at the IRR) whilst profitability index (being based on NPV) may produce a different ranking.

It is usually assumed that NPV (and its derivative, the profitability index) provide the best guidance because the cost of capital re-investment assumption is more conservative and likely to be more realistic.

Discussion of techniques

First, it is by no means certain that the NPV method is definitely better than the IRR approach. It is certainly conceivable that the IRR re-investment assumption is as realistic as the NPV assumption — any business which could only invest its funds at the cost of capital would not be in business for long! And, in a capital-rationing situation there may be other projects readily available which would generate returns well in excess of the cost of capital. The IRR re-investment assumption could be more realistic in this situation and a technique which favours early inflows (as IRR does) could be preferable because it makes finance available with which to fund the other projects. The point can also be made that the technique which favours early inflows is also more risk averse — because earlier cashflows are more certain than later ones.

Having defended IRR on theoretical grounds it can be pointed out that it is, arguably, more 'meaningful' than NPV. A manager presented with an NPV of £6,500 may well ask what this figure 'means' — what investment? How long? etc — an absolute number cannot easily be assessed in isolation. The same manager presented with an IRR of 12.7 per cent immediately has a 'feel' for the project — if money can be borrowed at, say, 5 per cent, then the project is probably sound. If the cost of capital is 10 per cent then there does not appear to be much margin for error.

These considerations are borne out in practice. A survey by Pike (1980), reported by Pike and Dobbins (1986), revealed that 41 per cent of firms surveyed used IRR as their primary method of investment appraisal compared with only 17 per cent which used NPV as their primary method.

To sum up, IRR is criticised because it is complex, there may be multiple IRRs, it can mislead where projects are mutually exclusive and its re-investment assumption may be optimistic. Nevertheless, provided that the method is thoroughly understood, none of these objections is insuperable and there are reasons why IRR may be preferred to NPV.

It is interesting to compare the result obtained using IRR with that produced by the accounting rate of return (ARR) method. Remember that the accounting rate of return was 16 per cent but the IRR was 12.7 per cent. This is typical. On the basis of ARR it may appear that the project is profitable if the cost of capital is, say, 14 per cent. However, this is erroneous; the project is only viable if the cost of capital is less than 12.7 per cent.

Note that the IRR and the ARR are comparable but IRR is less than ARR. This is what one would expect because ARR treats all future inflows as equally valuable whilst IRR takes account of the time value of money. If ARR were calculated in other ways, for example based on initial investment rather than average (depreciated) investment, the comparison between IRR and ARR would not make sense.

Given that accounting rate of return does not take account of the time value of money, one might assume that it should not be used. However, this does not necessarily follow. Remembering that analysts often use return on investment to evaluate business performance, a change in the ROI ratio could actually affect the company's share price!

If an investment were big enough to have repercussions on published P & L and balance sheet it would be foolish *not* to calculate the ARR!

Having made a case for at least considering IRR and ARR we can consider the payback technique. As discussed earlier, payback is often used in practice, probably because of its simplicity.

However, it may also be used because of its risk aversion — early cashflows are given full value, late cashflows are ignored.

The usual textbook advice is to take account of risk in both the following ways:

1 If payback is used by decreasing the required payback period.
2 If IRR is used by increasing the required 'hurdle rate'.
3 If NPV is used by increasing the discount rate to take account of the 'risk' associated with the project. The capital asset pricing model provides a means of assessing the premium which ought to be added to the 'risk free' discount rate.
4 To assign probabilities to 'best', 'most likely' and 'worst' values for each variable and calculate a range of possible outcomes together with their probabilities. (This approach can be refined by establishing distributions for the input variables and 'simulating' the project many times in order to build up a distribution of possible outcomes).

The relatively straightforward methods of handling risk if payback or IRR are used are cited as advantages of these techniques. However, none of the techniques described above deals with the important point that early cashflows are likely to be more certain than late ones. The discounting techniques take account of the time value of money but they assume that whatever cashflows are projected are *certain*. Only the payback technique clearly favours early cashflows much more than later ones and this may partially account for its popularity. (The IRR approach favours early inflows when compared with the NPV approach because of its re-investment assumption. However, this is a very fine point compared with payback which ignores late cashflows altogether.)

Continued on page 50

Conclusion

It could be argued that much of the discussion is so academic as to be irrelevant in practice. Studies of investment decision-making in practice reveal that financial analysis is only a part of the decision-making process and social factors are equally important. However, accepting this point and the need for a rounded, pragmatic, approach to investment decisions does not excuse management accountants from thoroughly understanding the tools of their trade.

The arguments put forward here suggest that *all* the techniques of investment appraisal need to be well understood if they are to be wisely used.

In summary:

1 NPV is the principal theoretical recommendation and should be used if the cost of capital is a realistic re-investment assumption.
2 IRR, like NPV, incorporates discounting principles and, for some managers, may be more obviously meaningful than the absolute NPV of the project. However, IRR needs to be thoroughly understood because of possible difficulties concerning multiple IRRs and its use if projects are mutually exclusive.
3 Payback is much used in practice and, aside from its obvious simplicity, it can also be recommended if a risk-averse decision is needed (or if liquidity is a major problem).
4 ARR takes no account of the time value of money and could lead to an incorrect decision if compared with the cost of capital. However, because of the extensive use of the return on capital employed or return on investment ratio in practice it could be foolish not to calculate it.

The analysis suggests that there may be a place for all the techniques of investment appraisal in the management accountant's armoury. However, a thorough understanding of their theoretical nuances *is* important. □

CARSBERG, B. V. and HOPE, A. (1976): *Business Investment Decisions Under Inflation*. Institute of Chartered Accountants in England and Wales.

PIKE, R. H. and DOBBINS, R. (1986): *Investment Decisions and Financial Strategy*. Philip Allan, p. 274.

'Discordant voices: "accountants" views of
investment appraisal'

David Dugdale and Colwyn Jones

Reproduced from *Management Accounting*,
Journal of the Chartered Institute of
Management Accountants

November 1991

Discordant voices: accountants' views of investment appraisal

David Dugdale and Colwyn Jones explore the gap between theory and practice in relation to the selection and use of investment appraisal techniques. Their study is based on loosely structured interviews with an accounting lecturer, industrial accountants at plant and divisional level in two companies and a financial adviser in local government, aimed at identifying different perceptions of investment appraisal.

It has become a commonplace observation that one of the current problems of management accounting is a gap between theory and practice (e.g. Scapens 1983, 1988). This article explores this gap in relation to one specific issue — the selection and use of investment appraisal techniques.

In a previous article one of the authors discussed the theoretical ramifications of techniques of investment appraisal such as 'net present value', 'payback', 'accounting rate of return' etc (Dugdale 1990). Here we examine differences in practitioner and academic views of this subject, drawing on a pilot study conducted in Summer 1990. This study used loosely structured interviews aimed at identifying different perceptions of investment appraisal and relating these to different roles occupied by academics and practitioners.

Our comments are based on detailed analysis of interviews with an accounting lecturer, industrial accountants at plant and divisional level in two companies and a financial advisor in local government.

An academic voice

> 'The strength of NPV is that it gives the right answer . . . NPV is the only really sensible way of doing it . . . I don't think NPV is difficult to understand, most managers have actually heard about NPV — they do a quants course and they study accounting or whatever.'
>
> *Academic Accountant*

The 'academic' interviewed was an Oxbridge graduate who teaches financial management on final year degree, MBA and professional courses. He thought that investment appraisal theory 'ought' to be applied in practice and the only 'sound' method of appraisal was calculation of NPV. Payback was naive and had merit only in those specific circumstances where it could produce the same result as NPV (where constant cash inflows in perpetuity

David Dugdale is Principal Lecturer at Bristol Business School and Colwyn Jones is Principal Lecturer in the Department of Social Science at Bristol Polytechnic.

follow a single cash outflow). The possibility that payback might provide a check on NPV calculations was conceded only after prompting and no particular difficulties were envisaged in explaining NPV. Our interviewee felt that everyone would have heard of it, all accountants would be able to calculate it and the tedious nature of the calculations should no longer be a problem given the widespread availability of IBM personal computers.

If the organisation required other methods of evaluation (such as payback) our inverviewee still expected the accountant to calculate NPV. At first he thought the accountant should challenge the company policy but, on reflection, thought this might not be necessary so long as the 'correct' decisions were taken.

The 'correct' decision was the one which would maximise NPV in the long term — so that shareholder wealth would be maximised. If the accountant was satisfied that a project was viable it was almost his or her duty to ensure that it was accepted — and this may involve some 'manipulation' if, for example, a payback-style analysis was required by the company.

Any difficulties in using NPV were expected to revolve around establishing the appropriate discount rate — which ought to reflect the cost of capital for that class of projects which was as risky as the project under consideration. Academic research might be useful here and this was the area in which practical difficulties could be anticipated.

An plant accountant's voice

> 'Payback? Its strength is it is simple and if you can justify something on simple grounds then why make them more complicated? I've always been a bit sceptical of DCF . . . who would I present it to? My local management wouldn't understand that, I'm sure they wouldn't understand that.'
>
> *Plant Accountant*

At 'plant' level the interviewee was a CIMA qualified chief accountant (the 'plant' being a division of a larger group).

In this company the payback technique was specified as the means of evaluation when investment proposals were submitted (to group) for approval. The accountant was aware of the drawbacks of payback — taking no account of inflation or interest rates — but he did not regard these technical deficiencies as important. He argued that the data, especially that concerning product volume (marketing) assumptions, was uncertain, the result of any analysis would be very sensitive to such assumptions and, therefore, sophisticated analysis was not worthwhile.

This accountant felt that the use of DCF techniques would be counter-productive: first, because the results would be difficult to explain to other managers and, second, because the complexity of the analysis would distract from the main task — interrogating the cashflow projections (especially the product volume assumptions) on which the analysis was based. (Our interviewee also admitted that, if required to carry out NPV calculations, he might have to buy a book or 'buy someone a pint' to explain the subject to him!).

When pressed as to the possible usefulness of discounted cashflow methods he conceded that they might provide a check on payback (the reverse of the usual academic view!) and such calculations were probably carried out at head-office — 'in their role as bankers'. He had no motivation to 'second guess' the head-office calculation because, in his experience, projects were not rejected (although they were occasionally delayed whilst more information was requested).

Although investment proposals submitted to group were not turned down this did not mean that capital funds were freely available. Group signalled its intentions to division in two ways: first, in agreeing the annual capital budget — where funding of broad areas was established — and, second, in the stipulated 'payback period' — which could range between eighteen months and three years.

Our interviewee had seen policy change when the plant had been owned by different companies, capital was plentifully available when expansion was intended but lacking when the owner chose to treat the division as a 'cash cow'.

Two divisional accountants' voices

> 'Investment appraisal techniques? Somebody, somewhere is going to ask you for all of them, for each in turn. Invariably, you'll end up doing them all'
>
> *Senior Divisional Accountant*

> 'From a theoretical point of view the time-value of money is important and DCF is more responsive to uncertainty . . . Divisional Managers ought to be doing DCF (but) I think I'm a victim of my training more than anything else and I might have a different view in a year if I find I've been spending a lot of time doing this with no practical satisfaction that it has helped decision making at all.'
>
> *Junior Divisional Accountant*

This interview was with two accountants (one a recently qualified graduate) at the UK headquarters of a (relatively small) American multinational.

These interviewees placed very little emphasis on financial analysis in the decision-making process. Instead they emphasised the process itself which seemed to be remarkably procedure-free. The process consisted of pushing a proposal up through the hierarchy until it received the required level of authorisation — although the 'level' was hardly clear. Small projects might be authorised with very little justification whilst major projects needed approval by the company president.

Decision-making was recognised as slow and a proposal only reached the president after much vetting, cross-checking and the involvement of anyone who had a contribution to make; the process could 'loop' from higher to lower levels in the hierarchy more than once. The process could be frustrating for managers who wanted a decision — while the president failed to understand their frustration 'because I've never turned down a proposal which reached me'.

As part of the vetting process 'someone' was almost certain to ask for NPV, payback etc and so it was normal to calculate all the investment appraisal measures for important projects. Such calculations were regarded as relatively trivial and, given the company's policy of recruiting highly qualified staff and encouraging them to study for degrees such as the MBA, no difficulties of understanding were anticipated. One of the interviewees did feel that DCF appraisal methods 'ought' to be used but she said that she might hold this view because of her training. Her view might change after a year or so of actualy doing such calculations.

While investment appraisal calculations might be part of the process it was emphasised that they were a small part. The original proposal would usually be 'driven' by perceived market forces — to meet capacity, quality, reliability etc — and the importance of such projects fitting into company 'strategy' was emphasised rather

than their financial justification. If a project 'felt' right but appeared not to meet financial criteria then the financial justification would be scrutinised for errors rather than reject the project. Again the uncertainty of cashflow projections was emphasised and attempts were made to quantify this uncertainty by having managers estimate the probabilities of certain events.

While DCF techniques might have an important, if relatively small, role in the appraisal process it was recognised that, at plant level, different criteria could predominate. The company measures divisional performance by profitability and growth (and *not* by return on investment) and, because accounting 'profit' is a key measure, managers wish to understand the projected profit consequences of an investment decision.

A local government accountant's voice

> 'We always use NPV for appraisals. But we express each project [to elected members of the county council] in terms of its payback, because most of our members are farmers and small businessmen who find that more acceptable — in fact they talk in those terms.'
>
> *Local Government Accountant*

This interview was with a financial adviser in local government, an economics graduate who had worked in local government throughout his career.

This interviewee was clear as to the virtues of DCF analysis and the drawbacks of payback. He understood the nuances of DCF, spelling out the importance of using money cashflows with a nominal (money) discount rate or using 'real' cashflows with a rate which excluded inflation. He used DCF techniques himself and expected other financial advisors to do so.

However, he did not expect non-accountants either to use or to understand DCF methods. Proposers of projects almost certainly used payback as their method of evaluation. And, although he used DCF to establish the viability of projects, presentation (to the original proposer and to elected representatives) was based on payback (although it was made clear that a DCF analysis had, in fact, been carried out). Eventual evaluation of accepted projects was also based on payback — comparing the 'payback' actually achieved with that anticipated when the project was accepted.

The interviewee did not think that conflicts arose between the NPV 'analysis' and the payback 'presentation'. He pointed out that, so long as 'real' discount rates were used in the DCF calculation quite 'long' payback periods could be justified — certainly of the order of 5 to 10 years. Since capital was invariably 'rationed' marginal projects were unlikely to be presented for consideration and those projects which were considered would be viable on both NPV and payback criteria.

The importance of differing roles in the decision-making process was emphasised. Elected representatives made decisions — first, how much capital would be allocated to 'budgets' (energy-saving, school building etc) and, second, which specific projects would be undertaken? Operational managers presented possible projects for consideration while the treasurer's department evaluated the projects, using appropriate techniques, and presented this evaluation in terms understandable to the proposers and decision-makers. The importance of doing the analysis 'correctly' was emphasised, but the adviser had no responsibility for the eventual decisions — which might be based on financial advice or on other considerations.

Analysis of the interviews

Whilst practitioners might differ as to the relative importance of investment appraisal techniques, the most striking feature of these interviews was the emphasis they gave to the *process* of investment decision-making. Theoretical issues might be well understood or poorly understood; that accountants 'should' use the 'best' theoretical technique might be regarded as important or unimportant; explaining the results of theoretical analysis might be considered difficult or trivial. But what practitioners *did* agree on was that financial analysis was a relatively small part of the whole decision-making process.

In the three organisations visited decisions were made within the context of a 'strategy' which was only tenuously connected to the idea that companies would 'maximise shareholder wealth' or that local government would 'maximise the cost/benefit return'. The divisional accountants placed great emphasis on company strategy — the fit of new investment with company technologies, protection of markets and customers etc. The plant accountant emphasised marketing assumptions and recounted the manner in which funding could vary depending on the owner's expansion plans (or lack of them) and, in local government, strategic decisions such as that to invest in energy conservation were taken prior to any detailed analysis.

Operationalisation of strategy was partly achieved through the annual capital budget — where funds were allocated to divisions or, in local government, to operational areas such as 'energy saving', 'school building' etc. Generation of projects was undertaken within a framework which effectively 'rationed' the availability of funds encourages the search for suitable projects, this mechanism tends to steer an organisation in the direction dictated by 'strategy' (whether strategy be explicit or implicit).

If 'strategy' shapes the general investment direction one might still expect financial analysis to determine which specific projects were selected. However, this did not seem to be the case either. Although, in local government, only projects which met the requisite NPV criteria were put forward, it seemed more important to company accountants that projects 'felt' right than that they generated substantial net present values. No doubt the uncertainty prevalent in both commercial organisations contributed to this view — ranking projects on the basis of 'profitability index' or 'payback' might be considered spurious given the uncertainty of the underlying data. And, in local government, it was recognised that political considerations could easily outweigh any financial analysis when decisions were made.

Previous studies

Textbooks generally emphasise the techniques of investment appraisal with (for example) Drury (1988) devoting 30 pages to theoretical techniques but only two and a half pages to the wider context of investment decision-making. However, a review of the literature reveals a tradition of research into investment decision-making processes which dates back at least 30 years. Haynes and Solomon (1962) noted that capital budgeting consists of at least five managerial functions:

'1 continuous and creative search for investment opportunities;
2 forecasting the supply and cost of funds for investment purposes;
3 estimating each project's cashflows and other benefits;
4 ranking and choosing among competing projects; and
5 post auditing already committed investments.'

They concluded that attention had been devoted to the fourth and second functions but the others had usually been neglected. Subsequent researchers confirmed these findings and called for more emphasis on the whole process of investment decision-making. King (1975) argued that the implicit assumption of much 'theory' (that all projects could be defined and choice exercised on the basis of their economic worth) was impracticable. He emphasised the whole process of decision-making, the majority of which he claimed was largely unexplained.

Hastie (1974) expressed a personal view based on his experience (he was Assistant Treasurer of the Bendix Corporation at the time of writing): 'I am continually amazed at the academic community's preoccupation with refining capital expenditure analyses rather than improving decision making . . . It is suggested here that the use of incorrect assumptions has been a more significant source of bad investment decisions than the use of simple measurement techniques. Investment decision-making could be improved significantly if the emphasis were placed on asking the appropriate strategic questions and providing better assumptions rather than on increasing the sophistication of measurement techniques . . .'

A number of studies (e.g. Ackerman (1970), Scapens, Sale and Tikkas (1982)) have concluded that, in practice, 'strategic' considerations often override financial

analysis in investment decision-making. One recent study, however, runs counter to this 'traditional' view. Marsh et al (1988) question the influence of strategy and, in three case studies, they found that projects did not even match the corporations' divisional strategies, let alone their overall one.

Some researchers have emphasised the importance of social and political factors in the decision-making process (as opposed to the 'technical' emphasis implied by the conventional textbook treatment). Hall (1979) commented that '[in this environment] it seems apparent that the *analytical power* of a tool like discounted cashflow analysis is far less significant than the *managerial power* which can be employed to get the relevant investment alternatives generated, approved and properly executed in a complex organisation'. Ackerman found that '. . . authorisation was a function of the availability of funds and political power in the organisation'. And Cooper (1975) drew attention to differing rationalities (of social man, administrative man and political man) in the decision-making process.

One concrete finding of previous researchers is that proposals which are formally submitted to top management are unlikely to be rejected. Scapens et al confirmed the findings of Morgan and Luck (1973) in that 'very few capital projects appear to be rejected at the stage of formal authorisation by corporate management'.

Conclusions

Our study, together with those of previous researchers, indicates that investment 'appraisal' is but a small part of the whole process of decision-making. Strategic considerations are often cited as the most important determinants of capital investment decisions and such considerations may be communicated by an explicit statement of strategy, through the rationing mechanism of the capital budget and by the implicit message of stricter financial criteria or higher organisational levels for authorisation. Although Marsh et al question the influence of strategy, two points might be made. First, if projects do not 'flow' from a pre-defined strategy this does not prevent strategic considerations being very important in the decision-making process and, second, even if 'strategy' is not objectively so important as traditionally assumed, it is certainly *perceived* to be important by some practitioners.

Operational managers 'trigger' investment proposals and it has been suggested that the manner in which managers are controlled and evaluated will influence which projects are 'triggered' and how much commitment they generate. Our evidence is equivocal. While managers might wish to predict the effect of a new investment on evaluation criteria (such as 'profit' or 'growth') we had no indication that this information determined their level of commitment. Our impression was rather that top management *could* determine the

direction of investment and that managers had only limited discretion (for example, if a customer was at risk then an investment might *have* to be made even if it meant a deterioration in short-term performance measures).

Our own and previous studies suggest a limited role for financial analysis in the approval process. There are varied perceptions on the importance of DCF techniques but it does seem important that financial analysis is undertaken in order to *complete* a capital expenditure proposal before submission to higher levels of management. Other writers have suggested that such analysis might be biased in favour of projects which already have substantial commitment within the organisation but here again, our findings were equivocal. While our academic seemed prepared to 'manipulate' a presentation so long as the fundamental (NPV) evaluation was sound, practitioners were at pains to emphasise that they would not 'fiddle' the numbers and that ethical and professional standards should be observed.

It seems that practitioners could face a dilemma if a favoured project did not meet financial criteria but our feeling was that this would be addressed by asking the project sponsor to reconsider the project cashflow assumptions or by attempting more sophisticated analysis (perhaps trying to quantify 'intangible' benefits). If these approaches failed then it might be admitted that the proposal could not reasonably be justified on financial grounds (although it might be justified on other grounds).

Specific appraisal techniques did not seem to be a major issue for our 'divisional' and 'local government' practitioners, who were happy to combine various measures in order to make the case as clearly as possible to decision-makers. These practitioners did not anticipate conflicts between discounting measures and 'payback'. The plant accountant felt that the use of discounting techniques would be counterproductive in his particular environment and this is an indication of the importance of social as well as financial systems.

If a proposal can generate sufficient management commitment to be put forward for final approval then both our own and previous studies indicate that it is most unlikely to be rejected (although it may be delayed). To reject a proposal which had gained a high degree of managerial commitment would be to question the judgement of the entire management team and it is therefore perhaps not surprising that projects which reach this final stage are almost invariably approved. The fact that final approval is likely makes it particularly important that top management is able to influence the selection and evaluation processes — and this may be a partial explanation of the emphasis on 'strategy' as a determinant of investment acceptability.

Our research builds on and provides selective support for the findings of previous researchers.

Continued on page 59

Accountants' views of investment appraisal

Continued from page 56

Longitudinal case studies are now planned to investigate the factors which influence the introduction of modern manufacturing technology in specific firms and this should allow the relationship of individual perceptions to organisational structure and pedures to be investigated. We hope that this will help redress the traditional emphasis of management accounting investment 'theory' by placing the emphasis on the whole *context* of investment decision-making (where context embraces both the organisational situations of practitioners and their personal experiences and skills). □

ACKERMAN, R. W. (1970); 'Influence of integration and diversity in the investment process', *Administrative Science Quarterly*, September, pp. 341-352.

COOPER, D. J. (1975): 'Rationality and investment appraisal', *Accounting and Business Research*, Summer, pp.198-202.

DRURY, J. C. (1988): '*Management and Cost Accounting*', 2nd edition. VNR International.

DUGDALE, D. (1991): 'Is there a 'correct' method of investment appraisal?', *Management Accounting*, May, pp.46-48.

HALL, W. K. (1979): 'Changing perspectives on the capital investment process', *Long Range Planning*, February, pp.37-40.

HASTIE, K. L. (1974): 'One businessman's view of capital budgeting', *Financial Management*, Winter, pp. 36-44.

HAYNES, W. W. and SOLOMON, M. B. JR. (1962): 'A misplaced emphasis in capital budgeting' *Quarterly Review of Economics and Business*, February, pp.39-46.

KING, P. (1975): 'Is the emphasis of capital budgeting misplaced?', *Journal of Business Finance and Accounting*, Vol 2, pp.69-82.

MARSH, P., BARWISE, P., THOMAS, K. and WENSLEY, R. (1988): 'How investment decisions are made', *The Economist*, 9 July, pp.68-70.

MORGAN, J. and LUCK, M. (1973): *Managing capital investment*. Mantec.

SCAPENS, R. W., SALE, J. T. and TIKKAS, P. A. (1982): *Financial control and divisional capital investment*. CIMA.

SCAPENS, R. W. (1983): 'Closing the gap between theory and practice', *Management Accounting*, January, pp.34-36.

SCAPENS, R. W. (1988): 'Research into management accounting practice', *Management Accounting*, December, pp.26-28.

READER ARTICLE 4.1

'Evaluating and controlling investments in advanced manufacture technology'

Graham Motteram and John Sizer

Reproduced from *Management Accounting*, Journal of the Chartered Institute of Management Accountants

January 1992

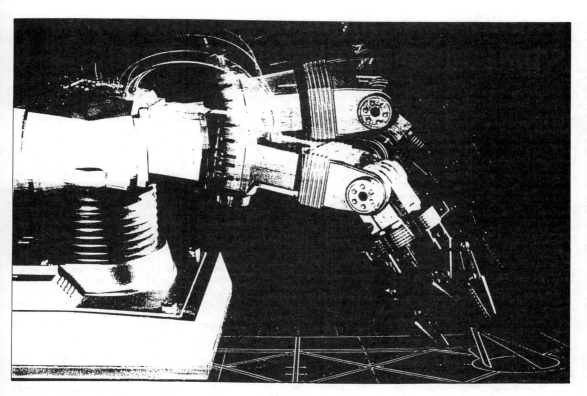

Evaluating and controlling investments in advanced manufacturing technology

Graham Motteram and John Sizer observe that successfully evaluating and controlling investments in AMT is not easy. No matter how sophisticated the analysis, some companies will continue to invest in projects that over-spend, run late and under-earn. They advocate an eight-step approach for evaluating investments in AMT which should assist management accountants in making an effective input into financial evaluations and therefore minimising the likelihood of this happening in their companies.

Many chief executives and boards of directors are making, or contemplating, major investments in advanced manufacturing technology as part of a world-class manufacturing strategy in order to strengthen or sustain their competitive advantage, in both global and niche market segments. Such decisions are particularly difficult during recessions, but are equally important if companies are to take full advantage of growth markets.

The careful evaluation of alternative

Graham Motteram FCMA is Engineering Business Manager, Civil Engine Group, Rolls Royce plc, and John Sizer CBE, DLitt, FCMA is Professor of Financial Management and Director of Loughborough University Business School.

investments is a crucial first stage in successfully employing AMT, and management accountants should make a significant input as part of a structured team approach. Decisions made will substantially affect a sector of the business's performance when implemented, and if the incorrect judgments are made, it is unlikely the decision process could be reversed, and therefore a damaging, negative business performance is likely to be the outcome.

We should recognise at the outset that, even in companies employing sophisticated systems of appraisal, capital projects generally tend to overspend, run late and under-earn. This may partly reflect 'ego trips' of managements preparing proposals and/or internal competition for scarce funds. Statements such as the following are

not uncommon and must be guarded against:
'We will just have to find a way of getting this project through.'
'Our competitors are going to have one, so we must.'
'We must have one before our competitors.'
Furthermore, many operating managers and accountants have limited experience of evaluating major capital projects; it is not something they do every day. Add the complexities and uncertainties of new technologies, temptations of salesmen and sales literature, shorter product lifecycles and global competition, and the difficulties and dangers become apparent.

In this article we examine eight major sequential steps (Figure 1) involved in successfully evaluating and controlling

26

proposed major investments in AMT, which we believe will assist management accountants in making effective inputs to the work of 'expert teams' created to oversee the selection, implementation and maintenance of AMT (Currie, 1991).

Step 1 — Determination of corporate strategy

The strategic decision to invest in AMT and related management techniques, such as just-in-time (JIT), materials requirements planning (MRPI) and manufacturing resource planning (MRPII) should flow from an assessment of corporate strategy; in particular, how to create and sustain competitive advantage in global and/or niche market segments. This must be a board-level decision based on hard-nosed strategic analysis rather than detailed investment appraisal. Furthermore, investment in AMT has to be part of a continuous programme of strategic improvement, *not* a one-off event.

In her recent reports on the findings of her research into the management methods and practices of Japanese companies, Currie (1991) observed that it was common practice for companies to devise long-range strategic plans for AMT implementation. The assessment of corporate strategy should lead to the formulation of inter-linking product-market, development, manufacturing and financial strategies. The formulation of a manufacturing strategy will include evaluation of strategic make or buy decisions, and manufacturing organisation and methods choice.

A full discussion of strategy formulation and manufacturing policies is beyond the scope of this article but it will be recognised that manufacturing investment policy should flow from the assessment of corporate strategy, in particular manufacturing strategy.

For many large manufacturing companies the analysis will lead the Board to conclude, if it is to be internationally competitive, that its strategy must be one of a low-cost producer achieving continuous cost improvements and value improvements to its customers in specific chosen

areas of production. For many manufacturing companies this necessitates that investments in AMT should be controlled from the centre, thereby enabling:

- a global view of manufacturing investment strategy to be maintained;
- the integration of new technology whilst allowing maximum utilisation to be made of existing physical assets and labour skills.

This policy may be best administered by an investment committee of the board.

Step 2 — Establish investment funding available and prioritising investment cases

Social and environmental pressures are resulting in an increasing proportion of many companies' capital investment programmes being in respect of non-profit adding projects, e.g. improved welfare facilities, safety and environmental expenditure etc, and for replacement investments. It is important to establish at an early stage the likely scale of investments in AMT required to implement the manufacturing strategy, and whether adequate funding will be available.

A capital-investment company should formally have:

- a detailed two-year investment project profile which is reviewed quarterly;
- a strategic investment plan in reasonable depth for five years, which is reviewed at least annually, and
- an outline investment plan to at least a ten-year horizon which is also reviewed annually.

These profiles and plans should be employed by treasury management in preparing short-term cash budgets and forecasts and longer-term financial plans. These provide the basis for determining external funding requirements and determining the company's cost of capital and hurdle rates for capital-investment projects. They should take into account any foreign-exchange risks.

Once the strategic decisions have been taken, funding availability determined and investment policy formulated, the evaluation of alternative AMT systems prior to

final approval is the key stage. In large companies it is preferable to undertake initial investment feasibility studies on major investments before giving agreement to move to detailed evaluation of alternative systems. Acquisition of individual items of equipment should flow from this evaluation.

Step 3 — Undertake initial investment feasibility study

It is likely that not only will limited funds be available for investment, but so also the resources to evaluate and successfully implement projects. Therefore, it is essential that only key important projects are worked upon.

It is advisable that prior to any detailed technical and financial work being undertaken, an outline of the proposed investment should be submitted to the investment committee of the board or its equivalent. This should ensure not only that control is exercised via 'top down' approval in principle, but it also allows the central strategy to be refined by recognition of 'bottom up' proposals. It will also assist the committee in ranking of projects for detailed evaluation and for building into investment plans.

Step 4 — Prepare detailed business case

Business case preparation on the subjects selected for detailed analysis is the crucial stage in the successful evaluation of AMT projects, when realism should not be driven out by 'starry eyed' optimism. The components of the detailed financial evaluation are summarised in Figure 2. Close examination and determination of the sensitivities of the assumptions made on each aspect is considered essential. We discuss important aspects of each element.

Investment costs
Investment costs include costs of planning, purchasing, installing and commissioning plant and machinery, and related computer hardware and software. As overspends tend to occur because of these items, it is advisable to test the sensitivity of cashflows and measures of project profitability for variations in both initial spend and time scales. If alternative manufacturing systems or types of machinery have different initial capital costs/operating costs/maintenance costs. structures it may be necessary or worthwhile to undertake a life cycle cost analysis. If the equipment is to be purchased from a foreign supplier, exchange-rate risk is an obvious, but frequently overlooked, point. Where major projects are being considered it may be worthwhile undertaking them on a turnkey basis with the selected major supplier. Whilst this may add a little to the investment costs, resultant implementation may be more successful.

Running costs
It may be sensible at this stage to recognise the need to operate a separate cost centre and build a cost model for the new system.

Figure 1: Major sequential steps in evaluating and controlling investments in advanced manufacturing technology

STEP 1	Determination of corporate strategy
STEP 2	Establishing investment funding implications and prioritising investment cases
STEP 3	Undertake initial investment feasibility study
STEP 4	Prepare detailed business case
STEP 5	Project authorisation
STEP 6	Effective control of authorised projects
STEP 7	Undertake post-implementation review
STEP 8	Develop action plans for continuous improvement

When building the cost model, we would advise:

- Do not simply accept *manufacturers' cycle times* when evaluating alternative systems, and make sure penalties are built into subsequent contracts for both delivery and technical performance.
- Do not be over-optimistic about *learning curves*; the greater the complexity the longer the curve.
- Ensure you will not have the problems *feeding* the system and *bottlenecks* out of the system, which would result in under-utilisation of capacity levels and higher levels of working capital.
- Given *high fixed cost/total cost ratio* associated with AMT, and therefore high break-even volume/capacity, recognise the importance of maintaining high levels of capacity utilisation, but also accept this may result in lower utilisation of support equipment in order to maintain an even flow through the high-cost equipment.
- Consider the *costs of maintenance*, perhaps in the form of a contract once the guarantee period has expired.
- Determine if there are any other cost factors which should be taken into account which are peculiar to an individual project proposal, e.g. programming costs.

It is important, therefore, to test the assumptions in your forecast cashflows and profitability measures for these elements of the cost model.

Figure 2 Components of financial evaluation of business case

1	**INVESTMENT COSTS** — including costs of planning, purchasing, installing, commissioning plant and machinery and related computer hardware and software.
2	**RUNNING COSTS**
3	**BENEFITS OF INVESTMENT**
	— Cost savings
	— Increased flexibility
	— Reductions in working capital
	— Market factor benefits
	— Taxation and investment grants
4	**CONSEQUENCES OF NOT INVESTING**
5	**TEST SENSITIVITY** of cashflows, DCF returns or NPVs and payback periods to variations in key assumptions

Benefits of investments in AMT
When evaluating the benefits to be derived from investing in AMT systems, you could usefully differentiate between: cost savings, reductions in working capital, and market factor benefits.

Cost savings normally arise from *reductions in direct labour, scrap, space requirements, and the benefits of increased flexibility*. We would again emphasise, do not simply accept manufacturers' cycle times and efficiencies when estimating *direct labour savings*; be careful to ensure that subsidiary

managements have not made such savings the balancing item to make investment worthwhile. If the reductions will necessitate changes in working practices and/or redundancies, do not be over-optimistic about work force reactions. *Reductions in scrap* result from a move towards zero defects, which result in savings in direct material costs and inspection costs. Additional capacity may be created which should generate additional contribution. A *reduced space requirement* will either reduce occupancy costs or result in benefits from the additional contribution generated by alternative use. *Increased flexibility* allows merging product lines, reduced diversity of components, simplified and common product designs, reduced engineering overhead, and benefits of designing for manufacturability and customer service. These benefits are difficult to quantify; understanding the factors that drive or determine these costs will provide assistance. Remember, unless the benefits of increased capacity or available space can be utilised as realisable saleable output, there is no benefit.

Reductions in working capital are usually a significant benefit arising from investments in AMT systems, particularly if linked to JIT and MRP systems. Reductions should occur in raw materials and bought-in component stocks, and in the length of the work-in-progress cycle. However, it is important to recognise these benefits will only be realised if production lines are balanced. It is easy to be over-optimistic on the timing of working capital savings and therefore sensitivities should be tested. The more complex the system, the greater the step change, therefore the longer the time taken to realise working capital savings.

Market factor benefits: the competitive advantages to be gained in the marketplace are the most difficult benefits to quantify. They are reflected in higher product quality, greater reliability in the hands of the customer and improved customer service. The three key questions are:

- Will these benefits to customers result in higher contribution ratios, i.e. per cent contribution to sales or higher volumes at current contribution ratios or both?
- Will it be necessary to share benefits with customers in order to maintain *competitive advantage* or improve *market share?*
- What offsetting factors are likely to result from competitors' actions? There may be a gain for a period of time but this may then be partially or fully offset.

The answers will depend partly on the countervailing power and expectations of customers. Major customers are likely to expect and want to share in the benefits! It also depends on the strategies and investment plans of competitors. Hence the importance of competitive benchmarking and continuous monitoring of competitors' plans and actions.

If the system increases capacity, evaluate carefully where the *additional volume* is coming from and the level of contribution

(sales revenue less variable product costs) it will generate. If it implies increasing your market share, ask yourselves, who will lose it and how will competitors react? It is all too easy to assume all of the market factor benefits will be retained in the business, and that market share can be increased, which is unlikely to be the case. It is also important to take account of forecast market trends, not only in terms of growth, but also recession and product lifecycles, and the impact of these on market share.

Consequences of not investing
The questions posed about market factor benefits also lead into the *consequences of not investing*: possibly rising real costs, falling real selling prices, squeezed contribution ratios and loss of market share. It is important not to be over-optimistic about the market factor benefits and at the same time over-pessimistic about the consequences of not investing. One risk-averse approach is to insist that all claimed market factor benefits and consequences of not investing pass the 3M test, i.e. they must be *meaningful, measurable* and *monitorable*.

Taxation and investment grants
Investment projects should be assessed on post-tax and investment-grant basis. In international businesses it is important to recognise that the timing of investment allowances, rates of taxation and availability of investment grants may vary significantly between countries, and of investment grants within a country. If there are political changes on the horizon and/or taxation policy changes under consideration, you should identify and assess the possible impact of these.

Test sensitivity of cashflows, DCF rates of return, and payback periods
In the preparation of the business case, it is important that key assumptions are identified, and the sensitivity of cashflows and DCF rates of return or net present values, and of simple or discounted payback periods, to these key assumptions are tested, so that the board is presented with a complete picture of the range of possible project outcomes. The board should *not* be presented with a single 'most likely' or, even worse, 'most optimistic' set of cashflow and profitability measures.

Step 5 — Project authorisation
The completed business case should be presented to the investment committee of the board, and subsequently for the board of directors, for approval. Given the increasing proportion of non-profit-adding projects in many companies' capital investment programmes, the board should recognise that this increases the return required from profit-adding projects, and therefore increases the gap between its cost of capital and the minimum hurdle rate for profit-adding projects.

Faced with a business case that presents a most likely return and range of possible returns derived from the sensitivity analysis, the board will have to exercise judg-

READER ARTICLE 4.2

'Post-completion auditing: a source of strategic direction'

Alison Kennedy and Roger Mills

Reproduced from *Management Accounting*, Journal of the Chartered Institute of Management Accountants

May 1992

Post-completion auditing: a source of strategic direction?

Alison Kennedy and Roger Mills believe that, although the academic literature on investment decision-making is vast, post-auditing has been relatively, if not completely, neglected. They outline the objectives of their forthcoming CIMA-funded in-depth analysis of the post-completion auditing practices of a number of UK companies, from which they aim to discover whether companies are gaining the benefits expected.

The business environment of the 1990s is an 'interesting' one — using that word in the sense of the Chinese curse 'May you live in interesting times'. As the recent results of companies in the UK show it has been a rare event to report a significant increase in profits in 1991. Many company chairmen and financial analysts are now focusing on the ability of companies to contain the decrease in profit rather than looking to any short-term increase in earnings.

The competitive environment in recent years has undoubtedly been a hostile one. The ability of UK companies to survive the next few years will not only be influenced by future actions but will also be heavily dependent on decisions taken in the past. By analysing the quality of those past decisions, companies may learn useful lessons for the future.

The systematic analysis of past capital expenditure decisions is known as a 'Post-completion audit'. In 1990, CIMA published Management Accounting Guide 9: *Post-Completion Audit of Capital Expenditure Projects*. This was commissioned by CIMA's Research and Technical Committee in 1987, with the aim of providing a publication which would 'assist managers in working out how, when and why information (on the performance of current projects) is fed into the company's decision making system with the aim of improving future company performance from both current and prospective projects'. The guide was prepared by the present authors following detailed discussions with a number of UK companies.

The academic literature on investment decision-making is vast, but post-audit has been relatively, if not entirely, neglected. Prior to publication of the guide, post-auditing practice had been surveyed by a number of authors, often as part of a wider survey into aspects of capital investment appraisal (e.g. Scapens and Sale 1981; Pike 1982, 1988; Neale and Holmes 1988, 1990). They revealed that post-auditing was common among companies in the USA. In the

J. Alison Kennedy BA(*Hons*), ACMA *is Senior Lecturer in Accounting at the University of Salford and Roger Mills* PhD, MSc, BTech (*Hons*), FCMA *is Professor of Accounting at Henley, The Management College.*

UK it was less popular overall and, although it was practised most frequently by large firms, even in the largest companies less than 50 per cent employed it on a regular basis.

However, it would appear from the results of a recently reported survey (Neale 1991) that a significant increase in the UK usage took place during the period in which the guide was being prepared. This survey found that 79 per cent of the 291 respondents (all companies in the Times 1000 listing) were post-auditors, a much higher percentage than reported in earlier UK surveys. The large increase in adoption rates between this and earlier surveys could be attributable to the lack of strict comparability between the samples. However, when questioned as to the date at which post-auditing was first adopted, over 40 per cent of firms in the later survey reported that it had taken place during the period 1986-1990.

The results would seem, therefore, to reflect a *genuine* increase in the use of post-completion audits. This shows an acceleration of the trend noted by Neale and Holmes (1988), whose 1985 survey of 385 firms identified that '21 per cent of respondents had adopted the process within the last three years'. These results are consistent with the increasing level of adoption reported in earlier surveys in the UK (Pike 1988). It thus appears that there has been a rapid and accelerating trend towards the use of post-completion audits in the UK in the 1980s and early 1990s.

We have recently been awarded a grant by CIMA to conduct an in-depth analysis of the post-completion auditing practices of a number of UK companies. As has been noted above, many companies have a relatively short history of post-completion auditing. We wish to discover whether companies are gaining the benefits which were expected from it. We also wish to identify any major differences in the expected benefits of post-auditing, e.g. do companies *primarily* view the post-completion audit as a mechanism for project control, or do they view it as a part of their overall system/control procedure?

It is our view that the main benefits to be gained from post-completion audits are from the improvement to *future* decisions rather than through the improved perform-

ance of the project under review. In the guide we suggested that the post-completion audit could be made up of a number of separate audits: the decision audit, the commissioning audit, the implementation audit and the final audit. We recognise that only few companies would adopt our particular terminology, but many others may nevertheless carry out activities which would fit within our definitions.

Face-to-face interviews will enable us to establish where differences in company practice are more apparent than real, and arise only from semantics, and where they are substantive. We shall seek to explore the reasons for substantive differences. If post-completion audit is seen mainly as a mechanism for project control, then its emphasis may well be on making improvements in the project under current review. A systems orientation would focus on future projects as well as the current one.

In producing the guide we attempted to emphasise the importance of a future orientation in post auditing, our definition of post-completion auditing being as follows: 'An objective and independent appraisal of all phases of the capital expenditure process as it relates to a particular project. It includes consideration of the appraisal process leading to the project's acceptance or rejection. For accepted projects, it also includes a review of the project's commissioning and implementation phases. The objective of post-completion auditing is to feed information into the company's decision-making system to improve future company performance from *either current or prospective projects*'.

In learning lessons for the future, it is important that the correct interpretation is placed on what has happened in the past. For example, if expectations of sales on a new project are not met, it may be stated that the original forecasts were over-optimistic. However, this alleged over-optimism may be attributable to a variety of causes, and it is the *source* of the over-optimism which is important if the post audit is to be useful in helping to avoid similar errors in the future. Possible causes would be:

- straight wishful thinking on the part of the forecaster. An implication for the future may be to reduce forecasts provided from this source;

- implementation errors, e.g. failure to distribute sufficient quantities of the goods to meet demand. An implementation audit may identify this problem in time for corrective action to be taken;
- adverse changes in environmental circumstances between forecast and implementation date. If a post-audit system is orientated towards the present project this may merely be noted. However, if a future orientation is adopted, the question as to whether the initial assessment of environmental conditions was realistic should be assessed, in order to improve future forecasting where possible. Further, and more importantly, the consideration given to the robustness of the project in the face of environmental turbulence should be investigated. Forecasts of the future will *always* be inaccurate, and a system which encourages exploration of the consequences of errors in forecasting is likely to be more successful than a system which merely ignores the possibility of error.

One possible explanation for the rapid increase in the use of post-auditing in recent years may lie in the dissatisfaction which firms may have had with the returns which they have been obtaining from their investments. Most investments involve the forecasting of both costs and revenues. Once the investment has been undertaken, the ability of a company to influence the outturn of these cashflows is usually fairly limited.

For example, it has been estimated that, for large-scale engineering projects, around 80 per cent of the total project cost is unalterably fixed at the final approval stage, i.e. if the plans are followed, there is only limited scope for altering the costs. In other types of project, approval may fix a much higher percentage of the total investment cost — for example, approval to buy a particular machine at a specified price would imply a commitment to 100 per cent of the project's total costs.

It can thus be seen that, as the bulk of project costs are committed at the acceptance of the plan at the approval stage, project cost control is more effectively exercised *before* this point is reached, rather than during implementation. This may explain why relatively few of the respondents to the survey by Gitman and Forrester (1977) regarded implementation as the most critical or difficult phase of the capital budgeting process.

The survey referred to above is one of very few to have made any attempt to ascertain which aspects of the capital budgeting procedure in practice present most difficulty to managers, and which aspects are considered by them to be most critical to an investment's success. They divided the capital investment process into four stages, as shown in the table. Despite its overwhelming prominence in the academic literature, 'financial analysis and project selection' (which equates to evaluation) was considered to be the most difficult aspect of the appraisal process by a mere 15

Most difficult and most important stages of capital budgeting process

Stage	Responses	
	Most difficult %	Most critical %
Project definition and cash flow estimation	64	52
Financial analysis and project selection	15	33
Project implementation	7	9
Project review	14	6
Total responses	100	100

per cent of the respondents, and only 33 per cent considered it to be the stage most critical to a project's success.

The results of this survey, which are consistent with the findings of Fremgen (1973), clearly show that project definition and cashflow estimation were regarded as both the most difficult *and* the most critical part of the capital budgeting process. It is interesting to note that project review — which we take to be broadly equivalent to post-completion audit — is seen as the *least* important contributor to the success of a project.

If the focus of the review is on improving the *current* project, then this is self-evidently true; if the scope for affecting cashflows is limited once implementation has begun, then it is clear that a project review will be of much less importance to the project's success than the original decision to accept the proposal. If the original estimates of cost built into a plan turn out on implementation to be unrealistically low, even the most effective project management will not turn a bad investment into a good one: efficient implementation can never be a substitute for proper planning.

The scope for obtaining revenues whose forecast was based on a mis-reading of the marketplace is similarly small. The increased use of post-completion audit may reflect an acceptance by companies that its primary role is to help with the first — and arguably most difficult — stage of future investments: project definition and cashflow estimation. Experience gained from past investments may be very helpful in future deliberations. Our guide stressed the importance of assessing the strategic impact of any investment and we believe that post-completion audits offer an ideal mechanism whereby the validity of company strategies can be explored.

It will be taken as axiomatic by most readers that capital investments would usually not receive approval unless they were expected to yield a positive net present value (NPV). However, it must be remembered that such positive returns represent a reward to the suppliers of funds in *excess* of that which is necessary given the risk which is being accepted.

Positive NPV's imply a market imperfection which enables the supplier of funds to earn an excess return. Before capital expenditure is authorised, it is good practice to require project sponsors to explain the source of the imperfection which will enable the excess return to be earned. For

example, if the proposal is to introduce a product innovation, this will give the supplier a degree of monopoly power which justifies the belief that excess returns will be earned in the period before others are able to enter the market.

If there are barriers to others entering the market, such as a patent on the innovation, then this competitive advantage is sustainable over a long period. If a sponsor is unable to elucidate the source of the competitive advantage which gives rise to the forecast positive NPV, then the suspicion must always be that it has been made possible by inflating revenue predictions, underestimating cost predictions, using a discount rate which does not adequately reflect the risk — or some combination of all these factors!

Post-completion audits should uncover blatant manipulation of forecast figures, and the knowledge that the audit will take place should discourage excessive claims. Perhaps more importantly, the post-completion audit provides an opportunity to consider whether the company's competitive advantage is as strong as expected. Sometimes the advantage may be weaker than expected, sometimes it may be stronger. If the reasons are documented and discussed — even in a qualitative way — this may be invaluable in steering the course of the company's future direction.

The importance attached to discussing the actual results of an investment within the context of a pre-determined strategy may vary from project to project and company to company. Differences in approach to post-audit may in fact be a function of differences in wider management styles.

In *Strategies and Styles* by Goold and Campbell (1987), a number of management styles, or ways in which the corporate centre attempts to add value to the company's business units, were defined. The main styles discussed were labelled strategic planning, strategic control and financial control. These were defined in terms of the two primary ways in which the centre influences its business units: by helping shape the plans of the businesses (planning influence) and through the control process (control influence).

The chart illustrates the nature of planning control influence under three styles.

In companies that follow the strategic planning style, the centre is involved and influential in the formulation of plans for the businesses, and stresses long-term objectives in the control process. These

Main management styles

Strategic management style	Responsibility for strategy	Need for measures of overall business performance	Importance of short-term profits in control process	Nature of controls
Strategic planning	Shared	Lower	Important, but part of a wider assessment	Strategic controls
Strategic control	Delegated	High	High, but not paramount	Strategic controls
Financial control	Highly delegated	Very high	Paramount	Profit controls

companies are flexible about the achievement of short-term targets. By contrast, financial control companies are highly decentralised in their approach to planning their strategies but exercise tight short-term financial control.

Strategic control companies fall between the other two styles. In terms of planning influence, they are less decentralised than financial control companies, but less hands-on than strategic planning companies. In terms of control influence, they see the need for long-term, strategic objectives and the use of strategic 'milestones', but they also place considerable emphasis on delivering short-term profit targets.

A primary objective of our research is to establish to what extent post-completion auditing is influenced by the strategic management style adopted. Goold and Campbell (1987) and Goold and Quinn (1990) have illustrated that, in general, control differs, depending upon the management style adopted, and it is our intention to look at this specifically within the context of post-completion auditing.

We are therefore basing our sample of companies on those investigated by Goold and Campbell, and subsequently by Goold and Quinn.

We will draw upon the definition developed in the Management Accounting Guide that we developed for CIMA (given above) in carrying out our research.

By conducting face-to-face interviews we hope to overcome the semantic problems of discussing post-auditing that we highlighted in our earlier article in *Management Accounting* (Kennedy, Mills 1988). Also, by conducting interviews at both the centre and divisional level we will be able to form a judgment as to the role of post auditing, as broadly defined, in the strategic control process.

The interviews we have undertaken so far are supportive of Neale's (1991) findings that post-auditing has increased in recent years. However the companies which we have visited may well have been respondents to Neale's enquiries and may therefore not represent new evidence.

Our interviews to date are supportive of Goold and Quinn's (1990) work and suggest that a process with all of the characteristics of post-completion auditing operates at a strategic level as part of a strategic control process in many companies.

Our findings thus far are based on a small number of interviews and are therefore highly tentative. They can in no way as yet be taken as indicative of widespread practice. Our research is intended to be complete by 31 December 1992, after which we shall publish our findings in *Management Accounting*. □

FREMGEN, N. J.: 'Capital budgeting practices: a survey', *Management Accounting*, May 1973.

GITMANN, L. J., FORRESTER, J. R.: 'A survey of capital budgeting techniques used by major US firms', *Financial Management*, Fall, 1977.

GOOLD, M. and CAMPBELL, A.: *Strategies and styles: the role of the centre in managing diversified corporations.* Blackwell, 1987.

GOOLD, M. and QUINN, J. J.: *Strategic control: milestones for long-term performance.* Hutchinson Business Books, 1990.

KENNEDY, J. A. and MILLS, R. W.: Post auditing and project control: a question of semantics?', *Management Accounting*, Vol. 66, No. 10, 1988, pp. 53-54.

KENNEDY, J. A. and MILLS, R. W.: *Post-completion audit of capital expenditure projects.* CIMA, London, 1990.

NEALE, B.: 'A revolution in post-completion audit adoption', *Management Accounting*, November, 1991.

NEALE, C. W. and HOLMES, D. E. A.: 'Post-completion audits: the costs and benefits', *Management Accounting*, March, 1988.

NEALE, C. W. and HOLMES, D. E. A.: 'Post-auditing capital projects,' *Long Range Planning*, Vol. 23, No. 4, pp. 88-96.

PIKE, R. H.: *Capital budgeting in the 1980s: a major survey of the investment practices in large companies.* CIMA, London, 1982.

PIKE, R. H. and WOLFE, M.: *Capital budgeting for the 1990s.* CIMA, Occasional Paper, 1987.

SCAPENS, R. W. and SALE, J. T.: 'Performance measurement and formal capital expenditure controls in divisionalised companies', *Journal of Business Finance and Accounting*, Autumn 1981, pp. 389-419.

READER
ARTICLE 5.1

'Make or buy decisions: a simpler approach'

Gordon Ellis

Reproduced from *Management Accounting*, Journal of the Chartered Institute of Management Accountants

June 1992

MAKE-OR-BUY DECISIONS: A SIMPLER APPROACH

Gordon Ellis responds to an earlier article on make-or-buy decisions. He shows that the textbook rules can be unreliable since they emphasise production aspects whilst ignoring the buying aspects of the problem. He suggests that the advantage-in-making approach will simplify the task of reaching a cost answer, although it will not make a decision for you!

The November 1991 issue of *Management Accounting* featured an interesting and thought-provoking article about make-or-buy decisions by Ron Bassett. The article sought to show how textbook rules may be misleading when faced with limiting factor problems.

The approach adopted was logical. First, the textbook rules were followed, as far as the situation permitted. Then, a second analysis was carried out to determine 'purchase price contributions', with purchase price contribution expressed as a percentage of product contribution. Finally, the information from the purchase price contribution analysis was used to amend the outcome of the textbook rules exercise. In essence, the approach separated the *buying* aspects of the problem from the *production* aspects.

Inadequacy of textbook rules

The textbook rules are usually stated in the form:

1 Calculate product contributions.
2 Convert product contributions to contributions per limiting factor.
3 Rank the limiting factor contributions in order of production priority. The product with the highest contribution per limiting factor ranks first.
4 Use the rank order to determine production (up to sales demand) on each product, until all available limiting factor is used up.
5 Buy in those products where the purchase price is below the marginal cost of production.

Ron Bassett's approach demonstrated very clearly that rigid adherence to these rules may result in misleading — and suboptimal — conclusions.

The basic problem with the rules is that they are concerned with the allocation of scarce resources for *production*; they are not geared to the *choice* between *making* and *buying*. In other words, the rules, as commonly expressed, are not really appropriate to the make-or-buy decision.

The textbook rules pay insufficient attention to the *buying* aspect of the decision. As Ron Bassett's example shows (see example data) rule 5 may not apply

Gordon Ellis ACMA, MBIM is a lecturer in accounting in the Faculty of Business, Luton College of Higher Education

Example data

Product	P1	P2	P3	P4
Demand (units)	10,000	15,000	12,000	13,000
Machine hours per unit	4	6	5	4
Selling price	£20	£25	£22	£30
Marginal cost	£10	£15	£12	£20
Product contribution	£10	£10	£10	£10
Selling price	£20	£25	£22	£30
Purchase price	£16	£20	£18	£22
Purchase price contribution	£4	£5	£4	£8
Purchase price contrib as percentage of product contribution	40%	50%	40%	80%

Machine hours available 225,000

Note: The purchase price contribution as a percentage of product contribution is not required by the approach adopted in this article. It was used in Ron Bassett's approach to determine an order of preference for buying-in. This gave a rank order of P4, P2, P3, P1 — with P3 taking precedence over P1 on account of higher sales demand.

since, as is often the case, it may not be possible to buy *any* product at below the marginal cost of product. Rules 1 to 4 *will* make best use of available resources — *as long as there is no necessity to make good any shortfall in production by buying-in.*

The assumption that sales demand may be left unsatisfied is not usually realistic. In practice, a company may have no option but to buy-in products to make good any shortfall in its own production, since failure *fully* to meet sales demand incurs the risk of cancelled orders and permanent loss of customers.

Where shortfall in own production *must* be made good by buying-in then the textbook rules will prove inadequate.

Ron Bassett overcame the inadequacy of the rules by calculating a purchase price contribution for each product (selling price − purchase price = purchase price contribution). The purchase price contribution was then expressed as a percentage of the product contribution. This revealed preference for buying-in — the product with the highest percentage being favoured for purchase to make good shortfall in production.

There is, however, an alternative

approach which is more direct and consequently simpler and easier to understand.

Advantage in making

In situations involving limiting factors but in which we must fully meet sales demand we have only two choices:

1 make the product ourselves;
2 buy-in the product from outside.

The easiest approach to the problem is to ask ourselves: what *advantage* is there to the company in making the product? For this, we need only compare the purchase price with the marginal cost of production.

Then we can ask: how does this advantage relate to the use of limiting factors? From this we can determine a rank order of priority in using available resources based on advantage to the company.

We can then allocate available resources to meet sales demand on each product until resources are used up. The remaining shortfall is bought-in.

You will notice that this approach combines features from both the textbook-rules approach and the purchase-price approach. The combination of *both* production *and* buying aspects of the problem renders unnecessary their separate consideration.

The approach can be summarised as a series of steps:

Step 1 Measure the advantage in making rather than buying.

Step 2 Express the advantage as an advantage per limiting factor.

Step 3 Use the advantage per limiting factor to determine a rank order for the use of available resources. Product giving greatest advantage per limiting factor is ranked first.

Step 4 Allocate available resources and determine number of units to be made and number to be bought-in.

For the purposes of illustration we will make use of the same basic data as used by Ron Bassett in his article, as follows:

Step 1: Measuring the advantage in making

Step 1 merely requires the comparison of the purchase price of each product with its marginal cost of production.

Product	P1	P2	P3	P4
Purchase price	£16	£20	£18	£22
Marginal cost of production	• £10	£15	£12	£20
Advantage in making	£6	£5	£6	£2

All that our statement tells us at this stage is that it is preferable to make *all* products since in no case can we buy-in for less than the marginal cost of production. Any negative advantage (i.e. disadvantage) in making would reveal a product where marginal cost exceeds purchase price — textbook rule 5 above tells us that such a product should in any event be bought-in.

Step 2: Advantage and the limiting factor
Step 3: Determine rank order

Step 2 involves expressing the advantage in relation to the limiting factor. We can do this by extending our workings from Step 1.

Product	P1	P2	P3	P4
Purchase price	£16	£20	£18	£22
Marginal cost of production	£10	£15	£12	£20
Advantage in making	£6	£5	£6	£2
Machine hours per unit	4	6	5	4
Advantage per hour in making	£1.50	0.83	1.20	0.50
Ranking	1	3	2	4

We have quickly arrived at a position where we can allocate available resources. The ranking gives the order of priority for using up available resources, to the greatest advantage for the company.

It is interesting to note that the rankings obtained are in the reverse order to those obtained by looking at purchase price contributions, expressed as a percentage of product contributions (see note below

example data). This should not be surprising since the product with the greatest advantage-in-making *should* be the least favoured for buying-in. In fact, purchase price contributions could themselves be misleading since they take no account of the use of the limiting factor. The great gain from using the advantage-in-making approach is that we have *combined* consideration of purchase price (and marginal cost of production) with consideration of the limiting factor.

Step 4: Allocation of resources

Step 4 enables us to allocate resources in order of advantage in making. We know that there is a shortfall in hours:

	Sales demand (units)	Hours per unit	Total hours required
P1	10,000	4	40,000
P2	15,000	6	90,000
P3	12,000	5	60,000
P4	13,000	4	52,000
Hours required			242,000
Hours available			225,000
Shortfall in hours			17,000

It is easy to see that we shall be able to meet the demand in full for three products but will be short of time for the fourth. We will therefore need to buy-in a part of our requirements for the product with the lowest advantage in making, P4.

This results in the following:

Product	P1	P2	P3	P4
Hours (total 225,000)	40,000	90,000	60,000	35,000 (balancing figure)
Make (units)	10,000	15,000	12,000	8,750
Buy-in (units)	—	—	—	4,250

Note: P4 Make 35,000 ÷ 4 = 8,750 units
P4 Buy-in balance of sales demand 13,000 − 8,750 = 4250

This gives the solution to our make-or-buy problem. All that remains to do is to calculate the total contribution, as follows:

Make P1	10,000 × £10 =	100,000
Make P2	15,000 × £10 =	150,000
Make P3	12,000 × £10 =	120,000
Make P4	8,750 × £10 =	87,500
Buy P4	4,250 × £5 =	34,000
Total contribution		£491,500

And that's it. Easy, isn't it?

Conclusion

Textbook rules for make-or-buy decisions can be shown to be unreliable since they emphasise production aspects whilst ignoring buying aspects of the problem.

Purchase price contribution provides one way of looking at the buying aspects of the problem and may be helpful when used in conjunction with the textbook approach. However, purchase price contribution may itself be an unreliable indicator in some situations. It takes no account of the way in which each product uses resources, concentrating only on the buying aspects of the problem.

In the example above purchase price contribution was able to determine the correct order of preference for buying-in — but only by chance, since P3 was ranked before P1 on the basis of higher sales demand. Sales demand can tell us nothing about relative use of scarce resources in production. Purchase price contribution should therefore only be used with an awareness of its limitations.

In contrast, the advantage-in-making approach suggested here offers a way in which the production aspects and the buying aspects of the problem are effectively combined. This ensures reliability and shows very clearly what advantage there is to the company in making a product rather than buying-in. Priority for the use of resources is clearly indicated; the product with the *greatest* advantage in making is *made* first, and when internal capacity is used up the product with the *least* advantage would be *bought* first. The approach also has the virtues of speed and simplicity.

The advantage-in-making approach lends itself to more complex situations than the one illustrated above. For example, in cases where there are opportunity costs associated with the use of resources we could still follow the approach described — we would merely need to substitute incremental cost of making *plus* opportunity cost of scarce resources in place of straightforward marginal cost of production.

Finally, it might be worth reminding ourselves that the cost 'answer' is *not* a decision but merely one piece of evidence (albeit an important piece) to be used in arriving at a decision. For make-or-buy decisions a range of other considerations may be of vital importance — for example, the need to maintain control over supply, the reliability of suppliers, quality, the possibility of cost or purchase price change and so on. Hopefully, the advantage-in-making approach will simplify the task of reaching a cost answer; unfortunately, it will not make a decision for you. □

READER ARTICLE 5.2

'Considering the time value of money in breakdown analysis'

Mark Freeman and Kerrie Freeman

Reproduced from *Management Accounting*, Journal of the Chartered Institute of Management Accountants

January 1993

Considering the time value of money in breakeven analysis

Mark Freeman and Kerrie Freeman show that it is inconsistent to appraise investments using discounted cashflow techniques like net present value and then make operating decisions using breakeven analysis based on profits. They demonstrate that operating at the breakeven profit level will in fact destroy value. This can only reduce the chances of survival and growth.

In a recent article on financial management in *Management Accounting* (May 1992), David Allen identified the time value of money as the key aspect of financial management. This follows because 'the discipline of the capital market is harnessed as a basis for the allocation of resources within the enterprise, thereby maximising its chances of survival and growth'.

But the worrying thing is that management accountants are often ignoring this key link when they use two of the most common tools of financial management — net present value (NPV) and breakeven (BE) analysis.

It is our contention that the common practice of using BE analysis without considering the time value of money is likely to result in business ventures losing value instead of adding it. This can only reduce their chances of survival and growth.

The purpose of this short note is to show how easily the latter can (and probably does) occur.

How NPV is typically used

NPV analysis is typically used to appraise the worthiness of potential business ventures. The relative merits of NPV for investment appraisal have been well documented elsewhere. What is worth repeating is the interpretation of what NPV means. Consider firm ABC plc which are considering investing £120,000 in a new venture.

The details are in Table 1. ABC is currently valued at £1,000,000 (i.e. a market share price of £10 and 100,000 shares on issue).

If investors agree with ABC's appraisal that the investment has an expected NPV of £9,000 then the market share price is likely to rise by £0.09 (i.e. the NPV of £9,000 divided by 100,000 shares) on announcement of the venture to the stock exchange. This rise reflects an expectation that the future benefits of the venture are sufficient to recover the money invested (here £120,000) *plus* 10 per cent per annum extra to compensate for the opportunity cost of the money tied up.

Mark Freeman BA, MEC, ASCPA, ACIM *and Kerrie Freeman* BA, ASCPA *are with the Faculty of Business, University of Technology, Sydney.*

Table 1 NPV calculations of new venture

Equipment costing £120,000 will be financed 100 per cent by equity. It is expected to produce 42,000 units per annum for three years and then have a zero scrap value. Depreciation can be assumed to be straight line for accounting and tax purposes. Extra working capital shall be ignored for simplicity. Expected selling price is £3 per unit and variable costs per unit are £1.08. Fixed cash expenses are expected to be £25,000 per annum. In reality these costs would change (e.g. due to inflation or efficiency gains). Tax rates are 25 per cent per annum. The opportunity cost of capital or risk adjusted discount rate has been estimated to be 10 per cent per annum. Numbers are expressed in thousands of pounds in the calculations below.

	Year 0	Year 1	Year 2	Year 3	
Capital cost	−120.0				
Sales revenue		126.0	126.0	126.0	(£3×42,000)
Variable costs		−45.4	−45.4	−45.4	(£1.08×42,000)
Contribution margin		80.6	80.6	80.6	(£1.92×42,000)
Fixed cash expenses		−25.0	−25.0	−25.0	
Depreciation		−40.0	−40.0	−40.0	(£120,000÷3)
Operating profit		15.6	15.6	15.6	
Tax (25%)		−3.9	−3.9	−3.9	(0.25×£15,600)
Operating profit after tax		11.7	11.7	11.7	
Add back depreciation		40.0	40.0	40.0	(non cash item)
Operating cashflow after tax		51.7	51.7	51.7	
Total cashflow	−120.0	51.7	51.7	51.7	
Present value factor	1.000	0.909	0.826	0.751	
Present value	−120.0	47.0	42.8	38.9	
Net present value	£8.7 (say £9,000)				

Table 2 Breakeven sales level based on profits

Breakeven sales volume	=	Total fixed costs		
		Contribution margin per unit		
	=	65,000/1.92		
	=	33,854 units		
where CM/unit	=	£1.92 from above		
and Total FC	=	25,000 cash FC + 40,000 depreciation		
	=	£65,000		

Proof	Year 1	Year 2	Year 3	
Sales revenue	101.6	101.6	101.6	(£3×33,854)
Variable costs	−36.6	−36.6	−36.6	(£1.08×33,854)
Contribution margin	65.0	65.6	65.0	(£1.92×33,854)
Fixed cash expenses	−25.0	−25.0	−25.0	
Depreciation	−40.0	−40.0	−40.0	(£120,000÷3)
Operating profit	0.0	0.0	0.0	

The NPV effect is much like the instantaneous effect on the price of my property if I discovered that it was located above a huge gold deposit. Even though no product has been produced or sold yet, the value of the firm, or shareholders' wealth, will increase immediately by the amount of the increase in the share price multiplied by the number of shares (equal to the NPV of the venture).

How breakeven is typically used

Planning for value to be added does not

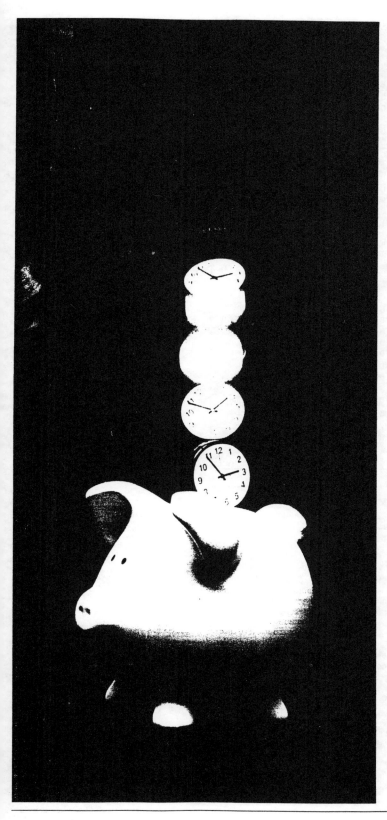

necessarily mean value will be added. The daily, weekly, monthly operating decisions play a critical role in whether the expected net present value is achieved. This is where breakeven analysis comes in. Management accountants typically use BE analysis to advise what level of sales volume/price mix is necessary in order for sales revenue to cover costs — that is to break even. If the venture subsequently proves unable to break even, it should be discontinued.

As Table 2 shows, the breakeven level of sales for the above project is 33,854 units for all three years of operation since the cost-volume-profit relationships are constant over the life of the venture.

But here is where the problem lies. Let's say management operated the venture so as to sell 33,854 units per annum. As Table 2 shows, ABC would generate sufficient sales revenue (i.e. £101,600 per annum) to just cover total expenses (i.e. variable cash expenses of £36,600 p.a. plus fixed cash expenses of £25,000 p.a. plus fixed depreciation of £40,000 p.a. to recover the cost of the equipment). *But this is insufficient to break even in terms of NPV as Table 3 shows.*

As Table 3 shows, ABC will be £21,000 worse off by taking the venture on and operating at the 'breakeven' level. Or put another way the share price would decline by £0.21 (i.e. NPV of –£21,000 divided by 100,000 shares). This result occurs because calculating breakeven using the standard method only allows for the cost of the equipment to be included. It ignores the implicit opportunity cost to the firm (and therefore shareholders) of having £120,000 tied up in equipment.

The opportunity cost of capital was included in the original investment appraisal and it is inconsistent (and destroying value!) by making operating decisions which do not include this opportunity cost. In fact, ABC have to sell at least 39,583 units and make at least £8,300 profit each year to break even in NPV, as Table 4 shows.

How did we get 39,583 units to make the BE analysis consistent with NPV analysis? Table 5 is only marginally different to Table 2. It recognises that tax depreciation is insufficient to recover the full cost of the equipment in total fixed costs. Not only does the historic cost of the equipment need to be recovered (i.e. £40,000 p.a.) but also an extra amount (i.e. £8,300) representing the cost of the money tied up. When both components are together, they are sometimes labelled economic depreciation.

Another potential mistake arises when equipment is partly debt-financed. When calculating breakeven sales level based on profits, it would make sense to include interest as it is a fixed cost. Such costs, however, represent only part of the full cost of financing the equipment and thus will always result in the breakeven sales level being understated. If calculating breakeven sales level based on present values then interest costs should be excluded as they are already implicit in the opportunity cost of capital.

Table 3 NPV calculations for breakeven sales level based on profits

	Year 0	Year 1	Year 2	Year 3	
Capital cost	−120.0				
Sales revenue		101.6	101.6	101.6	(£3×33,854)
Variable costs		−36.6	−36.6	−36.6	(£1.08×33,854)
Contribution margin		65.0	65.0	65.0	(£1.92×33,854)
Fixed cash expenses		−25.0	−25.0	−25.0	
Depreciation		−40.0	−40.0	−40.0	(£120,000÷3)
Operating profit		0.0	0.0	0.0	
Tax (25%)		0.0	0.0	0.0	(0.25×£0)
Operating profit after tax		0.0	0.0	0.0	
Add back depreciation		40.0	40.0	40.0	(non-cash item)
Operating cashflow after tax		40.0	40.0	40.0	
Total cashflow	−120.0	40.0	40.0	40.0	
Present value factor	1.000	0.909	0.826	0.751	
Present value	−120.0	36.3	33.1	30.0	
Net present value	−£20.5 (say −£21,000)				

Table 4 NPV calculations for breakeven sales level based on present values

	Year 0	Year 1	Year 2	Year 3	
Capital cost	−120.0				
Sales revenue		118.8	118.8	118.8	(£3×39,583)
Variable costs		−42.8	−42.8	−42.8	(£1.08×39,583)
Contribution margin		76.0	76.0	76.0	(£1.92×39,583)
Fixed cash expenses		−25.0	−25.0	−25.0	
Depreciation		−40.0	−40.0	−40.0	(£120,000÷3)
Operating profit		11.0	11.0	11.0	
Tax (25%)		−2.8	−2.8	−2.8	(0.25×£11,000)
Operating profit after tax		8.3	8.3	8.3	
Add back depreciation		40.0	40.0	40.0	(non-cash item)
Operating cashflow after tax		48.3	48.3	48.3	
Total cashflow	−120.0	48.3	48.3	48.3	
Present value factor	1.000	0.909	0.826	0.751	
Present value	−120.0	43.9	39.9	36.2	
Net present value	£0				

Table 5 Breakeven sales level based on present values

Breakeven sales volume $= \dfrac{\text{Total fixed costs after tax}^*}{\text{Contribution margin per unit after tax}^*}$

= 57,000/1.44

= 39,583 units

where CM/unit after tax = £1.92×(1−0.25 tax rate)

= £1.44

Total FC after tax = (25,000 cash FC + 40,000 depreciation) × (1−0.25 tax rate) + 8,300 premium for excess of economic over tax depreciation† (or opportunity cost of money tied up)

= £65,000 (0.75) + 8,300

= £57,000

Previously, it made no difference if before- or after-tax figures were used to calculate breakeven. This time it does matter. The extra 'cost' or premium for economic depreciation over normal depreciation is not tax-deductible as it is not part of the historic cost of the equipment.

Excess depreciation = £48,300−£40,000

= £8,300

† Economic depreciation can be calculated as the equivalent annual payment including a 10 per cent p.a. return that would make investors indifferent to tying the £120,000 up for three years. Here

Equivalent annual annuity $= \dfrac{120,000}{2.487}$ (i.e. present value of equipment cost)

(i.e. three year annuity factor at 10 per cent)

= £48,300

Conclusion

We have demonstrated that it is inconsistent to appraise investments using discounted cashflow techniques like net present value and then make operating decisions using breakeven analysis based on profits. We have shown that operating at the breakeven profit level will in fact destroy value. In our example of a £120,000 investment, a zero profit over three years destroyed £21,000 in present value because such an operating level failed to ensure the firm (and investors) received a return on their money tied up. At higher interest rates, the value destroyed increases. □

READER ARTICLE 6.1

'ABC in retail financial services'

Colin Drury and David Pettifer

Reproduced from *Certified Accounting*

February 1993

ABC IN RETAIL FINANCIAL SERVICES

The late 1980s saw a need arise for management accounting systems that could analyse product and customer profitability and help manage costs more effectively. Colin Drury and David Pettifer examine the impact of such systems on retail financial services organisations

Traditional product costing systems were designed by manufacturing organisations decades ago when most companies manufactured a narrow range of products and direct labour and materials were the dominant factory costs. Overhead costs were relatively small and the distortions arising from overhead allocations were not significant.

Information processing costs were high and it was therefore difficult to justify the use of more sophisticated methods of tracing overheads to products. Deregulation, increased competition, changing cost structures and an expanding product range changed all this. Today, companies produce a wide range of products, and overheads are the dominant costs. Simplistic overhead allocations can no longer be justified, particularly when information processing costs are no longer a barrier to introducing more sophisticated systems. Hence the claims that traditional systems are obsolete. It is against this background that activity-based costing has emerged.

A recent survey of 300 British manufacturing companies indicated that over 90% of them produced monthly profit statements. This means that a cost system must track costs on a day-to-day basis so that monthly costs can be allocated between the cost of goods sold and inventories. Inventory valuation is not an issue in the financial services sector. Therefore, product costing systems should not be driven by financial accounting requirements. Instead, their sole purpose should be to provide management information for strategic and operational decisions.

Periodic cost audits

The detailed day-to-day tracking of costs is unnecessary for strategic decision making and profitability analysis. A cost audit should be undertaken to determine at periodic intervals (say, once or twice a year) the cost and profitability of products, product lines, customers, market segments and branches. The aim is to design a cost system that accurately traces the resources consumed by different cost objects. A cost object represents any activity for which a separate measure of cost is required (for example, products, customers, market segments).

There are four alternative approaches that RFS organisations should consider when designing cost systems; the choice depends on the circumstances, the cost of operating the system and the benefits arising from the information. The alternatives are:

- Assigning only those costs that can be directly attributed to individual products
- Reporting incremental/avoidable costs
- Tracing all costs to products using traditional cost systems that make extensive use of arbitrary cost allocations
- Implementing activity-based costing systems that focus on measuring the resources consumed by individual products.

The first approach should be adopted if direct costs represent a high proportion of total costs. But most RFS organisations have large amounts of support costs that are not directly attributable to products, so the direct costing approach will represent only a partial measure of product profitability.

The incremental/avoidable cost approach is the one normally advocated in the management accounting literature but it is more appropriate for undertaking special studies when specific products have been identified that require decisions on product introduction, abandonment or pricing. It should be adopted only by those financial service organisations that have a small number of product or customer categories.

The third alternative (traditional product costing systems) makes extensive use of arbitrary overhead cost allocations. The deficiencies of these systems have been widely publicised — it is unwise to use the output of such systems for profitability analysis and strategic decision making.

Activity-based costing

It was not until the late 1980s that activity-based costing (ABC) systems were developed. RFS organisations have shown great interest in ABC and some banks and building societies have already introduced activity-based systems. These organisations operate in a highly competitive environment. They incur a large amount of support overhead costs that cannot be directly assigned to specific cost objects and their products and customers differ significantly in terms of consuming overhead resources.

ABC emphasises the need to obtain a better understanding of indirect cost behaviour and therefore ascertain what causes the overhead costs to be incurred. The focus is on what is generating the cost rather than the traditional approach of merely allocating cost. ABC systems assume that activities cause costs to be incurred and that products (or other selected cost objects, such as customers and branches) consume activities in varying amounts. A link is made between activities and products by assigning the cost of activities to products based on an individual product's demand for each activity.

Designing an ABC system involves the following stages:

- Identifying the key activities that take place in the organisation
- Creating a cost pool/cost centre for each major activity
- Assigning costs to activity cost pools
- Determining the cost driver for each activity cost pool
- Determining the unit cost for each activity
- Assigning the costs of activities to selected cost objects (for example, products) according to the cost object's demand for each activity.

The first stage requires that an activity analysis is undertaken in order to identify the major activities performed in the enterprise. Activities are simply the tasks that people or machines perform in order to provide a product or service; for example, processing a deposit, issuing a credit card, processing a cheque, setting up a loan, opening an account or processing monthly statements.

The next stage requires that a cost pool (or cost centre) be created for each activity. Costs are then analysed and assigned to the appropriate activity pool. For example, the total cost of processing a deposit might constitute one activity

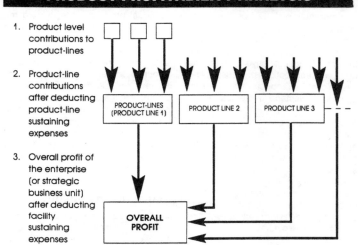

FIGURE 1
ACTIVITY-BASED PRODUCT PROFITABILITY ANALYSIS

1. Product level contributions to product-lines

2. Product-line contributions after deducting product-line sustaining expenses

3. Overall profit of the enterprise (or strategic business unit) after deducting facility sustaining expenses

cost pool for all deposit processing related costs. But separate cost pools should be created for each type of deposit account if different types of deposits consume resources differently.

The fourth stage is to identify the factors that influence the cost of a particular activity. The term 'cost driver' is used to describe the events or forces that are the significant determinants of the cost of the activities. For example, if the cost of processing deposits is generated by the number of deposits processed then the number of deposits processed would represent the cost driver for deposit processing activities.

The cost driver selected for each cost pool should be the one that, as closely as possible, mirrors the consumption of the activities represented by the cost centre. Examples of cost drivers that might be appropriate include:

- Number of applications processed for setting up a loan
- Number of statements mailed for processing monthly statements
- Number of mortgage payments past due date for processing activities relating to mortgage arrears.

The next stage divides the cost traced to each activity cost pool by the total

number of driver units in order to calculate a cost per unit of activity.

Finally, the cost of activities is traced to products (or other cost objects) according to a product's demand for the activities by multiplying unit activity costs by the quantity of each activity that a product consumes.

A product or service can be viewed as a bundle of activities. Thus the cost of a product of service consists of the sum of the individual costs of the activities that are required to deliver the product or service. In other words, ABC focuses on the costing of activities and the bundling of these activities into products, customers or any other cost objects.

ABC seeks to measure accurately resources consumed by products whereas traditional systems merely allocate costs to products. For example, a traditional costing system might allocate deposit transaction processing costs to customers, or different types of deposit accounts, on the basis of the number of customer accounts. This approach will lead to distorted product costs if deposit processing costs are driven by the number of transactions processed. Allocating costs according to the number of customers will lead to low value deposit accounts that involve numerous 'over-the-counter' transactions being undercosted, whereas high value long term savings accounts requiring very few transactions will be overcosted. In contrast, an ABC system would establish a separate cost centre for deposit processing activities, ascertain what causes the costs (that is, determine the appropriate cost driver, such as the number of transactions processed) and assign costs to products on the basis of a product's demand for the activity.

Activity-based profitability analysis should be based on a hierarchical approach. **Figure 1** illustrates the approach for product profitability analysis. The costs of undertaking the various activities should be listed, analysed by products and deducted from revenues, so that a contribution to profits can be reported at the product level (see **line 1** in **Figure 1**).

At the next level, product line (or product group) contributions to profit are reported. For example, deposit accounts and loans would represent the different product lines and the different types of deposits and loan accounts represent the individual products within the product line. Some expenses are incurred at the product line level and are common to all products within the product line but are not identifiable with individual products.

The activity-based profitability analysis classifies these expenses as product-line-sustaining expenses and traces them to product lines but not to individual products within the line. On the other hand, an advertising campaign aimed at one specific type of loan would be assigned to the individual product.

A product line contribution is computed in **line 2** by deducting product-line-sustaining expenses from the sum of the individual product-level contributions sold within the line. This calculation shows whether the products sold within the line earn a sufficient contribution to cover the expenses of activities performed to sustain the product line.

ABC systems recognise that not all costs can be assigned to products. Some costs are common and joint to all products. These costs are called facility-sustaining expenses and include such items as top management salaries and maintenance

of head office premises. At the final level in the hierarchy (see **line 3** of **Figure 1**), facility-sustaining expenses are deducted as lump sum from the total of all the profit margins from all the individual products lines to yield the overall profit of the enterprise or a particular strategic business unit.

ABC has attracted a considerable amount of interest because it provides not only a basis for more accurately determining the cost and profitability of individual products, product lines, customers and branches, but also a mechanism for managing costs. It is in the area of cost management and cost control where ABC could have its greatest potential.

Managing the business

Traditional accounting control systems are not particularly helpful for controlling non-variable costs. Activity costing concentrates on managing the business on the basis of activities that make-up the organisation. By collecting and reporting the costs consumed by the significant activities of a business, it is possible to understand and manage costs (including non-variable costs) more effectively.

With an ABC system, costs are managed in the long-term by controlling the activities that drive them. In other words, the aim is to manage the activities rather than the costs. By managing the forces that cause the activities (that is, the cost drivers), cost will be managed in the long term.

It is claimed that ABC results in organisations reaching a better understanding of costs and their causes. This opens up opportunities to reduce or eliminate activities that do not add value. For example, knowing costs by activities is a catalyst that eventually triggers the actions necessary to become competitive.

Traditional management accounting reports do not show how much activities cost. Charting the flow of activities and estimating the activities' costs enables management to see the costs being incurred and the waste that has been tolerated in the past. Managers are frequently surprised at how many activities are performed within their

organisation that do not add value to any product or service but consume significant resources. These non-value added activities have continued because they have been hidden by traditional cost systems. ABC makes them visible so that steps can be made to eliminate them. Furthermore, by merely knowing the costs of activities potential activities are highlighted so that steps can be taken to improve profitability.

Consider a situation where loans staff, as a result of costing activities, are informed that it costs £100 to process and maintain loans of less than £500. They become aware that it is questionable to provide loans of less than £500 unless more cost effective ways can be found of undertaking this activity. Similarly, if the cost of processing and maintaining low value and high value mortgages is the same, management is made aware that it is more profitable to focus on high value rather than low value mortgages.

It is important to note, however, that process improvements should lead to actions that reduce resource spending or the creation of extra resources that lead to higher profits. There is nothing to be gained from merely creating unutilised resources.

Our experience indicates that many banks and building societies have only recently turned their attention to designing and implementing cost management systems. Many of the constraints imposed on manufacturing organisations, such as having to meet financial accounting stock valuation requirements or a reluctance to change or scrap existing cost systems, do not apply.

Furthermore, they have begun implementing and experimenting with new systems at the very time when the deficiencies of traditional systems and the experiences of firms implementing innovative new systems are being widely publicised. Financial service organisations have the opportunity to be at the 'leading edge' in the development of contemporary management accounting systems. ∎

Professor Colin Drury, University of Huddersfield and David Pettifer, Price Waterhouse.

READER ARTICLE 6.2

'ABC: the right approach for you?'

Robin Cooper

Reproduced from *Accountancy*

January 1991

In my article in September 1990, p 86, I showed that ABC systems costed manufactured goods more accurately than conventional systems. In November 1990, p 78, I detailed the steps that should be taken in designing an ABC system. I shall now explain when it is appropriate to install one.

ABC systems use a number of different second-stage cost drivers to trace costs to the products. Unfortunately, every second-stage cost driver requires measuring some unique attribute of each product. For example, the cost driver number of engineering change orders requires measurement of the number of change orders consumed by each product. Measuring these attributes can be expensive, and there is no guarantee that the additional measurement costs required by an ABC system will be justified by the benefits. Consequently, I will discuss three factors to consider in determining whether the benefits of an ABC system will exceed its implementation and operating costs:

1. The sophistication of the company's information systems.
2. The cost of errors.
3. The diversity of the company's products.

1. Sophistication of the company's information systems

Increased accuracy is bought only at the cost of rapidly increasing measurement costs. Ultimately, the trade-off between measurement costs and the cost of errors means that the optimal cost system (which minimises the total of measurement costs and costs associated with making poor decisions because of inaccurate product costs) is not the most accurate cost system. Rather, the point at which the marginal cost of an improvement just equals the marginal benefits of the improvement (in terms of more accurate product costs) defines the optimal cost system.

The position of the optimal cost system is affected by changes in the measurement costs, cost of errors, and product diversity.

If measurement costs can be reduced while the other two factors remain unchanged, more accurate product costs are reported for the same price. Similarly, if the cost of errors increases (because, perhaps, of increased competition) while the other two factors remain constant, it can be shown that more accurate product costs are reported for the same price.

Finally, an increase in product diversity will reduce the accuracy of reported product costs. The effect of this will be to increase the cost of errors and hence justify additional measurements.

Conditions that favour ABC systems. Measurement costs, the cost of errors and product diversity all change continuously over time. Understanding how and why these changes occur provides insights into the conditions that favour the use of ABC systems.

Decreasing measurement costs. High measurement costs often make it uneconomical to undertake measurements solely for product costing purposes. Fortunately, virtually all the information needed for ABC is already available. Given this, measurement costs typically consist of two elements: the cost of routing the information to the cost system and the cost of making the calculations needed to compute product costs.

Measurement costs are changed by the introduction of new information technology, such as computerised shopfloor planning systems, numerically controlled machinery, and more powerful, less expensive, computers.

With a computerised production floor scheduling system, more information about products exists in electronic form. This information can then be supplied to the cost system at virtually no cost. For example, the control system for the shopfloor captures information about the number of production runs. This information can be used, in turn, to estimate the number of movements of material that occur.

Cost systems also typically perform many calculations to arrive at product costs. These calculations can comprise a major component of overall measurement costs. The cost per calculation has fallen dramatically in recent years with improvements in information processing technology. Indeed, this cost reduction has effectively removed any computational barrier to the development of ABC systems. For example, a powerful microcomputer can now run the cost system of a sizeable facility. Ten years ago, a mainframe computer would have been required; 20 years ago, such a system would have been impossible.

2. The cost of errors

The cost of errors can take several forms. These include the following:

● Making poor decisions about products (for example, aggressively selling unprofit-able products, setting prices inappropriately, or introducing new products into unprofitable niches).

● Making poor product design decisions (for example, increasing the number of unique parts in a product to reduce its direct labour content when the cost of maintaining those parts exceeds the labour savings).

● Making poor capital investment decisions based on overhead savings that do not materialise.

● Making inaccurate budgeting decisions about the level of operating expenses required.

Changes in competition. The major cause of changes in the cost of errors is variation in the level of competition faced. Increased competition ordinarily increases the cost of errors, because there is a greater chance that a competitor will take advantage of any errors made. For example, an apparently low profit margin of an overcosted (but actually profitable) product – a product, moreover, which a competitor is chasing aggressively – might lead a company to abandon that product, which could prove to be a costly mistake.

More focused competition. By reducing the diversity of products offered, focused manufacturing makes the product costs that conventional cost systems report less distorted. The more accurate product costs that result allow focused manufacturers to make better pricing decisions than full-range manufacturers. They can thus develop superior marketing strategies. Therefore, full-range manufacturers that suddenly face competition from more focused firms require systems that report more accurate product costs.

More creative competition. Creative competition can also change how a product is sold. This change alone can render a cost accounting system obsolete.

To illustrate this consider the case of a company that bundled two products together: the first was a machine that customers rented, and the second a fastener that customers purchased in large volumes and attached using the machine. Rental fees for the machines were set low purposely to attract customers.

Since the machines and fasteners were customised and had to be used together, customers became 'captive'. The company set the price of the fasteners high enough to cover not only the costs of the fasteners, but also the unrecovered costs of the machines, plus a profit. Reflecting this bundled product marketing strategy, the company cost system overcosted fasteners by tracing all overhead costs (including overheads related to the attaching machines) to fasteners and none to the machines.

A competitor, in an attempt to increase market share, found a way to unbundle the two products. It sold the fasteners at a 20% discount, which was approximately the amount by which the fasteners were over-costed by the first company to subsidise the machines with which they were bundled. The competitor's unbundling of the fasteners and the machines forced the first firm to redesign its cost system so that

ABC:
THE RIGHT APPROACH FOR YOU?

What are the factors to consider when deciding whether an ABC system is appropriate?

Robin Cooper

it would report separate product costs for the machines and the fasteners.

Deregulation. Deregulation can also force firms to compete in new ways. When a company's products and the prices that it charges are regulated, it survives by controlling its overall efficiency, not by managing its competitive position.

The cost systems of many regulated companies reflect this reality by measuring the cost of functional activities, not the cost of products. However, a more accurate knowledge of product costs becomes imperative when unregulated competitors appear, cut prices, and start 'cherry picking' products. Therefore, when deregulation looms on the horizon, managers of regulated companies often display a sudden, intense interest in knowing their product costs.

Formerly captive suppliers. Companies that were once captive suppliers, but are suddenly allowed (or forced) to compete, face a situation virtually identical to deregulation. The companies' transfer pricing systems, which were formerly used to 'price' products, often act much like a regulated pricing system.

One company that recently went through this experience, for example, discovered that its cost system was causing it to price products inappropriately. The prices attracted business that it did not want and caused it to refuse business that was actually profitable. Realising that the cost system was the culprit, the company's management decided to develop a new product costing system that more accurately reported product costs.

Changing overhead structures. A more subtle way in which the cost of errors increases over time can be found in the changing overhead structure of most companies. Over the past 150 years, overhead costs have relentlessly increased as a percentage of value added. This increase has caused many cost systems based on direct labour hours to report increasingly distorted product costs.

As overhead costs become more important, so does their effective management. Traditional cost accounting systems, with their reliance on one (or a few) allocation bases that are derived from the number of units produced make it difficult (if not impossible) to understand the relationship (considering both mix and volume) between the products produced and the appropriate level of overhead. An ABC system, in contrast, provides insights into these relationships and thus leads to better management of overhead costs.

3. Product diversity

As was demonstrated in my first article, traditional cost systems can report highly distorted product costs when the products that a company manufactures consume a diverse mixture of inputs. The following actions increase product diversity, and can reduce the overall accuracy of reported product costs:

● introducing new products;
● adopting new marketing strategies;
● improving production processes.

New products. The introduction of a new product or product line whose cost structure differs significantly from the cost structure of existing products can increase the distortion of reported product costs. The distortions occur because cost systems report average product costs; the new averages are less representative of actual costs of both the old and new products produced than the old average was of the old products alone.

A classic example of this problem occurs when a cost centre contains both manual and automated machines. As long as the products that pass through the centre use different types of machines in about the same proportion, reported product costs are not significantly distorted. However, if a new product is introduced and it uses the automated machines more intensely, it will be undercosted if direct labour hours are used to allocate costs.

Costing distortions can increase gradually over time as the new products are produced in greater volumes relative to existing products. For example, one firm introduced a new line of plastic products. Since the firm did not have enough volume to justify

> **'** The prices attracted business that it did not want and caused it to refuse business that was actually profitable **'**

doing its own moulding, it purchased moulded parts. However, the company fabricated its older, metal products by purchasing sheet metal, which was then cut and welded to create the desired shapes. The company's cost system, which was based on direct labour, spread the support overhead for metal fabrication over both metal and plastic products, thus undercosting the metal products and overcosting the plastic ones. As the production volume of plastic products increased, so did the distortion in reported product costs.

New marketing strategies. Changing strategies for a product can also make a cost system obsolete. The decision to market in low-volume niches requires increased production of low-volume products. Conversely, the decision to produce standard parts in a speciality shop requires increased production of high-volume products. These changes result in distorted product costs if the cost system is not designed to trace overhead costs appropriately.

Unit-based cost systems generally cannot differentiate adequately between overhead consumed by high-volume or low-volume products. (See my first article for discussion of batch size diversity.) Fortunately, as long as the difference in volumes produced is low (for example, a ratio of 5-to-1 for the number of items in the largest to smallest

batches), product costs are usually still reasonably accurate. But if the ratio exceeds 10-to-1, the risk of significantly distorted product costs increases.

For example, one company had a large variety of products. Some of the products were sold, in high volumes, so some production lots contained thousands of items. Other products sold in low volumes and were produced in production lots containing as few as 10 or 20 items. As a result, the company's unit-based cost system produced highly distorted product costs. The reported product costs would have led management to believe – erroneously – that the low-volume products were highly profitable.

New production processes. Introducing a new production process can also cause a cost system to give distorted product costs. For example, the introduction of automated production processes (such as flexible machining) leads to the use of less direct labour but to an increase in the use of support functions such as programming and special engineering. As a result, the products manufactured on the new machinery are undercosted if direct labour is the only allocation base used. Conversely, products that are not manufactured on the new machines are overcosted.

One company, for example, completely revamped its production process. Machines that required continuous direct supervision were replaced with machines that required little supervision. This replacement allowed machine operators to watch over several machines at once, perform off-line set-ups, and also do inspections. But the company's cost system, which was based on direct labour, was not completely revamped at the same time. As a result, it failed to capture the changed economics of the company's production process and thus reported distorted product costs.

Cost system obsolescence. Even though a company's measurement costs, cost of errors, and product diversity often change, companies seldom redesign their cost systems. So as the years go by the changes in the three factors accumulate.

For example, a company may install a computerised system for controlling the shopfloor. A few years later, it may face increased competition. Finally, the firm may add one or more new products over the course of the years. In combination, these changes can render the company's cost accounting system obsolete. Consequently, deciding if an ABC system is justified requires taking into account all the changes that have occurred since the existing cost system was installed.

Cost of a new system. A cost system is obsolete and should be changed when the net present value of the benefits of having improved product costs exceeds the net present value of redesigning a new costing system.

Typically, cost accounting systems seem to last 10 years or more. However, a cost system's longevity depends on the perceived costs of redesigning a new cost system. These costs create a significant barrier to the introduction of a new cost system. Total costs of a new cost accounting system include the following:

- obtaining the support of management for a new system;
- identifying a team (whether internal or external) to design the system;
- designing and implementing the new system;
- tying the new cost system into the company's other information systems;
- training management in the use of the new system;
- creating a team to maintain the new system.

An ABC system is justified whenever the costs of installing and operating the new system are more than offset by the long-term benefits that would be derived from the new ABC system. These benefits are real, though they are often difficult to quantify. This trade-off differs for every company and depends on the factors already mentioned that affect the optimal cost system and the adequacy of the existing cost system.

It is therefore impossible to generate a set of simple decision rules to answer the question: 'Do I need an ABC system?' However, it is possible to define the conditions when ABC is most likely to be justified. Specifically, implementing an ABC system is advisable if the existing cost system was designed when measurement costs were high, competition was weak, and product diversity was low, but measurement costs are now low, competition is fierce, and product diversity is high.

Decisions to implement ABC

Any company about to redesign its cost system should consider implementing an ABC system even if all of the conditions do not exist. The best reason for following this argument is that companies tend to keep their cost systems long after they have become obsolete. The long life expectancy of most cost systems and the time that it takes to install a new cost system make it dangerous to wait for all the appropriate conditions to occur.

Companies should monitor how well their cost systems perform and how much the three factors have changed over time. In other words, they should anticipate the obsolescence of their cost systems before major problems occur. By doing so, a company will have enough time to decide whether an ABC system is required. Ideally, an ABC system can be designed and implemented before an obsolete system can do too much damage. □

This article is based on material appearing in the four-part series 'The Rise of Activity-Based Costing', Journal of Cost Management, *summer 1988 to spring 1989.*

Robin Cooper FCA *is associate professor of business administration in the Graduate School of Business Administration at Harvard University and provides consultancy services to KPMG Peat Marwick.*

72

READER
ARTICLE 6.3

'ABC in the UK – a status report'

Brent Nicholls

Reproduced from *Management Accounting,*
Journal of the Chartered Institute of
Management Accountants

1992

ABC IN THE UK—A STATUS REPORT

Brent Nicholls describes a survey carried out as part of an MBA which attempted to shed light on the extent of ABC implementation and the associated benefits and barriers. The project involved a detailed implementation case study within an engineering company and also a survey of UK companies, by questionnaire and by subsequent follow-up telephone interviews.

How widely accepted and implemented as a management decision tool is activity-based costing (ABC)? What is the current status of ABC implementation in the less well known companies and what problems are they experiencing? Such are the kinds of question being asked by managers considering ABC implementation.

With these questions in mind, an MBA project entitled 'ABC — a product review' has been completed in an attempt to shed light on the extent of ABC implementation and the associated benefits and barriers. The project involved a detailed implementation case study within an engineering company and also a survey of UK companies. A questionnaire was sent to 179 companies all of which had attended a major seminar on ABC in May 1990. Consequently, when the questionnaires were completed in January 1991 seven months had elapsed since the seminar — enough time to evaluate and start implementing ABC.

The questionnaires were sent to a range of industrial organisations, from which 62 usable replies were received covering a wide cross section of UK companies. The response, in excess of 35 per cent, reflects the significant interest currently being shown in ABC. A series of follow-up telephone interviews was conducted with respondents to probe responses to the questionnaire in greater depth. In each case the contact was with the individual who attended the seminar in May 1991 and in the majority of cases this was the financial director.

The questionnaire was completed by a cross-section of companies from less than £15m turnover to more than £100m, with the number of employees varying from fewer than 150 to more than 1000. The general engineering and manufacturing sector accounted for over 36 per cent of those who replied.

The results of the survey are set out below.

Method of overhead allocation

In the area of current methods of overhead allocation, over 80 per cent of respondent companies used traditional methods of overhead recovery based on labour content, unit volume, machine hours or a combination. Over 55 per cent of all respondent companies used direct labour content as a method of overhead allocation while 17 per cent of respondent companies used cost drivers as a method of allocating overhead to products.

Status of ABC implementation

The questionnaire established that over 90 per cent of respondent companies had implemented, were currently implementing or were investigating ABC to determine suitability for their environments. 10 per cent of companies (three out of six respondent companies from the financial/insurance sector) indicated they had implemented ABC, whilst the majority of companies — 62 per cent — were investigating ABC techniques to determine suitability and the remaining 18 per cent were piloting ABC techniques. Companies that positively did not intend to implement ABC comprised some 5 per cent. Of these:

- one company had developed a brand reporting system;
- three companies questioned the suitability of ABC for their type of industry and
- one company stated 'current criticism of standard costing whilst justified is even amplified in ABC'.

Reasons for initially considering ABC

This question caused many companies to state several reasons for their initial interest in ABC. In order of respondent priority the following summarises the percentage of total replies that agreed with the statements:

- requirement to understand true product costs (65 per cent);
- not being entirely satisfied with their current system (50 per cent);
- business requirement to identify and reduce product costs (45 per cent);
- increasing proportion of overhead as opposed to direct cost (32 per cent);
- improvements not financially recognised (7 per cent) and
- make versus buy decisions (7 per cent).

It can be concluded that there is a strong requirement in UK industry to understand true product costs rather than using a traditional method of allocating overhead, which often serves to obscure actual product costs. To support this statement, over 50 per cent of the respondents stated that they were not entirely satisfied with their existing costing system. It should be noted that the dissatisfied cost system users use a traditional method of allocating overhead.

Proposed method of ABC implementation

There was a mixed response to this question. 58 per cent of respondent companies either had used outside help or intended to do so. Half simply stated that they were unclear of the best way forward. This is

probably a reflection of the fact that ABC is perceived to be a complex new management tool. The ABC approach, although stated as 'simple' by many authorities on the subject, is clearly not considered to be simple to implement. One successful approach to implementing ABC is to undertake a pilot study first, and 27 per cent of respondent companies considered this as their favoured approach.

Benefits gained or hoped for from ABC

Again this question caused a mixed response, with several companies stating a concern over benefits expected and those promised by the advocates of ABC. In order of respondent priority the following summarises the benefits gained or realistically expected from ABC implementation:

- greater understanding of product cost (65 per cent);
- focused overhead reduction via activity analysis (60 per cent);
- greater understanding of customer profitability (47 per cent);
- anticipated change of product portfolio and/or pricing strategy (43 per cent) and
- identification of non value adding activities (40 per cent).

This question also invoked a series of comments from respondent companies which can be summarised as:

- greater understanding of product family and market segment profitability;
- justification of overhead charges to customers requiring 'open book' costing and
- ability dynamically to model our business.

Problems and pitfalls of ABC implementation

This question without doubt generated the greatest number of comments from respondent companies.

As before, the following summarises the percentage of total replies that agreed with the statements:

- unavailability of adequate detailed data (38 per cent);
- lack of resources (33 per cent);
- reluctance to change traditional accounting method (27 per cent);
- departmental resistance to change or provide information (25 per cent);
- lack of knowledge, training or information (17 per cent) and
- lack of clear direction on how to implement (12 per cent).

In support of these responses the following comments were made:

panies who had not initiated any positive work towards ABC implementation trials or data collection confirmed the following:

- a dissatisfaction with the information currently provided by existing cost systems, particularly relating to confidence in determining individual product profitabilities;
- a reluctance to initiate any change in the short term due to a lack of resources and the pressure of other commitments and
- a realisation that they will have to 'do something about their costs perhaps when ABC is more widely accepted or made simpler to maintain'.

Those companies which are currently piloting or implementing ABC provided a mixed response to the telephone interview. In each case they were perfectly clear about the benefits they were driving towards but said that the task of implementing ABC was more involved and consumed more management time than first anticipated. It was also felt that insufficient time was allowed for training, which subsequently reduced the acceptance of 'new measures inflicted' upon cost centres. In each case they also confirmed that information was difficult to obtain. In some cases the plan was to retain the existing costing systems for valuation of stock and to design the ABC systems to run independently. Each company was confident, however, that ABC would eventually yield the desired objectives and benefits.

Finally, a comment made by a company who has implemented ABC: 'companies who implement ABC without fully understanding the behavioural issues of new performance measures or cost drivers may underestimate the impact of change internally'.

Survey conclusions

- Over 80 per cent of respondent companies still used traditional methods of allocating overhead based on labour content, unit volume or machine hours.
- Over 90 per cent of respondent companies were now considering ABC as a way forward for their costing system and 10 per cent indicated that they had implemented ABC.
- A requirement to determine true product costs is given as the prime reason for considering ABC followed by 50 per cent of companies stating they were not entirely satisfied with their current costing system.
- The principal benefit required from implementing ABC was to identify true product profitabilities followed by focused overhead reduction.
- Problems and pitfalls encountered centre around unavailability of detailed data, lack of resources and training or ownership issues.
- Some 38 per cent of companies stated that they had adopted total quality initiatives (TQC/TQM).

Managerial issues and actions

As a direct result of the telephone conversa-
Continued on page 28

- 'the data was difficult to obtain initially but the system now works quite well';
- 'administration of manual records difficult';
- 'lack of managerial understanding of how to run business in this totally different way';
- 'unwieldy in large organisation, expensive to maintain, causes conflict on methodologies';
- 'whole regiment of accountants required to support it';
- 'unwillingness to see value in ABC';
- 'problem of selling "benefits" to already submersed line managers';
- 'sheer volume of data to be processed and the consequent difficulty in obtaining accuracy'.

Clearly these comments and the even spread of respondent replies to the questionnaire indicate a genuine concern on

behalf of companies in three areas:
- data collection and the resources to carry this out;
- willingness of existing line and operations management to participate in change commonly viewed as 'the domain of the accountants' and
- the maintenance of such a system once established.

These areas centre around firstly the commitment to change from the top and hence investment in thorough education and training of key operations staff, and secondly striking the right balance between collecting enough detail and the benefit of a simplistic system.

Telephone enquiries

Telephone enquiries were made to a number of companies to gain supporting detail to the questionnaire responses. The com-

ABC in the UK
Continued from page 23
tions with respondent companies, and the examination of ABC case studies, the following list of actions are likely to be suggested to managers by ABC:

Manufacturing and logistics
- focus factories concentrated on reduced product range;
- just-in-time manufacturing with reduced complexity (less waste, product line focus and streamlined material and information flow);
- flexible manufacturing systems (FMS);
- computer integrated manufacturing (CIM);
- electronic data interchange from retail outlet to manufacture and
- cost drivers measured over time to indicate true cost reductions.

ABC helps to indicate the potential overhead cost reductions possible in the above systems that would be difficult to justify using traditional costing methods.

Product innovation and development
- fewer component parts;
- common components;
- design for ease of manufacture or reduced transactions and
- variety in the process.

Marketing and sales
- repricing of products;
- modified trading terms and conditions;
- different or shifting product emphasis and mix;
- standardise the sources of variety on the market and
- customer and segment product planning and budgeting with 'owned' credible costing system.

Behavioural
- induce (positive or negative) behaviour through cost drivers/performance measures;
- endorse world-class manufacturing initiatives or continuous improvement team-based cultures;
- emphasise manufacturing and corporate strategies;
- understand and eliminate complexity in the operation and
- improved understanding of the economics of production and activities performed by an organisation.

The way forward
Without doubt any company able to identify true product costs will have a tactical advantage over a competitor who is unable to do so. Consequently, companies not entirely satisfied with their existing product cost systems (and this survey suggests over 50 per cent fall into this category) should be actively encouraging their managers to develop a product costing system that will provide them with the tactical information.

Brent Nicholls is a senior consultant in York MDM Ltd, a management consultancy specialising in the manufacturing and distribution sectors of industry.

READER ARTICLE 7.1

'Budgeting and cost management: a route to continuous improvement'

Robin Bellis-Jones

Reproduced from *Management Accounting,* Journal of the Chartered Institute of Management Accountants

April 1992

Budgeting and cost management: a route to continuous improvement

Robin Bellis-Jones, a director of management consultants Develin and Partners and a member of CIMA's Council, reviews the weaknesses in budgetary control and highlights how budgeting can contribute to the process of continuous improvement.

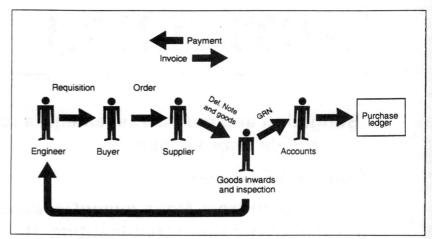

The basic techniques for developing budgets and monitoring progress against them are long established and deeply embedded in the culture and management philosophy of must UK companies. They have a powerful influence on how people behave and, given the extensive experience of its practical use, one might expect it to be a well regarded management tool.

However, a recent survey* of senior managers has revealed a serious issue for finance managers. Only 10 per cent of respondents believed conventional budgets, cost centre and variance reporting to be a 'very effective' control mechanism, while over three times this number believed it to be 'poor', particularly in relation to overhead. Even this might be regarded as an optimistic view as 80 per cent of respondents were in the finance function.

Many would accept that the most important feature of budgetary control is that it should help senior management to plan and co-ordinate the efforts of disparate functions and departments to achieve predetermined, clearly understood targets. If this is so then the survey findings indicate that budgetary control, as currently practised, is failing management to a fairly spectacular extent.

The problem with conventional budgeting

All too frequently, budgetary control is seen as a costly and burdensome routine, reinforcing bad practice and constraining response in a rapidly changing commercial environment.

The trouble is that conventional approaches to cost management through budgetary

* Activity Based Cost Management: The Overheads Revolution. A CBI/ Develin and Partners Survey.

control seem carefully to avoid the potential benefits and emphasise its disadvantages. Why should this be so?

I would like to suggest the following reasons:

Constraint, not control
Psychologically it is not that people dislike change, rather they dislike *being changed*. In the same way they dislike *being controlled* through such mechanisms as budgetary control; rather they would prefer to *be in control* of their area of responsibility. However, all too often *control has become constraint*, suffocating managerial initiative and running completely counter to the empowering philosophy of total quality and continuous improvement. As a result, there is little affection or confidence in a process which they perceive as constraining them from acting in the best interest of the company.

ar
Based on limited knowledge
A major assumption in conventional budgetary control is that departmental managers know what goes on in their department at an appropriate level of detail.

Sometimes this assumption is valid, particularly when managers have 'worked their way up' in a department and do know the detail; however, this is not always the case. Too often managers settle for basing this year's budget on last year's, rather than judging what is right for the business or seeking to improve effectiveness.

Compromises in budget-setting
Budgets are generally poor at translating strategy into action. Strategy generally expresses the organisational plan with reference to the operating environment, while budget and cost centres are constructed to reflect the hierarchical and functional nature of the structure of the organisations and its subdivisions. Elements of the strategy need to be translated into the broad requirements of each function or department for the overall strategy to succeed. In turn these requirements are translated into a statement of the resources required in each area. The sum of these resources across the organisation inevitably exceeds the total available and a process of negotiation and adjustment follows, modifying

the budget proposals to the point where some form of agreement is reached for each cost centre. By this stage individual departmental budgets often bear little connection with the strategy which spawned them.

The resulting budgets are then monitored against outturns, and variances reported on a function-by-function basis by the finance department. Performance against each budget is examined separately, totally ignoring the cross-functional impact that departments have on each other in practice.

Lack of performance measures
Conventional budgets have an over-emphasis on inputs, to the exclusion of outputs. Examination of a wide sample of departmental budget statements will typically reveal that they are expressed in financial terms against established ledger headings. A cynic might suggest that this form is more for the convenience of the finance function than for the benefit of the departmental managers who have to use the information. It is still the exception to find useful non-financial performance measures integrated into the month-

Management Accounting, April 1992

ly performance reporting package.

Too inward-looking

Most budgeting processes fail to recognise the crucial role of cross-functional business processes. The business process of purchasing is illustrated here. This process involves a number of different groups, some of which are external to the organisation, which perform a variety of related activities to effect the completion of a transaction. The activity of each group is dependent on the output of the preceding one, therefore the process as a whole is only as strong as its weakest link.

Consequently, the effectiveness of budgetholders is dependent on three factors:

- their ability to influence directly the way their own departmental staff operate;
- the volume of work placed on their departments by others;
- the problems and errors in the work presented to their department which directly influence the amount of unnecessary checking and correcting their staff have to do.

The latter two are beyond the immediate jurisdiction of the budgetholder.

It is usually significantly more expensive to correct an error than to avoid it. Yet, especially under the competitive pressures generated during a recession, management are tempted to reduce department budgets crudely, unaware that the immediate consequence is a reduction in the quality of work done and an increase in error rates.

This in turn causes resources to be expended on correcting these errors elsewhere in the organisation. Even worse, product or service quality can be directly affected, causing customers to incur unnecessary rectification costs: they therefore may be tempted to seek better quality elsewhere.

It is efficient, effective and responsive business processes which provide the foundation of service quality and cost effectiveness. These are rarely recognised in the budget process.

First steps to a solution

To overcome these weaknesses and develop a budget process which actively encourages continuous improvement, we must recognise that:

- staff costs are only as fixed as

management are prepared to allow, and activities drive cost and *can* be managed;
- not all activities add equal value and staff do not usually undertake non-value-added activity for the fun of it: they do it because of the circumstances in which they have been placed by others;
- the majority of activity within a particular department is driven by demands and decisions beyond the immediate control of the budgetholder, upstream in a business process;
- the role of a manager must be to improve the business processes in which his staff have to operate, focusing on the quality of their activities and how such activities link cross-functionally into a business process. Related measures of performance should focus on the factors which drive activities, the quality of the activity undertaken and responsive-

ness to changing customer requirements.

The benefits

The net effect of getting these things right is a tangible improvement in both product and service quality and a major re-balancing of resources. As quality improves, so resources are released for re-investment in new activities which will secure the future at no extra cost. Alternatively costs may be reduced over time, thereby improving the competitive cost position of the organisation.

In addition there is a significant change in culture from one where managers are *controlled* to one where they are *in control*. By focusing on *how* people's activities inter-relate to deliver tangible results managers become much more supportive of the notion of continuous improvement *because it is in their interest to do so.*

If the introduction of such

improvements to the budget process was easy then adoption would probably be universal already. It does require a serious commitment of time and effort. However, there is a growing recognition that the benefits of so improving the budget process significantly outweigh the burden of the change itself, to the point where the question is not 'can we afford to do it?' but 'can we afford *not* to do it?'. □

A one day course on 'Budgeting and Cost Management: A Route to Continuous Improvement' will be presented by Robin Bellis-Jones on 18 June in London. It will analyse the weaknesses inherent in using conventional budgetary control for cost management purposes and explore how budgeting can make a direct contribution to the process of continuous improvement. Further details may be obtained from CIMA Mastercourses 071-637 2311, ext 2318.

READER
ARTICLE 7.2

'Evaluating Performance'

Dr Graham Morgan

Reproduced from Certified Diploma

Evaluating performance

Budgets are now a fact of life for most managers. Dr Graham Morgan of Birmingham Polytechnic looks at the way performance against budget is evaluated, and the importance top executives place on achieving budget.

THE accountant has popularised the use of budgeting by emphasising its usefulness in helping to plan and control financial commitments at a departmental and organisational level.

Variance analysis has been promoted as a diagnostic tool for understanding performance against budgetary standards, and information is provided to the manager to promote greater control over the manager's area of responsibility. In practice, when actual performance is compared with budget standard, it is possible for the accountant, either consciously or inadvertently, to use this information to appraise the performance of the individual manager as opposed to evaluating the performance of the operating department.

Furthermore, there is also the possibility that the line manager will in turn use budgetary information as a means of evaluating the performance of subordinates. In effect, the budget review process becomes a system of performance evaluation of the individual manager and may operate in a way which undermines schemes such as management by objectives advocated by personnel specialists.

Hopwood [1] in his study of a US steel making company, defined three distinct ways of using budgetary information in the evaluation of managerial performance:

1. Budget constrained style of evaluation.

Under this style of evaluation a manager's performance is primarily evaluated on his ability to meet the budget on a short-term basis.

The manager will receive unfavourable criticism from his superior if actual costs exceed the budget costs regardless of other considerations.

2. Profit-conscious style of evaluation.

Under this style of evaluation the manager's performance is evaluated on the basis of his ability to increase the general effectiveness of his units operation in relation to the long-term purpose of the organisation, eg reducing long-term costs. Budget information has to be used in a flexible manner.

3. Non-accounting style of evaluation.

Under this style of evaluation the budgetary information plays a relatively unimportant part in the superior's evaluation of the manager's performance.

While budgetary information obviously indicates whether or not a manager has succeeded in meeting his current budget, it does not necessarily indicate that he is achieving it in the intended manner or, indeed, if he is behaving in a manner consistent with achieving the organisation's longer term effectiveness.

With the profit-conscious style of evaluation, the superior is concerned with wider information and not just the magnitude of variances. The budget is seen more as a means to an end rather than an end in itself.

Hopwood observed that the different styles had an influence on important aspects of performance which are presented in Table 1.

It can be seen that while the budget-constrained style encourages a high degree of involvement with costs, it has several negative aspects, eg high job related tension, extensive manipulation of reported figures and poor relationships with supervisors and colleagues.

The profit-conscious style of evaluation still encourages a high degree of involvement with costs but overcomes the problems highlighted above. Hopwood's study also identified the fact that the budget-constrained style of evaluation was passed down through the organisation. This was not necessarily the case with the other two styles.

Subsequent research by Otley [2] questioned whether Hop-

TABLE 1

	Style of evaluation:		
	Budget constrained	Profit conscious	Non acc'ting
Involvement with costs	high	high	low
Job related tension	high	medium	medium
Manipulation of figures	extensive	little	little
Relations with supervisors	poor	good	good
Relations with colleagues	poor	good	good

TABLE 2

	Top three rankings: (Most important 1 etc)					Combined ranking
Managing Directors A	B	C	D	E	F	
The effort they put into their job	1		3	3	3		2
How much profit they make	3	1	1	1			1
Their concern with quality	2			2			4
How well they meet their budget		2				2	4
Their employee relations					3		7
How efficiently they run their unit	3			1	1		3
Their attitude towards the work		2		2			4

TABLE 3		Profit conscious style of evaluation:					
Managing directors –	A	B	C	D	E	F	Hopwood
Involvement with costs	high	high	high	high	high	high	high
Job related tension	med	high	med	low	med	med	medium
Manipulation of figures	mod	mod	little	little	little	little	little
Relations with supervisors	mod	good	good	mod	mod	mod	good
Relations with colleagues	mod	good	good	good	mod	mod	good

wood's findings were universally applicable. Otley's studies in the British coal industry showed that there was no or little interdependence between organisation's units (as in the case of coal pits), the adverse consequences of the budget-constrained style did not apply.

In fact, many of the more successful mines were operating under a 'budget-constrained' management style. Otley's contention that the appropriate management style depends on the degree of interdependence between organisational sub-units, the toughness of the unit's operating environment and its size and profitability, is now widely accepted.

In response to Hopwood's questionnaire, the answers given by the managing directors as to how they judged the performance of subordinate managers was interesting. In only two companies was the performance criterion of budget achievement given a top three ranking out of seven.

There was unanimous agreement with the suggestion that a rigid performance evaluation based on the achievement of the budget can lead to an emphasis on the short-term at the expense of the longer term. In the view of managing director C, the balancing of performance through time was critical. However, in his view, there was inevitably a general tendency to focus on the short-term. He stated: 'Budgets tend to focus on the short-term; however the short-term is extremely important because if you do not manage the short-term then often you do not have a long-term'.

Overall, it would appear that on the basis of ranking the 'profit-conscious' style was pre-ferred. In assessing the consequences of this style there is broad agreement with Hopwood's assessment of its impact, as is shown in Table 3. Total consistency only occurs with regard to 'involvement with costs'. The other assessments overlap, the greatest divergence occurring in judging 'relations with supervisors' which would be classified as moderate overall.

The managing directors' assessments of how they themselves were evaluated produced a more consistent pattern of response and a higher ranking for budget achievement. The response of each managing director and a combined ranking is given in Table 4.

While the performance criteria of managing the budget has risen to second ranking, all managing directors were unwilling to accept that they operated under a 'budget-constrained' style. Yet at other times in the interviews the managing directors stressed the importance of budget achievement. Indeed, one referred to a group

> **'With the profit-conscious style of evaluation, the superior is concerned with wider information and not just the magnitude of variances. The budget is seen more as a means to an end rather than an end in itself'**

culture where 'the non-achievement of the budget attracts an inordinate amount of criticism'.

Despite the higher priority assigned to budget achievement for managing directors themselves, it would appear that this was not transferred downwards – which is at variance with Hopwood's study. For example, the managing director quoted above did not give budget achievement a place in his top three performance criteria ranking.

The budgetary process was not specifically designed as a means by which the performance of an individual manager is to be assessed. However, given that budgetary information is the principal and most accessible quantifiable information within an organisation, its use in the above manner seems almost inevitable.

The managing directors in this study were of the opinion that budget achievement should not become an end in itself. To counterbalance this tendency, the accountant should be will-ing to highlight the dysfunctional behaviour (eg, manipulation of figures, interdepartmental conflict and sacrificing long-term position for short-term gains etc) which can arise from concentrating on a single incomplete measure of performance.

The accountant should attempt to ensure that reporting systems are used in ways which complement rather than dominate, that organisational culture which best supports the organisation's strategy and long-term development is therefore important if the accountant is to act in a fully supportive role for top management.

References:
[1] Hopwood AG: *An Empirical Study of the Role of Accounting Data in Performance Evaluation. Empirical Research in Accounting*, supplement to Journal of Accounting Research volume 10.
[2] Otley DT: *Budget Use and Managerial Performance*. Journal of Accounting and Research vol 16.

TABLE 4	Top three rankings: Combined (Most Important 1 etc) Ranking					
Managing directors	A	B	C	D	E	F
How much profit I make	1	1	1	1	1	1
How well I meet my budget	2	2			2	2	2
My concern with quality	3				3		5
My attitude towards my work			3	2			3
The effort I put into my job				3	2		3
How efficiently I run my unit						3	3	5
Long-term development of the business						1	7

READER ARTICLE 7.3

'Activity-Based Budgeting'

Mike Harvey

Reproduced from *Certified Accountant*

July 1991

ACTIVITY-BASED BUDGETING

MIKE HARVEY claims that budgetary control systems will need
to be changed in the 1990s to assist business survival,
and discusses the advent of activity-based budgeting as
part of the orientation process

THE question is often asked about the so-called 'new' management, including accounting techniques, as to whether they merely concern a flavour of the month or are really useful!

The past generation has seen the introduction of numerous new ideas and their associated buzz words. For example, in the area of budgeting there has been zero based budgeting (ZBB), priority based budgeting (PBB), planning programming budgeting (PPB).... to name but a few.

The sceptic will ask whether such have been dreamed up by academics or consultants - and wonder whether the objective of their initiator has either been to get his/her name in the history books or to provide an income-generating vehicle through writing about and teaching the newly developed technique!

This view is frequently reinforced by the fact that either many of the ideas have been in use before under a slightly different guise or shortly after their 'introduction' they sink without trace. The cynics also remind one that even in the case of a widely approved major technique like management by objectives (MBO) (1), this did not save one of its major proponents, John Humble's, organisation from problems!

Whatsoever, for his continuing professional development (CPD) the management accountant must keep up with potential progress and needs to ascertain what, if any, the new ideas are likely to offer to his organisation. In this it should be remembered that frequently such developments are supplementary to existing ones and, although they may never supplant the old completely, they can frequently help in the provision of additional, more relevant information.

Surgery needed

For survival in the 1990s, systems will need to be changed and sometimes surgery, rather than medication, will be necessary.

One aspect of this concerns the traditional budgetary control system. It is suggested that budgets would be better if they were established in a way which focussed on activities. Activity-based costing (ABC) is where costs are related to activities, and the variability of this is based on an assessment of cost behaviour and the related resource consumption. Many benefits would flow from focusing budgets on activities.

One such recent development which enables this new orientation concerns activity-based budgeting (ABB) (2). In the field of budgetary control it is clear that the traditional systems have several shortcomings. A major concern is the relevance of the information that the system produces. Because of this management has increasingly been asking its management accountants how the system could be improved, especially as far as the provision of better information for decision making, planning and controlling purposes is concerned.

Industrial application

The response of ABB may be used in tandem with an existing budgetary control system to supplement the information produced – although writers such as Michael Morrow and Tim Connolly forecast that in appropriate situations the activity-based approach will... 'replace rather than supplement traditional cost reporting when it comes to preparing the budget' (3). The application of ABB can be to any industry whether in manufacturing, services or the public sector. For example, in relation to

Figure 1: Simplified stages of the basic budgetary, control model

STAGE	ACTION
One	Divide the organisation into units (departments, etc)
Two	Establish short-term objectives for each unit consistent with overall strategy
Three	Provide terms of reference for unit operations
Four	Ascertain the cost of last year's actual operations based on resource consumption
Five	Discuss with local managment the likely cost of any new activites or ask them to tell about, and with luck they may, any likely reductions in resource requirements coming from shrinking activities
Six	Add in something for inflation
Seven	Take a line-by line approach to build up a unit's budget
Eight	Consider any constraints, *eg* profit requirements
Nine	Mesh the unit budgets together to establish the overall budget, reiterating as necessary
Ten	Monitor, explain variances and control – make sure overspending is 'punished' and claw back , but conveniently forget to praise under spending!

Management accounting

Figure 2: objectives of organisational and management processes

OBJECTIVES/ACTIONS RELATED TO	STRATEGY	TACTICS
Establish overall objectives (these may concern:)	Profitability; Markets; Products	Resource use; Training: research
Management	Define roles and responsibilities	Build a team
Consider customs and environment	Does organisational culture impose constraints?	What is the influence of organisational climate?
Information systems (develop and establish)	Management information system	Lines of communication
Integration, ensuring goal congruence	Of strategic business units	Eliminate adverse knock-on effects
Operations	Establish targets	Monitor and control performance
Cost reduction	Improve efficiency	Reduce costs; eliminate waste
Marketing avareness	Define market(s); ensure marketing orientation	Establish customer satisfaction, etc.
Production	Design products; improve	Establish cost-effective production

Figure 3: a systems approach to focus on activity-based budgeting

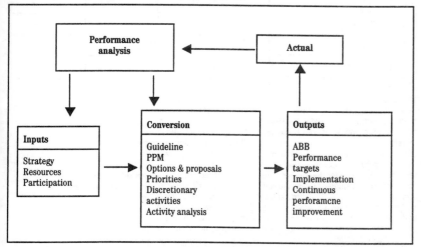

though it does incorporate budgetary control as one of its ingredients and tends to put this into a longer-term planning context.

One authority who highlighted the importance of developing a relationship between long and short-term planning some 30 years ago was Ralph Lewis, who wrote '...the long-range plan and the budget go hand-in-hand. The long-range plan is the vehicle for quantifying where a business should be headed and the best route to follow in order to arrive at that destination ... the budget indicates the specific steps to be taken in the near future which will lead to accomplishment of the long-range plan' (6).

It is possible for all the time horizons related to planning, *eg* long-term (strategic planning), medium term (tactical planning) and short-term (operational or administrative planning) to provide a focus for budgetary control. However, in spite of Ralph Lewis' statement, few organisations have developed a sufficient relationship between their long and shorter-term planning time horizons.

One major objective and benefit of ABB is to be found in its ability to provide an interface between long-term planning and budgetary control through the establishment of activity level drivers which provide a linkage in this respect.

Since the development of ABC there has been renewed interest in the use of activity analysis in other ways. One of the 'many benefits that can flow from the operation of an ABC system – probably the major one – will stem from the enhancement of the costing information produced ... The process also provides helpful information related to the establishment of budgets, with a concentric development coming next through the add on of activity-based budgeting (ABB) which takes ABC further' (7).

Cost behaviour
An aspect of this improvement of information provision is related to something that the student of accountancy is taught early on in costing, cost behaviour. This may seem to be rather theoretical and so is put on the back burner by many management accountants. However, ABC shows the importance of analysing cost behaviour and provides a greater understanding of the benefits of putting this into practice.

There are two features about earlier and current approaches to budgetary control which could be improved through the use of ABB. One concerns the mechanism for establishing the budget, the other is related to improving performance and efficiency.

A simplified, basic version of the traditional budgetary control model, with its orientation towards building up the budget on a departmental basis (generally with a

the public sector Derek Holford and Lawrence McAulay state that 'typical examples of activity measures may be numbers of patients, occupied bed days or pathology tests' (4).

One of the benefits of basing budgets on activities concerns the dilemma of the manager who is responsible for the resources that an activity consumes but does not have authority over the factors which cause the volume of the activity. That is the situation which goes against the well known management principle of

the correspondence of authority with responsibility. ABB helps to provide a structure which reduces this conflict.

Horizons interface
One approach to planning and control is to use profit planning and management (PPM) (5). This concerns a refined approach to profit management based on the substance of break-even analysis. However, although PPM shows the possibilities of profit gains it has no relationship to the gap analysis of corporate planning, even

backward- looking emphasis) is depicted using the 10 stages provided in Figure 1. In applying this, a high profile is rarely given to the distribution of resources throughout the organisation. Also, if any overall long-term strategy is brought into play this is only likely to be funnelled downwards in a broad sense.

As far as operational activities are concerned, the aim should be to continually improve the performance of these rather than undertaking to make improvements on a crisis basis such as when things get tight either generally, as in a recession, or when the organisation is facing unique difficulties.

Initially, when there are problems related to the non- achievement of a budget, 'axe wielding' takes place – those things which are easy to cut, and can be cut almost instantaneously, eg research, marketing and training, face the chop.

However, this does not concern genuine cost reduction. Concurrently (and here any savings will take longer to work through) cost reduction schemes (8) will be introduced. For example, those related to work study (to gain savings related to production processes); value analysis (to achieve savings related to material inputs) and organisation and methods (O & M) (to obtain savings related to administrative work).

Cost reduction endeavours need to lead to results. Nevertheless, related to cost reduction exercises, the question should be asked whether continual gains in cost savings can be made, or will they be subject to diminishing returns? Some lateral thinking must be employed in this respect, remembering that cost savings can be related to improvements in such ways as eliminating unnecessary work, better time management and improving organisational structure and methods at all levels. As far as cost savings related to resource use are concerned, the application of the cost benefit analysis (CBA) technique may help.

Information tests

As well as being developed from ABC, ABB can also bring in aspects of other established techniques as appropriate to the organisation and its situation, including zero-based budgeting (ZBB) (9), priority-based budgeting (PBB) (10) and total quality management (TQM) (11).

In the introduction of ABB the organisation's existing systems should be appraised to ascertain whether they are able to cope with an activity approach. Tests should be undertaken to establish how capable the organisation's information system is of providing its activity information requirements. This will all be helped if the information system is computer-based and an appropriate database can be established.

Before any form of budgeting can be used

Figure 4: simplified stages of the basic budgetary control model

STAGE	ACTION
One	Indentify the major cost drivers associated with the main and support activities, sub-dividing these as appropriate.
Two	Establish objectives for units once aware of the implications of alternative courses of action
Three	Construct a matrix based on the major cost drivers and their sub-divisions, which shows the resources associated with activities. An example of such a matrix's layout is provided in Figure 5.
Four	Establish the volume of an activity expected for the next period and from this establish its cost related to the resources it is likely to consume in budget terms. The level of activity should be ascertained on a ZBB/PBB basis as is appropriate.
Five	Reiterate as necessary, simulating the system, and apply sensitivity analysis until budgets for all activities are happily integrated.
Six	Monitor – look for variances based on activity

Figure 5: activity-based budgeting matrix

		ACTIVITIES				
		SUB ACTIVITIES			SUPPORT ACTIVITIES	
		Dept 1	Dept 2	Dept 3	Maintenance	Personnel
R E S O U R C E S	Eg Personnel					
	Materials					
	Equipment					
	Utilities					

to maximum benefit, it is important to establish clear objectives which will initially be drawn up at the strategic level and then, keeping consistent with these, formulated for tactics and operations for each of the enterprise's strategic business units (SBU). It goes without saying that these must be appropriate for the whole and its parts as far as acceptable targets and constraints are concerned. There are likely to be financial objectives, eg profit targets, and non-financial objectives such as market objectives, eg related to customer care, and welfare objectives.

Although not comprehensive, Figure 2 provides an indication of some of the objectives and actions which are associated with organisational and management processes. The aim of any budgetary control system must be to help achieve the goals established.

Once objectives have been developed and defined, processes related to the establishment of ABB can be considered. Figure 3 summarises an overall strategy related to this which takes a systems approach. Mike Bromwich has discussed the

benefits associated with using this concept in analysis (12).

Analysis techniques

The basic procedure underlying ABB concerns its use of activity analysis techniques combined with responsibility analysis. In discussing how the activity approach comes into budgeting, Michael Morrow and Tim Connolly state that this is '...by defining the activities underlying the financial figures in each function and using the level of activity to determine how much resource should be allocated, how well it is being managed and to explain variances from budget' (13).

In establishing the ABB, resources consumed will be associated with the level of the services used and in analysing this the level of the service supplied can be associated with the technique of TQM. The steps in ABB are provided in Figure 4.

Budgeting focused on activities provides a number of benefits, including:
● Has the ingredients of simplicity and usefulness.
● Improves the quality and effectiveness

of management information.

● Provides an increased understanding of how profitability is affected.

● Enables the resources required for consumption by an activity to be established more easily.

● Can help decisions related to the distribution of resources when combined with ZBB.

● Highlights the cost of an activity (14).

● Facilitates the allocation of resources in a way which ensures that the management principle of the correspondence of authority with responsibilities is adhered to.

● Highlights changes in resources requirements related to activities where environmental factors and influences cause these to increase or decrease.

● Makes it difficult to 'hide' resource consumption into some 'whole' because the ABB approach attempts to avoid the arbitrary allocations of overhead, which are unlikely to mirror cost behaviour.

● Facilitates the management of the cost of activities more effectively.

● Continually looks for improvements in efficiency.

● Helps cost reduction, such as through process improvement, but also points to new approaches in the way an activity can be undertaken.

● Enables target budgeting.

● Facilitates achieving improvements in efficiency through establishing appropriate targets such as those related to production and sales.

● Enables cross organisational questions, such as where there are inter relationships between units, to be dealt with and where these are likely to cause problems helps avoid them.

● Assists monitoring and control procedures, as the variances highlighted from this approach frequently indicate areas where improvement would be beneficial.

However, as with the majority of techniques, ABB has disadvantages and problems associated with its application, including the following:

● Where an activity is changeable over short periods, or seasonal, is invariably difficult to apply.

● It may be that where activities swing, for example on a seasonal basis, the fixed components of these will have a corrupting effect and activities may not provide a suitable vehicle for monitoring purposes (15).

● In the justification of the allocation of a resource to the activities that they support there must inevitably be some subjectivity.

Conclusions

Today, success in business comes from efficiency and effectiveness and, from management's point of view, this is gauged using appropriate performance measures.

Derek Holford and Lawrence McAulay write the following about activity-based

accounting: 'Management accounting systems, costing systems and management information systems all require a clear understanding of the nature of cost and unequivocal measures of activity in order to provide information for planning, control and decision-making (16).

The management accountant must compare the existing techniques that are being used within his organisation with the best developing practices available and, as appropriate, move towards them. ABB falls into this category.

Why and how it is done becomes less important than the beneficial results it will give.

ABB at its current stage of development provides a supplementary approach to, rather than replacing, the traditional budgetary control model.

The use of ABB is at its best where the cost of the activities varies over the medium to long-term rather than in the short term, and where the activities are distinct and frequently repeated. It helps achieve efficiency and effectiveness by focusing on the cost level drivers related to activities which enable improvements to be directed towards these.

All in all ABB provides an ideal approach to integrate long-term planning with budgetary control, relevant information on activities to management and helps in the planning of resource use.

Another major advantage is that it enables benchmarking and shows trends, and from this it associates targets with levels of activities which are realistic because they can be closely related to a change in activity. ■

Mike Harvey is profesor of accounting at the City of London Polytechnic and director of academic course development at E W Fact plc. He is also a former ACCA Education Committee chairman

REFERENCES

1 John Humble, *Management by Objectives*, Management Publications Ltd, 1969.

2 Jim Brimson and Robin Fraser, *The Key Features of ABB*, (Management Accounting, January 1991), writing about ABB state that this approach was '..developed by consultants Coopers and Lybrand Deloitte'.

3 Michael Morrow and Tim Connolly, *The Emergence of Activity- Based Budgeting*, (Management Accounting, February 1991).

4 Derek Holford and Lawrence McAulay, *Activity-Based Accounting in the National Health Service*. (Management Accounting, October 1987).

5 For a discussion of PPM see. for example, Mike Harvey, *Planning for Profitability*, (Accountancy Age, June 1981).

6 Ralph Lewis, *Planning and Control For Profit*, (Harper and Row, 1961, pages 4 and 5).

7 Mike Harvey, *A New Era in Costing*, (Certified Accountant, May 1991).

8 It is surprising what cost reduction savings can be made when there is a crisis on the horizon. It is a pity that such savings were not identified when things were going well - think of all the additional profit that the organisation would have made if it had done so!

9 Zero based/Priority based budgeting: 'A method of budgeting whereby all activities are re-evaluated each time a budget is set. Discrete levels of each activity are valued and a combination chosen to match funds available'. CIMA Management Accounting Official Terminology, CIMA, 1991, page 73)

10 ibid

11 TQM is 'a process of continuing improvement'. Malcolm Smith, *Management Accounting for Total Quality Management*, (Management Accounting, June 1990). 'The basic principle of TQM is that the cost of prevention (getting things right first time) is lower than the cost of correction (not getting things consistently right first time). Robin Bellis-Jones, *Are Total Quality Management Programmes a Fact or a Management Fad?*, (Management Accounting, May 1989).

12 For example see Mike Bromwich, *Standard Costing for Planning and Control,(* The Accountant, 19 & 26 Apl 1969 and 3 May 1969).

13 Michael Morrow and Tim Connolly, op cit

14 For example the cost of servicing a customer when combined with the technique of customer profitability analysis (CPA). Robin Bellis-Jones says 'CPA demands that all costs relevant to the trading relationship with any particular customer outlet are taken into account'. Robin Bellis-Jones, *Customer Profitability Analysis*, (Management Accounting, February 1989.) Therefore, with a customer as the unit of activity, CPA provides some of the information required for ABC. This approach can be developed on a matrix basis and activities, such as order acceptance, could be costed. It could also be used to help decisions related to such things as how goods and services were priced to different customers.

15 For example the knitting yarn trade is seasonal and the spinners (the manufacturers of the product) in a crude analysis of warehouse activity many years ago, offered retail customers discounts to bring their orders forward into the off season and so spread warehousepeople's work loads. Although this had a cost on the form of 'lost' profits there was a benefit as far as reduced overtime, etc. was concerned, with a cost benefit analysis approach showing an overall gain to the spinners.

16 Derek Holford and Lawrence McAulay, op cit.

READER
ARTICLE 8.1

'Cost Control: the manager's perspective'

C. Graham, D. Lyall and A. Puxty

Reproduced from *Management Accounting*, Journal of the Chartered Institute of Management Accountants

October 1992

Cost control: the manager's perspective

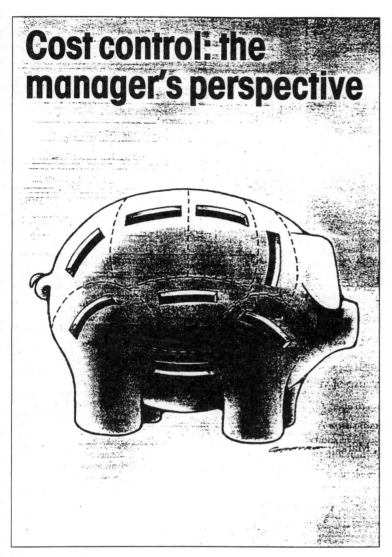

C. Graham, D. Lyall and A. G. Puxty of the University of Strathclyde present the findings of their recent CIMA funded research study into non-accounting managers' views on the effectiveness of cost control systems in industry. Accountants, it seems, are no longer seen as 'dead hands'.

Questions have been raised recently in the literature on the usefulness of traditional cost information for controlling modern manufacturing industry. Johnson and Kaplan,[1] for example, claim that cost accounting information is generally produced too late and is too aggregated and too distorted to be relevant for management control and decision-making purposes.

Moreover, as the pace of development in the automation of production processes has quickened, criticisms about the failure of existing cost systems to cope with the changed manufacturing environment have increased. Hendricks,[2] for example, states that increased factory automation has exposed and highlighted cost accounting problems related to investment justification, product costing and performance measurement.

These views, however, contradicted the findings of our earlier survey among accountants in industry (reported in *Management Accounting*, February 1990). We found that accountants, generally, were quite satisfied with the information produced by traditional cost systems. On reflection, given their close involvement in the implementation and operation of cost systems, their satisfaction with existing systems was not surprising. A better test of the adequacy of industry cost systems would have been to ascertain the opinion of non-accounting users.

Questionnaire

Accordingly, 2,000 questionnaires were distributed to 500 companies with a request that copies of the questionnaire be given to four managers who were not in the accounting or finance functions in each company. The questionnaire was concerned mainly with aspects of the standard cost and budgetary control systems in operation in these companies; 231 useable responses were received, mainly from individuals in the more senior levels in the organisation.

To augment the information given in the completed questionnaires and to improve our understanding of managers' views on these systems, visits were arranged to a number of companies and questionnaire results were discussed with individual managers. This article reports on our findings.

Of the 90 per cent of respondents who knew whether their companies used standard costing, three-quarters said that it did. Contrary to expectations, managers' perceptions of its usefulness generally mirrored that of the first survey; indeed, they were strongly supportive of it, although five unhappy managers thought it 'worthless'.

A manager's area of operation clearly determines the extent of his interest in standard cost information. One personnel manager we interviewed had little use for standard cost information. His interest was primarily focused on information about employee absences, sickness levels and overtime levels. Although he sought and received information from the accounting function on a regular basis, this information had little to do with standard costing. On the other hand, one general manager commented that standard costing information was essential in the operation of any large production process. It was essential in many processes to establish standards and monitor achievements continuously against standards. This view was supported by a production manager who claimed that, 'if you can't measure production output, you can't control it'. The standard cost system was for him a proven way of controlling output.

Although standard cost information can be used to assess a manager's performance, almost half of the respondents denied that this was so in their case. The picture that might be given, therefore, of organisations where continuous evaluation of employees is undertaken using cost information, seems not to be justified. Three respondents, however, did claim that they were judged *solely* on these reports (which seems to place a major onus on the accountant to ensure that the results are reliable and appropriate).

Dissatisfaction

Respondents were asked to indicate reasons for dissatisfaction with their standard costing system. A set of possible objections to the way in which information was received was presented to them and they were invited to check more than one, if they wished. Accountants who pride themselves on accuracy may be disturbed to learn that a lack of accuracy was the most commonly reported cause for dissatisfaction.

Reason for dissatisfaction	Number	%
Not wholly accurate	55	23.9
Not timely	41	17.8
Not wholly relevant for decision making/control	40	17.5
Predominantly numerical	29	12.6
Unsuitable form	21	9.1
Not detailed enough	17	7.4
Too detailed	16	7.0
Not intelligible	6	2.6

Motivation

It was clear from our results that standard cost data motivated many employees to perform better and this was taken up at the interview. The process of monitoring actual performance against standard was agreed to be a strong motivating factor, especially where reports showed adverse trends. But standard costing was only one of a number of instruments used to motivate employees.

Financial incentives were used widely in the companies visited to motivate employees as were improvements in conditions of employment. But good man-management was thought to be an equally important motivating factor. Being close to employees, explaining what was happening in the organisation and trying to instill in them the ideas of an efficient operation was considered by one manager to be more important in motivating staff than the application of a standard cost system.

Volume of information

Turning to the frequency with which standard cost reports were produced our questionnaire survey found that only half are produced at monthly intervals. One in 12 companies produced the reports daily, while almost a quarter produced them at intervals other than the normal monthly, weekly or daily rates. In the companies visited, daily reports showing production volume were available and were essential for those involved in production control. Production cost information, however, was produced only on a weekly basis. Asked if they could cope with additional cost information most managers indicated that they would probably just not get round to reading it. One production manager merely scanned daily reports and if a problem was identified, he would go into the details of the report more thoroughly. In his case, the daily report was used to confirm his own assessment of the day's performance. Any difference between his assessment of performance and that portrayed by the report was investigated.

Importance of standard costing

To gauge the overall importance of standard costing, managers were asked how much more difficult their job would be and how much they felt the company would be harmed if the standard costing system were abandoned. Although some managers felt they would be unaffected — unsurprising since some functional managers have little contact with the standard cost system — others said that the company would be harmed more than they themselves would experience difficulty. This is best interpreted as suggesting that they could find alternative sources of information but the company as a whole could not.

Budgeting systems

Almost all respondents (97 per cent) reported that their companies had budget systems. Generally budgets were perceived to be more useful for most purposes than standard cost information. When interviewed, respondents indicated that budgets were generally examined less frequently than standard cost reports and there was a tendency to regard them as targets, the achievement of which was less important than adherence to a strict standard. If, for example, additional expenses were incurred and these were more than offset by the resultant benefits, then exceeding the budget was quite acceptable. One possible explanation for the lower concern about budgets was that management built slack into them and they were consequently less difficult to achieve than standards.

Participation

Previous studies would lead us to believe that participation in budget-setting is essential if managers are to be committed to their budgets. It is interesting to compare this with the similar question on standard costing where 72 per cent said that they had the opportunity to participate. The latter is perhaps seen as more technical and hence beyond the scope of managers to understand. The survey also asked those managers who felt that they did not have enough opportunity to participate whether they would like to participate more; 80 per cent said that they would.

What is more interesting, however, is that 20 per cent said that they had no wish to do so. Of these, four had reported that their performance was assessed using the budget results and one respondent even claimed to be monitored solely on the basis of budget results. This appears to show a remarkable faith in his/her superior's fairness in setting the budget target.

Non-routine information

Managers frequently asked the accounting department for information, over and above that provided on a routine basis. Examples of this included a break-down of cost incurred in the manufacture of a special product and the profitability of individual customers accounts, especially where the customer had asked for additional services. Sometimes managers also asked for a different presentation of existing information.

A good indication of the satisfaction with the service provided by accountants was that managers seldom by-passed the accounting function in the search for additional information. Occasionally, when a manager's priority had not accorded with the accountant's priorities, the accountant had been by-passed. More usually when accountants were by-passed it was because of the nature of the information being sought. An example of this was when a customer complained about the quality of a product, information was sought from other customer who had purchased from the same batch to see if they had found the quality deficient. This information was not kept by the accounting department.

Conclusion

It was reassuring to find from the study that, generally, managers are strongly supportive of standard cost and budgetary control systems and regard the information that they provide as essential for running large organisations efficiently.

From our discussion with managers, it would appear that accountants have become increasingly involved in the production side of business in recent years and that they are no longer regarded as 'dead hands' or 'obstructionists'. Indeed they are widely perceived to have a positive contribution to make in the way that businesses operate.

JOHNSON, H. T. and KAPLAN, R. S.: 'The rise and fall of management accounting', *Management Accounting* (USA), January 1987.
HENDRICKS, J. A.: 'Applying cost accounting to factory automation'. *Management Accounting* (USA), December 1988.

ABCO TROUT FISHERIES

'I knew there had to be a catch in it somewhere . . .'

READER ARTICLE 8.2

'Feedforward control for competitive advantage: the Japanese approach'

Malcolm Morgan

Reproduced from *Journal of General Management*, Volume 17, No. 4

Summer 1992

Journal of General Management
Vol. 17 No. 4 Summer 1992

Feedforward Control for Competitive Advantage: The Japanese Approach

by
Malcolm J. Morgan, European School of Management, Oxford

41

Traditional control systems based on feedback have the obvious disadvantage that it takes place after the event and valuable time is lost putting things right. Feedforward control is preventive rather than remedial and may help explain the success and quality of Japanese production methods.

In the past decade many 'experts' on Japanese management and manufacturing techniques have isolated distinctive practices that have accounted for the continued economic success of Japan. Since modernization during the Mieji period (1868-1911), the forms taken by Japanese economic organization as that country became industrialized have fascinated and captivated Western observers. Even the earliest Western commentators saw the Japanese enterprise as different. As far back as 1915, Vehblen outlined some of these differences regarding organizations in Japan [1].

Contemporary Western commentators and observers of Japan point to practices like Just-in-Time production [2], the idea of harmony [3,4], total quality control [5] and the aggressive use of flexible manufacturing technologies [6] as the basis for the continuous out-performance of their Western counterparts by Japanese manufacturers.

What has been under-represented in this analysis is the contribution that information systems have made to the continued economic success of Japan. The explanation for this is that the vast coverage given to the Japanese economic success story has concentrated in the main on Japanese production control techniques. It has not addressed itself to the control information aspects of that story. The questions which we intend to ask in our analysis are the following. In what ways are Japanese information control systems different, if at all? If they are different, do they make a significant contribution to the Japanese economic success story? Finally, and perhaps most importantly, should they be emulated in a British management information systems context?

In order to answer these questions, we will first examine the traditional
approach to ideas of control and then re-evaluate it in terms of more recent
thinking about the management process.

The Traditional Approach to Planning and Control

Figure 1 shows the concept of control that has traditionally guided managers.
It illustrates the idea of feedback information being used from the output
side of a system to guide decisions on corrective action to be taken by
managers to control that system [7]. It is the classic decision model aimed
at controlling operations within the business. Indeed, a random selection
of management textbooks on information systems showed every one with
an entry for 'feedback control' in the index.

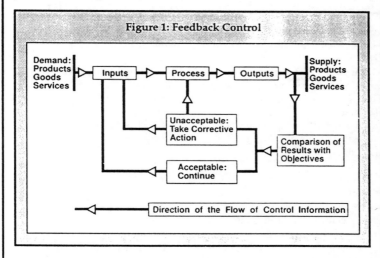

Figure 1: Feedback Control

The major problem with feedback control however, is that such action as is
taken happens well after the event to which it relates. This means that there
are invariably even more consequences of the original problem still
unwinding in the system.

The Modern Approach to Planning and Control

It has been argued recently that the emphasis of modern management has
moved away from the control of physical operations to the control of time
[8]. Because of this change of approach the feedback model now has less
relevance as a control tool. The main reason for this is because it operates
on the output side of the system. Under this approach information is

Journal of General Management
Vol. 17 No. 4 Summer 1992

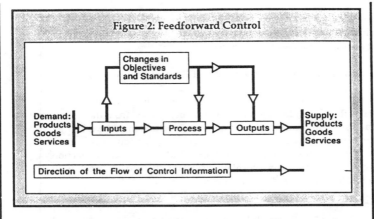

Figure 2: Feedforward Control

43

produced at the end of the system's cycle. As a result, control data is received relatively late and valuable time is lost in the corrective process.

The answer to the question of the difference between Western and Japanese information systems which we posed earlier can be found in this area. The Japanese approach is to use control information in conjunction with planning to give a more proactive, rather than a reactive, emphasis. It has been argued that this single characteristic explains much of the difference in emphasis in the approach to control in Western and Japanese information systems [9,10].

As a result of this approach, it is feedforward control which dominates Japanese information systems rather than feedback control. The most obvious difference between the two is the anticipatory character of feedforward control. This is illustrated in Figure 2. In effect, feedforward control is preventive in nature, whereas feedback control is remedial. In terms of systems effectiveness, prevention must be better than cure and so feedforward control represents an improvement on the more widely discussed and implemented technique of feedback control [11,12].

Why is there a need for the inclusion of feedforward information in a control system? It has already been noted that feedback control can be costly because of the time lag involved in making corrections to operations. Consequently, some writers suggest the use of feedforward control because it provides lead-time to solve problems before they have had an impact on operations and create overspends. Illustrations of this approach are most evident and widespread in the fields of cash planning and stock control.

With respect to cash planning, a cash plan's deviations from its

Journal of General Management
Vol. 17 No. 4 Summer 1992

expected parameters (receipts, expenditures, etc.) could be anticipated under a feedforward system before they affect the cash balance at a specified future time. Such anticipation of changes from the expected cash balance, and with the expected corrective action taken in advance, could be beneficial in terms of negotiating short-term credit facilities well ahead of their need, thus possibly reducing the costs of borrowing.

Illustration of Feedforward Control

The management of finished goods, or any other inventory for that matter, can be used to illustrate the two techniques of control. Under a feedback system of control, the level of inventory is checked periodically against an established standard - the periodic review method. If the level begins to exceed the established standard at some point, production schedules are altered to reduce output. Investigation may reveal that the rate of sales has declined, despatch delays have occurred, and so forth. Although the inventory build-up has been stopped, the excess inventory remains. The consequences are unnecessarily increased investment, which also results in higher insurance payments to protect the higher value of stock, and more space needed to accommodate the finished goods. Similarly, if the inventory falls below the established standard, corrective action is taken under feedback control.

The difficulty with feedback control is the time lag involved in the information system unwinding to provide a measure of the adverse variance. It may not even be possible to take effective corrective action in time to prevent those adverse variances occurring or even getting worse.

The basic idea behind the use of a feedforward system of control is that factors which affect inventory levels are well known and can be recognized before their consequences have had a full impact on inventory. For example, if the rate of sales begins to decline, that information can be fed forward as an order to reduce the level of finished goods inventory by reducing the rate of production before inventory exceeds established levels. Under feedforward control, lead-time is gained and more immediate, if not total, achieving of objectives and standards is possible.

Relationship Between Feedback and Feedforward Controls

In advocating the extended use of feedforward control, we should maintain a sense of perspective. The superiority of feedforward over feedback controls would suggest that managers should opt for the former and abandon the latter. This is not feasible, however. These two types of control are not mutually exclusive, nor are they interchangeable. Instead, they are supplementary and, as such, to a certain extent complementary.

Journal of General Management
Vol. 17 No. 4 Summer 1992

Feedback from operations is also used to correct budget projections. If actual sales appear to be running at the rate of 110 per cent of last year rather than the 105 per cent predicted, then the revenue projections may be altered, additional production expenditures budgeted, and provision made for increased purchases of raw materials and supplies.

If managers are aware of anticipated events which may affect the budget in the next time period, these too are considered. For example, available information may suggest strongly that a major competitor will be the victim of a long strike in the next six months and the sales and expense projections may be increased further in anticipation of an exceptional, if temporary, increase in demand.

To summarize this process, the budget establishes feedforward controls, the expense information in the reports provides feedback to measure actual achievement versus projections. As a result, the new budget period allowances are changed to take into account corrections made by the feedback and feedforward systems of control in previous periods.

Thus, it appears that although the idea of feedforward control in management is a relatively new one, it is one that has been practised for a long time. Managers often simply did not realize that when they prepared budgets they were using feedforward control in addition to feedback to manage their operations. The idea is, however, that budget preparation is not seen as the end of the role that the budget plays in the process of control. Recent ideas in the areas of differentiating between planning and operating variances owe a great deal to the clarification of the distinction between feedforward and feedback control systems, as does the emergence of the use of revision variances to quantify these effects.

A Comparison Between the Different Approaches to Control

Figures 3 and 4 illustrate the basic differences between feedback and feedforward control and uses our stock control example for its inputs and outputs. In the feedback system, as Figure 3 shows, information is generated as a by-product of outputs and is literally fed back into the process on the input side. It indicates either to continue as is or to take corrective action. The choice to continue or change is made by comparing actual outputs with the established objectives and standards of the system.

In feedforward control, the information flow is reversed. Information available at the input stage is fed forward as representative of changes in objectives and/or standards. This is done in anticipation of the need to change outputs, or operations to ensure expected results are achieved.

Journal of General Management
Vol. 17 No. 4 Summer 1992

Risks involved in implementing and using feedforward control have to do with the inability to predict exactly how much should be done and when. Hence it is easy to under- or overestimate what is needed at some future date. As in most activities, practice and experience tend to make for improvement but not perfection. Nevertheless, there may be a gap between what is desired and what is achieved. Feedback control usually helps eventually to eliminate or narrow that gap, another example of the two approaches going hand in hand.

While these costs of planning quickly become evident, the benefits are not so obvious. The major benefit should be that which is sought in the use of feedforward control - more accurate achievement of organizational objectives and standards. One test of that achievement would be an estimate of the cost of adjusting the organization to changed circumstances through the use of feedback controls only, in effect asking, what would have happened if no anticipatory corrective action had been taken? The longer the time required for corrective action, the higher the cost and the lower the probability of making timely changes through feedback control.

The flexibility that comes as a by-product of the implementation of feedforward information is as important as the improved control. Feedforward planning conditions managers to constantly anticipate change and they have a lead-time to consider alternative strategies, even to build up an inventory of strategies, so that they are prepared to deal with a reasonable range of contingencies. It is in this context that the Japanese practice of target costing rather than standard costing has been used to great effect [14].

Other by-products of planning are the mutual expectations that are developed between and among organizational managers as they contemplate alternative strategies to adjust the organization's supply capabilities to environmental demands for its products, or services. Organizational change requires time and understanding to overcome the commitment to past policies, strategies, and operational levels.

Summary and Conclusions

A review of the arguments and implications of this comparison between feedforward and feedback controls suggests the following:

- It is easier to anticipate environmental demands with feedforward control than to react only with feedback control.
- Feedforward control is not an intervening variable between planning and control; planning is feedforward control.

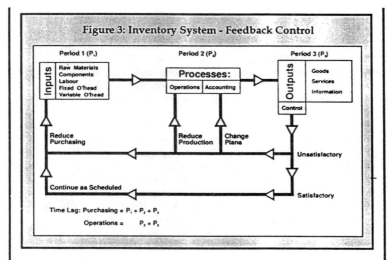

Figure 3: Inventory System - Feedback Control

Separation and Integration of Planning and Control

This belated recognition of the use of feedforward control is the consequence of the erroneous separation of the idea of planning from the idea of control in management literature [13]. It was a simple semantic problem. Control was defined as focusing on feedback; planning, therefore, was some other kind of management technique.

But planning, including budgeting, is a method of feedforward control, albeit possibly the most widely used method. We are only belatedly recognizing this identity because of a narrow definition of control that has dominated the literature of management, the assumption that it was based solely on feedback. Indeed, recent discussions of feedforward control persist in identifying it as a technique to use between planning and feedback control.

These writers are saying: first you plan, then you correct your plans with feedforward control, then you correct the results of operations with feedback control. But the amendment of a plan is hardly different from the preparation of a plan.

Among other components, a properly prepared plan contains a statement of objectives and standards, an assessment of the market and other sectors of the environment, forecasts of demand, delineation of strategies, a programme of action, a budget, and a reporting system. Correction of a plan through feedforward control is simply a change of any one or more of these components - an increase or decrease in the market

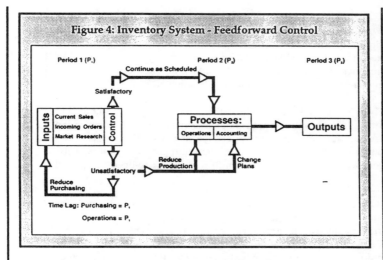

Figure 4: Inventory System - Feedforward Control

share objective or the detection of a new trend in the environment. The result of changing an original plan through the use of feedforward control, in effect, results in a revised plan. Therefore planning is simply a technique of feedforward control.

Belabouring the identity of planning as a control technique may appear to be merely a semantic or academic exercise. However, it is far more important than that. It is important because if managers think they can manage effectively on the basis of feedback information, they will view planning as an additional, and perhaps unnecessarily expensive management tool, or even a luxury. On the other hand, ensuring the incorporation of feedforward control into the process supports the idea of anticipating rather than reacting to unexpected results. Otherwise it smacks more of tinkering with the whole management process than of effective management.

The real difference between feedforward and feedback control is the difference between foresight and hindsight. With feedforward control exemplified by planning, managers are constantly looking forward to minimize the need for corrective action when the results are known, when it may be too late. With feedback control only, managers are constantly looking backwards, possibly heading into deeper trouble while wrestling with problems that have already overtaken them.

Informal Use of Feedforward Control

We know, of course, that in real life, while relying on feedback controls to

Journal of General Management
Vol. 17 No. 4 Summer 1992

manage operations, many managers observe changes in the environment and take anticipatory corrective action. For example, noting a trend to increasing sales, a managing director may informally explore the need for expanded production facilities. Limited expansion may be carried out in an *ad hoc* manner. If considerable additional facilities are needed, a formal planning effort to build a new plant may be initiated.

There is every reason to believe, then, that managers in fact tend to rely on feedforward control to anticipate some changes in their organization and its environment. They anticipate the obvious. When sales keep increasing steadily and the production lines are approaching full capacity, managers will not ordinarily wait until they are knee-deep in unfilled orders.

But to the extent that there are no obvious indicators of change in the environment - or if managers simply fail to observe them - then such sporadic responses to feedforward control are not likely to satisfy the control needs of the organization. That is why there is so much prescription of planning by academics and practitioners alike. It must be remembered that not all organizations plan, although the practice of planning has been spreading for decades.

Costs of Feedforward Control

One barrier to the spread of planning already noted is the understanding of its role in control. Another important one is cost. As suggested earlier, feedback information about the results of organizational operations is the minimum condition for control. If only one kind of control were possible, feedback would be the most useful because it is ultimately the most complete. Feedforward is a supplement to feedback but could not exist on its own because exact control would not be exercised. As a result feedforward control involves incremental costs. These costs are reflected in:

- The additional time and effort that the organization invests in planning; and
- The risks that are incurred by making organizational changes in advance of actual needs.

The clearest indication of the additional work required to implement feedforward control is the old adage that 'operations drive out planning'. Since there is often no slack time available for planning, personnel must be hired either to plan or to relieve planners of routine work. In these circumstances there may be a reluctance on the part of managers to incorporate an additional staff function within the finance function leading to the further neglect of feedforward control.

Journal of General Management
Vol. 17 No. 4 Summer 1992

[11] Merriam, D.W. and Wilkinson, Joseph W., 'Model for Planning and Feedforward Control', *Managerial Planning*, March-April 1977, pp. 31-36, 40.

[12] Koontz, H. and Bradspies, Robert W., 'Managing Through Feedforward Control', *Business Horizons*, June 1972, pp. 25-36.

[13] Drucker, P.F., *Management: Tasks, Responsibilities, Practices*, New York: Harper and Row, 1973-1974; the separation of planning and control is also the rule in management texts and periodical literature.

[14] Monden, Yasuhiro, and Sakurai, Michiharu, *Japanese Management Accounting: A World Class Approach to Profit Management*, Cambridge, Mass. Productivity Press, 1989.

READER ARTICLE 9.1

'Bench-marking in divisionalized companies'

Roy Skinner

Reproduced from *Certified Accountant*

April 1993

The criterion most often referred to as a bench-mark is the performance of other, similar, businesses. But the yardstick used for measuring performance could be comparison with past performance of a business, or it could be the business's budgets and standards.

At best, comparison with past performance indicates how a business is performing relative to the past. It gives no indication of how good or bad current performance is in any absolute sense.

Budgets embody what managers consider to be good performance, but their judgement may be limited for two reasons. Firstly, budgets are likely to be related to recent past performance, so two firms in an industry may achieve their budgets but one may be performing at a significantly higher level than the other because its budgets are set at a substantially higher level.

The other problem is that it is only possible in some areas of performance for managers to judge with any degree of objectivity what good performance involves. It may be possible to find out, for example, the minimum level of material wastage and maximum level of labour efficiency achievable given the best possible circumstances.

In many areas of performance, objective information is impossible to obtain, such as on the correct amounts that should be spent on research and development, advertising, employee training and administration to achieve the firm's goals.

Using the performance of other firms as a bench-mark has the potential to give what no other evaluation method can give: comparison with what is currently best possible practice. Best practice in an industry may be only second best, due to the firms being protected from competition by such things as high tariff barriers. But that difficulty is, in principle, surmountable by comparison of businesses across different countries.

Inter-firm comparison

Using the performance data of other firms as a bench-mark, commonly known as 'inter-firm comparison' (IFC), is a

long-established method. (IFC as a management accounting rather than an investment evaluation technique has a longer history and is better developed in the UK than in any other country.)

Ideally, there should be a formal IFC scheme operated by the relevant trade, industry or professional association. In the UK, schemes are also operated by the National Centre for Inter-firm Comparison. Some British schemes are co-operative efforts between the centre and the relevant associations. The first formal IFC scheme was set up in the UK by the British Federation of Master

Printers (now the British Printing Industries Federation) in 1958.

In the absence of a formal scheme, the only information likely to be available about companies is that designed for financial accounting purposes, which is not suitable for management accounting.

In IFC schemes run by industry associations, information tends to be disseminated on an anonymous basis under code numbers. Each participant firm or division knows its own code number but not that of any other business. Under each item of information, participants are ranked in order of results and significant characteristics of the distributions are identified, such as the upper quartile, median and lower quartile positions.

These features are based on the assumption that a participant may wish

Although the term bench-marking is relatively new, the practice it refers to has a long history.

Roy Skinner reports on its usage

BENCH-MARKING
IN DIVISIONALIZED COMPANIES

to compare its performance on any item primarily with the business in a particular position, say, at the upper quartile level.

The information consists primarily of ratios. There are two reasons for this: ratios enable the results of businesses of different sizes to be compared, and they preserve anonymity: (dollar amounts would often identify a business to anyone familiar with the industry).

Businesses participating in any IFC scheme belong, of course, to a particular industry, trade or profession. Given sufficient members, the results can be analysed by sub-industries. So, for example, a firm which prints colour magazines can compare its performance not only with all other printing firms in the scheme, but also with those involved with just its own type of production. The object of sub-grouping is to give greater comparability of results.

development expenditure would be included in their central fixed costs, whereas in companies where that activity was decentralised central fixed costs would include very little of the R&D expenditure.

Comparability

Apart from the availability of suitable management accounting data, the other major problem involved in IFC is the lack of uniformity in the data that is available.

The industry association should specify the nature of the data to be supplied for the major areas. It needs to be determined how the ratios used as bench-marks are to be defined and where alternative definitions are possible.

Investment, for example, can be total assets, net assets (total assets less current liabilities), or ordinary shareholders' funds; profit must, of course, be measured in a manner consistent with that of the denominator. The deciding factor in choosing a definition is often the issue of what matters are typically most subject to the control of a business's management.

In the case of a division, the investment base is unlikely to be ordinary shareholders' funds, because long-term credit is typically not controlled at divisional level. If short-term credit is also controlled centrally in most of the companies, total assets is more likely to be used than net assets as the measure of divisional capital.

External investments, often controlled centrally, are sometimes excluded from the divisional capital base. Care must be taken in making exclusions, however, since one of the objects of an IFC scheme may be to show up any comparatively large amounts of low-yielding investments. One possibility is to show rates of return including and excluding external investments.

Fixed asset values are sometimes computed gross rather than net of accumulated depreciation, but that is not due to control considerations, but to give more comparability between business with fixed assets of different average ages.

Measures other than conventional financial accounting ratios are often used, such as those based on conversion cost (manufacturing cost less direct materials), value added (sales value less the materials and services purchased externally) and productivity measures (such as sales per employed person).

Uniformity in the data used in an IFC scheme needs to go well beyond the types of ratios used and the ways they are computed. Problems are caused by two types of diversity — in accounting methods and in business practice — and the industry association needs to maximise comparability in both areas.

In many areas of performance, objective information is impossible to obtain

For example, modified historic cost may (or may not) give acceptable results in financial accounting, but the lack of comparability it produces is not acceptable in IFC schemes. Current replacement cost is needed for valuing and depreciating fixed assets. Rather than requiring appraisals, it may be satisfactory for the industry association to specify use of insurance values.

In the case of divisions, the bases used for valuing transfers of goods between them need to be specified. The dominant basis is likely to be external market price, but some other basis needs to be selected for goods that do not have external markets.

An example of diversity of business practice is the fact that some businesses own their land and buildings whereas others rent them. To convert all business to the same basis (whether ownership or rental), it is common to use local government rating valuations.

In the case of divisions, as pointed out in the preceding section, the costs of central services need to be allocated in order to give comparability with divisions which supply their own services. The basis of allocation for each type of service needs to be specified .

Accounting uniformity preceded IFC by many years. In 1913, the printing industry association in Britain, mentioned above, introduced a uniform costing system. The scheme's rationale was that 70-80% of firms in printing use cost-plus pricing.

If firm X is more efficient than firm Y on all types of production, its product costs computed for managerial use ought to be consistently lower. That will not necessarily be the case if the firms use different costing methods.

On some types of job, for example, letterpress printing rather than colour printing, or on short runs as opposed to long runs, firm X may compute its product costs as being higher than those of firm Y (X's product costs on the other types of job are likely, of course, to be significantly lower than Y's).

The objective of uniform costing is to allow differences in efficiency between firms to be reflected in product costs and, therefore, selling prices. In this way, firms compete on the basis of relative performance and not on the basis of their costing systems. Typically, the amount of uniformity needed for an IFC scheme is significantly less than that needed in a uniform costing system.

Inter-firm comparison by divisions is more common than would generally have been expected, given the shortage of suitable information. This type of bench-marking would be more common if more data were available. Greater availability of suitable data depends on the more widespread use of formal IFC schemes operated by industry, trade and professional associations. Efforts should be made to expand the divisional coverage of such schemes, ideally incorporating both national and international data. ∎

Roy Skinner is a lecturer in the Department of Accounting and Finance at Monash University, Melbourne, Victoria, Australia.

READER
ARTICLE 9.2

'Transfer pricing comes to Barts'

Roger Halford

Reproduced from *Management Accounting*,
Journal of the Chartered Institute of
Management Accountants

May 1992

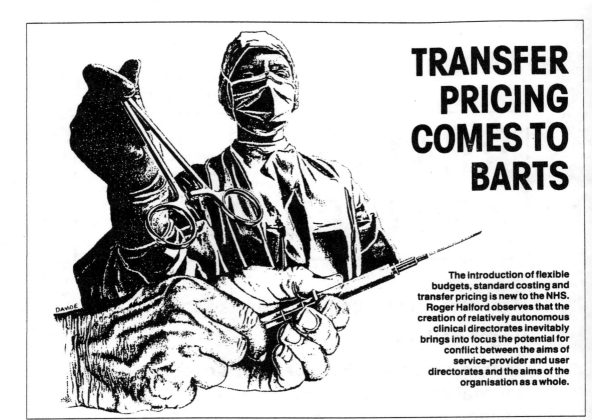

TRANSFER PRICING COMES TO BARTS

The introduction of flexible budgets, standard costing and transfer pricing is new to the NHS. Roger Halford observes that the creation of relatively autonomous clinical directorates inevitably brings into focus the potential for conflict between the aims of service-provider and user directorates and the aims of the organisation as a whole.

The introduction to the Barts NHS Trust[1] of a system of transfer pricing has been brought about by a number of factors:

Decentralisation

'Transfer pricing is inevitable whenever one division supplies product(s) to another.'[2] Barts management recently reorganised the then health authority into clinical directorates. Quite how the authority was organised before that is not clear. There were all manner of organisational entities: specialties, departments, units, firms and site service points as well as the more recognisable wards, theatres and clinics.

All of these entities still exist but now they all belong to one of the directorates and it is easier to see how they relate to each other. Directorates have more autonomy than previous organisational elements and are encouraged, amongst other things, to think strategically and be resource-conscious.

The introduction of directorates has raised the question for accountants of the financial aspects of their inter-relationships. Other aspects include, for instance, the right of users to buy on the open market (so-called sourcing decisions). For example, should a doctor be able to get a lab test done by a private laboratory?

Roger Halford is Systems Development Accountant with the City and Hackney Health Authority, St Bartholomews' Hospital, London

A useful perspective to apply in this situation is Thompson's threefold categorisation of forms of interdependence into pooled, sequential and reciprocal types.[3] Hospitals appear to consist of the first two types: there are directorates that do not interact directly but share certain common resources such as wards and theatres, and we have directorates, such as pathologies and laboratory services that provide services for what are styled 'end users', i.e. patient-admitting consultants.

As Emmanuel and Otley[4] have pointed out, 'Interdependence between operating units can be handled either by cost allocation or transfer pricing . . . Not to allocate costs relating to sequential . . . interdependence leads to 'free' goods and services being provided by divisions . . . and results in financial reports being meaningless' (pp.192-193).

There *has* been a system of cost allocation in the NHS for the past few years but the cost objective for this system is the specialty bed day and the cost ascertained is a partial absorption cost. This system is not linked to the present system of budgetary control.[5]

Budgeting

There is widespread agreement here amongst managers and clinicians that the present system of budgetary control is discredited. It has two glaring deficiencies.

First, it is based on fixed, allocative, incremental budgets, which means that the only control information that budget holders are provided with is presented in terms of over- and underspends. If a department does more work than was implicit in its fixed budget, and does it more efficiently, but as a result overspends, then this overspend is all that the present system reports. And clearly, overspends are bad things.

Conversely if a department does less, and less efficiently, but underspends then all that matters is the underspend. Underspends can lead to subsequent budget reductions or be viewed against other departments' overspends so nobody in their right mind would plan to underspend.

Second, budgets do not cover the clinicians. We have a set of functional budgets where doctors are not regarded as a function. All areas of hospital activity have budgets, except the people who control the level of activity — the doctors. By increasing activity levels doctors can force other departments, such as theatres, to overspend. But because budgets are not flexed to reflect activity we cannot ascertain what part of the overspend is due to the increased activity (which is beyond the theatre management's control) and what is due to factors more within the theatre management's control — theatre input prices and efficiency.

Motivationally this system is a disaster. Key staff are completely let off the hook in terms of financial responsibility and those that are made responsible have no incentives to provide healthcare at a given level of quality more efficiently.

To try to improve the quality of financial

information being provided to clinicians and management we are attempting to introduce three related mechanisms familiar to all accountants: flexible budgets, standard costing and transfer prices. And doctors will become budget holders.

By providing budget holders with flexible budgets and by using standard costing to report on variances rather than spending differences we hope to overcome some of the problems inherent in the present system. Transfer prices will be the standard costs of resources provided by facility directorates to user directorates. For facility providers the transfer price will measure cost recharged and for users, costs incurred by using hospital facilities. Are we hoping for the impossible?

Initial problems

Having decided in principle to introduce transfer pricing as part of a package of improvements to the management accounting system we have encountered a number of problems.

First, most of the accounting literature on transfer pricing assumes that goods and services are being transferred between divisions of profit-maximising firms operating in markets of varying degrees of perfection. This assumption is understandable in view of the absence, until recently, of transfer pricing in the public sector, in which the NHS has been no exception.[6] (We have found one exception at Barts where the Central Sterile Supplies Department, which makes up and provides sterile packs of dressings and instruments to wards and theatres, charges these packs out at standard cost. This system was apparently introduced in the late 1960s but nobody can remember why.)

Second, it is not yet clear what are the objectives of a clinical directorate. Different hospital doctors emphasise different objectives. This in itself is not necessarily a problem — as Haire has observed, '... organisations persist ... in spite of recurrent conflict as to the nature of their goals'.[7]

What we do know is that directorates cannot, under the present rules of the game, formulate objectives in terms of profitability. Transfer prices will therefore be at cost. (We have discounted the idea of a dual transfer pricing system[8] using some sort of market price for performance evaluation as being beyond our resources.) Our working assumption will be that a directorate's financial aim is to recover its costs, although we will distinguish between those directorates that provide services to clinicians and those that treat patients.

Third, we have sought to clarify if there are any constraints on our initiatives. To date we have no indication from the Department of Health as to whether it would want to introduce any constraints in designing a transfer-pricing system. The only pronouncement that is of any relevance has come from the NHS Management Executive, which has laid down the fundamental principles of cost allocation

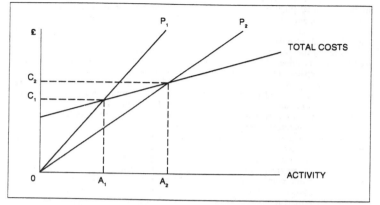

Figure 1 Costs. activity and prices for service provider departments assuming total absorption costing

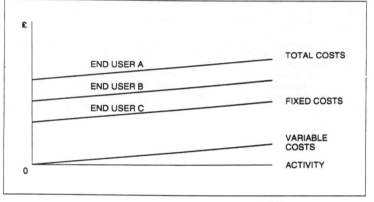

Figure 2 Costs. activity and prices for service provider departments assuming two-part costing

that should underlie contract costing and pricing:
- contracts should generally be priced at cost;
- costs should include all costs and
- there should be no planned cross-subsidisation.[9]

These principles clearly relate to the financial relationship between service providers and purchasing authorities. However, the existence of the above principles would make it extremely complicated to designate our responsibility centres as profit centres and operate a set of transfer prices based on market prices. How, for instance, would profits and losses be interpreted under such a system?

Fourth, we have needed to clarify the kind of responsibility centre that a clinical directorate constitutes. Under the present rules they are clearly cost centres but are they also investment centres? The answer to this question is a top-level management policy decision.

What kinds of transfer price?

The next problem is one that recurs within accounting in many different guises. While it has been relatively easy to decide that transfer prices will be based on standard, as opposed to actual costs, a more difficult

issue has been to decide on the treatment of fixed costs in a situation where most costs are fixed staff costs.

The choice is between combining fixed and variable costs into a total cost or charging them both out separately. This second alternative is usually referred to as a 'two-part tariff transfer price'[10] or 'incremental cost plus fixed fee'[11] and appears to have been developed to counter the disadvantages associated with full cost transfer pricing in the private sector.

Under this method a proportion of the supplier department's budgeted fixed costs will be allocated on a periodic basis to users. This is interpreted as a fixed fee or rental payment for the existence of an in-house service. Each item of service will then be charged at standard variable cost.

It appears that we have the freedom to choose between these methods. The choice of approach will depend partly on the activity objectives of the parties to agreements. There may be cases in a hospital setting where an aim of the pricing structure is to act to minimise activity, e.g. out-of-hours pathology tests, and to maximise activity, e.g. use of theatre sessions.

It seems to us that conventional total-cost approach will be appropriate if the aim is to

Continued on page 57

437

Transfer pricing comes to Barts

Continued from page 35

constrain demand for a service. However, if this policy is successful it may mean that the facility department will under-recover its costs. If the policy is unsuccessful and demand exceeds plan we have the problem of interpreting the over-recovery of costs. We have had to dampen the enthusiasm of some facility departments who have misinterpreted over-recovery of costs as surpluses which can be used for investment funding to make up for the lack of investment funds from elsewhere.

These two alternative treatments of fixed costs can be illustrated diagramatically. The use of total costs to calculate transfer prices is depicted in Figure 1. Points A_1 and A_2 on the activity axis are different levels of planned activity and points C_1 and C_2 are the levels of total cost associated with the corresponding activity levels. The slopes of the 'revenue' lines $0P_1$ and $0P_2$ are the average total costs at each level of activity (C_n/A_n).

This diagram shows the familiar result that the total cost per unit of activity is dependent on the level of activity chosen. The higher level of activity (A_2) leads to a lower average unit cost (shown by the shallower slope of the line $0C_2$). This is brought about solely because the fixed cost per unit is reduced as activity increases, the variable cost per unit remaining constant.

We envisage following the convention of assuming a normal level of activity to solve this problem.

Two-part charging is shown in Figure 2. Having charged its users with its fixed costs on a periodic base, the transfer price for each unit of service is then the standard variable cost.

One objection that might be raised against this approach is that it gives the provider no incentive to minimise its fixed costs. A way round this would be to allow any favourable fixed cost expenditure variance (equivalent to an underspend) to be split between the provider and users and allow the provider to utilise it to fund investment expenditure.

Pricing under this system provides the user with an incentive to maximise inputs in order to reduce the fixed fee per unit, which may, however, have the effect of placing excess demand on the service provider.

Conclusion

The introduction of flexible budgets, standard costing and transfer pricing is new to the NHS and appears to have a momentum independent of political concern with provider and purchaser splits, trusts and GP fundholders. The creation of relatively autonomous clinical directorates inevitably brings into focus the potential for conflict between the aims of service provider and user directorates and the aims of the organisation as a whole. In general it seems that any transfer-pricing mechanism will reflect these conflicts but when particular methods are applied these conflicts may be exacerbated. $\square$

1 Barts was originally a colloquial name for St Bartholomew's Hospital but is now enshrined in the formal name of the Barts NHS Trust.
2 KEEGAN, D. P. and HOWARD, P. D.: 'Transfer pricing for fun and profit', *Price Waterhouse Review*, Vol. 30, No. 3, 1986, pp.37-45.
3 THOMPSON, J. D.: *Organisations in Action*. Mcgraw Hill, 1967.
4 EMMANUEL, C. and OTLEY, D.: *Accounting for Management Control*. VNR, 1985.
5 This takes place in the preparation of the annual financial returns, known as the Körner Accounts, after Edith Körner, who chaired the NHS/DHSS Steering Group on Health Services Information whose sixth report focused on the Collection and Use of Financial Information.
6 PERRIN, JOHN: *Resource Management in the NHS*. Chapman and Hall, 1988, pp.139-40.
7 HAIRE, M.: 'What is organised in an organisation' in *Organisation Theory in Industrial Practice*. Wiley, 1962.
8 See, for example, COLIN DRURY: *Management and Cost Accounting*. VNR, 1988, pp.757-8.
9 Department of Health Executive Letter EL(90)173.
10 SOLOMONS, D.: *Divisional Performance: Measurement and Control*. Irwin, 1965.
11 KAPLAN, R. S.: *Advanced Management Accounting*. Prentice Hall, 1982.